The Germans in Normandy

The Germans in Normandy

Death Reaped a Terrible Harvest

by

Richard Hargreaves

Pen & Sword
MILITARY

First published in Great Britain in 2006 by
Pen & Sword Military
an imprint of
Pen & Sword Books Ltd
47 Church Street
Barnsley
South Yorkshire
S70 2AS

Copyright © Richard Hargreaves, 2006

ISBN 1 84415 447 5

A CIP catalogue record for this book is
available from the British Library.

Typeset in Sabon10/12 by
Lamorna Publishing Services

Printed and bound in England by
Biddles Ltd., King's Lynn

Pen & Sword Books Ltd incorporates the Imprints of Pen & Sword Aviation,
Pen & Sword Maritime, Wharncliffe Local History, Pen & Sword Select, Pen
& Sword Military Classics and Leo Cooper

For a complete list of Pen & Sword titles please contact
PEN & SWORD BOOKS LIMITED
47 Church Street, Barnsley, South Yorkshire, S70 2AS, England
E-mail: enquiries@pen-and-sword.co.uk
Website: www.pen-and-sword.co.uk

I felt like anything rather than rejoicing at the downfall of a foe who had fought so long and valiantly, and had suffered so much for a cause, though that cause was, I believe, one of the worst for which a people ever fought, and one for which there was the least excuse.

Ulysses S. Grant

Contents

Acknowledgements		*ix*
Abbreviations		*xi*
Introduction		*xiii*
Chapter 1	Every Night We Wait for Tommy	1
Chapter 2	The Last Opportunity to Turn the Tide	20
Chapter 3	My God, it's the Invasion	33
Chapter 4	Up Against an Irresistible Force	41
Chapter 5	Approaching a Catastrophe	65
Chapter 6	Further Sacrifices Cannot Change Anything	86
Chapter 7	The Unequal Struggle	105
Chapter 8	The Blackest Day in German History	138
Chapter 9	Only the Dead Can Now Hold the Line	164
Chapter 10	Death has Reaped a Terrible Harvest	189
Chapter 11	Out-Generalled and Out-Fought	223
Chapter 12	This Cannot be the End	243
Appendix		*252*
Bibliography		*253*
Index		*261*

Acknowledgements

Jamie Wilson of Spellmount Publishers for permission to quote from *Heaven and Hell*; David Higham Associates for permission to quote from *The Rommel Papers*; Stephen Walton and his colleagues in the Department of Documents at the Imperial War Museum, London; National Archives, Kew; George Malcolmson, Royal Navy Submarine Museum, Gosport; Stephen Brooks, formerly curator of the D-Day Museum, Portsmouth; the staff of the following libraries: University of Nottingham, University of Manchester, University of Sussex, University of Portsmouth, University of Warwick, and Lancashire, Portsmouth, and Nottinghamshire; New York Public Libraries; British Newspaper Library; Commander Eddie Grenfell RN (Retd); Jason Pipes and his colleagues at www.feldgrau.net; Jason Mark; Howard Davies for his inestimable knowledge of the German language; Lawrence Paterson for his expertise on U-boats; Andy Brady for the maps; Darren Beck, Helen Craven and Allison Tupper for proofreading (and much encouragement). For all their help, and for the input of countless others I am eternally grateful. If there are any errors in the work which follows, they are mine, not theirs.

Abbreviations used in references

AL   Reference used by the Imperial War Museum
AOK   *Armeeoberkommando* - Army High Command
BA/MA   *Bundesarchiv Militär-Archiv* - Bundesarchiv Military Archive, Freiburg
BdU   *Befehlshaber der U-Boote* - Commander-in-Chief of U-boats
CAB   Cabinet Office Papers, National Archives
CSDIC   Combined Services Detailed Interrogation Centre
HGr   *Heeresgruppe* - Army Group
IWM   Imperial War Museum, London
Kdo   Kommando - Command
KTB   *Kriegstagebuch* - War diary
Mar.Grp   *Marinegruppen* - Naval Group
MS   Manuscripts prepared for the US Army by German officers post-war
NA   National Archives, Kew
NHB   Naval Historical Branch, Portsmouth
OKH   *Oberkommando des Heeres* - German Army High Command
OKW   *Oberkommando der Wehrmacht* - German Armed Forces High Command
SD Meldung *Sicherheitsdienst* report on public morale
Skl   *Seekriegsleitung* - German Naval Staff
TB   *Tagebuch* - Diary

Author's Note

German ranks throughout, with the exception of *Generalfeldmarschall* – field marshal – have been left in their original language. An explanation of the comparative ranks can be found in the appendix.

21

2

Pen & Sword Books Limited
FREEPOST SF5
47 Church Street
BARNSLEY
South Yorkshire
S70 2BR

1

*mandy will forever be
books.*

Kurt Meyer

:he main Caen–Cherbourg
untryside between Bayeux
meticulously maintained.
e, roughly cut black stone
grouped around a great
s is La Cambe, last resting
fended Normandy against

rever German; cemeteries
:he burial sites of a further
'44 *'für Führer, Volk und*
l. Death had indeed reaped

Jormandy and perhaps the

the actions of the German
ns of occupied France and
Arguably the finest new
divisions Germany formed or re-formed in the winter of 1943–44 were
sent west to bolster the second-rate units who had watched over the
English Channel since 1940, holding the much-vaunted Atlantic Wall.
On these divisions, the *Panzer Lehr*, the *Hitlerjugend*, 21st Panzer and
a handful of others, the Third Reich entrusted the defence of France.
The flower of the German Armed Forces, the *Wehrmacht*, of 1944
vintage would fight and, if necessary, die on French soil to safeguard the
future of the Fatherland.

Of course, it never came to pass. The Allies were not destroyed on the beaches. By Thursday, 8 June 1944, when the beachheads had merged, the enemy had a firm foothold on *Festung Europa* – Fortress Europe. He would not be driven out.

In the years since American, British and Canadian soldiers swept over the beaches of the Seine Bay, Normandy has been seen more as an Allied victory than a German defeat. The men who defended Caen and Cherbourg, who escaped the hell of the Falaise pocket, have been poorly served by history and historians. Perhaps this is not entirely surprising. British, Canadians and American accounts focused on the achievements of their respective armed forces. Beyond divisional historians, German writers have concentrated their researches on the Eastern Front – and rightly so; even when the Battle for Normandy was at its peak, the number of men involved on the German side never came close to matching the Third Reich's commitment in the titanic struggle with Russia. From 1941-45, the Eastern Front was the engine of the war in Europe.

Yet in 1944 it did not appear that way. The gaze of the German public, of Germany's leaders, of her generals, was fixed towards the west, not east. The Reich's strategy for the year could be neatly summed up as: thwart the invasion then shore up the Eastern Front. And the Reich was confident of its strategy. Those who believed the invasion would succeed were in the minority in the spring of 1944. From Adolf Hitler down, the leaders of the Third Reich were confident the Allies would be smashed on the beaches. It would be a ferocious battle, yes, but the invader would be driven back whence he came.

The story of Europe's liberation has been told many times in the past six decades,[1] but rarely from the German viewpoint – despite the exhortation of the *Hitlerjugend*'s leader, Kurt Meyer.[2] It is a story which deserves to be told.

And it is a story which can be told in detail. Copious official and unofficial documents and accounts exist to allow us to recount the struggle for Normandy, from the private and public thoughts of Germany's political and military leaders, to the heroics and privations of the ordinary German soldier, the *Landser*.[3] Readers seeking a detailed tactical and strategic history of the struggle for Normandy, of unit actions, of individual companies, regiments and divisions, should look elsewhere. The account which follows is a human history of the men who fought, and in many cases died, defending *Festung Europa*, how they acted, and reacted, from Hitler and Erwin Rommel down to the lowliest soldier digging in for his life in the Norman bocage under a hail of Allied mortars and bombs.

The story of the struggle for Normandy is an appalling one; the battle was, in Erwin Rommel's words, 'one terrible blood-letting'.[4] However

Introduction

The German soldier's performance in Normandy will forever be immortalized in the history books.

Kurt Meyer

At the foot of the Cotentin peninsula, just off the main Caen–Cherbourg highway which cuts through the Calvados countryside between Bayeux and Carentan, is a sprawling cemetery, meticulously maintained. Overshadowed by oak trees and small, simple, roughly cut black stone crosses, lie the graves of 21,160 soldiers, grouped around a great funereal mound which dominates the site. This is La Cambe, last resting place of soldiers, sailors and airmen who defended Normandy against invasion.

Four more patches of Norman soil are forever German; cemeteries scattered around this historic French region, the burial sites of a further 38,000 men who died in the summer of 1944 *'für Führer, Volk und Vaterland'* – for leader, people and Fatherland. Death had indeed reaped a terrible harvest.

Had these men succeeded sixty years ago, Normandy and perhaps the rest of France might yet be forever German.

In 1944 the fate of Western Europe rested on the actions of the German forces which held the shores and fortifications of occupied France and the Allied troops sent to dislodge them. Arguably the finest new divisions Germany formed or re-formed in the winter of 1943–44 were sent west to bolster the second-rate units who had watched over the English Channel since 1940, holding the much-vaunted Atlantic Wall. On these divisions, the *Panzer Lehr*, the *Hitlerjugend*, 21st Panzer and a handful of others, the Third Reich entrusted the defence of France. The flower of the German Armed Forces, the *Wehrmacht*, of 1944 vintage would fight and, if necessary, die on French soil to safeguard the future of the Fatherland.

Of course, it never came to pass. The Allies were not destroyed on the beaches. By Thursday, 8 June 1944, when the beachheads had merged, the enemy had a firm foothold on *Festung Europa* – Fortress Europe. He would not be driven out.

In the years since American, British and Canadian soldiers swept over the beaches of the Seine Bay, Normandy has been seen more as an Allied victory than a German defeat. The men who defended Caen and Cherbourg, who escaped the hell of the Falaise pocket, have been poorly served by history and historians. Perhaps this is not entirely surprising. British, Canadians and American accounts focused on the achievements of their respective armed forces. Beyond divisional historians, German writers have concentrated their researches on the Eastern Front – and rightly so; even when the Battle for Normandy was at its peak, the number of men involved on the German side never came close to matching the Third Reich's commitment in the titanic struggle with Russia. From 1941-45, the Eastern Front was the engine of the war in Europe.

Yet in 1944 it did not appear that way. The gaze of the German public, of Germany's leaders, of her generals, was fixed towards the west, not east. The Reich's strategy for the year could be neatly summed up as: thwart the invasion then shore up the Eastern Front. And the Reich was confident of its strategy. Those who believed the invasion would succeed were in the minority in the spring of 1944. From Adolf Hitler down, the leaders of the Third Reich were confident the Allies would be smashed on the beaches. It would be a ferocious battle, yes, but the invader would be driven back whence he came.

The story of Europe's liberation has been told many times in the past six decades,[1] but rarely from the German viewpoint – despite the exhortation of the *Hitlerjugend*'s leader, Kurt Meyer.[2] It is a story which deserves to be told.

And it is a story which can be told in detail. Copious official and unofficial documents and accounts exist to allow us to recount the struggle for Normandy, from the private and public thoughts of Germany's political and military leaders, to the heroics and privations of the ordinary German soldier, the *Landser*.[3] Readers seeking a detailed tactical and strategic history of the struggle for Normandy, of unit actions, of individual companies, regiments and divisions, should look elsewhere. The account which follows is a human history of the men who fought, and in many cases died, defending *Festung Europa*, how they acted, and reacted, from Hitler and Erwin Rommel down to the lowliest soldier digging in for his life in the Norman bocage under a hail of Allied mortars and bombs.

The story of the struggle for Normandy is an appalling one; the battle was, in Erwin Rommel's words, 'one terrible blood-letting'.[4] However odious the regime he served was, the German soldier in Normandy fought bravely, for the most part honourably, and always against over-whelming enemy material and numerical superiority. The story which follows is his story.

Portsmouth, January 2006

Notes

1. The best accounts of the struggle for Normandy remain Carlo d'Este's *Decision in Normandy*, Max Hasting's *Overlord*, and the official American history, *Breakout and Pursuit*.

2. Paul Carell's flawed but readable popular history *Sie kommen! – Invasion: They're Coming!* – remains the standard work consulted by many English-speaking writers on Normandy, despite being nearly half a century old. The most trustworthy, though not especially readable, account of the 1944 battles is Ludewig's *Der deutsche Rückzug aus Frankreich*.

3. The German equivalent of the British 'Tommy' or French '*poilu*'.

4. Rommel, *The Rommel Papers* p.496.

Chapter 1

Every Night We Wait for Tommy

Day after day nothing. Nothing happened but the waves coming and going, coming and going.
Hauptmann Joachim Lindner

In the tiny village of Mollière d'Aval on the southern bank of the Somme estuary, *Gefreiter* Heinrich Böll penned a letter to his wife. Böll was a prodigious writer. Daily, almost without fail, he would write to his beloved Annemarie, a schoolteacher. Only writing and the arrival of the post alleviated the boredom for Böll, a reluctant soldier at best. Up at midday, the soldier and his comrades would eat, exercise, work on their bunker and surrounding positions and from 10 p.m. take it in turns to stand watch over the Atlantic in four-hour shifts. Böll had spent three years on and off in France, first standing watch in a bunker on the Cap Gris Nez at the narrowest point on the English Channel, now on the Somme estuary. It was monotonous, tedious. The tension gnawed at the men's nerves. 'If just once we could come face to face with the English it would be something different from this waiting, eternal waiting,' twenty-five year old Böll wrote to his wife Annemarie in August 1943. 'If the English tried to attack here on the Channel and suffered a defeat, it might perhaps bring about a decisive change in this war. Given the state of our fortifications right here they probably won't dare. But who knows how everything will turn out.'[1]

For almost four years, soldiers like Heinrich Böll 'lived like a god in France'. France was a backwater, far from the horrors of the Eastern Front, the sands of Africa, the mountains of Italy and snows of Finland. But by the spring of 1944, the ordinary German soldier, the *Landser*, knew that the days of his comparatively idyllic existence were drawing to a close.

There was evidence along the French coastline. In less than six months 500,000 obstacles, wooden and metal crosses, had been installed on the beaches, plus more than six million mines. Overlooking them on the

1

cliffs the coast was peppered with machine-gun nests, linked by trenches and hundreds of miles of barbed wire, interspersed with mighty concrete bunkers housing artillery pieces and heavy machine guns. And beyond them, a belt of mines 1,000 yards wide, low-lying land flooded to restrict movements, concrete anti-tank obstacles – dragon's teeth – fields covered with booby traps; stakes and other obstacles fitted with obsolete shells on the tip to prevent airborne landings.

There was evidence far beyond the coast; in the railway stations and junctions, bridges, marshalling yards, supply depots and ammunition dumps, gun emplacements and batteries, radar and radio sites. In the opening months of 1944, the infrastructure of the German Army in France was subjected to systematic destruction by the Allied air forces. And not just the infrastructure. In sweeps of up to 750 aircraft at a time, low-flying Jabos – *Jagdbomber*, fighter-bombers – ranged across north-west France seemingly at will, attacking trucks, trains and carriages. By the time June arrived, more than 76,000 tons of bombs had been dropped, almost cutting off western France from the rest of the Third Reich.

There was less tangible evidence; a soldier's natural instinct. Near Bayeux, artillery commander *Major* Werner Pluskat gathered his men for one of his regular pep talks. But this one, machine gunner Hein Severloh remembered, was different, darker, more fatalistic:

> Pluskat...talked about fulfilling our duty and used the usual phrases to motivate us, but his words suggested an imminent attack. Usually, such addresses finished with the phrase 'to the last drop of blood', indicating to soldiers that they should not surrender, but Pluskat used a phrase he had never uttered before at the end of his speech: A rotting German corpse can no longer save its Fatherland.[2]

A few miles to the west near the small Norman coastal town of Colleville, eighteen year old Franz Gockel gazed across the English Channel. Home to Gockel was a cramped bunker, its ceiling reinforced by more than six feet of concrete, completed as May drew to a close. 'Only once or twice a week would two German aircraft be seen flying along the coast,' Gockel recalled bitterly, then added with the *Landser*'s typical black sense of humour: 'We named them Max and Moritz.' But there was a growing sense of urgency along the Normandy coastline. New gun positions were going up, real and dummy. The alert status was raised. Veterans not much older than Gockel were certain. 'Something's in the air,' they muttered.[3]

In the balmy days of the summer of 1940 there had been no thought of an invasion in the minds of Germany's soldiers basking in the glory of victory over their traditional foe. The German Army in the west settled down to the task of occupation. At its moment of triumph, it stood just short of 100 divisions strong, ten of them armoured. There was an 'aura of invincibility' about the *Wehrmacht*; and an air of finality. The German Army's command declared confidently: 'With the decisive success in the west the tasks assigned to the Army here are completed for the time being.'[4]

Campaigns in the Balkans, North Africa and Russia soon drained the reservoir of forces in the west. When the *Wehrmacht* advanced into the Soviet Union in June 1941, just thirty-seven second-rate divisions, not a single armoured one among them, guarded the western shores. By the following spring, the number had dropped to a mere two dozen, holding the coast and interior of the Netherlands, Belgium and France, from the German border to the Spanish frontier. Quantity wasn't the only problem facing Field Marshal Gerd von Rundstedt, *Oberbefehlshaber West* – Supreme Commander, West – known simply as *OB West*. Quality was also lacking: his divisions were second-rate, units exhausted by the fighting in Russia re-forming, or new formations as yet unfit for battle.

Gerd von Rundstedt had arrived in France in March 1942 to take over command of the German Army in the West. Aristocratic, irascible, aged – he was now sixty-six – Rundstedt was the doyen of Germany's Officer Corps, a soldier for fifty-two years. He had led groups of armies to victory across Poland and France, then into the Ukraine, until he was sacked for retreating with his men at the gateway to the Caucasus in November 1941.

His unemployment had been brief. Never a Nazi – the field marshal frequently referred to Hitler as 'the Bohemian lance corporal'– Rundstedt would also never act against the regime. And that made him reliable – and employable. When called upon to safeguard the west against the invader Adolf Hitler knew would come across the Channel, von Rundstedt gushed: '*Mein Führer*, whatever you order, I shall do to my last breath.'

Rundstedt took up his post as *OB West*, at his headquarters buried beneath a slope under a school in the suburb of St Germain-en-Laye in the north-west quarter of the French capital. The marshal himself lived in a nearby home commandeered from its owner. He enjoyed the lifestyle of his command in France. Rundstedt lacked the drive of many of his fellow marshals; he rose in mid-morning and never worked beyond 8 p.m., but he also lived a modest life beyond his fondness for cigars and alcohol. As a commander, the marshal rarely made a decision on the battlefield – and never acted without consulting his staff – yet by all accounts Rundstedt was sharp, had an excellent grasp of strategy and a photographic memory. His staff were unusually fond of the veteran marshal they dubbed 'the last knight'. They were convinced his name alone 'influenced the morale and behaviour of his troops as did no other'.

The elderly field marshal quickly found his time in France frustrating; 'waiting for the "others"' gnawed at his nerves. Worse still, Rundstedt found he had no authority, despite his grandiose title. Hitler and his closest advisers on the *Wehrmacht* High Command, *Oberkommando des Wehrmacht* or OKW, oversaw operations in the west, while command of the air and naval units in his domain remained firmly in the hands of the *Luftwaffe* and German Navy, the *Kriegsmarine*. 'You see the guard posted outside,' Rundstedt once complained. 'If I want to post him on the other side of the house, I must first ask permission of Berchtesgaden.'[5]

With victories seemingly being won daily in Russia during the summer of 1941 and 1942, occupation troops left behind in France settled into a routine which was relaxed – 'a carefree life' by comparison with the rest of the Reich. 'There was entertainment,' one sailor stationed in Cherbourg recalled. 'Theatre tickets at the ready. Numerous soldiers' billets and convalescence homes had a holiday atmosphere.' It was hardly surprising, then, that *Landsers* in Russia, Italy and North Africa often accused their counterparts of '*Leben wie Gott in Frankreich*' – living like a god in France. But the German soldier billeted in the west did not live like a god. Visits to Paris, for example, were severely restricted, not merely because the city offered so many temptations; Nazi leaders didn't want German soldiers 'overrunning' the French capital, upsetting French sensibilities. Contact with the French was limited, such that one infantryman complained: 'We didn't sample the culture of France.' Slowly but surely, propaganda minister Joseph Goebbels observed, life in France was eating at the soul of the German soldier. 'Not once has living in France been good for troops on occupation duties. What I hear about our occupation forces there is anything but flattering.' A 'long rest period in a rich land', one division's war diarist complained, was not good for the discipline of the German soldier. As the occupation dragged on, inactivity, alcohol – which invariably played 'a key role' – and the temptations of French girls, led to a worrying rise in attacks, rapes, assaults and misdemeanours. Duties were monotonous; the endless *Wacht am Kanal* – guard over the Channel. Lethargy permeated every command, every army, every corps, division, regiment and battalion. *Hauptmann* Joachim Lindner, of 302nd Infantry Division holding the coast around Dieppe, captured the mood perfectly. 'Day after day nothing,' he complained. 'We had a problem with the men guarding the coast, the poor man walking with his rifle along the cliffs. Nothing happened but the waves coming and going, coming and going.' Heinrich Böll wrote home in a similar vein: 'We wait, every night we wait for Tommy, but he doesn't seem to want to come yet. I am really curious to see if he will come in the end.'[6]

Only once did 'Tommy' come in any strength. He came at Dieppe. His aim was not to invade, at least not permanently. His aim was to see if he could forge a bridgehead, if he could seize a port in occupied territory. The raid on 19 August 1942 failed almost entirely, especially around the port itself. Tanks trundled on to the beach, but got no further. They could not get around the high sea wall and, under murderous German fire, engineers could not blow a hole in the barrier. By mid-morning it was clear the landing had failed, and by 2 p.m. it was all over. An army major watched as the Allied warships laid down a thick smokescreen and turned to head back to Britain, then he ventured down to the water's edge to begin rounding up prisoners. 'In my battalion's sector alone prisoners were brought in in their thousands,' the major wrote. 'All Canadians, young, well-built chaps.' On the beach were shot-up tanks and landing craft. 'Between them hundreds of dead and the badly wounded,' the major observed. 'I have not witnessed images more terrible. In one landing craft the entire crew of about forty men had been wiped out by a direct hit. On the water we could see bits of wrecks, ships in ruins, corpses floating and soldiers wrestling with death. In Paris there was jubilation. The enemy's operation was smashed in just over nine hours!' *OB West* gloated. Shortly before 6 p.m., Hitler's head-quarters was told: 'No armed Englishman remains on the Continent.'

The Allies had lost thirty-three landing craft, 106 aircraft, every one of the twenty-eight tanks which put ashore, plus one destroyer sunk offshore. Of the 5,000 Canadians who set foot on French soil on 19 August 1942, barely 2,200 returned to Britain. All the Allies had to show for the raid were a smashed coastal battery, forty-eight downed *Luftwaffe* aircraft and around 600 German casualties. The day after the raid Rundstedt's chief-of-staff, Kurt Zeitzler, found dead Englishmen 'everywhere – mountains of bodies'. Dieppe, Zeitzler observed, 'presents a picture like Dunkirk.'[7]

Even before the Allied raid on Dieppe, an idea had begun to crystal-lize in the mind of Adolf Hitler: to build an impregnable shield along the coast of Europe – a great wall; an Atlantic Wall. A wall 'built with fanatical zeal' which would stand firm 'under all circumstances'. The Führer had been struck by the remarks of a construction worker during a tour of his defences in the west. '*Mein Führer*,' the man told him. 'I hope we're never going away from here. After all this tremendous work, that would be a pity.' Not merely would the wall defend the western shores, but it would inspire the German soldier to fight. On 13 August 1942, Hitler summoned his military and political leaders to explain his grand scheme for the west. 'The Führer wants to prevent the opening of a Second Front at all costs,' noted Alfred Jacob, the German Army's head of engineers and fortifications. 'The British might cause us difficulties at critical moments. The Führer has decided to build an impregnable wall along the Atlantic and Channel Coast.' Within this impregnable wall of 15,000 fortifications and bunkers – 10,000 of them in France – the German soldier would eat, sleep and fight. Fight and be protected. 'The most precious thing of all is German life,' Hitler declared. 'The blood spared in building this fortress is worth the billions spent on it.'[8]

Dieppe had been a warning, a portent of what was to come, as the Führer explained at length to a select group of his Western commanders and political leaders on the penultimate day of September 1942. The British would go away and lick their wounds, but they would be back. Hitler continued:

The enemy will not abandon attempts to form a Second Front, for he knows that it is the only chance he can still achieve total victory. Therefore, I regard it as my mission to do everything humanly possible to improve the defensive capability of the coast immediately.

Building an Atlantic Wall would be the 'most decisive factor' in determining the war in the Reich's favour, the Führer told his audience:

I cannot sleep securely at night if I think that the Americans and English have landed in France before I've brought the war in Russia and Africa to a victorious conclusion. I will not give up one foot of ground which is soaked in the blood of German soldiers. I will take root in France like scabies.

It would, of course, take time to build this great bulwark – until the spring of 1943, Hitler estimated. After that 'nothing more can happen to us'.[9]

The dream was eclipsed by reality. The Atlantic Wall as Adolf Hitler envisioned it in the summer of 1942 was beyond the means of the Third Reich. May 1943 was an impossible deadline for completing 15,000 new fortifications. The *Organisation Todt*, responsible for major construction projects in the Reich, believed that at best it could build just 6,000 of the positions the Führer expected of it. When building the West Wall, the line of fortifications hastily erected to protect the Reich on its border with France before 1940, one construction worker had been allocated to each metre of the wall; on the Atlantic, there would be one worker for every seven metres.

Despite its misgivings and shortages, the *Organisation Todt* set to work. There were already almost 5,000 bunkers, gun positions, trenches and other fortifications in the west. By the middle of 1943, there were more than 8,000, as a workforce 250,000 strong toiled. The Atlantic Wall was centred around hundreds of strong points – sizeable fortifications housing artillery positions, machine-gun nests, bunkers and shelters, surrounded by a network of trenches, barbed wire and anti-tank barriers.

The press described the Atlantic Wall as 'the greatest and strongest line of fortifications military history has seen'. It was regarded as a 'shield of steel and concrete and a safeguard of the values of Europe'. Gerd von Rundstedt was less impressed. The Atlantic Wall, he later declared, was 'sheer humbug'. Adolf Hitler expected his coastal bulwark to hold out for a month or more. Von Rundstedt believed at best it could delay the enemy for just twenty-four hours.[10]

Fortunately for von Rundstedt and his men, the Allied landings in 1943 were concentrated in the Mediterranean, first in Sicily, then in mainland Italy. But the asset stripping of France to feed the mincing machine of the Eastern Front now extended to feeding Italy as well. Work on the Atlantic Wall slowed, too, as the Reich's labour force was called upon to make good the effects of the enemy's air offensive against the Fatherland. It could not go on. 'The limit of what is possible and bearable has been reached and in some places has been surpassed,' Rundstedt complained to Berlin.

Each week von Rundstedt had reported with growing concern about the state of affairs in France. By October 1943, intelligence reports suggested that the Allies had a seventeen-division advantage in the west. If the enemy did its sums as the German High Command was doing, he didn't have 'a single reason for not attacking'. It was time to stop, the field marshal told Berlin, the constant 'diluting' of his forces, taking away the best men, replacing them with worn-out troops from the east, old men, non-Germanic 'volunteers'. Things had gone too far. 'Do not be surprised if – in spite of the Atlantic Wall and the total commitment of men and commanders – there's no defensive success in the event of a major enemy attack supported by all his material strength,' he warned bluntly in a report intended specifically for Adolf Hitler's eyes.[11]

For once, the Führer took note of his field marshal's warnings. 'There's no doubt that the attack in the west will come in the spring,' he told his staff. 'If they attack in the west, this attack will decide the war.' Barely a week after Rundstedt's report arrived on his desk at his headquarters in East Prussia, Adolf Hitler had issued a 'directive for the conduct of the war', his fifty-first:

The hard and costly struggle against Bolshevism during the last two and a half years has demanded extreme sacrifices. The scale of the threat there and the overall situation demanded them. Since then, the situation has changed, however. The threat in the east still exists; an even greater threat exists in the west: an Anglo-Saxon landing!

In the East, the sheer scale of land allows us to lose ground – even on a large scale – without a fatal blow being dealt to Germany.

Not so in the west! If the enemy succeeds in penetrating our defences on a broad front, the immediate results would be staggering. Everything points to the enemy launching an offensive against the Western Front in Europe, at the very latest next spring, perhaps even earlier.

Therefore, I can no longer take responsibility for weakening the west any longer in favour of other theatres of war. Rather, I have decided to strengthen its defences... For it is here that the enemy must – and will – attack, and it is here, unless all the signs are wrong, that the decisive battle against the invasion forces will be fought.

The Reich would be protected by a ring of iron, steel and concrete. The Führer promised new artillery, anti-tank weapons, machine guns, mines, panzers, fresh troops – regular infantry, grenadiers, panzer, and *Waffen SS*. 'Everything we have in Germany which is fit for battle,' Hitler declared, 'will be hurled against the invader immediately.' In 1944, the Third Reich would concentrate its efforts and the flower of its youth on the Western Front.

Adolf Hitler had just the man in mind to lead this impending battle against the invader: Erwin Rommel.[12]

For twelve months Erwin Rommel's star had been on the wane. In two years he had risen from the relatively lowly rank of divisional commander to field marshal. But since attaining Germany's highest military rank for seizing the fortress of Tobruk in June 1942, the war had turned against Erwin Rommel. Now on the cusp of his fifty-second birthday the Desert Fox, as the British liked to call him, was inspired once again. Born the son of a schoolmaster in Ulm, near Wurttemberg, in November 1891, Rommel had enlisted in the Imperial Army as an officer candidate aged nineteen. The young officer impressed. 'Rommel is built to command and lead men in war,' an early instructor wrote. 'Without doubt he will become an extraordinary officer.'[13] And so it proved. Rommel fought with distinction in France, Romania, but especially Italy during the 1914-18 conflagration, earning Imperial Germany's highest military honour *Pour le Mérite* for the capture of

8,000 Italians in the autumn of 1917.

The young officer remained in the rump of the German Army permitted after the Versailles Treaty, but in peacetime his progress up the ranks was slow. Rommel spent nine years as a company commander, then on to Dresden as an infantry instructor. Not even the Nazis' assumption of power in 1933 propelled the officer's career. Only when he set down an infantry manual, *Infanterie Greift an – Infantry Attacks* – based on his Great War experiences, and served as Hitler's escort at the Nuremberg rallies of 1936, did the officer come to the Führer's attention. In March 1939 he was summoned to command Hitler's mobile headquarters, first in Czechoslovakia, then at Memel, and finally in Poland.

But it was Erwin Rommel's lightning thrust through France in May and June 1940 with 7th Panzer Division – the 'Ghost Division' – which truly captured the public's, and Hitler's, imagination. The prize was command of German forces being sent to assist Italy in the spring of 1941, the *Afrika Korps*. Within three months, Rommel had his troops at the gates of Tobruk. There they stayed, until the British drove them back that winter to where they had begun their campaign of 1941. In the late spring of 1942, Rommel struck again. This time Tobruk fell and the road to Egypt opened up. His feat earned him the rank of field marshal; it also unsettled the British commander Claude Auchinleck, who told his men 'Rommel is no "bogey man" with superhuman powers; he is merely energetic and capable, that is all.'[14] Rommel was indeed no bogey man. Auchinleck brought him to a stop at a small railway halt near the Mediterranean coast: El Alamein.

That July, the Axis advance in North Africa finally ended. With it, Rommel's health cracked. Prone to spells of fainting caused by low blood pressure, by the middle of September 1942, Erwin Rommel was no longer fit to command. He was still recovering from his stomach complaint in an Austrian spa when a new British commander, Bernard Montgomery, struck at Alamein. The field marshal flew back to Africa, but once his lines broke, so too did his spirit. 'The battle is going heavily against us,' he wrote to his wife Lucie. 'We're simply being crushed by the enemy weight. The dead are lucky. It's all over for them.'[15] Rommel rallied. His men rallied. But the tide had turned against the Axis in North Africa. For five more months Anglo-American forces pushed the German-Italian Army back across the desert. By the end of February 1943, Rommel's health had collapsed too. He had rheumatism and his heart and nerves could stand the strain no more. On 9 March 1943 Erwin Rommel left North Africa. He would not return.

For four months, Erwin Rommel had no employment. He was a frequent visitor to Hitler's headquarters in East Prussia, where the field marshal and the Führer talked about the outcome of the war, about the fate of Italy, about the defence of Europe. When the Allies invaded Sicily on 10 July, Hitler decided it was time to employ his field marshal again. The name 'Rommel' meant too much to friend and foe alike. 'However history will judge him, Field Marshal Rommel has always been much loved by his soldiers, especially German troops,' the Führer told Mussolini. 'What is more, he has been, and always will be, greatly feared by the enemy.'[16] Rommel would take charge of Axis forces in central Italy, but pessimism dogged his appointment, convinced as he was an Axis collapse in Italy was 'just around the corner'. At the end of October 1943, Hitler decided an optimist was needed and replaced Rommel. His unemployment lasted barely a week. On 5 November 1943 came a summons to *Wolfschanze* – the Wolf's Lair – in East Prussia.

Rommel's mission, as the Führer explained, would be to inspect the defences of the west, from Denmark to Brittany, and decide how to defeat the Allied invasion which would come in 1944. The field marshal was left in no doubt about the importance of his task. 'When the enemy invades in the west it will be the moment of decision in this war,' Hitler impressed on him.

Rommel set about his task immediately. In the dying days of 1943, the field marshal was almost constantly on the road, inspecting the defences of the Atlantic coastline. The much-touted Atlantic Wall was not all it seemed. True, there were thousands of gun emplacements, bunkers and fortifications partially or wholly completed. But Rommel and his staff had expected much more from this supposed bulwark, as the field marshal's naval adviser Friedrich Ruge complained. 'The wall, so highly praised by the propaganda, existed in harsh reality only in a few places.' Only around Calais and Boulogne were there any fortifications which merited the title 'wall'. The divisions defending France left a lot to be desired too. Each one was marked on the map with a small flag, but the flag took no account of the differences in training and quality, and there were, Ruge noted, 'virtually no high-quality field divisions' in the west.[17]

Not high quality, but surprisingly high spirited. The festive season of 1943 found the German soldier in France and Belgium in remarkably good heart. Each man knew that 1944 would be the year of decision in the west. 'As black as 1943 was for us, we confidently begin the year of victory,' a *Gefreiter* with a flak unit scribbled enthusiastically to his wife. 'There's no doubt there'll be a storm in the west, which will be no weaker than the one in the east, but will not last as long. With it will come the decision, and since there can only be victory, it can only come for us.' A young officer cadet from Osnabrück posted to the Channel coast wrote in a similar vein: '1944 will see us steadfast and victorious on all fronts, although the struggle will be hard. Our faith in the Führer is boundless, and we know that at the end of this struggle the only victory will be ours.'

In Belgium, SS *Untersturmführer* Hannes Philipsen listened intently to Hitler's New Year appeal – 'wherever the Allies might land, they will be given a suitable reception'. Philipsen's 101st SS Panzer Battalion was training with ten new Tiger tanks for the impending invasion. 'The world struggle is raging more fiercely than ever,' he wrote home. 'Today marks the end of another year of exertion and sacrifice for our people. It has demanded much of all of us. The coming year shall find us even more ready in unshakeable faith in our Führer. He will lead us into a happier future.' 1943 had been bitter. But 1944 would be the year of Germany's victory.[18]

Erwin Rommel was nearly three weeks into his new appointment when he called on the irascible Commander-in-Chief, West. The Desert Fox was full of confidence ahead of his new task; Rundstedt full of pessimism. Rommel, the elderly field marshal explained, would be disappointed by 'the poor quality of the troops, the dangerous weakness of the *Luftwaffe*, the complete lack of a powerful reserve'. In English, Rundstedt turned to his young upstart. 'It all looks very black to me.' Black or not, Rommel was strangely encouraged by the meeting. 'He seems very pleased and I think it's all going well,' he wrote to Lucie.[19]

The differences between the two marshals could not have been greater. Rommel was a thunderball of energy, normally on the road by 6 a.m., inspiring, cajoling, encouraging or berating. Rundstedt, by contrast, rarely rose before 10.30 a.m., left most of his work to his team of dedicated staff officers, and rarely got involved in the day-to-day affairs of his armies in the west. The elderly field marshal, Hitler's chief of operations Alfred Jodl bitterly commented, would do well to swap his life of luxury for 'a command post where he can see the skies, where the sun shines and where it smells fresher'. Such indolence seemed to characterize all the headquarters in the west, Jodl found during an inspection tour. 'The military spirit is completely missing. Fancy chairs and carpets lead to the lifestyle of a royal court.' The general returned to Hitler's headquarters with a damning assessment of the commanders in France. 'The west is full of officers who would rather live in the eighteenth century than in National Socialist Germany.' Rundstedt, Jodl declared, 'must not only identify the dross,[20] but get rid of it. Not even Hercules was spared this task before he entered Mount Olympus.'[21]

Erwin Rommel began the new year turning his ideas into reality. His tour of the Pas de Calais had convinced him that the invader had to be

11

defeated at the water's edge. 'The most difficult moment for the enemy occurs during the moment of landing itself,' he declared. 'He has to be overpowered before he reaches the rim of the coast.' And so the beach would be turned into the first stage of a great zone of death. Stakes were driven into the sand, with mines fixed to the end, concrete and steel crosses dug in to tear the bottom out of any landing craft. The beach was only to be the beginning of Rommel's great plan for the west, however. What he proposed was far more comprehensive than the Atlantic Wall's waterfront bunkers and gun emplacements. The entire coastline would become a fortified strip five to six miles deep, crammed with mines, guarded by machine guns, anti-tank weapons, mortars, heavy artillery. As things stood at the end of 1943, Rommel was convinced that the invader would succeed. But come the summer of 1944, things would be different. 'I believe we shall win the defensive battle in the west if we still have time to prepare,' the field marshal wrote to his wife Lucie. 'I believe we can repulse the onslaught.'[22]

The greatest concern in the west, Erwin Rommel quickly learned, was the *Luftwaffe*. Its shortcomings were typified by its commander, the portly, arrogant and lazy Field Marshal Hugo Sperrle. Sperrle had commanded *Luftflotte 3* – Third Air Fleet – the senior air unit in the west, since the fall of France in the spring of 1940. Everything about the fifty-nine year old field marshal gave the impression of a man who had enjoyed four years of luxury in a backwater of the war, from his head-quarters in a château outside Paris to his nightly banquets. Hitler considered sacking Sperrle. 'Like every other *Luftwaffe* general he withdrew to a château,' the Führer rasped. 'He was less interested in the air war against England than a fine lunch or dinner.' Sperrle at least 'understood the situation clearly, especially the weakness of the *Luftwaffe*,' according to Friedrich Ruge; he could, however, 'give no hope that the situation would improve markedly.' Erwin Rommel was less impressed than his naval adviser. 'From what I heard before, I had expected much more of this service.'[23]

Like Rommel, the *Luftwaffe* had a grand plan to defeat the invasion: *Drohende Gefahr West* – Threatening Danger, West. In the weeks and months preceding the landings, when an Allied aerial onslaught was expected against *Luftflotte 3*'s bases, the *Luftwaffe* would withdraw from its forward airfields and scatter to temporary bases across northern France, the Low Countries and Germany. Formations were dispersed, stripped to the bare bones, given additional flak units to fight off the Allied raids, while dummy airfields were established across north-west France and the Low Countries to divert the enemy air raids. And, when the invader came, the *Luftwaffe* would flood into France for the decisive aerial counter-punch. 'The moment the British try and invade France to establish a second front, I will not leave a single fighter aircraft to the defence of the Reich,' Hermann Goering, the *Luftwaffe*'s vainglorious leader, boasted. 'Every single aircraft which is airworthy will be sent forward, and the Reich itself will not have an aircraft to its name – come hell or high water.' All the scattered units would return to the invasion front to strike a decisive blow and *Luftflotte 3* would also 'borrow' formations from the south of France, Italy, Denmark, the western and southern parts of the Reich, even Greece, to smash the invasion.[24] Such was the plan...

The German Navy, the *Kriegsmarine*, had also drawn up grandiose plans to defeat the impending invasion. Its commander-in-chief, *Grossadmiral* Karl Dönitz, expected his men to 'prepare a bloody welcome for our enemies and bar their entry to Europe!' The Navy, Dönitz told his commanders, would have a task 'which it will have to carry out fanatically summoning all its strength. There can be no withdrawals, not one metre.' If the invasion was defeated, the enemy would not repeat the attempt.

Words were just about all that Karl Dönitz could offer his commander in the west. No one knew the weakness of his forces better than *Vizeadmiral* Theodor Krancke, the man charged with defeating the invasion at sea. It was a hopeless task, the fifty-one year old admiral concluded. Since April 1943, Krancke had commanded all surface forces in France and Belgium, along more than 1,200 miles of coastline, plus the 350 miles of shore on the French Mediterranean coast. And what did he have to defend them? A few thousand poorly-trained and badly-equipped sailors, a handful of destroyers, and a few score motorboats. Such was the strength of the grandly-titled *Marinegruppe West* – Naval Group West – as it faced its sternest test. It was not enough, the *Vizeadmiral* warned Berlin from his headquarters in Paris. 'The few available destroyers, torpedo and speed boats can only harass an enemy landing, but they cannot effectively impede it.'[25]

And so the burden of the struggle in the west would rest upon the shoulders of the German Army. But in this fifth year of the war, the Army was tired. Germany had suffered casualties nearing four million, three out of four of them on the Eastern Front. 1943 had been a punishing year in Russia. Since July alone, Germany had lost more than 1,200,000 men. The losses could not be made good. Even after stripping Italy and especially France, even after sending more than a quarter of a million men from the training schools, even after sending wounded men back to the front, the German Army in Russia still found itself more than 300,000 short.

Short of men in the east, short of men in the west, Germany turned to desperate measures to fill its thinning ranks. Hitler was convinced the rear areas, supply depots, offices and administrations would prove to be a rich source of untapped manhood. He ordered every division, every naval and *Luftwaffe* unit to comb out men who could be spared duties behind the lines so they could be sent to the front. But combing out the *Wehrmacht* could not solve all its ills. The losses had simply been too great. In 1943, the German military machine began calling up seventeen and eighteen year olds and relying more and more heavily on foreign 'volunteers': *Volksdeutsche* – ethnic Germans, born outside the Fatherland; *Freiwillige* – foreign volunteers sympathetic to the Nazi cause – and *Hilfswillige* or 'Hiwis' – auxiliaries, usually Russians or Poles pressed into military service from the occupied territories or recruited from the millions of prisoners of war wasting away in German camps. With the war turning against the *Wehrmacht* in the east, it was no longer safe to use anti-Bolshevik Russians on the Eastern Front. From the autumn of 1943 onwards, the High Command steadily began swapping German troops behind the Atlantic Wall for these so-called *Osttruppen* – eastern troops. By the spring of 1944, one in six infantry battalions along the Atlantic Coast was composed of *Osttruppen* and foreign volunteers – Russians, Poles, Italians, Hungarians, Romanians, Ukrainians among them. On the eastern coast of the Cotentin peninsula, 709th Infantry Division was typical of the second-rate divisions defending the west in 1944. One in five in its ranks was a volunteer from the east. Its commander, Karl Wilhelm von Schlieben, was sceptical. 'We are asking rather a lot if we expect Russians to fight in France for Germany against Americans.'[26]

And numbers alone would not be enough, Germany's leaders realized. The *Landser* had to believe in the cause he was fighting for. Almost every man did. He had sworn allegiance to the Führer. That was only the beginning of the soldier's indoctrination in National Socialist principles in the ranks. 'Faith in the Führer and his ideology is the bedrock for the life of all German people,' the ordinary soldier was told. But as the war drew on, as the enemy advanced in Russia, in Italy, as his air forces pummelled the cities of the Reich, faith in the Führer was not enough. The men needed constant National Socialist instruction, Adolf Hitler decided. It came in the shape of the *Nationalsozialistisches Führungsoffizier* – the National Socialist Leadership Officer – a political commissar in the ranks of the German Army, to spread the Nazi word. 'The only decisive factors are the high values possessed by a nation,' the commissars preached. 'Bravery, iron discipline, honour and the nation's consciousness of being the standard bearers and the protagonists of a lofty idea.' In short, the *Landser* had to be 'more than a fighter'.[27] He would fight to the last round rather than give up his post and retreat. 'The captain of a ship goes down with it, with the flag flying. German military tradition has never known it any differently,' Rundstedt ordered. And if he would not fight to the last – if he would not face Allied bullets – he would face German ones.[28]

Nowhere did indoctrination and political instruction fall upon more fertile ground than in the ranks of the *Waffen SS*. No soldier, no division instilled more fear in the enemy than the men and ranks of Heinrich Himmler's private army. The *Waffen* – armed – SS had begun the war as an insignificant fighting force. It had not even begun the war as the *Waffen SS*, rather the *SS Verfügungstruppe* – SS special duty troops – a small elite group of armed SS regiments created by their leader Himmler and placed at the army's disposal. Better physical specimens, better trained, at times better equipped, and better motivated than comparative army units, the growing SS formations proved their worth on the Eastern Front.

In the summer and autumn of 1943, four new SS divisions were taking shape in France and Belgium – three armoured, one armoured infantry, or panzer grenadiers. All were born out of the debacle that winter at Stalingrad and the Caucasus, where Germany's southern wing of the Eastern Front had all but disintegrated. The finest new division was the 12th SS Panzer, the *Hitlerjugend*, so named for its ranks were drawn exclusively from the Hitler Youth – boys born as recently as 1926. In the summer of 1943, near Brussels, the 12th SS began to take shape. There was no shortage of volunteers for the *Hitlerjugend*. By the beginning of June 1944, there were more than 20,000 'men' in its ranks. On paper it was one of the strongest divisions in the west. But only on paper. The ranks were full, but the *Hitlerjugend* had barely half its NCOs and lacked one fifth of its officers.

Youth characterized the other *Waffen SS* divisions forming in the west in 1943 – 9th, 10th and 17th. Two out of every three men in the new SS divisions were aged twenty or under. The Hitler Youth had proved to be a fertile recruiting ground for the *Hitlerjugend* Panzer division. 9th *SS Hohenstaufen*, drawing its name from ancient German emperors, and its sister motorized division, 10th *SS Frundsberg*, named after a sixteenth century military leader, were supposed to be raised from Germany's labour service, the *Reichsarbeitsdienst*. But of the 27,000 men recruited for the *Frundsberg* and *Hohenstaufen* in their formative months, fewer than half were volunteers.

Press-ganged into service or not, the physical requirements for the *Waffen SS* remained forbidding; no recruit under five feet ten inches was accepted – the minimum for the men of the elite 1st SS Panzer, the *Leibstandarte*, which would join battle in Normandy later in the summer, was an inch taller and one filled tooth was sufficient to ensure

15

rejection. Physical strength was matched by moral fortitude. Heinrich Himmler expected his men to stand by their motto – *Mein Ehre heißt treue*, loyalty is my honour. 'Never look deflated, never despair, always fight,' the *Reichsführer* told the ranks of the 17th SS Panzer Grenadiers, training in France in the spring of 1944. 'It is to be drummed into every man in this division down to the youngest recruit that the individual is never to capitulate, never to allow himself to become a prisoner.'[29]

Erwin Rommel believed in action, not words. In the opening months of 1944 there was a new energy driving German defensive efforts in France. The workload of officers and men mushroomed. In a two-week period in February, more than 4,000 orders, teletypes and special instructions had crossed his desk; in a single day, *OB West*'s headquarters had fielded 8,788 telephone calls. There was physical evidence too of Rommel's impact in the west. In four months upwards of four million mines were buried beneath the soil and sands of France, and a further 500,000 barriers littered the beaches. Adolf Hitler was impressed. He told propaganda minister Joseph Goebbels:

> Rommel has set an example in the west. He has an old score to settle with the English and Americans. Inside he burns with anger and hatred and has devoted all his skill and all his finesse to perfecting the defences there. Rommel is the old warrior again. He has fully recovered from his illness. There's no longer any hint of defeatism in him. On the contrary, he yearns for the day when he can grapple with his old enemies.[30]

General Erich Marcks was similarly impressed. 'Rommel is a tremendous force and full of ideas,' he told his wife. 'He's hot-tempered, often blows his top – he really puts the wind up his commanders. The first person to report to him in the morning is eaten for breakfast.' Marcks was among those 'eaten for breakfast'. His corps, LXXXIV, was one of the strongest in the west – five divisions defending 250 miles of shore, including the Channel Islands, as well as the interior of Normandy. The quality of the men varied – 319th Infantry Division in the Channel Islands had been stripped of most of its troops; the ranks of 716th and 709th Infantry Divisions defending the Caen area and the Cherbourg peninsula respectively were in places filled by men in their mid-forties. And yet for all this, Erich Marcks was confident. Confident that the invasion would come in Normandy, and confident that his men would defeat it. 'It's highly gratifying to see the number and quality of divisions that we can still turn out in this, the fifth war year!' he declared. 'We had nothing remotely like it left in 1918.' Rommel stopped the corps commander in his tracks. His troops, the field marshal said bluntly, were not working hard enough. 'It's a good thing that despite his frankness he's highly thought of by Adolf Hitler and has been entrusted with important tasks,' Marcks wrote, surprisingly buoyed by his meeting with the Desert Fox. 'I got the impression that he's not only a real adventurer, but also a great warrior.'[31]

But in the spring of 1944, the mood of the 'great warrior' fluctuated wildly. Confident one day, melancholy the next. 'Now that March is nearing its end without the Anglo-Americans having started their attack, I'm beginning to believe they've lost confidence in their cause,' he wrote to his wife on 30 March. A week later, he added: 'The tension grows greater and greater here. Probably only a few weeks separate us from the decisive event. I will make good use of the time and push things on as much as possible. Then we can, I think, face the attack calmly.' Three days later, he was less confident. 'There's an endless amount to do to be 100 per cent ready when the battle begins,' he told Lucie. 'I hope that we will pull it off.' And on the 16th, he confided fatalistically in his diary: 'What will history say in passing its verdict on me? If I am successful here, then everybody else will claim all the glory. But if I fail here, then everybody will be after my blood.'[32]

If Rommel had his doubts, so too did his men. Doubts about the impending battle, doubts about the war's outcome. Those who had never seen battle yearned for action. Nineteen year old Werner Kortenhaus had spent a year in France longing to get at the Allies with his comrades in 21st Panzer Division. 'We thought "Let them get here, we'll throw them out again",' he recalled. 'We genuinely believed that we were so strong we would throw them out again. We were young men and in a way we burned for a little action.' *Schütze* Jochen Leykauff also waited anxiously for his *Feuertaufe* – baptism of fire – with the *Hitlerjugend*. 'Our first action lay ahead,' he wrote. 'We were looking forward to it. The Allies planned to take apart the "baby milk division" as they called us. But we were not afraid.' Older soldiers, the veterans, were afraid, even fatalistic. 'We felt in our bones instinctively that something terrible was to come,' recalled *Fallschirmjäger* Karl Max Wietzorek, at nineteen already a veteran of the Eastern Front. Another *Ostfront* veteran, Helmut Gunther, a senior non-commissioned officer in the newly-formed 17th SS Panzer Grenadiers, knew the impending clash would be different from anything he had yet faced. 'In Russia we had fought men against men,' he remembered. 'We knew that in Normandy it would be men against machines. We no longer expected total victory, but we still felt an absolute sense of loyalty.'[33]

What neither rookie nor veteran could stand was the uncertainty; the interminable waiting. 'The inactivity was wearisome and dangerous,' recalled *Major* Hans von Luck. There were few places the aristocratic von Luck had not fought – Poland, France, Russia, Africa. His men, a regiment of panzer grenadiers billeted outside Caen, enjoyed butter, cheese, cider, meat and crème fraîche, the very best of what Normandy's farmers could produce. 'I was used to mobile actions,' the frustrated officer wrote. 'This waiting for an invasion that was undoubtedly coming was enervating.'

As May passed and the weather improved by the day, one senior non-commissioned officer wrote home:

> I hate this fleeting, uncanny quiet. There's the feeling that here we're waiting for something big. Sometimes I think there'll be an invasion, and then later I have my doubts. At the moment I believe that Tommy will come.[34]

Notes

1. Böll letters, 31/7/42, 21/8/43. Böll, pp.416, 850. Heinrich Böll would not see the 'English' – as the Germans insisted upon calling the British – 'dare' to land on the shores of France. He was transferred to the Crimea that autumn.
2. Severloh, p.19.
3. Gockel memoirs. search.eb.com/Normandy.
4. Das Reich, 26/5/40; KTB HGr.A Appendices, 26/6/40. IWM AL 1043/1.
5. *OB West: A Study in Command*, p.12; *Nazi Conspiracy and Aggression*, Volume B, p.1285; Messenger, *Last Prussian*, p.162; Geyr, p.205.
6. Tewes, pp.165, 205, 291; Bartov, p.68; Fowler, *Commandos at Dieppe*, p.123; Böll letter, 4/8/42. Böll, p.422; Tagebuch Goebbels, 1/3/42.
7. Fischer, Karl (ed), *Die Wehrmacht: Das Buch des Kriegs 1941-1942*, p.168; OB West report, 3/9/42. NA CAB 146/474; Ritgen, pp.10-15; KTB Skl, 20/8/42; OB West report, 3/9/42. NA CAB 146/474.
8. KTB *General* Alfred Jacob, 2/8/42, 13/8/42. NA CAB 146/480. Hitler's Table Talk, 13/5/42. KTB Skl, 17/8/42.
9. Heber, pp.271-4; Seidler, p.39.
10. Wilt, passim; Heber, pp.280-82; Seidler, p.47. Shulman, p.129.
11. Heber, p.343; KTB OKW, 25/10/43; OB West Report, 25/10/43. Cited in Heber, pp.370-89.
12. Heiber and Glantz, pp.311, 314; Directive No.51, 3/11/43. Author's papers.
13. Lormier, p.16.
14. KTB OKW 2/7/42.
15. Rommel to his wife, 3/11/42. Rommel, p.320.
16. Hitler to Mussolini, 14/3/43. NA CAB 146/26
17. IWM AL 768; Irving, *Trail of the Fox*, p.284; Ruge, p.33.
18. Buchbender, p.130; Mohrmann, p.137; Agte, p.236.
19. Messenger, pp.176-7; Rommel, p.461.
20. 'Scheisse'.
21. Müller and Volkmann, *Die Wehrmacht: Mythos und Realität*, p.378.
22. Ruge, pp.l5, 32; Rommel, pp.453-6; Rommel to his wife, 6/1/44, 19/1/44. NA CAB 146/336.
23. TB Goebbels, 9/3/43; Ruge, pp.37-8; Rommel to his wife, 29/12/43. NA CAB 146/336.
24. KTB OKW, Band 3, Pt.2, pp.1476-80; Boog et al, *Das Deutsche Reich und der Zweite Weltkrieg*, Band 7, pp.483, 485; Irving, *Rise and Fall of the Luftwaffe*, pp.249-50.
25. Salewski, ii, pp.410, 413-14; Nuremberg Trials Document D-443.

26. Carell, *Invasion – They're Coming*, p.104.
27. 'Mehr Kampfer'.
28. Messerschmidt, p.344; 'Instructions on National Socialist Leadership in the Army', 28/3/44. NA WO204/987; Wegmüller, pp.63, 191; Boog et al, *Das Deutsche Reich und der Zweite Weltkrieg*, Band 7, p.469.
29. Stöber, Band I, p.454.
30. TB Goebbels, 18/4/44.
31. Jacobsen, Otto, Erich Marcks, *Soldat und Gelehrter*, pp.159-60; Irving, *Trail of the Fox*, p.317; Ruge, pp.65-7.
32. Rommel to his wife, 30/3/44. Ryan, *Longest Day*, p.17; Rommel to his wife, 6/4/44, 9/4/44. NA CAB 146/336; Irving, *Trail of the Fox*, p.310.
33. Miller, *Nothing Less Than Victory*, p.86; Meyer, *12 SS Panzer Division Hitlerjugend*, p.10; McKee, p.23; Hastings, *Overlord*, p.78.
34. Luck, pp.169, 171; Buchbender, p.131.

Chapter 2

The Last Opportunity to Turn the Tide

We never talked about the invasion but we thought of it incessantly
– and of our death.
Oberleutnant Herbert Werner

In the headquarters of Seventh Army in Le Mans the teleprinter
chattered away furiously. With the feverish activity along the Channel
coast and across it, there was a flurry of messages arriving at
Generaloberst Eugen Dollmann's command post. This latest instruction
came with a caveat: at the right moment the message was to be read to
every soldier in France:

Soldiers of the Western Front.

The enemy has begun his long-awaited attack on Europe. His aim is
well known to all of us. You are called upon to frustrate him – thus
guaranteeing our national security, our existence and the future of
our nation. In the victorious western offensive of May and June
1940 the military and matériel preconditions for this clash were
created. Since then powerful fortifications have been built along
Europe's coast through years of work. Here, you will now defend
our continent. Here you will smash the attack by our enemies
against our people and our Reich.

Soldiers, in this historic hour, I appeal to your bravery, to your
proven courage and to the steadfastness of your hearts. Your task is
to deny the enemy entry to Europe at all costs. In this struggle, join
the strength of your weapons with the strength in your souls.
Defence against this attack is a matter of life and death for our
nation and a historic task, whose fateful dimension demands the
very utmost from every one of you. Here there can be no escape, no
manoeuvre. Here what counts is to stand, to hold or to die. Every
leader, every commander of a base, an island or a fortress or a ship
is honour-bound to me never to capitulate; he will continue the

struggle to the last fighter, to the last shell, to the last round. In these days, the German people and the entire world are looking at you.

I know, my heroic soldiers, that each one of you is filled with the will to fight for a fortunate future for our people in the next few days – and ultimately to secure it. Wherever the enemy attacks, he must be destroyed. He will not succeed in gaining a foothold on a coast defended by us. Victory will therefore be ours! You are called upon to fight for it and so fulfil the legacy of our fallen comrades.

Adolf Hitler[1]

Adolf Hitler was enjoying a Bavarian spring in the Alps. The impending invasion was attaining almost mythical importance for the Führer and his staff. 'The Führer is convinced that the invasion will fail, in fact, that he can repel it in a grand fashion,' Joseph Goebbels recorded after a lengthy talk. 'He's convinced that the decision in this war might possibly be linked with the invasion.' His troops were better than the enemy's, battle-hardened, imbued with belief in the cause. His defences grew stronger by the day. Any landing, he confidently declared, would be 'nipped in the bud'. With Italian leader Benito Mussolini on 22 April, Hitler predicted that the English 'would have the shock of their lives if they landed in the west'. He told the Duce: 'When the invasion came there would only be one surprise and that would be the one the English would receive when they landed.' And to Goebbels again four days later: 'We are ready. Nothing particularly unpleasant can happen any more. The enemy's daily bluster doesn't impress him in the slightest.'[2] The Führer nevertheless believed his commanders in the west needed a pep talk, a final exhortation. He summoned Rommel, Rundstedt, Sperrle and Krancke to his alpine retreat at Berchtesgaden. He left none of them in any doubt about the importance of their historic task:

The enemy's entire landing operation must under no circumstances be allowed to last longer than a matter of hours, or, at the most, days. Once the landing has been defeated it will under no circumstances be repeated. Quite apart from the heavy casualties he would suffer, months would be needed to prepare for a renewed attempt. There would also be a crushing blow to morale which a miscarried invasion would give.

The destruction of the enemy's landing attempt means more than a purely local decision on the Western Front. It is the sole decisive factor in the whole conduct of the war and hence in its final result.

On every single man fighting on the Western Front depends the outcome of the war and with it the fate of the Reich. This must become part and parcel of the thought process of every single officer

21

and man.[3]

While Hitler briefed his military commanders, his senior military adviser, *Generaloberst* Alfred Jodl, addressed the nation's political leaders. The message was the same:

> Unless it's all a trick and we are not dealing with the greatest bluff in the history of the world, then we are faced with a major landing by the Western Powers and therefore a battle decisive for the outcome of this war and for our future. The enemy has completed all his military and political preparations. The path for us is clearly marked out. Before us stands either victory or destruction.
>
> We have burned our bridges. Our troops will now have to fight like never before. I have no illusions about the seriousness of the struggle. But on the enemy's side, divisions which are not experienced in battle will have to be used for the first time. I await the battle full of confidence. A defensive victory will change the military and political situation, for you cannot simply repeat such a landing, which you have been preparing for down to the minutest detail for years, to say nothing of the domestic consequences in England and America.[4]

In the impressive château which served as his headquarters at La Roche-Guyon, half way along the Seine between Paris and the great river's estuary, Erwin Rommel sat down at his desk to write a few lines to his beloved Lucie. Twice a week, letters winged their way eastwards to the Rommel family home in southern Germany. In each one the field marshal had confided the ups and downs of his assignment in the west, from apprehension at the turn of the year to growing optimism as 1944 dragged on and still the invaders had not come. 'Still no signs of the British and Americans,' he wrote to his wife on 6 May. 'Every day, every week, we get stronger.' Two days later, Lucie received another letter. 'The enemy's offensive appears to have been delayed. For us every day is worth a fortune,' her husband wrote. The field marshal addressed his son Manfred in similar fashion. 'We are engaged in a serious battle, the most decisive battle of this war,' he told him. 'Extraordinary things have been accomplished in the last few months and weeks.'

Time was what Germany needed that spring. Time to complete Rommel's death zone which was formidable but by no means impregnable that May. 'If the British give us just two more weeks,' the field marshal told his adjutant Hellmuth Lang, 'then I won't have any more doubts about it.'[5]

By the spring of 1944, Erwin Rommel was more than simply Hitler's

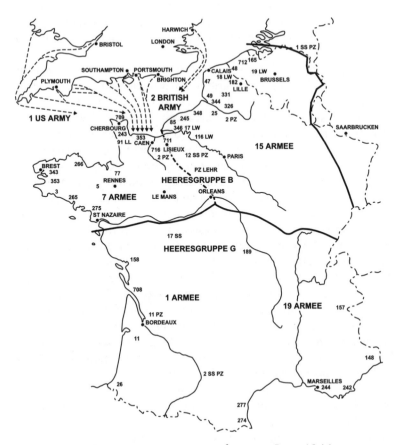

German Army units in the west, June 1944

inspector of the defences in the west. The Führer had also ordered him to take charge of defeating the invasion, commanding a new army group, B, overseeing the two best armies in France. Fifteenth Army guarded the Pas de Calais – where an invasion seemed most likely – and upper Normandy; the weaker Seventh Army protected 900 miles of coast from the estuary of the Orne north of Caen to the mouth of the Loire. The château at La Roche-Guyon, whose parts dated back to anywhere between the eleventh and seventeenth centuries, was part of the field marshal's new command. Rommel's staff grew too; in the network of tunnels which ran through the soft limestone under the castle, briefing rooms and communications centres were set up. But the field marshal found his new command frustrating; Gerd von Rundstedt was still his superior and, above all, Rommel had no authority over the

German Army's most potent weapon in the west, the armoured punch of *Panzergruppe West* – the combined might of Germany's panzer divisions in France. The Führer alone reserved the right to commit his panzers.

The struggle for the 'panzer reserve' dogged German strategy in the spring of 1944. Proponents of armoured warfare wanted to hold the panzer divisions back, draw the Allies inland and then smash the invader with sweeping armoured operations. It was a view most vehemently supported by the senior armoured commander in the west, the aristocratic, arrogant Leo Geyr von Schweppenburg. All Germany's armoured reserve was concentrated under Geyr's unwieldy *Panzergruppe West*, and Geyr had no intention of surrendering his divisions. The fifty-seven year old general had led armoured corps across Russia for two and a half years before being ordered west in November 1943 to train Germany's panzer divisions to smash the Allied invasion when it came. Geyr had nothing but disdain for Rommel, a 'pure tactician' whose strategy was 'indistinguishable from the trench-war soldiers of 1918'. To Rommel, Allied material superiority guaranteed the failure of a massed German counter-attack. The solution, he proposed, was a compromise: to hold the Atlantic shore as strongly as possible, holding an armoured counter-punch behind it, scattering Germany's panzer divisions in the west along the coastline. 'The war will be won or lost on the beaches,' as the Desert Fox famously told his trusted aide *Hauptmann* Hellmuth Lang. 'We'll only have one chance to stop the enemy and that's while he's in the water. The first twenty-four hours of the invasion will be decisive. For the Allies, as well as Germany, it will be the longest day.'[6]

Relations between Rommel and Geyr soured by the day. 'The panzer divisions are going to be moved forward whether they like it or not,' the field marshal fumed. After their latest clash on 29 March, Rommel told Geyr: 'I am an experienced tank commander. You and I do not see eye to eye on anything. I refuse to work with you any more.' Only Hitler could settle the affair, but despite promises in Rommel's favour, the Führer failed to issue any orders. Finally, the Desert Fox made a direct plea to Hitler. If he supported his ideas, Rommel assured his Führer, the enemy landing would be 'routed on the first day'. The field marshal continued: 'This will be the most decisive campaign of this war and will seal the fate of the German people. Failing the early engagement of all our mobile forces in the battle for the coast, victory will be in grave doubt.' Adolf Hitler fudged the issue. Half the armour in the west was turned over to Rommel – the highly-rated 2nd and 21st Panzers and the still forming 116th; the rest of the panzer divisions remained in Geyr's hands. The matter of the panzer reserve was finally settled by a solution which solved nothing and pleased no one.[7]

The armoured divisions were the cream of the *Wehrmacht* in the West. Gerd von Rundstedt had nine panzer divisions to meet the invasion, six standard army divisions, three *Waffen SS* units. Each division was different, different numerically, and different in constitution. Despite Hitler's predilection for the SS, man for man and panzer for panzer, the army and *Waffen SS* armoured divisions in France were pretty much equal. After five years of war, the standard tank remained the Panzer IV – more than 800 were ready for battle in the west – roughly on a par with the most numerous American tank, the Sherman. Almost as commonplace was the far superior, the Panzer V, or Panther. Fast, manoeuvrable, reliable, well-armoured, and equipped with a potent 75-mm main gun, the Panther was the backbone tank of the German panzer force in France in 1944; more than 600 would be committed in the battle for Normandy. No tank provoked more fear in the enemy than the Panzer Mark VI, the Tiger, the heaviest and most powerful piece of German armour deployed in any great numbers in Normandy. The Tiger was sluggish – its top speed of 24 mph was slower than its sister panzers – and at 57 tons it was more than twice as heavy as the Panzer IV. What the Tiger lacked in mobility and manoeuvrability, it made up for in firepower: its main armament was the devastating 88-mm cannon, capable of taking out a Sherman at 4,000 yards. No Allied armour was a match for the Tiger, tank for tank. Its armour was not impenetrable, but a Sherman had to close to within 300 yards to have any chance of penetrating the Tiger's defensive belt – and even then, the Allies' bitterly remarked, the Tiger was 'far less likely to brew up' than its American-built opponent.[8] Unfortunately for Germany, the Tiger was a complicated beast to produce; little more than 100 would see action in Normandy.

In the spring of 1944, four army panzer divisions – 2nd, 21st, 116th and the *Panzer Lehr* – were forming or re-forming in north-west France. Of the quartet, none was stronger than the elite *Panzer Lehr* – armoured training – division. 'Training' suggested a unit unworthy of battle, but the *Panzer Lehr* was formed by troops from the armoured training schools, 'a combat elite', regimental commander Helmut Ritgen wrote. Commanded by Rommel's former staff officer and a trusted friend of the field marshal, Fritz Bayerlein, in the late spring of 1944 the *Panzer Lehr* was spread across central Normandy ready for commitment against the invasion. When the invader came, the *Panzer Lehr* would throw more than 200 tanks and self-propelled guns against him.

No armoured division was deployed closer to the coast than 21st Panzer Division, deployed around Caen. The Allies had already destroyed 21st Panzer Division once. It ceased to exist in the sands of

Tunisia on 12 May 1943; the final remnants of a once great unit which had driven the British back to the gates of Alexandria marched off into captivity after destroying their equipment. Four months later near Versailles, a new 21st Panzer Division began to take shape, making use of captured French tanks, veteran Panzer IVs and a handful of Panthers rolling off the production lines. By the eve of invasion, 21st Panzer was short of just one in twenty-five of its 17,000 men. On 5 June 1944 its commander Edgar Feuchtinger confidently reported to superiors that his division was 'capable of carrying out any offensive task'. But Feuchtinger, a Party favourite, was overly confident. 21st Panzer was a solid unit on paper, but scratch beneath the surface and failings and shortcomings ran through it from top to bottom, from Feuchtinger's inexperience to the lack of training of his men, some too old and plucked from coastal defences, others plucked straight from the training schools.

There was, of course, more to the German Army in the west than panzers. The majority of Gerd von Rundstedt's fifty-eight divisions in France in 1944 were infantry. Fewer than half of them could be regarded as first-class. The infantry divisions in the west in 1944 stood anywhere between 7,500 and 17,000 men strong. The quality of the men fluctuated wildly too. There were elite units – the *Fallschirmjäger*, paratroopers, although paratroopers in name only; the days of large-scale airborne assaults had ended with the capture of Crete in May 1941. Unlike the rest of the German Army, the ranks of Rundstedt's three parachute divisions in the west were filled entirely by volunteers. Morale was excellent. So too was firepower. Seventh Army's chief-of-staff Max Pemsel regarded 3rd *Fallschirmjäger* Division the equivalent of two ordinary German infantry units.

The paratroopers were the exception, not the rule. All but one of the remaining twenty-five infantry divisions which would be thrown into the maelstrom of Normandy had never seen battle; they were fresh formations raised throughout the Reich, one *Luftwaffe* 'field' division, formed by combing out the ranks of the air force, and a solitary battle-hardened division, 331st Infantry, which was watered down with fresh blood by the time it was sent west to re-form in the spring of 1944. Every one of the infantry divisions in France in 1944 relied first and foremost on the horse for transport. The horse pulled field guns, ammunition wagons, anti-tank guns; horse-drawn vehicles in Normandy outnumbered their powered counterparts two to one in the summer of 1944. The poorest divisions in France that year even lacked horses. The 700 series, 'static' or 'fortress' divisions, were intended to do nothing more than hold the coast. Four held the Norman coast in the summer of 1944 and not one had been tested in battle. Worse still in many cases their ranks were filled with old men, some into their forties. But that was typical of the German Army in the west in 1944; the average age of the *Landser* was thirty-one and a half – six years older than the ordinary American soldier. One in three was aged more than thirty-four.

German infantry units at least had effective weapons. One weapon stood out above all others: the 88-mm flak gun, as effective against enemy tanks as it was against enemy air power. 'The Allies had nothing as good,' one US lieutenant lamented, 'despite one of them designating itself "The World's Greatest Industrial Power."'[9] In the hand-held *Panzerfaust* – armoured fist – and smaller *Panzerschreck* – literally 'tank terror' – the German Army enjoyed anti-tank weapons at least on a par with the Allies' bazookas and Piat guns as a last resort for knocking out enemy armour; they were just filtering through to the front-line troops too slowly. And the enemy had no counterpart to the *Nebelwerfer*, a multi-barrel rocket launcher which spewed more than sixty small shells through the air with a terrifying shriek. The standard heavy machine gun, the MG42, fired off upwards of 1,400 rounds each minute at targets nearly two miles away. It had no equal in any theatre of war.

And above all, the German soldier believed he had the measure of his enemy. 'We shall see who fights better and who dies more easily,' Alfred Jodl boasted on the eve of invasion, 'the German soldier faced with the destruction of his homeland or the American and British, who don't even know what they are fighting for in Europe.'[10] But it had been more than a quarter of a century since the fifty-four year old general had encountered an English or American soldier on the field of battle during his days as a junior artillery officer on the Western Front. What worried the *Landser* in the west was not the Tommy or Ami, rather their material superiority. Rommel confided in his old friend and commander of the elite *Panzer Lehr* Division, Fritz Bayerlein:

> Our friends from the east cannot imagine what they're in for here. It's not a matter of fanatical hordes driven forward in masses against our line, with no regard for casualties. Here we are facing an enemy who spares no expenditure of material and whose every operation goes its course as though it had been the subject of repeated rehearsal.[11]

There was no greater evidence of the material imbalance between the Allies and the Reich than the plight of the *Luftwaffe* in the late spring of 1944. Despite Hermann Goering's boasts, despite the grandiose plan to repulse the invader, the German Air Force in the west found itself simply overwhelmed by the task at hand. *Jagdkorps II* – Fighter Corps II – charged with defending the skies of north-west Europe, could offer only sixty to eighty fighters for battle against the Allied air armada on a daily basis. *Luftflotte 3*, the principal *Luftwaffe* organization in the west, was in no better condition at the end of May: of its 981 front-line aircraft, just 139 fighters and 185 bombers and fighter-bombers were fit for action. The *Luftwaffe*'s plight was hardly surprising. Its airfields were singled out for destruction; the German Air Force gradually inched eastwards to new bases, but the makeshift landing grounds it fled to were utterly inadequate for supporting a modern air force. 'The systematic destruction of the ground organization of the *Luftwaffe* was very effective just before the start of the invasion,' a staff officer later wrote. 'Hardly a single airfield of those intended for fighter operations is still serviceable.'[12]

Not only was *Luftflotte 3* weak in numbers, most of its aircraft were obsolescent. The *Luftwaffe* entered battle in the west for the most part with the same aircraft it had embarked upon the campaigns against France, Britain and Russia, with modifications. The backbone of the bomber forces, the Junkers 88 and Dornier 217 were in effect enhanced models of aircraft which had begun the war. The most common fighter in the west was the Focke-Wulf Fw190, capable of speeds in excess of 450 mph and the more venerable Messerschmitt Me109, veteran of all the *Wehrmacht*'s campaigns in numerous variants; model G deployed in the west was 50 mph slower than the Focke-Wulf, but was an easier machine to fly. The American Mustang outperformed them both; the latest variant of the British Spitfire was a match for the Fw190, and was superior to the Messerschmitt.

But what *Luftflotte 3* lacked above all was skilled pilots. Four years of war had taken its toll of experienced aircrew; now Germany's flying schools struggled to keep pace with the demands of the front line. *Oberfähnrich* Hans-Ulrich Flade, who trained to fly the Me109, was one of scores of new pilots heading for his first combat in the spring of 1944. Flade had been given little more than sixty hours' training in the air, three times less than trainee Allied pilots joining enemy squadrons. 'The front-line units were desperately short of experienced and capable fighter pilots,' he complained. It was hardly surprising. Since mid-February, the Allies had singled out the *Jagdwaffe*, the fighter force, for destruction. It cost the *Luftwaffe* more than 400 pilots each month. The training schools simply couldn't keep pace. And for their sacrifices, for their 'failure', all the fighter pilots heard from their commander-in-chief was chastisement. 'The success of the enemy's invasion would mean the death of the German people,' Goering told them in mid-April. 'Your life means nothing when the security of the Fatherland is in danger. If the *Luftwaffe* is smashed at the end of the day, but we have achieved victory, then our sacrifices will have been worthwhile.'[13]

The bomber force was in an equally parlous state. Goering had frittered what little punch his air force still had with fruitless retaliatory raids against the British Isles throughout the winter and spring of 1944. The 'Baby Blitz', as the British disparagingly dubbed it, brought neither the long-awaited revenge the Nazi propaganda machine had promised the German people, nor did it dent the Allies' military might. By the time the blitz had ended in late May, the *Luftwaffe* had little to show for its crews' exertions, other than the loss of more than 300 bombers it could ill afford in the west. The 'Baby Blitz' had achieved nothing, other than to serve as the *Luftwaffe*'s last hurrah over Britain.

The *Kriegsmarine* was no less overwhelmed by the magnitude of the task facing it than the *Luftwaffe*. In Paris, *Vizeadmiral* Theodor Krancke lamented the lack of forces under his command to defeat the invasion. At the end of May 1944 all he could muster from Boulogne to Brest were twenty-five motor torpedo boats and seventeen U-boats. The U-boat had always been the trump card of the *Kriegsmarine*. But 1943 had been a punishing year for the service – 'an iron year', Karl Dönitz called it – 241 boats had been sunk in all. The prospects were no brighter as 1944 opened. On paper the *U-Bootwaffe* was a potent force: nearly 450 submarines were in commission. But the figures were deceptive: two out of three boats were under training, another 120 or so were in refit or being repaired. On a typical day, barely forty boats could be offered for battle at sea. The only glimmers of hope were that the morale and spirit of the ordinary sailor, the *Matrose*, was unbroken – and that improved *Schnorchel* boats were beginning to filter through to the front line; boats fitted with air intakes which allowed the batteries to be recharged without surfacing. Without *Schnorchel* no U-boat could survive in the face of Allied counter-measures. But as Dönitz began shepherding his U-boats in his bases in Biscay and the Atlantic coast of France, just eight *Schnorchel* submarines were available to counter the invasion. The remainder of *Gruppe Landwirt*, codename for the U-boat force amassed to defeat the enemy landings, had no such advantage. Their commanders and crew alike knew the coming battle meant almost certain death.

As invasion loomed ever closer and successes at sea diminished, so the Supreme Commander of the *Kriegsmarine* issued appeals and orders which sounded increasingly desperate. First at the end of March:

Every commander must be aware that the future of the German people rests on his shoulders more than at any other time, and I demand of every commander that he has only one objective in his heart and before his eyes, irrespective of precautions which would normally apply: Attack! At them! Sink them![14]

A fortnight later, the Commander-in-Chief of the German Navy spelled out in no uncertain terms the sacrifice he expected from his U-boat men:

> Every enemy craft which supports the landing, even if it brings ashore only fifty soldiers or a single tank, is a target, which demands all-out action by the U-boat. It is to be attacked, even if it threatens the loss of your own boat...
>
> Every man and weapon of the enemy destroyed before landing reduces the enemy's prospects of success. The boat that causes the enemy losses in the invasion has fulfilled its highest task and justified its existence, even if it is lost.
>
> Every commander must be aware that no soldier can be given a more serious or more important mission; the future of Germany demands he summons all his strength.[15]

Dönitz's instructions were passed on in person to U-boat commanders by Hans Rösing, his trusted submarine leader in the west. In one port after another Rösing gathered his boat captains, then imparted the grand admiral's directive. Rösing arrived in the Brittany port of Brest in early May, home of 1st U-boat Flotilla. Fifteen submarine commanders were summoned to the imposing French Naval College, now the head-quarters of the flotilla. They listened as Rösing outlined their historic mission: attack and sink the invasion fleet. 'Once we could do no more,' U953's commander *Oberleutnant* Karl Heinz Marbach recalled Rösing say, 'then we should at least ram the invasion fleet, be it only the smallest dinghy.' At that moment 'deadly silence gripped the room,' wrote Herbert Werner, recently given command of U415. 'This was sheer madness. It was ludicrous to use a U-boat to accomplish what a torpedo should do.'[16]

Madness indeed, and Karl Dönitz knew it; he was losing three out of every ten boats he was sending to sea. 'The chances of success now are only slight,' Dönitz noted in his diary at the beginning of June. 'The chances of not returning from a patrol are very great.' And yet, the commander-in-chief of the *Kriegsmarine* took heart. 'That crews managed at all during this past year when we suffered the heaviest losses and achieved fewer successes, that their morale, their fighting spirit is unimpaired is fantastic evidence of courage and a result of the determination of the *U-Bootwaffe*.' *Oberleutnant* Herbert Werner shared none of his commander-in-chief's enthusiasm. He watched the activity in Brest as engineers worked feverishly to ready the fifteen U-boats, including his own U415. 'Under the concrete roof, the shipyard personnel worked around the clock to have the boats repaired, equipped and fitted out for their most vital mission, helping to put the boats in fighting condition.' When the call came, Werner knew it meant the death ride of the U-boats. 'We never talked about the invasion,' Werner recalled, 'but we thought of it incessantly – and of our death.'[17]

The German people were also filled with a sense of foreboding that spring. In the east, the Soviets continued their inexorable advance, the Germans their inexorable retreat. In the skies by day and by night, the Allied air forces laid waste to German cities. Not even the Nazi leadership could fail to notice the lowering morale. 'The majority of the people cling to the belief that whatever happens, they must keep going and grit their teeth,' the monitors of public opinion, the *Sicherheitsdienst*, observed. 'They do so simply because there is no other alternative. But there is also a feeling of impatience that something will happen soon, maybe the invasion and "settling the account" with England.' The tension was unbearable. 'It simply cannot go on like this any longer,' people were overheard to say. 'Let's hope they come soon so that there's an end to this never-ending uncertainty.' 'One way or another, they must come.' But the days passed, and 'they' did not come. There was widespread disappointment in the Reich – and widespread depression. As long as the western enemy had failed to set foot on the shores of the continent, the German public could see no end to war. 'The long period of waiting creates an even greater test of nerves for us – and ties us down in the west,' the *Sicherheitsdienst* recorded.[18]

That test of nerves was felt acutely by Germany's military leaders in France. It was obvious the Allies were ready to strike. But what no man could answer was when or where the invader would come. The obvious place remained the shortest Channel crossing: the Pas de Calais, anywhere between the estuaries of the Somme in France and the Scheldt in Belgium. But by mid-spring, Adolf Hitler was becoming increasingly concerned that the enemy might come ashore elsewhere. His gaze fixed on the shores of Brittany and Normandy. Reconnaissance and intelligence reports seemed to confirm the Führer's suspicions. But what neither Hitler, nor Rundstedt, nor Rommel, nor any German officer in 1944 expected was the full-scale invasion in Normandy; it would merely be a diversion, a secondary landing to the main event. And that would come, almost everyone agreed from the Führer down, in the Pas de Calais.

As late as Monday, 5 June, to Rommel and his staff the persistent enemy air raids still pointed to the Pas as the most likely site of an invasion. But the Desert Fox had a hunch. He knew his enemy. In the dying days of May he had continued his feverish tour of the Atlantic coast, giving heart to his men, addressing the ranks of 716th Infantry Division in Caen. 'Gentlemen, I've known the English since Africa and Italy,' he told the infantrymen. 'And I can tell you they'll choose a landing ground where they don't believe we're expecting an invasion. And that will be here, in this spot.'[19]

Notes
1. Ose, *Entscheidung im Westen*, 1944, pp.75-6.
2. TB Goebbels, 18/4/44, 27/4/44; *Akten zur deutschen auswärtigen Politik 1918-1945*. Serie E, Band 7, Dokument 236; Nazism, iii, pp.869-70.
3. Rommel, pp.465-6.
4. Ose, p.76.
5. Rommel to his wife, 6/5/44, 8/5/44. Ryan, *Longest Day,* p.17; Pimlott, *Rommel in His Own Words,* p.179; Rommel to his son, 21/5/44. NA CAB146/336; KTB Rommel, 5/5/44. Irving, *Trail of the Fox*, p.316.
6. Ryan, *Longest Day*, p.27.
7. Ambrose, *D-Day*, p.113; Irving, *Trail of the Fox*, pp.307, 314; Ruge, pp.109, 119, 154-5; Pimlott, pp. 177-8; Rommel, pp.468-70.
8. Hastings, *Overlord*, p.227.
9. Ambrose, *Citizen Soldiers*, pp.62-3.
10. Cited in Ambrose, *D-Day*, p.150.
11. Rommel, p.467.
12. Price, *Last Year of the Luftwaffe*, pp.22-30; Study by the German Air Historical Branch 'The Normandy Invasion, June 1944'. Cited in Ellis, i, p.110.
13. Price, *Last Year of the Luftwaffe*, p.15; Goering Tagesbefehl, 15/4/44. Author's papers.
14. 'Angriff-ran-versenken!'. Padfield, *Dönitz*, p.347; Tarrant, *Last Year of the Kriegsmarine*, pp.16-17; Salewski, ii, p.415.
15. Salewski, ii, pp.415-16; Padfield, *War Beneath the Sea*, pp.424-5.
16. Cited in Padfield, *War Beneath the Sea*, p.425; Werner, p.221.
17. KTB BdU, 15/6/44; Werner, pp.220, 223.
18. SD Meldungen, 30/3/44, 4/5/44, 11/5/44, 25/5/44.
19. Irving, *Trail of the Fox*, p.302; Wegmüller, pp.218, 219; IWM AL510/1/2; Perrigault, Jean-Claude, *21 Panzer Division*, p.225.

Chapter 3

My God, it's the Invasion

Our future will depend on how we fight this day.
Generalmajor Max Pemsel

General Erich Marcks had an uncanny knack; call it soldier's intuition. A stern, almost dour figure, Marcks was strangely popular with his men. Perhaps it was his refusal to eat sumptuous meals at his St Lô head-quarters in favour of the food the ordinary *Landser* was served. Perhaps it was his refusal to allow his disability to impede him; Marcks had lost a leg in the opening days of the campaign in Russia, yet continued to command a division and corps. Perhaps it was his refusal to buckle in time of adversity; 'I do not take part in retreats,' he told his wife. Whatever it was, for ten months Marcks' men had worked feverishly for him to improve the defences of the Seine Bay. The domain of LXXXIV Corps stretched from the Orne estuary north of Caen, running west along the shores of Calvados and the Cotentin peninsula, past Cherbourg, then south to Avranches, gateway to Brittany, including the Channel Islands; in all 250 miles of coastline. Every sign pointed to an invasion in the Pas de Calais, across the shortest stretch of the English Channel. But the one-legged artilleryman believed otherwise. On the first day of June 1944, Marcks paid one of his regular visits to the coast. Today he chose the 352nd Infantry Division in the picturesque town of Arromanches, sandwiched between the Norman cliffs north of Bayeux. Staring across the Channel, Marcks leaned on his stick. 'If I know the English, they will go to church on Sunday, and they will come on Monday,' he confided in a staff officer. 'Army Group headquarters is convinced that they're not going to come yet and when they do it'll be at Calais, so we'll give them a warm welcome right here on Monday.'[1] Monday would be 5 June.

Monday, 5 June, in France proved to be uneventful. The weather was bad. It was unseasonably cold. Squalls and showers drenched Normandy and the Pas de Calais. The forecast for 6 June was little better. This is not invasion weather, Field Marshal Erwin Rommel had already decided. Having read the latest meteorological report early on Sunday morning predicting 'unstable weather for the next few days,' the Desert Fox climbed into his powerful Horch open-topped staff car and headed for his home in southern Germany. The weather, tides and moon were in his favour. It would be 20 June at the earliest before the enemy would set foot in France. Plenty of time, Rommel reasoned, to return home with a gift for his wife, a fine pair of shoes from Paris, on her fiftieth birthday, Tuesday, 6 June.

Across Normandy, senior commanders were leaving their posts, not for home but for Rennes in Brittany for war games. The generals, too, had been prompted by the foul weather. The defenders of the Cherbourg peninsula were deprived of their leaders that Monday – divisional commanders, regimental commanders, staff officers. Only Erich Marcks remained. He would join them at the war games early on Tuesday morning. The aim of the exercise: to defeat an airborne landing.

At his headquarters in Paris, Theodor Krancke pored over the latest intelligence and aerial reconnaissance reports. For more than a year, the fifty-one year old admiral had been in charge of all the German Navy's surface forces in the west. They were not many. In June 1944, Krancke could summon just five destroyers, a handful of torpedo boats, and an assortment of minesweepers and patrol boats, defending a coastline from the Hook of Holland to the Franco-Spanish border. Across the English Channel the world's two most powerful navies were massing an invasion armada. But for the moment, Theodor Krancke was optimistic. In the Channel a gale was blowing. The Allied air campaign against northern France had still not reached its climax. Nor were there sufficient forces in England, he believed, to mount an invasion. This was just a guess; aerial reconnaissance had proved far from adequate, the admiral complained. Nevertheless, Krancke was confident in his judgment. 'I do not believe a major invasion is imminent,' he concluded, surveying all the information before him. 'The enemy's measures are a well-judged mix of bluff and preparations for an invasion he plans to carry out later on.'

The staff of Field Marshal Gerd von Rundstedt, also in the French capital, had reached the same conclusion as Krancke. That Monday, they sent their weekly report to Hitler's headquarters, outlining developments on the Western Front. Except that there was no front. Not yet. 'Where the enemy will strike remains unclear... As yet there is no immediate prospect of an invasion.'[2]

Rudolf von Ribbentrop was recuperating in the City of Light from wounds suffered in a fighter-bomber attack. The son of the Nazi Foreign

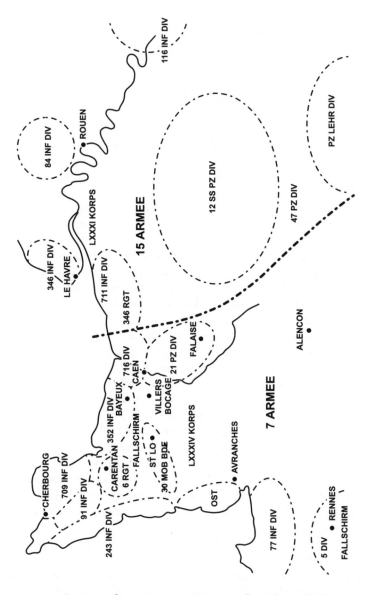

German dispositions in Normandy, 6 June 1944

Minister, the young *Waffen SS* panzer company commander was called upon by an embassy official: before 5 June was over, the invasion would come. Ribbentrop laughed it off: 'Another false alarm,' he told the diplomat as the two parted company. 'Be warned', the embassy official told him, 'the fifth is not quite over yet'.[3]

Near the town of Carentan, at the base of the Cherbourg peninsula, *Oberleutnant* Martin Pöppel trained his paratrooper company for the attack each man knew was coming. That afternoon, senior officers gathered for a map exercise: to defeat an enemy airborne landing. 'We disperse amid laughter,' he recalled. 'No one has any idea how near we are to the real situation.'[4]

Serving as a medical officer with a fortress division on the Norman coastline Heinrich Fürst awaited the invasion with a fatalistic view. 'It was not a very pleasant prospect, knowing you had a good chance to get killed,' he wrote. The invasion would come 'some time soon'. When and where no one knew, but it would come and it 'would come in force'. Fürst recalled: 'The situation was like sitting on a tropical beach, well protected, but expecting a huge hurricane to hit in the next forty-eight hours.'[5]

In the woods north of Chartres in central Normandy, panzer company commander Helmut Ritgen bivouacked with the rest of his troops. The men of the *Panzer Lehr* Division pitched tents next to their tanks, dug trenches for cover against air attacks. Leave was cancelled. Nights out in nearby villages were banned. The troops of the *Panzer Lehr*, in their striking black uniforms, ate alongside their tanks, slept alongside them, played sport and practical jokes in the clearings, watched film shows in barns and shelters. They waited...and waited.

Oberleutnant Herbert Werner checked into his office in Brest. There was no sign of an invasion. He headed into town to dine like a king: lobsters and snails, a 'classic Breton dinner'. Two months before, the young naval officer had been given command of U415, a U-boat which had 'already outlived too many patrols'. His new mission 'was as good as a death sentence – the life expectancy of a boat on battle duty had been reduced to four months or less'. In the safety of the vast concrete U-boat pen at Brest, U415 waited. Her crew waited. As Werner returned to his quarters that night he was convinced 'the hour for our last performance was very near'.[6]

Joseph Goebbels arrived at Hitler's mountain retreat in the Bavarian Alps near Obersalzberg. The day before the Nazi propaganda minister had rallied the masses in Nuremberg. In the bomb-scarred ruins of Adolf Hitler Platz, Goebbels sought to placate the faithful: 'I am convinced the greatest victory in history will arise for us out of the present crises and burdens in this war.' The word on everyone's lips was 'invasion'. In the late spring of 1944, Germany was wracked by tension. When would the Allies come? 'We can say only one thing,' the propaganda minister told his audience, 'We are ready! If the enemy comes, our soldiers will teach him a lesson.' Early the next morning, Monday, 5 June, Goebbels had climbed aboard a train bound for Munich. He read through the overnight reports. The Allies were on the verge of sweeping into Rome. 'It poses a terrible loss of prestige,' the minister noted with concern. 'The fall of Rome will certainly make a very deep impression upon the German people.' That afternoon, Goebbels found the German leader 'in a good mood'. The self-styled Führer brushed aside the loss of Rome – 'it's of no decisive importance for the conduct of the war'. Rome did not matter; France did. 'The decision undoubtedly will fall in the west,' Hitler told his trusted friend. It was the same message he had preached for seven months. 'Let's hope the enemy launches his invasion soon so that we can turn around the whole war in the west,' Goebbels confided to his diary.[7]

In the headquarters of LXXXIV Corps in St Lô, Erich Marcks' staff were preparing a surprise fifty-third birthday party for their general on the stroke of midnight. Nothing grandiose; a glass of Chablis. 'The battle will rage for sure in June,' he had predicted to his wife. But that did not trouble the one-legged general. 'I'm looking to the future in good heart, whatever they choose to throw at me,' he told her. 'We have nothing to blame ourselves about, in any event. Everything which is humanly possible has been done.'[8] It was now slightly before midnight. First there was a faint drone, then the low rumble in the skies over Normandy, the unmistakable sound of aero engines. Around St Lô, the flak blazed away at the Allied bombers streaming overhead. To a sound-track of 88-mm guns and the bells of the city's cathedral chiming twelve, the staff of LXXXIV Corps toasted their general's birthday. It was now Tuesday, 6 June.

Wakened by the humming, *Major* Hans von Luck peered out of the window of his billet, a small, spartan house in the village of Bellengreville near Caen. 'Flares were hanging in the sky,' the thirty-two year old commander of a panzer grenadier regiment wrote. The telephone rang. It was Luck's adjutant. '*Herr Major*, paratroops are dropping. Gliders are landing in our sector.'[9]

In the officers' mess at Cabourg, north-east of Caen, *Generalleutnant* Joseph Reichert and his staff were playing cards. It was time to end the game, the fifty-three year old general decided. But a drone began to fill the air, the hum of aero engines. 'The planes were flying so low, we had the feeling they might almost touch the roof,' Reichert wrote. The commander of 711th Infantry Division stepped out of the mess. 'It was a full-moon night and the weather was fairly stormy, with low-hanging black clouds, between which several low-flying planes could be distinctly observed,' the general recalled. And then a cry pierced the Norman night. 'Paratroopers!'

Machine-gunner Heinrich Severloh was asleep in the attic of his billet, a farmhouse north-west of Bayeux. His battery commander, *Oberleutnant* Bernhard Frerking, burst into his room on the stroke of midnight. 'It's happening!' Frerking said breathlessly. 'Come, Hein, I have been telephoned. We're off! Threatening danger...!' Severloh dressed and stepped out into the night, a rainy, blustery night filled with the drone of Allied bombers heading westwards across Normandy. A staff car took the two men the three-mile journey to their position: WN62, *Widerstandsnest 62* – nest of resistance number sixty-two – overlooking the western edge of the Seine Bay. 'We knew that the invasion would now come,' wrote Severloh. 'We'd been waiting for it for so long and there had been too many signs hinting at it recently.'[10]

It was the sound of gunfire, not aircraft engines, which woke *Major* Werner Pluskat in his billet near Bayeux. The artillery commander picked up the telephone and dialled headquarters. The staff at 352 Artillery Regiment were confused. They had no idea what was going on. Pluskat went back to bed. Around 12.30 a.m., the phone rang. It was headquarters. 'It seems the invasion is beginning.' The thirty-two year old officer got dressed, roused two colleagues and clambered into the staff car. 'I remember feeling very excited. We'd been waiting for this thing for so long that we were glad it was coming,' Pluskat recalled. Another half hour passed before the trio arrived at Pluskat's command post at St Honorine, overlooking the Normandy coastline. The officer picked up his binoculars and looked out to sea. 'There was absolutely nothing to be seen. Everything was terribly calm.' Pluskat turned to one of his colleagues, disappointed. 'Another false alarm.'[11]

Martin Pöppel looked at his watch: 2 a.m. The alarm rang in his observation post. From everywhere the same reports came in: enemy paratroopers falling from the skies. 'The night is stormy and wild,' Pöppel scrawled in his diary. 'From time to time the moon lights up the darkness. There are single cracks of rifle fire, but so far we've only detected the position of individual enemy soldiers.'[12]

It was the same across Normandy. A few miles north of Pöppel's observation post, paratroopers filled the skies. The men of American 82nd and 101st Airborne Divisions drifted slowly to earth. They fell upon the small town of St Mère Église, five miles from the lower east coast of the Cotentin peninsula. The American commander promised that before dawn the Stars and Stripes would fly over the town.

The telephone at LXXXIV Corps' headquarters jangled. Erich Marcks picked it up. 'Something important was coming through,' Marcks' intelligence officer Friedrich Hayn noted. 'The general stood up stiffly, his hand gripping the edge of the table. At last the suspense was over.'[13]

The phone jangled too at the headquarters of Seventh Army far from the front in Le Mans. Almost non-stop. At 2.15, the army's chief-of-staff, *Generalmajor* Max Pemsel, sounded the alarm, then picked up the telephone to waken his sixty-two year old commander, *Generaloberst* Friedrich Dollmann. Like Marcks, Dollmann believed Normandy was the obvious place to invade, although he had done little personally to improve its defences. '*General*,' Pemsel told him. 'I believe this is the invasion. Will you please come over immediately?' Max Pemsel picked up the telephone again and asked to be patched through to Rommel's headquarters at La Roche-Guyon on the Seine north-west of Paris. In the field marshal's absence, it was his wily chief-of-staff, *Generalmajor* Hans Speidel, who answered. There were widespread landings across Normandy, Pemsel told him. 'These actions point to a major action,' the Seventh Army chief-of-staff insisted. No, said Speidel, they did not. 'They're still localized encounters.' Speidel put the phone down.

Max Pemsel shared none of Speidel's complacency. He gathered his staff. 'I am convinced the invasion will be upon us by dawn,' he warned them. 'Our future will depend on how we fight this day.'[14]

Two hours had passed since Martin Pöppel's first encounter with the enemy. Now the bombers roared overhead again. And the paratroopers leapt out again. 'It all happens so quickly, we scarcely have time to shoot,' the paratroop officer noted. 'Slowly the day breaks, enabling us to survey the terrain through our field glasses. Here and there we can see the parachutes, camouflage colour for the paratroopers, pink for ammunition and yellow for the weapons.'

To the north the two-hour skirmish for the small town of St Mère Église had finally ended in the last minutes before dawn. As promised, the Stars and Stripes fluttered in the town square. 'Communications with St Mère Église are cut off,' Marcks reported. They would not be restored.[15]

Like Hans Speidel, Field Marshal Gerd von Rundstedt had dismissed the flood of reports pouring into his sumptuous headquarters in the grounds of a school in a Paris suburb. Was this the invasion, or was it merely a diversionary attack? The sixty-eight year old field marshal had been the most senior German soldier in the west for more than two years now, but had done little to prepare for an invasion. Gruff, sarcastic and prone to outbursts, throughout the night of 5-6 June he had been convinced the Allied landings in Normandy were not a large-scale operation. But Gerd von Rundstedt was also cautious. Large-scale operation or not, it would be wise to deal with it swiftly. The field marshal told Hitler's headquarters in Bavaria he would commit the elite force in the west, the panzer divisions held back from the front to deal with any invasion. 'If this really is a major operation, we can only deal with it successfully if we take action immediately,' Rundstedt pleaded. The panzers did not move an inch for the time being. That needed Hitler's permission. The Führer was still asleep. No one at Berchtesgaden thought the situation in Normandy serious enough to wake him.

The time was now shortly after 5 a.m. For four hours, Werner Pluskat and his men had peered through the darkness and seen nothing. But now night was slowly becoming day. 'As the first grey light of dawn began to creep across the sky, I thought I could see something along the horizon.' Pluskat grabbed his binoculars and swept the horizon. 'I saw that the horizon was literally filling with ships of all kinds. I could hardly believe it.' Stunned, the artillery officer passed the binoculars to a colleague in the concrete command post. 'Take a look,' Pluskat told him. He did. 'My God, it's the invasion.'[16]

Notes
1. Perrigault, Jean-Claude, 21 Panzer Division, p.225.
2. NHB 507; OB West Weekly report, 5/6/44. NA CAB 146/481.
3. Meyer, 12 SS Panzer Division Hitlerjugend, p.24.
4. Pöppel, p.174.
5. Miller, Nothing Less Than Victory, p.98.
6. Werner, pp.199, 224.
7. Goebbels' speech in Nuremberg, author's papers. TB Goebbels, 5/6/44, 6/6/44.
8. Irving, Trail of the Fox, p.317; Jacobsen, Otto: Erich Marcks, Soldat und Gelehrter, p.160.
9. Luck, p.172.
10. Severloh, p.18.
11. Miller, Nothing Less Than Victory, pp.243-4.
12. Pöppel, p.175.
13. Cited in Kershaw, p.88.
14. Ryan, Longest Day, pp.146, 153; KTB AOK 7, 0215 Hours, 6/6/44. IWM AL 528.
15. Pöppel, p.175; KTB AOK 7, 0330 Hours, 6/6/44. AL 528.
16. Miller, Nothing Less Than Victory, p.244.

Chapter 4

Up Against an Irresistible Force

Now we have them where we can destroy them.

Adolf Hitler

It began along the River Orne, north-east of Caen, with British gliders silently drifting down. They came to rest on a narrow strip of land between the Orne and a parallel stretch of water which ran from the sea to Caen, the Caen canal. Here between the villages of Bénouville on the west bank and Ranville on the east, lay the only bridges spanning these two waterways north of Caen. Just two men were on sentry duty on the canal crossing, Bénouville bridge. Seventeen year old Grenadier Helmut Romer paced up and down the bridge. Tonight was the same as every other night. Uneventful. Until the crash of Horsa gliders broke the silence. Within seconds, the men of British 6th Airborne Division were pouring out of them and charging the Orne and canal bridges. The first glider touched down at sixteen minutes past midnight; ten minutes later the two bridges were in British hands. They had not even been wired for demolition. It was typical of the German Army's half-hearted reaction which would characterize Tuesday, 6 June 1944.

The Americans came to Normandy from the east, across the base of the Cotentin peninsula. They came as low as 600 feet in gliders or DC3 Dakota transporters. They flew into a hailstorm of flak so intense that the American drops were scattered far and wide. Almost every man of the 82nd and 101st Airborne Divisions missed his intended drop zone around Carentan and the village of St Mère Église, three miles inland from what in a few hours would become Utah beach on the Cotentin's east coast. The paratroopers were spread across 375 square miles of the peninsula. 'The sky was filled with planes,' *Fallschirmjäger* Wolfgang Geritzlehner recalled. 'At one stroke there were soldiers coming out of all corners. It was like a swarm of maddened bees.' The men of 6th *Fallschirmjäger* Regiment around Carentan formed up to destroy the invader. 'We weren't afraid,' wrote Geritzlehner. 'We were convinced that everything would be settled in a few hours. Everyone was confident.'[1]

The landings were almost an hour old when the first reports began to filter through to Seventh Army's headquarters in Le Mans. The news was sketchy: fighting at the foot of the Cotentin, north and east of Caen. It was also encouraging: prisoners were being brought in; small groups of enemy paratroopers had been 'eliminated'. But the army's chief-of-staff Max Pemsel was in no doubt. 'This is a major operation.'[2]

Wolfgang Geritzlehner's confidence had been misplaced. The invader was sterner than he had been led to believe. The dispersed nature of the parachute drops at the foot of the Cotentin made it difficult for the Americans to form a coherent fighting force; it made it equally difficult for the Germans to wipe them out. And at one point, St Mère Église, enough men landed for the Americans to wipe out its small garrison, seize the village and raise the Stars and Stripes. The Americans had secured their first objective of D-Day. It was 4.30 a.m. and not yet light.

In Paris, Gerd von Rundstedt and his staff had been awake since before 3 a.m. Was this the invasion? The field marshal was not sure. Perhaps it was a diversionary attack. Diversionary attack or not, von Rundstedt had at least given orders for the *Hitlerjugend, Panzer Lehr* and 17th SS Panzer Grenadiers to prepare to move. Authority from Berchtesgaden was merely a formality, Rundstedt reasoned. But the Führer had retired to bed maybe an hour earlier after entertaining propaganda minister Joseph Goebbels. Hitler's long, rambling discussions, or rather monologues – the Führer did most of the talking – with his cronies typically dragged on long into the night. Today was no different. Rome had just fallen; the decision in the west was imminent. The first inkling of the landings in Normandy had filtered through to southern Bavaria before Goebbels went to bed. If this was the invasion, 'the decisive day in this war will have begun'. Goebbels grabbed a couple of hours sleep. He felt he would need all his strength to deal with Tuesday, 6 June. It would bring Germany 'fresh concerns and worries'. The Führer slept too. Now was not the time to inform him about events in the west, his naval adjutant Karl Jesko von Puttkamer decided. 'There wasn't much to tell him anyway.'[3] If the Führer was not awake he could not authorize the release of the panzer reserve.

The men of the *Hitlerjugend* had responded quickly to talk of an invasion. The 12th SS Panzer Division was scattered around eastern Normandy; it was not one of three armoured units released to Erwin Rommel when Adolf Hitler ruled on the fate of the panzer reserve. The *Hitlerjugend* could not be committed to battle without the Führer's permission. The unblooded division was eager for action, eager to prove itself. The division, regimental commander Kurt Meyer wrote, 'was ready for war and animated by the thought that its employment would be decisive for the defence of the homeland and for Germany's final victory'. The *Hitlerjugend* was an elite division and it relished the label. 'The young soldiers went to war superbly trained as no other division at that time,' Meyer recalled.

Sturmmann Oswald Beck was sleeping uneasily in full uniform when a colleague burst into his billet. 'Let's go, boys, get out! The Tommies have landed!' By 3 a.m. the division was ready to roll. But no order came from higher authorities. Beck was bemused. 'We were sent back to our quarters and stretched out on our beds, ready to go,' he recalled. 'Those who could slept. The others were talking quietly. When morning light came, we were all sitting on top of the armoured personnel carriers and expected that we would soon start out.'[4]

For nearly an hour battery commander Werner Pluskat had watched as the fleet grew ever closer to what hereafter would forever be known as Omaha beach. At a little after 5 a.m. on Tuesday, 6 June 1944, it was merely four miles of beach, four miles of sand littered with Rommel's 'death zone' – mines, steel crosses, wooden ramparts, barbed wire. And beyond that were the manned obstacles. Bunkers, trenches, gun positions armed with heavy machine guns, mortars, artillery pieces on the slopes and on the cliffs which towered over Omaha. In one of these bunkers at St Honorine, at the eastern end of Omaha, Pluskat picked up the telephone receiver to report to his superiors. The sight which had greeted him through his binoculars had filled the thirty-two year old major with both awe and fear. 'There must be ten thousand ships out there,' he told headquarters. 'It's unbelievable, fantastic.' At the other end of the line, 352nd Infantry Division's intelligence officer, one Major Block, told Pluskat to get a grip: 'The Americans and British don't have that many ships.' Pluskat slammed the phone down in frustration.[5]

Obergefreiter Heinrich Severloh had been waiting in a trench on a cliff top a couple of miles east of the village of Vierville since shortly after midnight. It was 5 a.m. when the early morning fog faded away to reveal 'the most powerful armada of all time – an endless line of gigantic battleships' stretching across the horizon. Before the war, Severloh had enjoyed a simple life as a farmer. Now the twenty year old *Landser* waited with his heavy machine gun at the ready in a strongpoint designated *Widerstandsnest* – nest of resistance – 62, or WN62, one of Pluskat's forward defences. As the silhouettes on the horizon grew closer, Severloh noticed the low drone of aero engines. 'The noise grew ever louder, and as the huge bomber fleet flew straight for us in a ghostly fashion through an overcast, grey sky, the sound of the engines grew to a hellish thunder,' he remembered:

Every man jumped into a bunker or dugout. Then the broad formation of heavy bombers roared over us and onwards. Their payload came whistling, howling and crashing down. The bombs fell like heavy rain. The first one landed barely 50m behind our position. Everything began to shake – even our small observation bunker built into the ground – and earth and lumps of chalk flew up all around us, but the bombers missed their target.[6]

The bombers had barely passed when the horizon rippled with flashes of fire as the guns of the great armada opened up.

It was maybe a little after 5.30 a.m. when the turrets of some of the 10,000 ships the Allies 'didn't have' slowly began turning to face the shoreline. Slowly the barrels of 5-in, 6-in, 8-in, 14-in, 15-in barrels were raised, then opened fire. In each broadside the veteran American battleships USS *Texas* and *Nevada* alone rained more than 12,000 tons of death and destruction on the German defenders. The bombardment shattered shelters, collapsed trenches, smashed field positions, buried some men alive, tore others to pieces. 'The ground of the entire cliff shook under the shelling,' wrote Severloh. 'The air shook too. Thick, bright grey chalk dust filled the air; smoke and the dirt flying around blackened the sky, interspersed with flashing bolts of lightning from explosions, and it seemed as if the whole world would disappear in a roaring, howling and crashing inferno of exploding shells.' Werner Pluskat's bunker was shaken to its foundations, he recalled: 'I was thrown to the ground and my binoculars were smashed. There was dust, powder, dirt and splinters of concrete all over the place. The bunker was swaying to and fro, filled with dust and dirt, and everyone inside was lying on the floor.'

Some twenty miles to the east, 716th Infantry Division sent a company of reinforcements to the coast at Bernières where landing craft were approaching. The company simply disappeared in the maelstrom. 'They were caught in the fire of the heavy naval bombardment and annihilated,' the division recorded matter-of-factly. 'Of the units employed, not one man returned.'[7]

Near Caen one educated *Landser* found time to write in his diary: *'L'invasion est arrivee!* Good morning Tommy! *Fallschirm Absprung ostwärts.'* The invasion's here. Good morning, Tommy! Paratroopers dropped to the east.

At Omaha, Heinrich Severloh had returned to his machine-gun post. The bombardment had caused him little more than a bump to the head from a shell splinter. Now he looked out upon forty-eight landing craft carrying troops bobbing and rocking in choppy waters. In each, thirty men, cold, wet, often seasick, waited for the endless six-mile journey to the beach to end. So these were the Tommies, thought Severloh, a veteran of the Eastern Front. But no; painted large in white paint on the bow of one of the boats sluggishly nearing the shore were the unmistakeable letters 'US'. Then down came the bow ramps on the craft and out came the GIs. The *Landser* recalled:

They jumped into the cold water up to their chests and shoulders. Some disappeared under the water for a moment, and half swimming, half wading, they began to move slowly on to the beach in front of our strongpoint. At this moment there was complete silence in the bay; not one shot was fired. We had strict orders to wait until the GIs were only about 400m from the edge of the beach and were wading in water up to their knees. I ran to the communications bunker about 15m away and reported: 'Now it's starting. They're landing!'

Once the Americans had firm ground under their feet, they waded in two long lines, one after the other, through the water, with the left hand firmly on the pack of the man in front. Everything was so calm, so organized, that you had the impression that they were merely carrying out an exercise.

The Americans struggled forward with their weapons and packs through the high surf of the cold sea, slowly and utterly unprotected. We were well aware that the GIs below us were being led like lambs to a slaughter.

Severloh's superior, *Oberleutnant* Bernhard Frerking, muttered: 'Poor swine…' And then, with the men just 400 yards short of journey's end, the order rang out in the bunkers and gun batteries which overlooked Omaha: '*Los!*' Open fire. Mortars, heavy machine guns, field guns opened up as one. Hein Severloh released the catch on his machine gun and opened fire. 'I could clearly see the water shoot up where my machine-gun bullets hit,' he wrote. 'When the small fountains approached the GIs, they threw themselves down. After just a few minutes, panic broke out among the Americans. All of them lay in the calm, cold water; some tried to get to the nearest beach obstacles.' Some assault craft burst into flames, others heeled over and sank. The American troops clambered over the sides, others waited for the bow ramp drop, then waded ashore. Whichever way they chose to escape the landing craft, they were greeted by a steel hail, as an American combat report graphically described:

As the first men jumped, they crumpled and flopped into the water. Then order was lost. It seemed to the men that the only way to get ashore was to dive head first in and swim clear of the fire that was

45

striking the boats. But as they hit the water, their heavy equipment dragged them down and soon they were struggling to keep afloat. Some were hit in the water and wounded. Some drowned then and there.[8]

Omaha beach curved softly for nearly four miles. A wide, gently sloping stretch of sand led to a 100-yard wide plateau before bluffs and cliffs rose from the Normandy shoreline. The GIs wading ashore had maybe 500 yards to cover before they even reached the foot of the cliffs. They faced the ranks of 352nd Infantry Division, a recently-raised unit formed by veterans of other divisions and raw recruits from the class of 1926. The 352nd was not a crack division, but nor was it filled with old men like many of the units defending the coast. Just four minutes after the landings began, an American patrol boat reported ominously: 'Entire first wave foundered.'

Into this maelstrom stepped nineteen year old American, Sergeant Robert Slaughter. The corpses of his dead comrades were washed in by the rising tide; the sea itself was stained with their blood. 'There were dead men floating in the water and there were live men acting dead, letting the tide take them in,' he recalled. 'Sand began to kick up from small-arms fire from the bluffs. It became apparent that it was past time to get the hell away from that killing zone and across the beach. Getting across the beach became an obsession. The decision not to try never entered my mind.'[9]

The American soldiers stumbling ashore expected to find the second-rate troops of the 716th Infantry holding the coast at Omaha; instead, they encountered the newly-raised and much stronger 352nd Infantry. On the heights overlooking the four-mile stretch of beach, the division's operations officer *Oberst* Fritz Ziegelman was trying to direct the battle as best he could from his bunker. Briefly, the staff officer gazed in wonder at the sight before him. 'The view will remain in my memory forever,' he said. 'The sea was like a picture of the Kiel review of the fleet. It's a wonder that German soldiers fought hard and stubbornly here.'[10]

This was no time to admire the spectacle of war. It was a time to kill. And the *Landser* did it in great abundance at Omaha, as Hein Severloh recalled:

The landing craft were now coming on in waves, a great swarm in an irregular formation. There was a break and then the next wave came. As the boats approached, I concentrated on the ramps. As soon as they came down for the GIs to jump out, I began to fire.

With the tide rising, the landing craft came ever closer to the edge of the beach. Quite a lot of them, some half sunken, drifted as wrecks on the waves. The GIs tried to find cover behind the beach obstacles which still towered above the waves, or corpses of their fallen comrades which were washing up and down. Often we could only see their heads and their helmets. After the landing craft had offloaded their living cargo on to the beach, they withdrew. Until the next wave arrived, I fired at everything which moved in the water and on the beach. I sometimes used my carbine, since I could fire aimed shots at individual soldiers and at the time give my machine gun a chance to cool down.[11]

At 8.30 a.m., *Gefreiter* Franz Gockel watched the American transporters off Omaha turn about. For two hours, the *Landser* had poured machine-gun fire on the oncoming invader from his pillbox. 'The beach became strewn with dead, wounded and shelter-seeking soldiers,' he wrote. 'The waves of attackers broke against our defences.' And now the American fleet was turning around. They are withdrawing, Gockel thought.[12] By 9 a.m. it appeared to the defenders of Omaha that the invasion had miscarried. The Atlantic Wall stood firm.

Ten miles to the west of Omaha, lay the long, flat straight sands of Utah, the Americans' other beach to assault this 6 June. There were no bluffs or cliffs here. The terrain at Utah, on the east coast of the Cotentin peninsula, was low-lying. There were no villages on the shoreline; the nearest was a good mile inland. But there were bunkers, which guarded the exits from the beach at breaks in the sand dunes and concrete sea wall, and behind which lay fields flooded by Rommel so that the only routes inland could be covered by German forces. There was nothing like the 352nd Infantry waiting for the American invader at Utah. Instead the elderly ranks of the 709th Fortress Division waited in the pillboxes, bunkers and trenches of the Cotentin peninsula's east coast. It had never seen battle; the average age of its men was thirty-six, and even then many were not trained, even though the division had been raised in 1941. On 6 June it was also leaderless; its commander Karl Wilhelm von Schlieben was away in Rennes for war games which never took place. Nor were its defences up to much. Of the forty-two strongpoints planned on the Cotentin, only one was finished by June 1944.

The boats at Utah went in five minutes earlier than at Omaha, at 6.30 a.m. precisely. The Americans' aim was to link up with the paratroopers landed four miles behind the beach at St Mère Église. Strong currents pushed the landing craft a good mile further south than intended. The error worked in the invaders' favour. Where the Americans waded ashore was even more lightly defended than the planned landing ground along the Cotentin. What defenders there were here were subdued by the preparatory bombardment. The occupants of the five bunkers over-looking Utah cowered in their concrete shelters. Some went mad. An elderly orderly ran around screaming: 'Everything is wrecked. The stores are on fire. We've got to surrender.' Just a few hours before *Leutnant* Arthur Jahnke had commanded a potent bunker in the form of *Widerstandnest 5* – Strongpoint 5. Jahnke's position boasted flame-throwers, pillboxes, heavy machine guns, a handful of light artillery pieces, concrete tank barriers, barbed wire, and a single 88-mm anti-tank/flak gun. Before the barrage was over only the flak gun could still be fired.

Jahnke and his men fought back as best they could, but within minutes of the first Americans setting foot on Utah, the guns of *Widerstandnest 5* were no longer firing. The invader did not attack the strongpoint directly. He streamed past it inland along the causeways which rose above the flooded landscape. 'It looks as though God and the world have forsaken us,' Jahnke muttered.[13]

The sun had still to rise over the horizon before company commander Peter Hansmann was on the move. Hansmann, an *Obersturmführer* in the *Hitlerjugend*, raced down the lanes of Calvados at the head of his column of armoured cars. It was a little after 6 a.m. when his eight-wheeled reconnaissance wagon reached the suburbs of Caen. The sound of battle could clearly be heard coming from the north-east. This, Hansmann told himself, was the invasion. 'Fighter-bombers attacked and fired randomly into the city,' the officer observed. 'French civilians were leaving their houses in panic and rushing out of the town.' Hansmann's company was ordered west, to defend Bayeux and counter the landings from Arromanches. The eight-wheelers rolled to a halt outside the historic town and from a farm watched 'the improbable, the really unimaginable spectacle'. Three miles away, in the Seine Bay off Arromanches, maybe 400 ships were massed. In the distance the regular, brief muzzle flashes of hundreds of guns were followed seconds later by gushers of mud and dirt 'as big as a house' rising up into the sky above Arromanches, then dropping. Hansmann grabbed his binoculars as he watched the landing unfold, transfixed:

A dark grey sea stretched between the beach and the armada of ships out there. White lines were racing at us through these dark masses of water from the endless line of ships.

These were fast boats with high, white foamy bow waves, landing craft which then spit out brown clumps of soldiers at the beach. They were wearing flat steel helmets so they were Brits. In groups, platoon strength, even whole companies, they were advancing slowly through the dunes towards us, seemingly without finding any resistance.

This was the invasion. There was no question. There were almost more ships than water. But who would believe it if he did not see it for himself.

The smell of war began to roll down the Norman coastline. Cordite and powder mingled with the morning mist, first from the fighting on the beach, then from the pounding of the Allies' naval bombardment. And under this barrage, Hansmann found himself admiring the Tommy:

> Each soldier had to first go through the water before reaching the beach. And through the wind today, almost a storm, which was whipping the seas down there. On top of that, there were the waves caused by the fast landing craft. Along the whole 20km wide coast, the bright wavy lines of the fast landing craft were constantly racing towards the beach. Hundreds of these boats were sitting in the shallow water, unloading. Vehicles dived into the sea and waded to shore. The beach was strewn with a lot of equipment and the Tommies were trying to reach the first houses by the beach quickly. [14]

Robert Vogt had been waiting in a trench high above what the British had codenamed Gold beach since before dawn. The nineteen year old infantryman lived just 500 yards from the water's edge at Arromanches, but still struggled to reach his position under a carpet of bombs. 'What I saw scared the devil out of me,' he recalled. 'Even though the weather was bad, we could see a huge number of ships. Ships as far as the eye could see. An entire fleet. I thought: "Oh God, we're finished! We're done for now!"' [15]

Gold's defences – natural and man-made – were by no means formidable, or impenetrable. Inland, behind the beaches and coast, there were heavy batteries protected by concrete emplacements, in many cases half-finished, and the more numerous *Widerstandsnester* containing light field artillery pieces and heavy machine guns. From Arromanches to Ouistreham, the stretch of coastline attacked by British and Canadian divisions on 6 June, there were just twenty-five guns immediately defending the beaches. In Normandy there was no Atlantic Wall as such, just a sporadic, incomplete line of defences.

The first landing craft set down on the sand and shingle at 7.35 a.m. in broad daylight, under overcast skies, but not under enemy fire. The Germans were slow to react. After just forty minutes, thirty-five British tanks were beyond the beach and racing towards Arromanches.

For three hours or more Peter Hansmann kept up his observation of the landing. In that time, he concluded, 10,000 British soldiers had come ashore. 'With every new second, more ships came in with soldiers, unloading them like ants. After only a short pause to catch their breath, they trampled our thin lines of defence.' It was 11 a.m. when the young officer was ordered to return to his division. 'It would probably take two days before it could get into action here,' he remarked ruefully.[16]

A few miles east of Gold, twenty-four landing craft were running behind schedule. They were due to put down on a three-mile stretch of beach between La Rivière and St Aubin sur Mer: Juno beach. Before the hour was out, twenty of the boats would be destroyed.

Only at Omaha did Allied soldiers pay a higher price for getting ashore on 6 June. At Juno, the defender had the advantage of a series of strongpoints and bunkers, whose guns concentrated their fire on Rommel's 'death zone' on the beach. If the ranks of 716th Infantry Division stood their ground, the invader would be destroyed at the water's edge.

The ramps of landing craft dropped on to Juno beach shortly before 8 a.m. For ninety minutes, the shore installations, bunkers and gun emplacements had been subjected to an unprecedented naval and rocket bombardment which only lifted as the assault craft went in. There was no response from the Germans. But as the ramps of their craft fell away on to the beach, the strongpoints opened fire exactly as planned. The Canadian soldiers walked into a hail of fire. 'The bombardment had failed to kill a single German or silence one weapon,' one soldier bitterly commented.[17]

Bodies lapped up and down the beach with the tide as their comrades waded through water, at least waist deep, to first reach the beach, then cross the obstacles and reach the sea wall, whose exits had been filled in with concrete. Beyond the wall, the Canadians could grapple with the enemy in his strongpoints. But only beyond the wall. Salvation came in the form of tanks, which began to arrive on the beach around 8.30 a.m. Forty-five minutes later, the sea wall at Juno was breached. The tanks and infantry could pass.

There was a five-mile gap between Juno and the last of the invasion beaches, Sword, which ran from the coastal village of Lion-sur-Mer to Caen's port, Ouistreham. British intelligence had predicted Sword would be the most heavily defended of the Normandy beaches. Men in the first wave were warned as many as five in every six of them would not come back. But the five-mile stretch of beach was defended by just three companies from the second-rate 716th Infantry Division, which had few anti-tank weapons and had never seen action in its three-year existence. There was little Atlantic Wall to speak of at Sword, beyond a handful of bunkers and a few light artillery pieces. A couple of landing craft were sunk, a third set on fire, and the initial 200 or so attackers at Ouistreham itself were massacred, but although 716th Infantry's commander Wilhelm Richter was confidently reporting 'very high' enemy losses within an hour of the first landings, British soldiers were moving inland. There was no answer to the Allies' material supremacy. 'For every round we fired,' one artillery observer complained, 'we got anything between 20 and 100 back.'[18]

Erwin Rommel was enjoying a quiet day at home in Herrlingen in southern Germany, celebrating his wife Lucie's fiftieth birthday. The relaxed mood changed in an instant. The telephone rang shortly after 10.15 a.m. It was Hans Speidel. The invasion had begun. In Normandy. The field marshal cursed, summoned his adjutant Hellmuth Lang and his driver. Shortly after midday the Desert Fox climbed into his Horch for the journey back to Normandy.

At Juno, bitter fighting raged for the strongpoints and bunkers. But the Canadians learned they did not have to wait for each pocket of resistance to be wiped out. They could simply bypass them. By 10.30 a.m. on 6 June, Canadian armour was rolling off the beaches. All roads led to Caen. By midday, the entire Canadian 3rd Division was ashore in Normandy.

Individual strongpoints held out until mid-afternoon. All were overrun, their occupants either killed or taken prisoner. Not all fought to the last man. One platoon commander told his men with Canadian soldiers upon his sector: 'This is it boys. We give up now.' Not one of his thirty men fired a shot in anger. Sherman tanks tore past Gustav Pflocksch's bunker near St Aubin before Canadian infantry surrounded the strongpoint and overran it. The junior officer marched off into captivity. 'I asked myself whether I should be happy or unhappy about the invasion, and I found out there was every reason to be somewhat happy. Now the war will very soon come to an end.'[19]

Three hours after the Americans had set foot at Omaha, their position remained precarious. Wounded and dead men littered the sands, their equipment at the bottom of the Channel or strewn across the churned up beach next to mortar craters. At the water's edge waves, turned a grey-red, lapped the bodies of the dead. The living were pinned down along shingle banks at the foot of the cliffs which led off the beach – and away from the murderous enemy fire.

From his strongpoint at Vierville, at the western end of Omaha, one of the 352nd Infantry Division's sector commanders excitedly called his headquarters. 'A great many vehicles – among them ten tanks – stand burning at the beach,' the officer telephoned Fritz Ziegelman, 352nd's chief-of-staff. 'The fire of our strongpoints and artillery was well placed and has inflicted considerable casualties among the enemy.'

In a lull in the fighting at Omaha, Hein Severloh took time to survey the scene on the beach below him:

> For the first time I realized how many dead had been washed up on the beach below by the high waves and rising tide in our sector. On a stretch of beach about 300m long and several metres wide lay hundreds upon hundreds of lifeless bodies of American soldiers, in places several on top of each other. The wounded moved slowly in the blood-soaked water, most of them crawled, to the edge of the beach where there was an embankment about one and half metres high, to find shelter behind it. I could only see about fifty to sixty GIs, who occasionally ducked and ran around on their own.

It was shortly after 10 a.m. when the deadlock was broken. It took landing craft to do it, forcing their way over the beach obstacles at high tide, pouring fire on the bunkers and pillboxes belching death and destruction on Omaha. Under gunfire from destroyers offshore, which picked off what German bunkers they could identify, US troops began to infiltrate their way off the beach at three separate points. Their comrades followed them ant-like up the slopes which led inland. It was maybe 11 a.m. when the first Americans reached the bluffs. They could not help but look back. 'The view was unforgettable,' Private Ray Moon recalled. 'The scene below reminded me of the Chicago stockyard cattle pens and its slaughter house.'[20]

Shortly before midday, the troops at Omaha were reporting German soldiers surrendering or abandoning their bunkers and streaming inland. *Landser* Franz Gockel slipped out of his surrounded strongpoint near Colleville on Omaha's eastern flank. Wounded, Gockel was sent to the rear in a hospital truck. As it stuttered down the Norman lanes, often blocked by the after-effects of Allied air attacks, he surveyed the countryside. 'Dead cattle lay in the pastures,' he remembered. 'The supply units had also suffered their share of casualties.' In five hours, Heinrich Severloh had fired at least 8,000 rounds from his machine gun. Severloh was running out of ammunition, so much so that he turned to using night-time bullets with tracers. The bullets were no less effective, but they revealed Severloh's position instantly. Four times in ten minutes, the machine-gunner was knocked from his post by shells landing close to his nest. Now it was time to go. The 'Amis' were filtering past, either on foot or in their Sherman tanks. It was the same along the cliffs overlooking Omaha. 'Gunfire barrage on the beach,' one strongpoint radioed. 'Every shell a certain hit. We are getting out.' One by one, Severloh and his comrades darted up the cliff slope away from WN62. Severloh jumped from one shell crater to the next, stooped down, never raising his head above the level of the earth, until he reached the road leading from the strongpoint inland to the village of St Laurent. A good 400m down the lane he stopped and waited for his colleagues to come. Only one made it. 'He was disoriented and, out of breath, told me that the others were all dead and somehow he had succeeded in getting through,' the *Landser* recalled. Somehow, Hein Severloh and his comrade reached battalion headquarters, three miles down the coast near the village of Colleville. As medics tended to flesh wounds in his face, the *Landser* overheard his battalion commander. 'We're waiting for the tanks. Then we'll kick those Americans out again.'[21]

The German soldier at Omaha gave his all. It was a tantalizing glimpse of what might have been on Tuesday, 6 June, had the *Landser* elsewhere in Normandy fought as doggedly. The price for the defence of this four-mile stretch of coast was high. US Sergeant Hyman Haas came across an enemy bunker overlooking the beach. 'There, lying on the parapet, was a German officer, bleeding from the mouth, obviously in his last moments of life, being held by another wounded German.'[22]

A few days after 6 June, British general Bernard Law Montgomery toured the sands of Omaha. 'If you saw Omaha beach, you would wonder how the Americans ever got ashore.'[23] There is no better epitaph for the defenders of Vierville, St Honorine and Colleville.

Leutnant Wolfgang Fischer had been enjoying a solid night's sleep in his billet, a small hotel near the airfield which was home to *Jagdgeschwader* 2's[24] Focke-Wulf Fw190s. It was 4.30 a.m. when a motorcyclist roused the young pilot from his bed. Before dawn, Fischer's Fw190 was airborne and heading for the staging ground at Creil, thirty miles north of Paris, where a dozen Fockes were armed with rockets. At 9.30 – three hours after the Allied invasion fleet began disgorging its troops and material on to the Normandy beaches – Fischer and his eleven colleagues lifted off and headed for Gold beach. The approach of the dozen fighter-bombers went unnoticed as the Fw190s slipped between the clouds at 10,000 ft above Normandy. As the great expanse of the Seine Bay stretched before the pilots' eyes, Fischer muttered to himself: 'Poor Germany.' The English Channel from the Orne estuary to the base of the Cotentin peninsula was filled with grey and black dots – 'an armada larger than I could ever have imagined' – as enemy fighters swarmed above the beaches. 'Such a concentration of firepower was impossible,' the *Leutnant* recalled. 'We took a conscious risk to continue our attack. Having fired our rockets, we attacked landing ships, then the shore. As far as I know, one of my rockets hit the bow of a troop transporter, probably a Victory-class ship.' JG2's attack lasted little more than a few minutes, before the Fw190s turned back for the Normandy heartland.

The raid had been little more than a pinprick, but Wolfgang Fischer was not disheartened. 'I kept faith in the future – as did most of my comrades,' Fischer admitted. 'We placed hope in the development of new weapons and their entry into action.'[25]

Wolfgang Fischer's fruitless attack was typical of the *Luftwaffe*'s disjointed, piecemeal response to the landings in Normandy. It rather made a mockery of Hugo Sperrle's grandiose order of the day which the pompous, bloated field marshal had issued that morning:

Men of *Luftflotte 3*! The enemy has launched the long-announced invasion. Long have we waited for this moment, long have we prepared ourselves, both inwardly and on the field of battle, by untiring, unending toil. Our task is now to defeat the enemy. I know that each one of you, true to his oath to the colours, will carry out his duties. Great things will be asked of you and you will show the bravest fighting valour.[26]

Adolf Hitler rose shortly before 10 a.m. Reports of an invasion did not trouble him. 'The news couldn't be better,' he told the *Wehrmacht*'s overbearing and arrogant chief-of-staff Field Marshal Keitel. 'As long as they were in Britain we couldn't get at them. Now we have them where we can destroy them.' Poring over the situation maps at the afternoon conference, the Führer quipped to his generals. 'So, we're off.' Kurt Zeitzler, Chief of the General Staff of the Army, left the briefing despondent. The invasion was not being taken seriously. 'That was typical,' he complained to a staff officer as he walked away. 'The invasion has begun. Time is of the essence. Instead of rushing officers to the front in an aircraft, instead of flying to the west immediately in person, instead of taking decisions or giving your commander in the west a free hand, every situation is discussed at length, we wait and hesitate.' Zeitzler's tirade continued. Hitler's staff only told him what he wanted to hear. It was as if a war game was being played out on the beaches of Normandy. 'We'll miss the right moment to strike back. And then it will be too late,' Zeitzler fumed.

The reason Hitler was buoyant, Goebbels guessed, was that the invasion had taken place exactly where he'd predicted it would: Normandy. 'I notice in him a change, which I have often seen before during grave crises, namely that he is depressed as long as the crisis has not been resolved but as soon as the crisis is resolved, a great weight is lifted from his shoulders,' Goebbels scrawled in his diary. The Führer's optimism was infectious. Goering, too, was confident. 'He has already almost won the battle,' the propaganda minister commented. 'But we don't want things to go too easily.'[27]

Throughout the day, Günther Blumentritt had pestered the staff at Hitler's headquarters for the release of the panzer divisions held in reserve. Only after Hitler emerged from his afternoon conference, at 2.30 p.m., did the order arrive for the divisions to move. Now the German Army in the west could mount its long-planned counter-attack against the invader.

21st Panzer Division had been on the move since around 6.30 that morning, roaring north-east of Caen towards the British paratroopers landed on the Orne – and away from the amphibious landings to the north of the city. What the division lacked on Tuesday, 6 June, was decisive leadership. It began the day with no leadership. Its commander Edgar Feuchtinger was enjoying the high life in Paris, as was his custom.

Few people were less suitable in command of a panzer division than Edgar Feuchtinger. He was not a typical German general. He was a Bohemian figure, a pleasure seeker, a sportsman who had helped to organize the winter and summer Olympics in Germany in 1936. He had no experience of armoured warfare, and little experience of command. Instead, Feuchtinger made few decisions; he let his subordinates command 21st Panzer Division on the battlefield. But Feuchtinger was also a Party favourite; in 1935 and 1937 he had been selected to arrange the *Wehrmacht*'s participation in the Nuremberg rallies. Feuchtinger had, Erwin Rommel bitterly commented, 'pull at Führer HQ'. In the small hours Edgar Feuchtinger made no decisions. His division, the closest armour to the beaches north of Caen, sat idly around. It was left to Erich Marcks to order 21st Panzer to move. He wanted the airborne troops on the Orne eliminated. The advance to the Orne was slow. The road was filled with refugees fleeing the Allied barrage and German units moving up. 21st Panzer never reached its objective. Four hours into its march, the division was ordered to double back through Caen and attack the British pouring ashore on Sword. Too late Marcks realized he had sent the panzers to deal with the wrong threat. 'The regrouping of the division took hours,' *Major* Hans von Luck, commanding a panzer grenadier regiment, recalled. 'Most of the units had to squeeze through the eye of the needle at Caen', which was 'under virtually constant bombardment from the navy and the fighter-bombers of the RAF'. Only Luck's regiment remained behind. It was to wipe out the airborne troops around Ranville – on its own.[28]

22nd Panzer Regiment and its 100 tanks were finally ready to strike west of the Orne in the early afternoon. As he prepared to move off, its forty-five year old commander Hermann von Oppeln-Bronikowski ran into Erich Marcks, who had come forward from his headquarters to watch the enemy driven back into the sea. The one-legged general seized the panzer leader: 'Whether the invasion is defeated or not depends on you.'

It was mid-afternoon when the men of 12th SS Panzer Division *Hitlerjugend* mounted their vehicles and began to move from south of Caen towards the beaches. The mood, *Sturmmann* Hellmuth Pock recorded in his diary, was confident. 'There is enthusiasm everywhere. "We'll show the Tommies", and similar lines dominate our conversation.' On the lanes and secondary roads of rural Normandy, the *Hitlerjugend* rumbled northwards. 'As far as the eye can see, and wherever there is a path a vehicle can drive on, units are moving in the direction of the coast,' Pock wrote. As the panzer division drew closer to the beachhead, the fighter-bombers struck. 'The number of our vehicles knocked out by the enemy keeps growing,' an anxious Pock noted. He continued:

They are sitting where they were hit, burnt out. Grenades are scattered about, shells, all types of ammunition, among them dead soldiers.

The march during the day becomes more and more dangerous. The pastures and fields are ploughed by bomb craters. We realize more and more that the enemy, as far as material is concerned, does not seem to be inferior to us.

The *Hitlerjugend*'s 25th Panzer Grenadier Regiment rolled down the Caen-Falaise road, its irrepressible commander, Kurt Meyer, at the head of the columns. Above, the hawkish enemy fighter-bombers watched every move of Meyer's regiment. 'We are hunted relentlessly, but cannot afford to take cover,' Meyer noted. 'The march must go on!' He continued in his diary:

A string of Spitfires is attacking the last platoon of 15th Company. Rockets and other weapons are reaping a grizzly harvest. The platoon is driving down a sunken road, evasion is not possible. A grenadier is lying in the road, a jet of blood shooting from his throat, an artery has been shot through. He dies in our arms. The ammunition in an amphibious vehicle explodes with a loud bang, the blast shoots flames high into the sky, the vehicle is torn to pieces. In a couple of minutes, the rubble is pushed aside. There is no stopping. On – always on![29]

Tuesday, 6 June, cost the *Hitlerjugend* eighty-three men, twenty-two of them dead. The division had yet to engage the enemy.

East of Le Mans, the 229 panzers and 658 armoured personnel carriers of the *Panzer Lehr* Division waited for the order to move. The *Panzer Lehr* was the best-equipped of all the *Wehrmacht*'s divisions in the west, but its commander Fritz Bayerlein was nervous. The Allies' air superiority alarmed him. When the order to strike north finally arrived shortly after 3 p.m., Bayerlein urged caution. Seventh Army wanted his division to cover 100 miles before daybreak on 7 June, then attack the British and Canadians west of Caen. Fritz Bayerlein did not want to move off before nightfall to prevent the *Panzer Lehr* being mauled. Max Pemsel overruled him. At 5 p.m., the division rolled. But Bayerlein was proved right. 'Even today,' panzer company commander Helmut Ritgen wrote years later, 'memories of this march still evoke nightmares for those who took part.' He continued:

> The division's columns had hardly got under way when they were spotted by enemy reconnaissance aircraft and attacked shortly afterwards by fighter-bombers with their on-board weapons, rockets and bombs. They flew in clear skies, the machines spotted the columns, attacked, called on other fighter-bombers to replace them. Soon mushroom clouds of black smoke rose from vehicles on fire, which lined the road we were following, for fresh waves of aircraft. The advance was slowed by every attack, columns were diverted, and the speed of advance was slowed further still by spreads of bombs dropped on the roads, on towns and on bridges.
> Flak was limited to some light anti-aircraft guns and our machine-gun fire. But we fired too little, hits on the targets were rare and we rarely recorded the destruction of an aircraft. Those who'd managed to find cover thought it was better to stay there. A lot of us thought: 'What use is it if we down a few aircraft among this mass of fighter-bombers?'[30]

It was gone 4 p.m. before Hans von Luck's panzer grenadiers struck to the east of Caen, and Hermann von Oppeln's panzers to the west. On both sides of Caen, the results were the same. Luck's regiment got nowhere near Ranville. 'All hell broke loose,' Luck wrote. 'The heaviest naval guns, artillery and fighter-bombers plastered us without pause. Radio contacts were lost, wounded came back.'[31] A few miles to the west Oppeln's men ran into a British ambush three miles short of Sword. 'The first Mark IV was blazing before a German tank had the chance to fire a shot,' one 21st Panzer soldier complained. In a matter of minutes, sixteen panzers had been shot up. Only a scratch group of panzer grenadiers met with success that afternoon. *Kampfgruppe*[32] *Rauch* – named after its commander, one Josef Rauch – slipped between the Allied forces landing at Sword and Juno beaches and drove headlong for the sea. At 7 p.m., Rauch's men beheld the promised land: the sweeping sands of Lion-sur-Mer. It was as far as any counter-attacking unit would strike on Tuesday, 6 June. The panzers did not follow. They got no closer than four miles from the coast, before being driven back. As 22nd Panzer Regiment fell back towards Caen, it left behind seventy of the 124 panzers it had started its dash to the sea with.

Far from the fighting, the picture at Seventh Army's headquarters in Le Mans was encouraging. First Erich Marcks had reported that, by and large, the landings from the sea had been 'utterly repulsed'. Then 716th Infantry Division's commander Wilhelm Richter had declared unequivocally that the attackers had been 'thrown back into the sea'. The optimism was pervasive. By mid-afternoon, Max Pemsel was confidently reporting to Rommel's headquarters that there was 'nothing to fear'. Nothing to fear or not, in the mid-afternoon of Tuesday, 6 June, the Allies had still not been driven back into the sea, despite the confident reports. From Paris, Rundstedt and his staff ordered the Allies wiped out before the day's end, otherwise the enemy would reinforce and the chance would be lost.

Karl Dönitz had been woken in the small hours of the morning at his headquarters, Koralle near Berlin. The fifty-two year old *Grossadmiral* was on leave in the Black Forest. The Dönitz family was still recovering from the loss of its eldest son, Klaus, killed in a torpedo boat in the Channel less than a month earlier. But duty called. Karl Dönitz raced back to Berlin. Shortly after 11 a.m., he was in Koralle. The mood was upbeat. 'The invasion has begun,' Dönitz told his staff. 'The unbearable tension has been lifted. For Germany, the war has entered its decisive phase. Once again, there is the chance of reaching a rapid decision in this war in a swift but powerful clash of arms.'[33] The *Grossadmiral* ordered every U-boat in the west committed to destroy the invasion fleet – thirty-six boats in La Pallice, St Nazaire, Lorient and Brest and twenty-two more from southern Norway. At 1st U-boat Flotilla's headquarters in Brest, the teleprinter churned out Dönitz's clarion call:

The enemy has started his invasion of Europe. The war has thus entered its decisive phase. If the Anglo-American landing succeeds, it would mean for us the loss of large territories vital to our war economy and an immediate threat to our most important industrial regions without which the war cannot be continued.

The enemy is at his weakest at the very moment of landing. Everything must be done to hit him at this moment and to inflict such losses on him that he will have no desire ever to try any landings again. Only then, furthermore, can the forces lacking on the Eastern Front be sent there.

Men of the U-boat arm! On you too the future of our German people depends, now more than at any other time. I therefore require of you the most unstinting action, and no consideration for otherwise valid precautionary measures. Each enemy vessel useful to him for landing is to be subjected to all-out attack, even when there is danger of losing your own U-boat. Every enemy man and enemy weapon destroyed before landing diminishes the enemy's prospect for success. In this crisis I know that you men of the U-boat arm – who have been tried in the toughest battles – are men on whom I can rely.[34]

Oberleutnant Herbert Werner picked up the orders for his *Schnorchel*-less U415: attack shipping off the southern English coast; the *Schnorchel* boats were to sail submerged into the mouth of hell and attack the invasion fleet. Werner was filled with foreboding. The orders demanded his boat 'remain on the surface and race unprotected towards the southern English coast at a time when the sky was black with thousands of aircraft and the sea swarmed with hundreds of destroyers and corvettes'. It was tantamount to a suicide mission.

The pen resounded to the voices of 800 U-boat men singing – men, Werner wrote, 'eager to sail against the enemy, even if it meant sailing straight to their deaths'. As night fell, the first of seventeen U-boats slowly slipped out of Brest harbour in single file, the *Schnorchel* boats first, then the 'underprivileged'. The sea was flat; the night lit up by the moon which 'illuminated the long row of U-boats and was sharply reflected in the calm sea'.

The U-boat procession out of Brest had barely been at sea more than a couple of hours when blips appeared on primitive radar sets: Allied aircraft. 'The Tommies,' Herbert Werner wrote. 'must have thought we had lost our minds.' At twelve minutes past one on Wednesday, 7 June, the battle off Brest began. 'Tracers spurted in various directions, then the sound of gunfire hit our ears,' U415's commander remembered. 'Fountains reached into the air. A spectacular fireworks display erupted, engulfing U-boats and aircraft.' First U413 careered wildly out of formation, then disappeared beneath the waves; riddled with bullets, the boat limped back to Brest for repairs. Then, U256 bringing up the rear of the formation was straddled by depth charges from a four-engined Liberator bomber, as Werner's 37-mm anti-aircraft gun opened fire. 'Four giant water columns leaped skywards behind the riddled aircraft as it tried to escape our fire,' the *Oberleutnant* recalled. 'Some shells from our 37-mm gun hit the plane broadside. It exploded in mid-air, then plunged into the sea.' But U256 was crippled, almost dead in the water. She too turned about and headed back to Brest.

At 2.20 a.m. it was U415's turn. Another Liberator dropped out of the skies and hurled four depth charges at the U-boat. 'Four savage

59

eruptions heaved U415 out of the water and threw our men flat on the deck plates,' Werner wrote. 'Then she fell back and the four collapsing geysers showered us with tons of water and sent cascades through the hatch. U415 lay crippled, bleeding oil from a ruptured tank, slowly coming to a full stop – a target to be finished off with ease.' On the conning tower, Herbert Werner waited for the Allies to deliver the *coup de grâce*. He only had to wait eight minutes. First a Sunderland flying boat, then a Liberator. Each one dropped four depth charges; each one was struck by ferocious fire from U415's flak guns. The Liberator spiralled into the sea in flames, the Sunderland vanished into the June night. And still U415 did not sink. As dawn neared, Werner's chief engineer reported the boat ready for diving. 'Quickly the men climbed up the bridge and dropped one by one through the round opening into their iron coffin,' the boat's commander remembered. 'I watched the deck gradually sink below surface. As the water crept up to the bridge I slammed the lid shut. Seconds later the floods engulfed the boat.'[35]

The phone at *Schlachtgeschwader* 4's[36] airfield near St Quentin rang shortly after 3 a.m: the enemy landing was imminent. It was another four hours before its thirty-eight serviceable Fw190s were readied to move to bases closer to Normandy. It was midday before they actually took off. To avoid the Allied fighter screen protecting the invasion armada, the Focke-Wulfs skirted south around Paris before turning for the forward airfields near Normandy. The fighter-bombers of SG4 were intercepted anyway by American Thunderbolts and Mustangs; four pilots were killed and one wounded even before the *Geschwader* intervened in Normandy. Their forward airfield was in no position to support a front-line squadron. 'There were no refuelling vehicles, no bomb-loading trolleys, no personnel to assist and above all no airfield defence,' the *Geschwader*'s diarist wrote angrily. Only thirteen aircraft were fit to attack the landings that afternoon, in three small groups bearing down on the beaches near the Orne estuary. Only two got through; the third flight was driven off by the Allied defences.[37]

Across western Europe, units like *Schlachtgeschwader* 4 began leapfrogging from airbases far from the coast towards the invasion area. The fighters of *Jagdgeschwader* 26 – the top guns of the *Luftwaffe* – were scattered all over France. It was long after dawn before they began to move forward in the direction of Normandy. Barely had the Messerschmitt Me109s and their entourage set down near Le Mans than the airfield was attacked by the Allies, as *Hauptmann* Hans Groos recalled:

The situation in Le Mans was indescribable. A group of fighters, which had just arrived from Germany, came to set up shop there, and of the twenty-five aircraft which made up the group when it set off, only four were fit to fly again. Others had been destroyed by fire shortly after landing. On the edge of the airfield, many Ju52s which had provided the technical means of transporting the group, were reduced to charred wrecks.[38]

The skies over Normandy on Tuesday, 6 June 1944, belonged to the Allies, whose aircraft had flown more than 14,000 sorties to safeguard the invasion; the *Luftwaffe* could muster just 319 flights. A mere 113 Allied aircraft were shot down; not one was the victim of the *Luftwaffe*. Flak was the only killer on 6 June.

By nightfall on 6 June, nearly 175,000 Allied soldiers were ashore. The British and Canadians at Gold and Juno had merged to form a sizeable beachhead which stretched to the gates of the historic town of Bayeux. To the east, there was a good two-mile gap between the Juno and Sword bridgeheads, the latter of which fell short of the city of Caen, objective for D-Day, by two miles. The Americans' foothold at Omaha was limited to a handful of scattered pockets no more than half a mile inland. Only at Utah had US forces enjoyed any great success. Around twenty-five square miles of the Cotentin peninsula were in American hands and the railway line to Cherbourg was cut.

The rapid success of the invasion, particularly at Utah, Gold and Sword, prompted taunts from the British propaganda machine. The German Army in the west had been taken by surprise, radio reports boasted. 'The English reported that German soldiers had to be hauled out of their beds in their bedclothes.'[39]

The price of the Allies' precarious foothold on French soil was fewer than 5,000 casualties. 'Bloody' Omaha cost the Americans 2,400 dead, wounded and missing, but the invading forces at Utah suffered fewer than 200 dead. The British lost 400 men at Gold, a further 630 troops were casualties at Sword, and the Canadians at Juno suffered 1,200 casualties. The German Army lost at least as many men defending the beaches and landing grounds that Tuesday.

One in five prisoners taken by the British on 6 June had been non-Germans, who showed little stomach for battle, rather they sought 'an early opportunity of giving up the fight'. Planners had expected 709th, 711th and 716th Infantry Divisions holding the Norman coast 'to be indifferent and full of foreigners – and so they have proved', one British report commented. *Oberst* Walter Köhn, a regimental commander on the Cotentin peninsula, complained of the *Osttruppen*: 'They fell to pieces completely. They held out for quite a while, but when things became critical, they took to their heels too.' Yet among the German captives, the British noticed a resolve. 'Morale seems to have been high,' one interrogator commented. 'All Germans are firmly determined to win the war.' But there was also some unease among the captives. The odd *Landser* conceded 'that when they saw what was being massed against them, they knew the game was up'.[40]

Darkness was falling across Normandy as Erwin Rommel's Horch arrived back at his headquarters in La Roche-Guyon. All day the powerful black open-top car had sped down the roads of Germany and France. Sporadically, it had stopped for the field marshal to call his chief-of-staff.

As Rommel stepped out of his saloon, his adjutant Hellmuth Lang buttonholed him. 'Sir, do you think we'll be able to manage it, hold them back?' Rommel nodded. 'Lang, I hope we can. I have always succeeded up to now.'[41]

From his artillery observation post overlooking Gold beach, *Oberleutnant* Werner Fiebig watched the British Army pour ashore with a sense of foreboding. 'I saw hundreds of English tanks but not one of our own,' he recalled. 'It became very clear to us that we were up against an irresistible force we could not hold back.'[42] Fiebig's commander, 352nd Infantry's commander Dietrich Kraiss, had watched his division disintegrate in the space of less than twenty-four hours. One in five of his men had been killed or wounded that Tuesday. With 6 June almost over, Kraiss picked up the telephone and called Erich Marcks at his headquarters in St Lô to report on the day's fighting. 'The losses of men and material in the pockets of resistance are total,' he informed Marcks. Marcks listened intently, then issued his terse orders. 'Every inch of ground must be defended to the last, until fresh reinforcements can be brought up.'[43]

To the north-east of Caen, Hans von Luck took shelter alongside his panzer. 'Even by night, "Christmas trees" hung in the sky, bathing the whole area in bright light. The air attacks never stopped; the navy laid a barrage of fire on our positions and bombarded the city of Caen, which was a focal point in our lateral communications.' The day had not gone well for 21st Panzer Division. One quarter of its tanks had been knocked out. As the day drew to a close, regimental adjutant Helmut Liebeskind and his comrades were melancholy. 'Things looked rather sad as we saw no possibility of throwing them out,' he recalled. 'The feeling of not being able to drive out the Allies, that everything was in vain, had already seeped into our thoughts.'[44]

As darkness descended at Omaha, Hein Severloh watched two horses draw a four-wheeled cart along the cliff top overlooking the beach.

Shots still reverberated around the battlefield, but the cursed fighter-bombers had gone. Only now did the cart's driver feel it was safe to venture to the bunkers. Slowly, he lifted the seriously wounded on to the wagon so they could be taken away for treatment. The soldier was still loading the wounded when it struck midnight.

Kurt Meyer reached Caen ahead of the rest of his men to confer with 21st Panzer Division's commander Edgar Feuchtinger whose men had achieved so little that day. It was 11 p.m. when Meyer drove into the city of the Norman dukes. 'Caen is a sea of flames,' he recorded in his diary. 'Harassed people are wandering through the rubble, streets are blocked, burning smoke is rolling through the town. Venerable churches are converted into heaps of rubble, the work of generations is now a sea of ashes and rubble.'[45]

It was getting on for midnight when *Oberleutnant* Martin Pöppel and his fellow paratroopers pitched camp near Carentan, ready for action if the alarm sounded. Pöppel's battle had ended at dawn. His men had captured or killed American paratroopers who had come down to the south of Carentan. 'We can see parachutes hanging and lying all over the area,' the young officer noted in his diary. 'This really is the Allies' big day, which unfortunately means that it's ours too.' The rest of the day was spent moving northwards towards the Utah landings but by nightfall, the *Fallschirmjäger* had gone no further than Carentan and were still a good three miles away from making contact with the enemy. The night sky had a reddish glow from fires burning on the horizon. 'I find it very difficult to sleep,' an exhausted Pöppel wrote. 'Everything is still too new. The impressions are still too fresh in my mind to let me drop off.'[46]

On the stroke of midnight the radio at 716th Infantry Division's head-quarters in a bunker near Caen sprang to life. 'The enemy is standing on top of my bunker,' the alarmed commander of 736th Grenadier Regiment, one *Oberst* Krug, screamed. 'I have no means to fight him, nor any contact with my units. What shall I do?' For the better part of twenty-four hours, *Generalleutnant* Wilhelm Richter had watched his division melt away. On the cusp of 7 June, it failed to exist as a fighting unit. Five out of its six battalions simply no longer existed. Richter was a broken man. 'I cannot give you any further orders. You may now act on your own initiative. Goodbye.'[47]

Notes
1. Ambrose, *D-Day*, p.218.
2. KTB AOK7, 0120, 0215, 0240 Hours, 6/6/44. IWM AL528.
3. TB Goebbels, 6/6/44; Ryan, *Longest Day*, p.185.
4. Kurt Meyer, *Grenadiers*, p.116; Hubert Meyer, op. cit., p.26.
5. Miller, *Nothing less than Victory*, p.244.

6. Severloh, pp.48-50.
7. Severloh, p.50; Miller, p.245; Kershaw, *D-Day*, p.94.
8. Severloh, pp.52-53, 54; Wilmot, *The Struggle for Europe*, p.277.
9. Neillands, Robin, *D-Day 1944: Voices from Normandy*, p.185.
10. Balkoski, *Beyond the Beachhead*, p.148.
11. Severloh, pp.59-61.
12. Ambrose, *D-Day*, p.380.
13. Carell, *Invasion – They're Coming*, pp.62, 68.
14. Hubert Meyer, *12 SS Panzer Division Hitlerjugend*, pp.29-31.
15. Steinhoff, *Voices from the Third Reich*, p.254.
16. Hubert Meyer, *12 SS Panzer Division Hitlerjugend*, p.31.
17. Ambrose, *D-Day*, p.534.
18. Kershaw, *D-Day*, p.173.
19. NA CAB106/975; Kershaw, p.171.
20. Severloh, p.62; Ambrose, p.442.
21. Ambrose, p.468; Severloh, pp.65-68; Carell, p.100.
22. Ambrose, p.439.
23. Montgomery letter, 13/6/44. Hamilton, ii, p.667.
24. 2nd Fighter Squadron.
25. Frappé, *La Luftwaffe face au débarquement allié*, pp.15, 16.
26. Sperrle Tagesbefehl, 6/6/44. Cited in Murray, p.374.
27. Irving, *Hitler's War*, 2nd Edition, p.638; Miller, *Nothing Less than Victory*, p.410; Heusinger, p.326; TB Goebbels, 7/6/44.
28. Cited in Perrigault, Jean-Claude, *21 Panzer Division*, p.215; Luck, pp.166-67; Luck, p.178.
29. Hubert Meyer, *12 SS Panzer Division Hitlerjugend*, p.34; Kurt Meyer, *Grenadiers*, p.118.
30. Ritgen, *Das Geschichte der Panzer Lehr Division im Westen 1944-1945*, p.105.
31. Luck, p.179.
32. Battlegroup. An ad hoc unit normally formed temporarily for specific tasks.
33. KTB Skl, 6/6/44.
34. Dönitz Tagesbefehl, 6/6/44. Blair, ii, p.581.
35. Werner, pp.226-32; KTB BdU, 6/6/44.
36. 4th Ground-attack squadron.
37. KTB Schlachtgeschwader 4, 6/6/44. Price, *Luftwaffe Data Book*, pp.202-03.
38. Frappé, p.59.
39. KTB AGp.B, 9/6/44.
40. NA WO208/4168; NA CAB 106/975.
41. Miller, *Nothing Less than Victory*, p.451.
42. Cited in Kershaw, *D-Day*, p.169.
43. Telephone log, 352nd Infantry Division, 2320 Hours, 6/6/44. MS B-432.
44. Luck, p.180; Miller, p.448.
45. Kurt Meyer, p.118.
46. Pöppel, pp. 177, 179.
47. Kurt Meyer, p.118.

Chapter 5

Approaching a Catastrophe

The war can now only be won by the politicians.
General Leo Geyr von Schweppenburg

The capital of the Reich awoke on Wednesday, 7 June 1944, to the Nazi party organ, the *Völkischer Beobachter*, screaming news of the Allied landings. 'Moscow's vassals had to begin the invasion,' ran the headline. 'The battle by our armed forces against the invaders was unleashed with full force immediately and is in full swing.' In full swing, and going in Germany's favour, the newspaper told its readers. The defenders were surprised nowhere; everywhere they fought 'with all their might'. Enemy paratroopers were captured 'as soon as they jumped'; enemy ships 'were under effective fire' – landing craft and battleships were hit by the guns of the Atlantic Wall. The lead article continued: 'Reports concerning the initial hours of the fighting show how determined the defensive will of the German leadership is, how superior their measures and how hard the first German counter-blows are.' Nevertheless, the *Völkischer Beobachter* left the German people in no doubt about the seriousness of the hour:

A great test of strength has begun, in which the enemy has committed the reserves on the grandest scale which he has built up and saved for years. The German leadership is prepared for this clash of arms, which affects the defence of Europe, its freedom and its greatness in perpetuity. The German people are aware that they have to summon all their inner strength to bring about a victorious conclusion, which is not merely a clash of arms. The nation begins this new chapter of the war with unshakeable courage and faith, which has filled them for almost five years of a harsh struggle which has demanded many sacrifices, which has given it great victories and given it the strength to withstand all the changes of fortune and to concentrate all its energies even more determinedly to secure its future.

In these hours the demands which the enemy's general offensive makes of us all have increased, as has the scale of the historic task which lies in our hands. We go into this battle with the ardent determination not to finish it before victory is ours, so that the lives, honour and freedom of our people are guaranteed for generations. The German people rallies around the Führer at this fateful hour in the firm belief in the victory of his just cause. He is our guarantee of victory and guarantee of a future which is worthy of our nation and fulfils our sense of history...

If the enemy's invasion succeeds, then the consequences for us would be obvious. It would mean the end. But if the German soldier drives back his attacker, then the consequences for the enemy side too are obvious. The decision for both the fate of our nation and the fate of our continent rests in the hands and in the heroic hearts of those fighting in the Atlantic Wall. The justification for holding out, for the German soldier on the Atlantic Coast resisting and striking back, lies in the terrible consequences of what will happen. But if the smoke from the guns finally disperses from the beaches and rocky coast of France, then we will also see the face of war take on an entirely new form.

The nation knows that this moment when this war dramatically intensifies, is also the moment for the greatest confidence, they know that in the chaos of the bitter battles of this summer, we will find the sword to deliver retribution.[1]

Standartenführer Kurt Meyer had no sleep on the night of the 6-7 June. Few soldiers were more hardened in battle than the thirty-three year old *Waffen SS* officer. Panzermeyer, as his men knew him, had fought in all Germany's theatres of war bar Norway and North Africa. But for more than a year, Meyer had seen no action. Instead, he had been charged with training and leading 25th SS Panzer Grenadier Regiment, freshly formed for the *Hitlerjugend* division. Now, on Wednesday, 7 June, Panzermeyer had orders to drive the enemy into the sea north of Caen. It was still dark when Meyer stepped out of 716th Infantry Division's command bunker to rejoin his regiment. 'The streets of Caen are empty of people, neither soldiers nor civilians can be seen,' he wrote in his diary. Caen was a dead city. 'The revolting smell of fire hangs heavily in the streets. Smouldering beams and houses are showering us with sparks as we go past.'[2]

At about the same time the telephone at Seventh Army's headquarters in Le Mans rang. The Army's harassed chief-of-staff, Max Pemsel, picked it up. The voice at the other end of the line was unmistakable; Erwin Rommel wanted to know how the battle was going. The battle was not going well Pemsel told him: 'The enemy is landing tanks at the rate of one per minute.' The field marshal listened intently, then issued his sweeping instruction: 'Everything possible must be done to ensure the enemy does not gain a firm foothold.'[3]

In the half-light of those minutes before the end of night and the beginning of the day yet to come, Hein Severloh lay in a damp hollow off a tree-lined lane outside the village of Colleville, just south of Omaha beach. Throughout the night, Severloh and a motley assortment of men from 352nd and 716th Infantry Divisions had struggled to head south to join up with their comrades. Outside Colleville, they were pinned down by heavy machine-gun fire and dived for cover in low-lying ground. The soldiers waited there, quietly contemplating their fate. Severloh recalled:

> We had to concede that the war had already moved behind us and now we were a small, lost group, with few weapons and few prospects, surrounded by enemies and were lying in a damp hollow somewhere at the end of the world.
>
> Now deep resignation took over me: was the whole struggle, the personal sacrifice, the enormous use of physical and mental strength, the fear, the pain and the terrible killing all for nothing? I thought too of Frerking and felt tears well up in my eyes and run warmly down my swollen face. Now it was all over.

With the first rays of light appearing on the eastern horizon, Severloh and his comrades stood up, climbed out of the hollow and through dense undergrowth into a neighbouring field. There thirty Americans, their guns and pistols at the ready, were waiting for the *Landsers*. Hein Severloh's war was over.[4]

Dawn shed light on the beaches of Normandy and revealed the full extent of the horrors of the previous day. American engineer Horace Henderson waded ashore at Omaha. 'The beach was covered with debris, sunken craft and wrecked vehicles,' he recalled. 'We saw many bodies in the water. The beach was literally covered with the bodies of American soldiers.' Dawn shed light on fields littered with crashed and wrecked gliders, their dead crews and airborne troops still inside; on panzers and half-tracks stopped dead in their tracks, the charred, often limbless bodies of commanders slumped half-in, half-out of their turrets; on trees with paratroopers slung from their chutes, arms by their side, necks broken. But light also brought hope. Hope for the Allies that the invasion would succeed; hope for the Germans that the enemy would be driven back into the sea. 'A bright morning dawns,' *Oberleutnant* Martin Pöppel wrote in a field near Carentan. 'Our tired eyes blink at that bright sky. At first we can hardly believe that today we'll be at war again.'5 On 7 June 1944, there was no Western Front as such, merely a handful of pockets; one around St Mère Église, to the east little more than a foothold at Omaha, Gold and Juno had promisingly merged, but then there was a gap which the Germans had failed to exploit to Sword around Ouistreham, and the slim bridgehead over the River Orne. Four separate beachheads; none substantial; none safe. There was one objective that Wednesday: destroy the Allies, crush the beachheads, send the Anglo-Americans back across the Channel whence they came.

To crush the beachhead, Erwin Rommel needed to concentrate his forces. Throughout north-west France, German units headed for the Cotentin peninsula and the beaches of the Seine Bay. In Brittany, the troops of II *Fallschirmjäger* Corps began moving towards the north-east and the Cotentin. Three divisions were on their way – elite paratroopers, SS panzer grenadiers and infantry. Only 77th Infantry made any progress. The majority of paratroopers of 3rd *Fallschirmjäger* Division were without transport and failed to set off, a problem not faced by the men of the 17th SS, whose march instead was halted by the Allied air forces pummelling the principal bridge the unit was using to cross the River Loire. On paper, 17th SS Panzer Grenadier Division *Götz von Berlichingen*6 was one of the strongest units in the west in June 1944. In reality, it lacked two out of five of its officers and many of its troops – more than half were aged under twenty – were still not fully trained. The division had 200 miles to cover before it reached the battlefield, but the *Waffen SS* men were confident as one staff officer recalled:

Everyone was in a good and eager mood to see action again – happy that the pre-invasion spell of uncertainty and waiting was snapped at last.

Our motorized columns were coiling along the road towards the invasion beaches. Then something happened that left us in a daze. Spurts of fire flicked along the column and splashes of dust staccatoed along the road. Everyone was piling out of the vehicles and scuttling for the neighbouring fields. Several vehicles were already in flames. This attack ceased as suddenly as it had crashed upon us fifteen minutes before. The men started drifting back to the column again, pale and shaky and wondering how they had survived this fiery rain of bullets. The march column was now completely disrupted and every man was on his own, to pull out of this blazing column as best he could. And it was none too soon, because an hour later the whole thing started all over again, only much worse this time. When this attack was over, the length of the road was strewn with splintered anti-tank guns, flaming motors and charred implements of war.

The march was called off and all vehicles that were left were hidden in the dense bushes or in barns. No-one dared show himself out in the open any more. Now the men started looking at each other. This was different from what we thought it would be like. It had been our first experience with our new foe – the American.[7]

Other troops of the *Götz von Berlichingen* moved to Normandy by rail. One *Unterscharführer* Kübel recalled: 'The mood was good, among the young lads who are not battle hardened, tense. The lads wanted to know a lot from the 'old hands'. The weather on 8 June was wonderful, the ride a pleasure.' It was late afternoon when the Allied fighter-bombers found the SS train. Kübel continued:

The Frenchmen on the train pulled the emergency brake, jumped off while we were still moving and disappeared into a forest. I was furious. But not for long...In an instant, our panzer crews realized what was happening. They fired at the aircraft with their machine guns without a thought for their own safety. Everyone else jumped off the train and ran into the forest. We ran for our lives.[8]

Around Caen, the *Hitlerjugend* was faring no better. The waves of air attacks had upset all of Fritz Witt's plans for any coordinated counter-attack against the British and Canadian forces. Witt stormed into the command post of 716th Infantry Division in Caen highly agitated. 'I have been on my way to you for eight hours, and I have had to spend four of these in a ditch because of air attacks,' he raged. 'The divisions' columns are suffering serious casualties in men and material.' It would now be Thursday morning at the earliest before the 12th SS Panzer Division launched any form of coordinated counter-blow.

Of the ranks of the *Hitlerjugend*, only Kurt Meyer's panzer regiment grappled with the invader on 7 June. The night before Edgar Feuchtinger, 21st Panzer Division's ineffective commander, had warned Panzermeyer not to move on his own, but to attack alongside the army armoured division. Meyer pored over the situation maps spread out in Feuchtinger's dingy command post. 'Little fish,' he sneered at Feuchtinger. 'We'll throw them back into the sea in the morning.'[9]

At 10 a.m. on Wednesday, 7 June, 25th Panzer Regiment rolled forwards to the attack. Meyer did not wait for Feuchtinger's division to move. Fifty Mark IV Panzers revved their engines under the constant shellfire of the Allied naval armada. The shells roared over the armour and crashed down upon Caen. From an observation tower, Kurt Meyer looked out upon an armada rolling up and down with the waves, sheathed by a protective umbrella of barrage balloons. 'Enemy tank units are forming up west of Douvres,' Meyer wrote in his diary. 'The whole terrain looks like an ant hill, and behind us? Smoking rubble, empty roads and burning vehicles. I can look down the straight Caen-Falaise road for kilometres. There is no German armour rolling along it.'[10]

The Canadians were rolling towards the village of Authie and beyond it to Caen's small airfield at Carpiquet across the Germans' line of advance. Further west, the historic town of Bayeux was about to fall to the British. Panzermeyer decided it was time to strike. The airwaves crackled with the order: *Achtung! Panzer marsch!* The advancing enemy armoured column was mauled. First fell Authie, a couple of miles west of Caen, then the panzers pushed on to the north towards another village, Buron. But there, Canadian anti-tank gunners were dug in and determined to stand their ground. The panzers turned about in a hail of anti-tank gunfire. 'Critically-wounded panzer comrades were coming to the rear,' *Sturmmann* Karl Vasold remembered. 'They had lost hands, suffered severe burns.' Kurt Meyer rode up to the front line on his motorcycle to watch the battle for Buron unfold. Or rather tried to. The village disappeared in a blanket of smoke and flames. 'I have never experienced such concentrated artillery fire before,' wrote Meyer. 'Inevitably I think of Verdun.' Meyer's men had set off with one objective in mind: the sea. But with 21st Panzer Division on his right advancing nowhere, 25th Panzer Regiment was out on a limb. It had to fall back – reluctantly. Panzermeyer was furious. 'Any properly coordinated attack would have been successful and the bridgehead north of Caen would have been crushed,' he angrily noted in his diary.[11]

To the south-east, the march columns of *Panzer Lehr* Division were refuelling in a forest near Alençon at daybreak, half way towards their objective of the beaches north of Caen. The armour had been on the move all night. At 2 a.m. Fritz Bayerlein's columns had rolled into the town of Argentan, thirty-five miles south of Caen. 'The scene was as bright as day,' the general recalled. 'The little town was quaking under the ceaseless hail of bombs. The whole of Argentan was burning. We were in a witch's cauldron. Behind us the road was blocked. We were trapped in a blazing town.' Thick smoke rolled off burning vehicles; blazing beams and rubble littered the roads. And overhead hung enemy bombers, dropping flares to light up the Normandy countryside. Bayerlein forced his way westwards to the small village of Flers. But he was on his own. There was no sign of the rest of his division.[12]

The 6 June cost the *Panzer Lehr* thirty vehicles. But it had to keep on moving on the 7th, regardless of the threat from the air. No sooner had the tanks moved off, than the fighter-bombers struck. 'The farther north I drove, the more I could see that the fighter-bombers had been busy,' company commander Helmut Ritgen wrote later. 'Here were the results of their work – burning vehicle wrecks on the side of the road spewing black smoke. At times, men would suddenly appear through the smoke as through a fog.' There was no hope of the *Panzer Lehr* entering the battle as a coherent unit, as its commander Fritz Bayerlein complained: 'By noon it was terrible; every vehicle was covered with tree branches and moved along hedges and the edge of woods. Road junctions were bombed and a bridge knocked out. By the end of the day I had lost forty trucks carrying fuel and ninety other vehicles. Five of my tanks were knocked out and eighty-four half-tracks.' Before 6 June, the *Panzer Lehr* had been just about the best armoured division in the west. Thirty-six hours into the battle for Normandy it was strewn out on Norman lanes, its wrecked vehicles festered long into the night. Bayerlein's adjutant, *Hauptmann* Alexander Hartdegen, recalled: 'Dozens of wrecked vehicles, now no more than steel skeletons, lay by the roadside burning and smouldering. The sector was a road of death. Burnt-out trucks, bombed field kitchens and gun tractors, many of them still smouldering, with dead bodies strewn alongside.'

Panzer Lehr covered more than fifty miles by nightfall on 7 June. It had still not reached the beaches, however.[13]

Friend and foe alike that Wednesday asked himself: Where is the *Luftwaffe*? But as on the preceding day, the German Air Force found the task facing it overwhelming. At first light on 7 June *Oberfeldwebel* Herbert Kaiser climbed in his trusty Messerschmitt Me109 and prepared to do battle again. Kaiser was one of two 'old guards' left among the senior non-commissioned officers in *III Gruppe, Jagdgeschwader 1*.[14] A veteran of around 1,000 sorties, Kaiser had downed forty Soviet aircraft on the Eastern Front, and nine Allied in North Africa, but the air battle over Normandy was something new:

> If the missions we had undertaken as fighters in the defence of the Reich until then had been tough and tested our nerves, the missions to follow on the invasion front were going to give us an insight into hell. I will never forget our first intervention that morning, skimming over the landing beaches at Caen. The surface of the sea was saturated with hundred of boats of all sizes, while the sky was filled with bomber formations going to attack our front, accompanied by countless fighters. Lost in the middle of all that, a handful of Messerschmitts: ours![15]

The Focke-Wulfs of *Schlachtgeschwader 4*, the specialist ground-attack squadron which had arrived in Normandy on the afternoon of D-Day, began taking off at 6 a.m. on 7 June to attack the beachhead. Just twenty-four Fw190s were able to attack the landing area. Of the four waves which set off, only one penetrated the Allied fighter cordon to actually make a run at the troop concentrations on the beaches; the remaining Focke-Wulfs jettisoned their bombs and returned to base, only to be pounced upon by Mustangs. 'Despite favourable weather, we achieved little,' the squadron's diarist noted sadly that night. 'Successful operations are impossible without effective fighter operation.' The next day was no better. One of three attacks on the beachheads was broken off early. All the squadron heard from above was criticism and admonishment. Orders were being issued, its diarist fumed, 'only by people who had no idea of the situation or the strength of the enemy defences'.[16]

Other *Luftwaffe* units were still moving up to their front-line airfields that Wednesday. *Hauptmann* Hans Groos had already witnessed the destruction of the aircraft of his JG26 on the first day of invasion at Le Mans. Now, he approached the beachheads in trucks as the fighter unit searched for a suitable airfield. 'On a long road, completely exposed, we passed a convoy of approximately twenty-five trucks, transporting 21-cm rockets, destined for the artillery,' the officer recalled. 'Before our eyes, this convoy was attacked by four Mustangs which, in roughly seven passes, tore them to shreds. A quarter of an hour later, there were only three or four vehicles intact; all the others were on fire at 100m intervals.'[17]

To Adolf Hitler in East Prussia, Gerd von Rundstedt was reporting that the battle for the beaches was making good progress. The invader would be defeated, the venerable field marshal assured his Führer:

> The troops engaged have fought bravely. Where ground has been lost this has only occurred because of the enemy's material superiority. This will now change. Strong forces with panzers, artillery of all types and mortars are being brought up, and the *Luftwaffe* will considerably increase its operations...
>
> Using its last man and last gun, Army Group B will attack and destroy the enemy forces which have landed...Not only will our attack continue, but will end in the final re-capture of the main defensive line.[18]

To the ordinary German citizen, the battle on the Channel coast was proceeding according to plan. The radio and newspaper accounts told them it was. The *Völkischer Beobachter* trumpeted 'heavy enemy losses'. Enemy paratroopers had been 'wiped out'; the Normandy terrain was littered with 'countless crashed gliders and dead paratroopers'. The Nazi Party newspaper continued:

After eliminating the troops dropped behind our coastal fortifications, our units drove against the landing points. Some smaller beachheads in the area of the Vire estuary as well as to the north of it, plus pockets of resistance in the Normandy peninsula were wiped out...

In the first twenty-four hours of the invasion, the enemy has been able to seize a stretch of coast around 40km wide, but just a few kilometres deep with some small landing areas, despite ruthlessly sacrificing strong forces and massive use of material provided by two empires.

He had to pay for this success with terrific losses in men as well as numerous ships, airplanes and weapons. The enemy has felt the strength of the German defence, and our troops respond to every step with counter-blows which become ever fiercer.[19]

Reaction to the invasion was not filled with shock; it was not laden with doom. The German public, much like the Nazi leadership, breathed a sigh of relief when the Allies stormed ashore. The monitors of public opinion, the *Sicherheitsdienst*, reported comments like 'Thank God that this endless tension is finally over', or 'Now we know at last where we stand,' or 'Now at last the decision has come. We will soon see that everything has not been for nothing and we are still here.'

The invasion was 'the sole topic of conversation'. The German people waited eagerly for the radio bulletins; they scrambled for the newspapers and read every inch of the reports from the invasion front. The *Sicherheitsdienst* continued:

The feeling that now 'things will be different' has not only given the depressed mood a powerful fillip, but also strengthened faith in our forces and in our leadership...Now they can see how right the Führer was 'to go easy'[20] in all other theatres of war, and to concentrate all our forces for the decisive blow in the west.

A large majority of the people now believe that the invasion will bring the decision in this war – and with it an end to the entire war, which is no longer too far away.[21]

The invasion – or rather the defence against it – was not running according to plan, however. It was being lost on every front: in the air, on the ground and on the sea. And now it was safe to talk of a western front; Commonwealth and American forces joined hands in the tiny Norman port of Port-en-Bessin, just north of the historic town of Bayeux. There was now a continuous enemy front in Normandy from east of Caen to the Cotentin peninsula north of St Mère Église. The separate beachheads had merged – and in doing so, the opportunity for defeating the invasion was disappearing. From the aged Gerd von Rundstedt there was a rare admission of failure. The field marshal had to concede that Rommel was right after all. The panzer reserves should have been concentrated on the coast. On D-Day they might have reached the coast; now, he conceded, they were being mauled by the Allied air forces. 'We've thrown a whole day away,' Rundstedt's operations officer, Bodo Zimmermann, acidly commented. 'Our tanks are lost in battles where they ought not to be.'[22]

Far from the invasion front at his Parisian headquarters, ardent Nazi Theodor Krancke was ready to concede defeat. The commander of all German naval forces in the west realized that there was no hope of defeating the invasion armada. There had, Krancke admitted, been 'no tangible successes' against the invasion fleet. Twenty three year old Heinz Sieder was among the failures. Sieder led his *Schnorchel*-fitted U984 out of Brest at nightfall on 6 June, bound for the invasion fleet in the Seine Bay. His boat was pounced upon north-west of Ushant the next day by Canadian destroyers. He fired off three torpedoes – unsuccessfully – before being driven below and subjected to a twenty-four hour depth charge bombardment. At 8 p.m. on 8 June, Sieder risked bringing his submarine to periscope depth. 'I decide to *schnorchel* a little to ventilate the boat. We have now been submerged continuously for nearly forty-two hours without a change of air, and for the last twelve hours breathing conditions have been extraordinarily bad. The men have literally been gasping for breath.' With his men – and batteries – exhausted, U984 slipped back into Brest the following day.[23]

Peter Cremer had also set sail on 6 June, not from Brest, but La Pallice. In two days his U333 covered barely 125 miles in the Bay of Biscay – never approaching the invasion area – as the boat spent days under water and nights warding off enemy air attacks as the full moon silhouetted the submarine's outline. 'We scarcely set foot on deck the whole time and were fully stretched fighting off aircraft,' Cremer complained. 'No trace of enemy surface forces. The only vessels we sighted were neutral fishing boats fully illuminated.' For five nights, the crew of U333 successfully thwarted all air attacks with minor damage to their boat. On the sixth, 11 June, the submarine was pounced upon by a Sunderland flying boat. 'With a single burst our gunner hit one engine of the aircraft, which at once burst into flames and crashed,' Cremer recalled. 'While it was going down we were still being fired at by the rear gunner. On impact, the bombs exploded in blazing columns. For a while, the wreck stayed afloat, the flames lighting up the surrounding sea and U333 as well, while behind in the darkness other planes were already circling, not daring to come close.' Trailing oil, with her tanks and conning tower shot up, U333 turned about and headed for La

Pallice. The next day, Theodore Krancke conceded defeat in the battle against the invasion fleet, ordering all *Schnorchel*-less boats to return to their bases. His torpedo boats were scoring no successes either. Sorties from Cherbourg into the Seine Bay simply ran directly into a wall of Allied destroyers. Two nights of attacks, 11 June and 12 June, cost Krancke two of his boats with nothing to show in return. Wherever they went, the S-boats were pounced upon by enemy warships and pounded by their guns. Even Krancke's master, Karl Dönitz, had to concede his navy had failed to stop the landings. 'The invasion has succeeded,' he told his staff. 'The Second Front has been established.'[24]

For all the setbacks, Erwin Rommel remained convinced of victory; if all his forces around the beachheads could be assembled and strike, they would defeat the Allies. The problem was that Germany's counter-strokes were going in piecemeal. After three days of battle, the German Army had failed to launch a single, coordinated counter-offensive.

And so it proved again on 9 June. North-east of Caen, along the River Orne, British airborne forces had held a tenuous foothold on the east bank since the early hours of D-Day. Like all bridgeheads and beach-heads in Normandy, the 6th Airborne Division had to be wiped out. The German counter-stroke on the 6th had miscarried because of confused orders. On the 9th, little was left to chance. The British lines were bombarded by a ninety-minute artillery barrage. Panzer commander Werner Kortenhaus expected the motley collection of panzers and panzer grenadiers to 'steamroller' through the British lines. The attacking Germans had barely jumped off when the airborne troops opened fire. 'Tank 432 was hit and lost a track,' Kortenhaus recalled:

Thirty seconds later, Tank 400 was hit and our company commander, *Leutnant* Hoffmann, was staring in horror at the bloody mess which had been his leg, while Tank 401 exploded, blowing open the hatches and literally flinging the crew out. We had seen three tanks, including the leader's, destroyed in a few seconds...The other tank drivers began hurriedly to reverse, under cover of a hail of fire from their turret guns and machine guns. Terrified, they watched the exploding mushrooms of earth and smoke shoot up around them, and saw too late the dead and wounded grenadiers lying around the road of retreat; some were squashed by the tanks. Perhaps six minutes had passed.[25]

The fighting east of the Orne that Friday, Kortenhaus recalled, was 'one of the hardest actions ever'. When it ended in failure, he was forced to concede the German Army would never drive the enemy back into the sea.

No factor weighed more heavily on the men defending Normandy than the Allies' power in the air. 'There's simply no answer to it,' Erwin Rommel wrote resignedly to his wife. Fritz Ziegelmann, operations officer of the 352nd Infantry defending ground between Omaha and St Lô, complained in a similar vein. 'The front line, as well as the troops' morale, was beginning to break up. The questions: Where is the *Luftwaffe*? And: When is the counter-attack going to begin? were often heard.'[26] A major in 77th Infantry Division told his American captors bitterly:

> The Führer said that if the invasion came he would send the whole [*Luftwaffe*] into action. That story was over as far as I was concerned after I had seen one single German reconnaissance aircraft in the air between 6th and 16th, and apart from that complete mastery of the air by the Americans. We can bring out whole armies and they'll smash them completely with their air forces within a week.[27]

The complaints and gripes reached the ear of Heinz Guderian, inspector of Germany's armoured forces. The gruff panzer general was blunt when Hitler summoned him for a regular briefing at the Berghof in the Alps:

> Any attempt to march by day has proved to be pointless. The countless burned-out vehicles on the roads are the result of attempting to move by day. Throwing the Anglo-Americans into the sea with the current forces and equipment seems impossible...Even the greatest courage by the panzer divisions cannot make up for the failings of the other two branches of the *Wehrmacht*.[28]

The difficulties in Normandy went beyond the lack of an effective air force. The *Landser* was experiencing a *Materialschlacht* – a battle of attrition – on an unparalleled scale. The sheer scale of the Allied attack and the pounding the German troops were suffering on the ground from fighter-bomber attacks, from naval gunfire, from mortars and field pieces the enemy had brought ashore was simply overwhelming. Entire cadres of junior commanders had simply been wiped out leaving Rommel and Rundstedt relatively in the dark about the fighting on the coast.[29]

After four days of battle, Geyr von Schweppenburg was finally manoeuvring his unwieldy *Panzergruppe West* into position around Caen for the great counter-stroke which Rommel would have launched on the day of the landings, had his views prevailed. Even now, on 10 June, Geyr was not ready. It was proving almost impossible to move the

Hitlerjugend, Panzer Lehr and 21st Panzer Divisions into position: 21st Panzer Division had fewer than half its tanks fit for action; the *Hitlerjugend* could only offer three out of four. Under such circumstances, Geyr expected little from his counter-attack. Expectations were irrelevant. At dusk on 10th, fighter-bombers pounced on Geyr's headquarters. All of *Panzergruppe West's* operations staff were killed; Geyr himself was wounded. Even if his divisions had been ready to launch a counter-offensive, *General* Geyr von Schweppenburg was not.

At his magnificent headquarters on the Seine, Erwin Rommel took a break from his visits to the front line to draft his first report on the conduct of the battle in the west for his Führer. The field marshal pulled no punches:

> The enemy has complete mastery of the air over the battlefield as far as around 100km behind the front. By day he cuts off almost all traffic on roads or by-roads or over open ground. Movements by day are therefore almost entirely ruled out, while the enemy can operate freely. Troops and staffs have to hide by day in sheltered areas to avoid the continuous attacks from the air...
>
> The troops of all branches of the *Wehrmacht* are fighting with the greatest determination and the greatest will to do battle despite the enemy's immense display of material.

Gerd von Rundstedt forwarded Rommel's report to Hitler's headquarters with a memorandum of his own attached:

> Despite the huge disparity in equipment and material, the troops of all branches of the *Wehrmacht* are fighting outstandingly and doing all they can. Their spirit and morale are good, but in the long term the Anglo-Americans' material superiority cannot fail to have an impact on the men... Like Field Marshal Rommel, I will leave no stone unturned to bring as many forces as possible into battle to offer the enemy a battle which will weaken him as much as possible. We will take advantage of every opportunity to score successes by attacking at a favourable point.[30]

The parlous state of troops in the west cut no ice with Adolf Hitler. 'Everyone must defend himself to the last round,' the Führer demanded. 'No orders to retreat may be given.' The Allied beachhead, he insisted, 'must be destroyed piece by piece'. He did, however, promise two panzer divisions, the 9th and 10th SS fresh from fighting on the Eastern Front. The promise of reinforcements did nothing to improve Erwin Rommel's mood. 'It's time for politics to come into play,' the marshal wrote to his wife. 'The long-husbanded strength of two world powers is now coming into action. The enemy's great superiority is beginning to tell. Whether the gravity of the situation is realized up above and the proper conclusions drawn seems to me doubtful.'[31]

At the western end of the Western Front, Erich Marcks realized that the beachhead could not be destroyed. The time for that had passed. The Americans had too strong a foothold. On 10 June troops landed at Omaha finally joined forces with their airborne counterparts north of Carentan, gateway to the Cherbourg peninsula. If the peninsula was to be cut off, Carentan had to be taken. Paratroops of the 101st Airborne Division began their assault on the town shortly after dawn on 10 June. The battle for Carentan raged to and fro, as Martin Pöppel and his fellow *Fallschirmjäger* hurled themselves at the attacking Americans. 'The men brace themselves one more time, advance again but are always driven back,' the officer recorded in his diary. 'The Americans continue to advance and fog makes any accurate assessment of the situation increasingly difficult.' By nightfall, the German defenders began to pull out of Carentan.[32] The Americans did not notice the *Fallschirmjäger* slipping out of Carentan; it was 2 a.m. on Monday, 12 June, before they began their final assault on the town. By 7.30 a.m. the Stars and Stripes were fluttering over Carentan's main square and the second major town in Normandy had fallen to the Allies.

Erich Marcks watched the situation at Carentan with concern. That morning he decided to inspect the front in person. Before midday he was dead, victim of a fighter-bomber attack. With his wooden leg, the general had been unable to escape from his staff car heading for Carentan.

Having lost Carentan, the German Army now prepared to re-take it. South of the town, 6th *Fallschirmjäger* Regiment formed up for a counter-attack, joined by the panzer grenadiers of the 17th SS Division. At 5.45 a.m. on 13 June, a fifteen-minute barrage opened up in the cauldron around Carentan. 'Everywhere there's an atmosphere of feverish excitement and expectancy,' wrote Martin Pöppel. 'The SS think they can do it easily – they've arrived with enormous idealism, but they'll get the surprise of their lives.' At the stroke of six, the artillery fire ceased and the SS moved forward, accompanied by tanks. The German troops poured over the American lines, then into the southern outskirts of Carentan.[33]

The attack went well for just short of four hours. Then the enemy delivered his counter-punch. *Oberstleutnant* Friedrich von Criegern, LXXXIV Corps' chief-of-staff, was furious. The *Luftwaffe* had promised to support his attack. It had promised to soften up the defenders the night before and support the *Waffen SS* advancing across the plains south of Carentan. 'What was decisive was not merely the lack of support, rather the effects of the absence of the promised support on the fighting will of the troops who were not yet battle-hardened,' he complained. Worse still, the Americans rolled over a battalion of *Osttruppen*, Russians and Poles, defending an important height on the south-west outskirts of the town. 'It ran away, leaderless, when its German commander was killed,' Criegern bitterly commented. 'The enemy was able to cross the hill unopposed.'[34] By the end of Tuesday, 13 June, Carentan was firmly in American hands. It would remain so.

The Americans had anchored themselves on the Normandy soil. They had a foothold in France. But in the great Overlord plan, Caen should have fallen into British and Canadian hands before the end of D-Day. A week into the invasion, Commonwealth forces still found themselves dug in at least three miles north of the Norman city. They ringed Caen to the north, east and west. Facing them were three German armoured divisions – the *Panzer Lehr, Hitlerjugend* and 21st Panzer – plus the first elements of I SS Panzer Corps, newly arrived from Belgium. But on 12 June, the British spied a gap in the German lines far to the west of Caen between the towns of Caumont and Villers-Bocage, on the boundary of the Commonwealth and American armies. Here was the opportunity to roll up the German front and take Caen from the rear. Late that afternoon, British 22 Armoured Brigade was sent into the gap. The tanks stopped short of Villers-Bocage at nightfall, then moved off again at first light on 13 June. Around 8 a.m., the British armoured column trundled into Villers-Bocage to be greeted by cheering locals. The road to Caen was open; the city was just fifteen miles to the west along the main highway. It was as close to Caen as the British would get that Tuesday.

On the outskirts of Villers-Bocage, thirty year old Michael Wittmann had passed a brief, but uneventful night. Most of the Tigers of his SS panzer company were resting in a sunken road, a mile or so north-east of the town. It was 8 a.m. when the *Obersturmführer* stepped out of his command post to see the might of 22 Armoured Brigade rolling past, barely 500 feet away. 'Never before had I been so impressed by the strength of the enemy as I was by those tanks rolling by,' the Tiger commander wrote. The enemy was driving unhindered towards Caen. There was no time to even form up his company. Wittmann leapt into his Tiger and rumbled down a dirt track which ran parallel to the main Caen highway the British were blithely rolling down. '[I] drove up to the column, surprised the English as much as they had me,' the *Obersturmführer* recalled. With his panzer on the move, Wittmann destroyed first one English tank, then a second, then a third, then troop carriers. 'They never left the road,' the Tiger commander reported. 'They were so surprised that they took to flight, but not with their vehicles, instead they jumped out, and I shot up the battalion's vehicles as I drove by.' The British Cromwells fired back when they could, but their rounds bounced off the Tiger's armour; every shot Wittmann fired was a direct hit. The front half of the advancing enemy column had been smashed, but Wittmann did not stop there. 'I drove toward the rear half of the column, knocking out every tank that came toward me as I went. The enemy was thrown into total confusion.' Tiger company commander *Hauptsturmführer* Rolf Möbius drove into Villers-Bocage in Wittmann's wake. 'The left side of the road was one pile of wreckage which was obscured by smoke from burning vehicles. To the right, in the direction of Caen, we discovered two Cromwell tanks. They began to turn around, but we were able to destroy them both. Terrified Englishmen were running everywhere.' Wittmann's Tiger rolled ever onwards, now into the centre of Villers-Bocage. The British were resting, dismounted from their armour. Three headquarters tanks fell victim to Wittmann's accuracy; a fourth careered wildly out of control into a front garden. Next a Sherman hove into view. Within seconds it was a smoking wreck. But Wittmann's luck was about to run out. As his Tiger rumbled past a clothing shop it was hit by a round from a 6-pound anti-tank gun. Still he continued the battle. 'I fired at and destroyed everything around me that I could reach,' said Wittmann, 'I then decided to abandon the tank.' On foot the Tiger commander and his crew covered ten miles to the command post of the *Panzer Lehr* Division, where Wittmann rallied his men for a fresh sortie with Tigers and panzers into Villers-Bocage. The British were now coming under pressure from the north, south and east as elements of two German armoured divisions – the *Panzer Lehr* and 2nd Panzer – closed in for the kill. *Panzer Lehr Gefreiter* Leo Enderle drove down the main Caen-Villers-Bocage highway. The dead lined the road. 'Knocked-out tanks and transport vehicles lay for kilometres,' he remembered. 'We drove into the town. At an intersection sat two Tigers, knocked out by a self-propelled gun which was positioned in the street to the left.'[35]

13 June belonged to Michael Wittmann. The British lost at least twenty-eight light and heavy tanks, three armoured cars and one personnel carrier that day at Villers-Bocage. Michael Wittmann had accounted for twenty-one tanks and single-handedly blunted the British thrust to encircle Caen. At midnight the shattered 22 Armoured Brigade pulled out of Villers-Bocage.

As night fell along the Normandy front line on Tuesday, 13 June, a great opportunity to breakthrough had been missed by the Allies. The gaping hole in the irregular German lines west of Villers-Bocage had been closed by scratch troops of 2nd Panzer Division near the small town of Caumont. The Germans pushed their luck. The next day, the armour prepared to roll forwards towards Caumont itself. The advance was stopped before it even began, as the Allies pulverized the German lines, first with artillery, then with aircraft. *Oberfeldwebel* Hans Erich Braun, from a tank destroyer detachment, wrote later:

> For fifteen minutes there was a continuous howling and shrieking in and around the orchards. Shells thunder-clapped, throwing up clouds of smoke and dust; red-hot splinters, lumps of earth, shattered branches, and splintered tiles from the farmhouse roof behind us, flew round our ears at each detonation. But this was only the beginning. Minutes later, after we had just carried two of our wounded to safety, it seemed that the very earth around us was going to burst.
>
> Hundreds of shells of all calibres literally ploughed up the gardens. Dozens of hits shook the walls of the farm and set its roof on fire. Thick smoke clouds as bitter as gall, from the high explosive, made breathing difficult and irritated our throats so that we developed a dry cough. A hurricane of fire raged through the countryside, wrapping everything in grey smoke and dirt.

As suddenly as it began, the barrage ended, and the fighter-bombers swept in. A group of seven Typhoons headed for Braun's position next to a stone wall. 'Flashes of light rippled along their wings as they fired,' the senior NCO recalled. He continued:

> Instantly, several of our vehicles, parked out of sight in a sunken road, went up in flames, marking our positions for the enemy with columns of jet-black ascending smoke.
>
> Hell broke loose. Machine-gun bursts mingled with the screeching of rockets. We lay huddled here, pulses beating, while the ricochets went chirping through the bushes, or hit with a crack against the stone walls. Then the bombs came whistling down, nearly bursting our eardrums, and men, weapons and fragments of shattered vehicles were thrown into the air. Explosive rockets came howling away from under the wings of some of them. They burst on the ground, brightly-glaring as a lightning flash, leaving behind a spray of a thousand splinters. For an eternity of minutes, the screaming of my wounded comrades and the terrified roaring of mortally-wounded cattle which had been grazing in the fields, was mingled with the chaotic sound of the low-level air attack.

Three days later, 21st Panzer found itself a couple of miles east of

Caumont, at Le Quesnay where the fighting was no less ferocious. Hans Erich Braun and his anti-tank unit lay in wait for the British along a sunken road, his gun disguised as a bush. As he waited for the enemy, Braun paused to survey the battlefield:

> The breath of decay and destruction lay heavy over the bocage. For days, the carcasses of cows and calves killed by the enemy's fire had lain in the fields. Bloated to bursting point like swollen balloons, their legs sticking up stiffly towards the sky, or with sides ripped, torn, and covered by a myriad of blue-shimmering flies, they exuded an indescribable smell and made life anywhere near them almost impossible. Some of the animals which were still alive were almost mad.

And then the turret of a Cromwell tank hove into view. Braun screamed: '*Feuer*!'

> A deep blue flame, surrounded by a bright flash, leapt up from the tank; there was a terrific explosion; and the Cromwell literally burst apart. We dived for the ground. Heavy armour plating and the complete turret flew in an arc through the air, howling and whistling, to land with a series of crashes in the bushes or the treetops. There was one more explosion as the petrol tank burst, and then a dense, black cloud of burning petrol welled up.

Braun and his gunners battled their way into the town itself. The fighting for le Quesnay raged 'house by house, cellar by cellar'. In one hour Braun lost nine comrades and another twenty-six wounded. 'Everywhere, in the road, on the paths, in the gardens, lay dead and wounded.' When the British laid down an artillery and aerial barrage, Braun pulled his men out. Le Quesnay was hidden by 'thick, evil-smelling smoke', under which lay 'burning houses, burning vehicles, burning rubber'. The barrage continued as the tank destroyer squad withdrew. Braun dived into a trench on the edge of town. He wrote later:

> At moments like these, when death seems so close and certain, one is incapable of thought. So close to the earth do you lie, that you feel as thin as a pancake. Every muscle is tensed, all breathing stops. The heart beats madly and the nerves are taut and vibrating. Waiting for the terrible pain, the tearing of the body; the impact of the razor-sharp, red-hot shell splinters. Cramped fingers claw the soil.

As the barrage ended, the British advanced into Le Quesnay again and for once, a brief panic swept through the German lines as the panzer grenadiers poured out of the town in headlong retreat. 'It could have been a catastrophe,' Braun wrote, 'but energetic officers and NCOs stopped the panic and the British attack was halted.' Le Quesnay was back in German hands the next day. But for what reason, Braun asked himself:

> What had we gained? A little ground, laughably unimportant, exchanged for irreplaceable manpower. When I sat down that evening in the cellar of a ruined farm house and looked at the few remaining men of my platoon, I saw in their faces the knowledge that this war in Normandy was lost for us. Privation, strain of battle and fear of death had marked their faces; but they faced with courage the three alternatives of the future: a grave, disablement or a prison camp.[36]

Having failed to break through at Villers-Bocage, the British and Canadians continued to search for a weakness in the German lines. The attacks by British 3rd and 49th, and Canadian 3rd Divisions reached their peak around Tilly-sur-Seulles, where the *Panzer Lehr* and *Hitlerjugend* held the line, on 16 and 17 June. But the barrages and bombardments had dealt their harshest blow to the 12th SS on 14 June. *Brigadeführer* Fritz Witt had been discussing the situation with his staff in the house which served as the *Hitlerjugend*'s temporary command post near Tilly when Allied naval artillery zeroed in on the location. Witt was the last man to dive for cover in a trench behind the house; the *Brigadeführer* was struck in the head by shrapnel from a salvo of naval shells, killing him instantly. Witt's loss was a severe blow to the *Hitlerjugend*. Into his shoes stepped Kurt Meyer.

Four days into his new command, Panzermeyer found himself defending another Allied attempt to pierce his lines near Tilly. The enemy hurled 3,000 shells at the lines held by a single company. 'The trees are uprooted and flung into the defenders' lines and a wave of tanks follows the barrage,' Meyer wrote. 'The tanks fire round after round into the wood.' As the British 49th Division came on, the *Hitlerjugend* fought back. The fighting, says Meyer, was hand-to-hand. His men were driven back, but the lines did not cave in. 'The division's front is stable but the losses have reached critical proportions,' wrote Meyer, who now toured the battlefield. 'Wounded lie behind an earth wall waiting for transport. Dead comrades are buried in the orchard. Thick ground mist cloaks the destruction.'[37]

The efforts of the 12th SS and *Panzer Lehr* on its left could not keep the Commonwealth troops out of Tilly. It fell on 18 June. Its loss or liberation was not vital to the outcome of the struggle for Normandy. It was one of a score of battles and skirmishes which flared up alongside the grand manoeuvres such as Villers-Bocage. But battles like Tilly and Le Quesnay were tearing the heart out of the German Army in the west. 'We know we are approaching a catastrophe,' Kurt Meyer recorded in his diary. His division was powerless in the face of the Allies' material supremacy. Each day he lost men and equipment, yet not a single replacement had arrived after ten days of combat.[38]

Meyer's superior, I SS Panzer Corps' commander Sepp Dietrich, addressed Erwin Rommel in the same vein. 'I am being bled white and getting nowhere,' he told the field marshal. 'We need another eight or ten divisions in a day or two or we are finished.'[39]

Notes

1. *Völkischer Beobachter*, 7/6/44.
2. Kurt Meyer, *Grenadiers*, p.120.
3. KTB AOK 7, 0400 Hours, 7/6/44. IWM AL 528.
4. Severloh, pp.76-8.
5. Ambrose, *Citizen Soldiers*, p.27; KTB Pöppel, 6/6/44. Pöppel, p.179.
6. Named after a sixteenth century German knight who lost his hand in battle and replaced it with an iron one.
7. Shulman, pp.151-2.
8. Stöber, Hans, *Die Sturmflut und das Ende,* Band I, pp.51-2.
9. Shulman, p.144.
10. Kurt Meyer, p.121.
11. Hubert Meyer, *12 SS Panzer Division Hitlerjugend*, p.42; Kurt Meyer, pp.123-4.
12. Carell, *Invasion – They're Coming*, p.122.
13. Ritgen, Western Front 1944, p.58; Ambrose, p.49; Carell, p.123.
14. Roughly the equivalent of an RAF wing within 1st Fighter Squadron.
15. Frappé, Jean-Bernard, *La Luftwaffe face au débarquement allié*, p.111.
16. KTB Schlachtgeschwader 4, 7-8/6/44. Price, Luftwaffe Data Book, p.204.
17. Frappé, p.59.
18. KTB OB West, 1300 Hours, 7/6/44.
19. *Völkischer Beobachter*, 8/6/44.
20. 'kurzzutreten'.
21. SD Meldungen über die Entwicklung in der öffentlichen Meinungsbildung, 8/6/44. Boberach, pp.512-14.
22. Irving, *Trail of the Fox,* p.342.
23. KTB U984, 8/6/44. Cited in Hessler, sec.439.
24. Cremer, pp.182-4; KTB Skl, 10/6/44.
25. McKee, *Caen: Anvil of Victory*, pp.83-4.
26. Rommel to his wife, 10/6/44. Rommel, p.491; Balkoski, p.163.
27. Murray, p.378.
28. Der Gen.Insp.d.Panzertruppen Vortrag vor Hitler, 10/6/44. BA/MA RH10/90.
29. Author's papers and Wegmüller, p.247.
30. IWM AL510/1/2; OB West, Ia, Nr. 361/44, 11/6/44, pp.2-3 - BA/MA RH 19 IV/47.

31. KTB AOK7, 12/6/44. IWM AL974/2; KTB OB West, 1250 Hours, 12/6/44; Rommel to his wife, 13/6/44, 14/6/44. Rommel, p.491.

32. KTB Pöppel, 10/6/44. Pöppel, p.204.

33. KTB Pöppel, 13/6/44. Pöppel, pp.206-09.

34. *Oberstleutnant* von Criegern, Chef des Stabes LXXXIV Korps, 'Die Kämpfe des LXXXIV Korps in der Normandie', MS B-784.

35. Agte, pp.319-324; Wittmann papers, author's collection.

36. McKee, pp.114-23.

37. Meyer, *Grenadiers*, p.133.

38. Ibid, p.134.

39. NA WO219/1908.

Chapter 6

Further Sacrifices Cannot Change Anything

Our Army generals are for the most part not worth a bean.

Joseph Goebbels

On Friday 16 June a giant four-engined Focke-Wulf Condor droned through the skies of Germany and north-west France, shepherded by three fighters. Inside sat Adolf Hitler, on his way to confer with his western field marshals. For ten days, the Führer had heard nothing but bad news from Normandy: enemy air supremacy, material superiority, towns taken, counter-attacks repulsed. Now, far from the battlefront, the Condor touched down at an airfield near Metz, followed by three more containing Hitler's staff. By road, the Führer and his entourage snaked through the Eifel mountains to a hillside near the village of Neuville-sur-Margival. Hidden among the trees lay *Wolfschlucht II*, Wolf's Gorge II, field headquarters built for Hitler to conduct the battle in the west the previous winter. It was 300 miles from the Normandy beaches.

It was 9 a.m. the next morning when Field Marshals Rommel and Rundstedt were ushered into the Führer's bunker. Erwin Rommel was not optimistic. In little more than a week of fighting, the field marshal's morale had crumbled. 'We must be prepared for grave events. The troops, SS and Army alike, are fighting with the utmost courage, but the balance of strength tips more heavily against us every day. Many hopes are having to be buried.' The Desert Fox did not expect much from his meeting with the Führer.[1]

Wolfschlucht II was a spartan headquarters. In Hitler's reinforced concrete bunker there was no conference table, no seats save a stool for the Führer. Hitler had become, Rommel's chief-of-staff Hans Speidel observed, 'old, bent, ever more nervous in his speech'. He ate a breakfast of rice, washed down with various medicines and pills.

Hitler sat down as Rommel, Rundstedt and their respective staffs stood around the sides of the shelter. Rommel took the floor, not his superior; in broad sweeps he presented a bleak picture of the situation. The enemy dominated the skies and dominated the sea. By day, the Allies poured ashore, by night the German forces slowly made their way to the invasion front. 'Movements by day are stopped by the enemy,' the field marshal complained. 'He bombs whatever and wherever he likes.' The *Luftwaffe* was rarely seen, and his men were being mauled by the Allies' naval and aerial artillery. 'In some cases, we cannot speak of divisions,' Rommel said bleakly, 'only of combat groups'. Hitler promised new weapons – new mines, new bombers 'in about six weeks' to blunt the invasion. Above all, the Führer exuded confidence. 'Don't call it a beachhead, but the last piece of French soil held by the enemy,' he told his marshals. Erwin Rommel seemed temporarily buoyed by Hitler's visit; the next day he wrote to his wife. 'I'm looking forward to the future with much less than anxiety than one week ago. A quick enemy breakthrough towards Paris is now barely possible.' Hans Speidel was not so sure. The Führer, he confided in author Ernst Jünger, 'had only unclear ideas about future events and seemed to hope – or perhaps to believe – that the favourable figure of Fate, which has already saved him from desperate situations on occasions, might recur here too'.[2]

What Rommel, Rundstedt and Hitler could not overlook was that after ten days of fighting the invasion had succeeded. And the Nazi hierarchy wanted someone to blame. When enemy newspapers reported that the German Army 'had been caught with their pants down' on D-Day, the Führer flew into a rage, demanded von Rundstedt answer for the actions of all his forces that morning. Who was surprised? Who failed to react? Every division attacked on Tuesday, 6 June, was ordered to account for itself. The witch hunt continued. Propaganda Minister Joseph Goebbels got in on the act. 'I cannot hide my disappointment about the many promises which the *Wehrmacht* made to us about the course of the invasion – and which were not kept,' he recorded with frustration. There had been no surprises on 6 June, no failures to react. The reasons for defeat were obvious, as *Generalleutnant* Wilhelm Richter pointed out. His 716th Infantry Division had all but melted away in the fighting around Caen since 6 June. Richter's men had not been surprised, merely overwhelmed by an enemy who outnumbered his troops in men and material. The general complained about 'the utter lack of support from the *Luftwaffe*' and 'the enemy's total air superiority'. Richter's report was forwarded as far as Rommel. The field marshal nodded in agreement. The invasion's success confirmed all his fears. He had been let down by the Navy and the *Luftwaffe*; his men 'were too weak and badly over-age'; and above all his pre-invasion plea to concentrate his forces on the coast had proved prophetic. As the field marshal had warned, his divisions had been mauled on their approach to Normandy. It took days, not hours for Rommel's reserves to reach the beachhead. By then, it was too late, the field marshal lamented. 'All the reserves that came up arrived far too late to smash the enemy landing by counter-attack.'[3] The witch hunt seemed to stop.

It was hard for Joseph Goebbels to come to terms with the fact that the Allies were lodged in Normandy and would not be driven back into the sea. It was even harder for him to convince the German people. For more than a week, the communiqués and newspaper headlines had talked of mopping up operations, of paratroopers destroyed behind the lines, of a bitter struggle, but one going in Germany's favour. Now Goebbels sought to account for the failure to destroy the enemy beachhead. In the Nazi's flagship weekly news magazine *Das Reich*, the propaganda minister gloated over 'mounds of dead British and American soldiers piled up along Europe's west coast'. He continued:

No-one can deny that English and American casualties in the battles on the French coast have been unbearably high. Even on the first day of the invasion, casualties were so high that war correspondents from London and New York sent back cries of horror. The English press tried to play down or hide the facts.

We saw it all coming. We know it cannot be any different. We must go through this inferno until we can see daylight at its end. It would be a fateful mistake if the German people believed that this great struggle in the west was an easy, safe operation which could – or would – change the balance of the war with a quick miracle. We are facing two world powers. Both have made preparations they believe will crush us and bring success. Our soldiers too are making great sacrifices. They are showing courage and heroism which is a match for all that has happened earlier in this war, even if it does not better it. We have reached the most serious and gravest point in the war. We should not be afraid, nor should we be over-confident. We are fighting for our lives in the east and in the west. Our soldiers realize that. They will not waver, nor lose their nerve. Our soldiers in the west are fighting as well as their fathers did in 1917 and 1918. The nation looks to coming events with calm. It knows that its fate and its life are in good hands.[4]

The public too put its faith in the *Landser* – and in Erwin Rommel – but the initial optimism which had carried the German nation in the first hours and days after the invasion was gone. Maybe, some argued, the invader was being allowed to come ashore en masse so even more enemy could be destroyed when the German counter-stroke was launched. Others adopted a 'wait-and-see' attitude. Each man and woman was convinced that soldier for soldier, the *Landser* was superior to any opponent. 'The German soldier enjoys an almost unbelievable reputation among the enemy troops,' Goebbels recorded in his diary. 'They are regarded as fanatical Hitlerites and Nazis, who by no means give an impression of being depressed or ill-fed. On the contrary, they appeared firm and assured and this image has a particularly impressive impact on enemy soldiers. A war correspondent quite rightly notes, that in Eisenhower's headquarters the words 'violent', 'stubborn' and 'strong' are constantly repeated, unfortunately not to describe the English and Americans, rather only to describe the Germans.'[5] Stubborn and strong, the *Landser* was, but he was not invulnerable to the Allies' material supremacy. No single factor had a greater impact on the morale of the German soldier in the west than enemy air superiority. 'No vehicle on the road is safe from the fighter-bombers and Lightnings,' Martin Pöppel complained. 'It's become virtually impossible to travel the roads by day. Despite all precautionary measures, the pilots are always finding new victims.'[6] Ewald Klapdor, a staff officer with 10th SS Panzer Division *Frundsberg*, recently arrived from Russia, was stunned by the disparity between the *Luftwaffe* and its foe:

> The air action is just unbelievable. Above all, it's very one-sided. Formations of silvery four-engined bombers form a continuous stream, an image of untamed might.
>
> Important supplies no longer reach the front. There's no peace, even at night. The roads are lit up from the sky with floodlights and flares. For the first time, the enemy has succeeded in paralysing the supplies for the front line across hundreds of kilometres. What a change in conditions from the Eastern Front! In Russia, the *Luftwaffe* still flies. Here the scene is different. There is effectively no German aerial support any more. In the invasion area, there's only one air force – the Western Allies'.[7]

The roads and lanes of Normandy were littered with burned-out panzers, self-propelled guns and half-tracks. The German soldier became increasingly frustrated at his feeling of powerlessness. 'It was a soul-destroying scene to watch the enemy air force fly as if on manoeuvres,' flak commander *Oberst* Hans Kessler wrote bitterly. The impact of the relentless enemy strikes was not lost on the Nazi leadership. The senior National Socialist Leadership Officer in the west reported to his superiors: 'If you have spent hours idly on a secondary road watching as English fighter-bombers circle continuously and attack not merely every vehicle, but also every individual, then you can only form the correct view. It's a depressing feeling to have to wait for the skies to be free for half an hour so you can move on a bit.' The one question on every soldier's lips was: where is the *Luftwaffe*? 'The mood of the troops is strained,' the officer warned. 'The soldiers realize that the enemy is the clear master of the skies.'[8]

It was hardly surprising the *Landser* rarely sighted a German aircraft over Normandy. Just two days into the invasion, *Luftflotte 3* could muster just 100 machines to counter the Allied aerial armada. The fate of the elite *Jagdgeschwader 26*, the 'Abbeville boys', was typical of many of the fighter units in the west that June. It was losing pilots at the rate of two a day, one killed, one wounded, but was downing an average of three Allied aircraft each day in reply. On 14 June alone, the *Geschwader* had shot down seven enemy fighters, mainly Lightnings, in the skies north of Paris, but JG26 lost seven Me109s for its efforts that morning. The attack, *Unteroffizier* Erhard Tippe recalled, had been 'a great success'. 'It had been 18 against 120 – the same odds we faced daily.'[9] The Allies could afford the losses; *Luftflotte 3* could not.

The Allied air forces were not merely punishing the troops in Normandy. The road and rail network, the bridges which were the lifeblood of the fighting front in Normandy were being hammered by day and night. 'A stretch of line which is still usable at the moment can be put out of action within a few hours,' the quartermaster general of Fifteenth Army complained. One week into the invasion, nine tenths of Normandy's railway system had been paralysed.[10]

From the lowliest *Landser* to Erwin Rommel, every soldier in the west realized that the war was lost unless Germany countered the enemy air force. 'The Allied air force is the decisive factor in the success of the invasion,' complained *General* Geyr von Schweppenburg, commander of *Panzergruppe West*, and himself the victim of air attack on 10 June which killed most of his staff. 'In effect, it is possible to attack any movement by day on the battlefield – and up to 60km behind the front – and so make movement impossible.'[11]

It was 1.30 a.m. when the telephone rang at the headquarters of Flak Regiment 155 near the French city of Amiens on the Somme. The date was 6 June, 1944. The invasion had begun. *Luftwaffe Oberst* Max Wachtel mulled over the news. For the past twelve months, Wachtel and his men had trained to defeat the invasion before it began. Now it was upon the *Luftwaffe* regiment. And the regiment was still not ready. Wachtel was undaunted. 'For the flying bomb,' the officer noted in his diary, 'the struggle has entered its decisive phase.'[12] Within ten days, a new era in warfare would begin.

Since the spring of 1942, the firm of Gerhard Fieseler had been working on a secret project for the *Luftwaffe*, the FZG76 – a pilotless aircraft, a flying bomb. The flying bomb would hurtle through the sky at nearly 500 miles per hour driven by a jet engine, at anywhere between 700 and 6,500 feet for up to 225 miles, then fall from the heavens, delivering a one-ton warhead. A prototype was thrust skywards on a ramp at Christmas 1942. Within a year, the *Luftwaffe* predicted, the flying bomb would be raining down on London. The reasoning of the air force's leaders was bluntly encapsulated by Field Marshal Erhard Milch, in charge of *Luftwaffe* production and development. 'Kill off a few million Englishmen! If only we could do that they would very quickly call off their attacks on Germany.'[13]

Through the summer of 1943, Max Wachtel's unit had tested the flying bomb at the rocket test centre in Peenemünde on the Baltic coast. But development of the new weapon was slow. When the production lines finally began moving that September, they churned out not the 1,000 bombs each month as predicted, but barely twenty. Nor did the production models match the prototypes; they exploded on the ramps, broke apart in mid-air, veered off course after take-off. In the autumn of 1943, the flying bomb was not a weapon to be built like any other. And with it, the dream of a Christmas offensive against London vanished.

It was the spring of 1944 before the flying bomb was reaching Max Wachtel in numbers. All over north-west France, strange looking 'ski ramps' began appearing on the Pas de Calais and Cherbourg peninsula, behind them bunkers and depots began storing the now-renamed flying bomb. But it was a slow process. Even with around 2,000 bombs per month now arriving in the west, it would be June before Wachtel could begin launching his wonder weapon. His preparations were severely hindered by almost constant air attacks through the first months of 1944. By the end of February alone, more than 19,000 bombs had dropped on the regiment's launch sites. Despite raids which dragged on through the spring, by mid-May the FZG76 was almost operational. Hitler was so confident it would be ready that he ordered an all-out offensive against London from the middle of June. 'The bombardment will open like a thunderclap by night.' Preparations were almost ready, but as June began Max Wachtel noted with frustration. 'The past few months have been a bitter, unremitting struggle with an enemy who enjoys the advantage of air superiority. The question is: shall we get in first, or will the enemy be across the Channel beforehand. Every man in the regiment is convinced that the rocket will be on the other side before Sammy and Tommy are over here.'[14] Sammy and Tommy got there first.

The invasion was seventeen hours old when the teleprinter at Wachtel's headquarters finally flashed into life. The codeword *Rumpelkammer* – junk room – meant that within ten days the flying bomb offensive had to begin. Great hopes were placed in the new weapon. For the past year, German newspapers and radio broadcasts had been promising revenge, retaliation, retribution for the damage the Allied air raids had inflicted on the Fatherland. For the past year, Wachtel's men had trained relentlessly. For the past year and more the *Luftwaffe*'s leaders had hoped the pilotless bomb would restore confidence in an air force which the enemy seemingly brushed aside. 'Just picture a large high-explosive bomb falling every half hour, and nobody knowing where it will come down next,' Field Marshal Erhard Milch told his men. 'Twenty days of that will have them all folding at the knees!'[15] *Oberst* Max Wachtel rose to the occasion with a stirring order of the day:

> When we fire our missiles today and in the future we shall be thinking of the misery and the damage which the enemy has caused us with his terror bombing.
>
> Men, the Führer and our homeland are watching us in the expectation that our operations will be rewarded with complete success.[16]

The offensive began with a whimper, not a bang. Twice the assault on London went off half-cocked, first on 12 June, again on 14 June because preparations were incomplete. The scene was set for the third attempt, beginning at 11.16 p.m. on 15 June. *Rumpelkammer* was on. The first of 244 flying bombs hurtled up a ramp, bound for Target 42, London. Forty-five of the new weapons, packing 1,800lbs of high explosive, crashed shortly after take-off; the remainder disappeared into the darkness over the English Channel humming through the June night, trailing a red flame behind them at just under 350 miles per hour. Richard Wolff-Boenisch, an administration officer with 116th Panzer Division still being formed behind the Normandy front, watched the flying bombs tear through the June night. 'A tremendous, thundering noise fills the air,' he jotted in his diary. 'We run into the street and in the dark we recognize several flying objects, trailed by long, fiery comet-like trails. It is the 'vengeance'. All night long these 'wild ducks' fly over our heads.' Max Wachtel was delighted. 'May our triumph justify all the expectations which front and Fatherland have bestowed upon our weapon,' he signalled his superiors.[17]

It was well into Friday, 16 June, before German newspapers and radio broke the news of the offensive. Joseph Goebbels wanted no mention of the word *Vergeltung* – revenge. He wanted to avoid raising false hopes. 'Southern England and the London area were bombarded with very heavy high-explosive missiles of a new type last night and this morning,' the German High Command reported tersely in its daily bulletin. Berlin's nightly newspaper, *Berliner Nachtausgabe*, reacted entirely differently. That Friday afternoon its headline screamed: 'The day which eighty million Germans have been longing for has arrived.' The national radio service, the *Reichsrundfunk*, was more measured. The missile offensive 'was the first turn of the screw – a screw which will be tightened more and more'. However the German propaganda machine reported the flying bomb offensive; it was the sole topic of conversation on both sides of the Channel. 'It's the greatest sensation in the Anglo-American media, even eclipsing the invasion,' Goebbels gloated. 'It provokes near ecstatic joy among the German people. Although we didn't use the word 'revenge' at all, the news of the 'revenge' spreads like wildfire through the population. People have the impression that with the use of this new secret weapon, a total change in the course of the war has begun.'[18]

In three nights, 500 flying bombs were thrown at London. The effects, German spies in the British capital noted, were devastating. 'Operations are a complete surprise to the British public,' one agent reported. 'The shock was very great, even panic in individual places. Very many dead. Considerable devastation. What is making the greatest impression on the British public is that at the moment there is no effective defence.'

This wonder weapon, Berlin declared, was the V1, *Vergeltung 1* – Vengeance 1. 'The number "1",' Goebbels proclaimed, 'suggests that other long-range weapons against Britain will follow.'[19] For Britons in June, the V1 alone sufficed. Goebbels noted:

It seems to be having a particularly depressing effect on English morale as the citizens of London must sit in their cellars for the duration of the air raid warning. Since Thursday evening the bombardment of London has not stopped...The German people are almost in a state of high fever. That comes not merely from the fact that our press made too much of the news of our new secret weapon being used, but also from the fact that with one blow tension welled up for so long has exploded.[20]

The Nazi Party newspaper celebrated the enemy's dance of death. On 19 June, war correspondent Wolfgang Küchler flew over London. 'All hell broke loose below,' Küchler wrote the following day for the Nazi Party organ:

Slowly the skies over London began to turn yellow and red. Just a few minutes after the first German explosive devices crashed into the sea of houses in the capital the individual fires became widespread blazes on a huge scale. The clouds over the target area were lit up by the huge, blood-red fires.

Almost the entire London conurbation is in flames. Everywhere fiery mushroom clouds rose into the sky...The English tried to shoot down the German devices with a mass of fire from light flak guns, but in vain.

Below however new explosions flared up. Devastating fires were raging there. When the German air crew began their way back, the huge fires from London were their companions for a long time. Even when we had long since passed the Channel, the glow of fire was still clearly visible. All the time the bombardment continued. The heavy devices repeatedly rained down on the city...

That is Germany's long-awaited response to the countless terror raids which the enemy has haunted the German people with.

And yet the same newspaper also struck a note of caution. The public should not place too much faith in the V1, it urged:

This war is a titanic struggle, in which individual events are not decisive on their own. Only every ounce of bravery, readiness and determination of a nation, only the combined strength of our weapons, will force the path to victory.[21]

It was too late. For months, Goebbels and his propagandists had promised revenge. Now vengeance had begun, the German *Volk* believed it would bring victory. People who just a few weeks earlier had considered the war lost, now 'talk big and already consider the war as over', the monitors of opinion noted. Away from the Western Front, the news of the V1 galvanized morale. 'Now the English are getting a bash on the head,' one *Gefreiter* in Italy wrote gleefully. 'This could possibly mean a decisive change in the war and bring about the end of the war. We must succeed in destroying the invasion army at the same time as using the new weapon against England herself, knocking out England and forcing her to make peace.'[22]

In France there was an air of reality about reaction to the flying bomb offensive. Soldiers watched the flying bombs tear through the skies by day and night, blazing an orange-red trail through the heavens. It was not so much revenge as relief that the soldiers of the Western Front demanded. 'We hoped that life would be a little easier for us,' Robert Vogt of the 352nd Infantry Division remembered; one of his comrades, a Nazi Party member, had insisted that the 'new weapons' trumpeted for so long by propaganda would one day come. Now the day had come, and Vogt and his fellow infantrymen expected great things, 'that the matériel imbalance would be addressed'. Vogt and thousands of others waited for the V1 to turn defeat into victory. But would it? 'If noticeable results of the revenge are not apparent at the invasion front,' warned the senior National Socialist Leadership officer in the west, 'then there will be a fresh moment of crisis.'[23]

And so it proved. The initial euphoria quickly passed. In his trench along the River Orne north-east of Caen, radioman Werner Kortenhaus was becoming increasingly despondent. 'The men know that the battle is lost already,' he jotted in his diary. 'There's not a chance anymore. Not even the first V-weapons which thunder across the night skies towards England give them any hope. The enemy gets stronger every day. Not a man, not a machine to replace our losses. The troops are bled to death. The survivors are completely exhausted. Our task is simply to hold the enemy; no longer can we attempt to drive him back.'[24]

To the west near Carentan, *Oberleutnant* Martin Pöppel was similarly fatalistic. 'If we haven't managed to drive the enemy back at all after ten days' fighting, how on earth are we going to get them out?' Pöppel scribbled resignedly in his diary. 'We are not very optimistic. Almost all of us are convinced that unless we succeed in driving the enemy out within three weeks at most, then we will have lost the war.'[25]

The pessimism filtered upwards. Erwin Rommel's morale had always been fickle at best. In the first two weeks of June 1944 it swung wildly from despair to hope, then despair again. The battle so far had cost him more than 24,000 officers and men dead, wounded and missing, and 1,676 Russians. In four days' battle 346th Infantry Division had lost half its strength, 21st Panzer suffered 2,100 casualties while the *Panzer Lehr* was losing 150 men each day, almost to a man victims of aerial attack and the enemy's artillery bombardment. Simple mathematics showed that the balance sheet was not in Germany's favour. Within days of his meeting with Hitler, Rommel was again facing disaster in the west. 'You can imagine how worried I am. We must be prepared for grave events,' he wrote home.[26]

Long before Hitler had finished conferring with his field marshals at *Wolfschlucht II*, the teleprinter at Karl-Wilhelm von Schlieben's head-quarters near Valognes had whirred away. The commander of 709th Infantry Division – the title was a misnomer, Schlieben's force consisted only of fortress troops, average age thirty-six, and three battalions of *Osttruppen* who could not be relied on in battle – read his terse orders: 'Holding Cherbourg at all costs is of the greatest importance. Every day is a gain for the overall conduct of the war. The enemy must be worn down by a fighting withdrawal. There is no question of giving up. I regard it as a matter of honour for every soldier from the general down to the lowest ranks to hold Fortress Cherbourg.'[27] The Führer was convinced that the fortress could be held 'until about the middle of July';

each day it held out would gain time elsewhere.

On paper, the prospects looked promising. Hitler had declared the port *Festung* Cherbourg – Fortress Cherbourg – and ordered every 'worker and inhabitant used to the last man for preparing defences', as well as preparing the harbour for destruction. And the newly appointed commandant of the peninsula, von Schlieben, had four divisions to defend the port. But all that was left of the 77th, 91st, 243rd and 709th divisions, however, were battered remnants of the units which began the defence of Normandy on 6 June, plus an assortment of ad hoc units including sailors, flak gunners and labour squads – 21,000 men in all from three battered divisions 'whose powers of resistance are not great', the general warned Berlin. As *Generalmajor* Robert Sattler, commander of Cherbourg's arsenal, acidly commented: 'A three year old boy does not grow a beard if you declare him to be a man and a town does not become a fortress by being declared a fortress.'[28]

For more than a week, American troops had battered their way westwards across the base of the Cotentin peninsula. 'The neck must be kept open at all costs,' Rommel had urged Seventh Army commander Eugen Dollmann. 'Throw everything into the gap to ensure the peninsula is not cut off.' But Dollmann had nothing to throw into the gap. His forces were tied down around Caen. Come the morning of 18 June, the Atlantic Ocean stretched out before the invaders. In his alpine retreat, fresh back from his visit to France, Adolf Hitler waited impatiently for news from Cherbourg. There was a certain irritability in his voice. 'Are they through now or not?' the Führer asked Jodl. 'Yes,' the general conceded. 'They are through.'[29] In those final bitter battles on the coastline American troops reported hand-to-hand fighting as they pounded the defenders, 77th Infantry Division, with mortar and artillery fire. The troops' commander, *Generalmajor* Rudolf Stegmann was struck in the head by 20-mm cannon fire from an enemy fighter-bomber as he drove his staff car. The next day, some of 77th's battered remnants, 1,400 men in all, smashed through the American lines southwards. They were the last Germans to escape the Cotentin peninsula. Cherbourg's fate was sealed.

Before dawn on 19 June, three full-strength American divisions of VII Corps swept forward across German field positions. Schlieben had no intention of fighting with the Americans in the open field; he would fall back on Cherbourg in a 'fighting retreat', making the enemy fight for every foot of ground so that the invader was worn down. By the end of Monday, 19 June, the defenders of Cherbourg were retreating, and in some instances still fighting. The port was ringed by bunkers and field fortifications some four to six miles from the port, guarding every approach to the city, and supplemented with anti-tank ditches and flak batteries.

As Schlieben's scratch force retreated northwards, it was hounded constantly by the enemy air forces. In the skies above the Cotentin, the *Landser* saw only the markings of the RAF and US Air Force, never the *Luftwaffe*'s swastika as one flak commander complained: 'The enemy smashed up everything with his aircraft. We didn't see one of our aircraft, no fighters, nothing. The last official communiqué that we heard was enough to drive you wild. The people in Germany who aren't in the know were bound to think: "Things are going splendidly." '[30]

In 'fortress' Cherbourg, Karl-Wilhelm von Schlieben grew more fatalistic by the day. 'Cherbourg isn't a fortress,' he privately confessed. 'Things were at their lowest ebb. All old men who had done nothing but stare at the Atlantic Ocean for three years, none of them soldiers.' Against the Americans 'with their masses', the general said forlornly, defence of Cherbourg was a 'hopeless affair'. His men were *verbunkert* – suffering from bunker-psychosis – in many cases 'more of a burden than an aid', while using 'Russians in France for Germany against America' was madness.[31]

It was not surprising, then, that Hitler had his doubts about Cherbourg's commandant; his *Wehrmacht* adjutant Rudolf Schmundt warned Rommel's staff: 'I'm worried about Schlieben. I don't get the impression that he's an iron personality. The honour and reputation of the entire German officer corps rests on how long we hang on to Cherbourg. The whole world is looking at Cherbourg.' Perhaps a stirring order of the day from the Führer might help. 'I expect you to lead this battle as Gneisenau once led the defence of Kolberg,' Hitler told Schlieben, referring to the epic defence of the Baltic city against Napoleon's forces 140 years previously. He continued:

> Even in the worst case, you are duty bound to defend the very last bunker and to leave the enemy not a port but a scene of devastation. The entire German nation, the entire world is watching your struggle upon which depends the conduct and success of our operations to eliminate the beachhead, the honour of the *Wehrmacht* and the honour of your very name.[32]

The Allies were determined that Schlieben should not hold out for long. Forty minutes after midday on 22 June, the Allies unleashed a ferocious aerial assault on Cherbourg and its environs. For twenty minutes, fighter-bombers strafed, fired rockets and dropped bombs on Schlieben's defenders. It was merely the precursor to more misery. For an hour from 1 p.m. wave after wave of enemy bombers, 375 in all, pummelled the Normandy port as Allied batteries loosed off shells. Then at 2 p.m. the inferno ceased as the Allied infantry moved off. The final assault on Cherbourg was beginning.

'The troops were worn down by the ceaseless enemy naval bombardment and air attacks,' one battalion commander recalled. 'Even some commanders were demoralized by the enemy's material superiority.' German soldiers deserted to the Allies in droves or disappeared into the Cotentin countryside. Those men who remained on the sorry withdrawal into Cherbourg itself were exhausted and weary, confused and demoralized. 'The total lack of our air force had a thoroughly depressing impact on the troops and encouraged signs of skiving.'[33] *Landser* Robert Wiegel captured the life of the encircled garrison of Cherbourg in a letter to his wife on 22 June:

My dear wife!

Although I'm writing to you today, I'm sure this letter will no longer get out of here. I want to record the hours I have to endure here in diary form. I don't believe we'll be relieved. The fortress is encircled on the landward side by the enemy. It'll be a matter of days before he attacks with his armoured forces. Yesterday two tanks penetrated the city – they were shot up by the flak guns. The artillery fire gets ever closer and today the Americans flew constantly from midday to knock out the flak positions...

The greater the danger, the more you reach a point where you are indifferent to everything. Only the thought of you, my dear, and the children, thrive every minute. I have just looked at your picture, with your dear face looking at me, as if it wanted to say: 'Don't leave me.' Nevertheless, I'm still alive and have not given up all hope that I will see you again, my love, one day. You only truly realize how dear someone is when you are about to lose them. In this war we've learned to steel our hearts. And yet yesterday I stood with tears in my eyes at the thought that I would never again see my little Hannelore. We don't want to give up the hope, however, until the last moment. I would dearly like to spare you the great pain, my love, but our Fate is predetermined. Only memories of happy times are left and give us the strength to start a new life, my beloved, for the future belongs to the living. The children now need their mother all the more...That is my prayer – that God may give you a strong heart, to take your fate again firmly in your hands. In our brief marriage you have made me happy – that is also a wonderful memory for you, my dear. Say hello to and kiss my Mausele, Willi and Inge. I hold you now, my beloved wife, with my love for ever and always.

Your Robert.

Wiegel was killed the next day.[34]

By the afternoon of 23 June it was clear that Cherbourg would not hold out to 'about the middle of July'. The rate the front was crumbling it would not hold out until the end of June. The Americans smashed through 709th Infantry Division, a fortress garrison full of 'old, untrained troops' who could do nothing more than defend bunkers. In the open field, they were cut to pieces. Officers began blowing up roads as hand-to-hand fighting raged in artillery positions and field headquarters. Schlieben now threw his final reserves into the battle – his staff and supply troops – to delay the inevitable. That evening, Hitler reiterated his order: Cherbourg would be held 'to the last man'. Last man or not, Erwin Rommel was convinced that Cherbourg would soon fall. So too was von Schlieben. The next morning, with his communications failing with his troops and eight batteries destroyed by the enemy, the *Generalleutnant* reported that the only question was whether the fall of Cherbourg could be 'postponed for a few days' or not. 'The troops are squeezed into a small area. They will barely be able to withstand an attack.'[35]

In the early afternoon hours of 25 June, the turrets of three battleships, four cruisers and destroyers of the Allied invasion fleet swivelled to face Cherbourg and the tip of the Cotentin peninsula. The battle for the city had been raging all morning as fighter-bombers swept down on the historic fortresses and redoubts which ringed the heart of the port. One by one, the ageing forts, batteries, emplacements, pillboxes and bunkers were cleared. In Berlin, Joseph Goebbels gloated over a bloodbath – not of German troops, but of the Americans storming into the city:

> The German garrison is fighting in every nook and cranny and has turned virtually every house into a machine-gun nest. The soldiers have all but cemented themselves into the fortifications and only openings for gun barrels and machine barrels are left open. There is unimaginable heroism by the *Wehrmacht*. In this fifth year of war, the morale of the German soldier is utterly unbroken.

In reality, only some German units put up a fight, others surrendered rapidly. US 9th Division alone took 1,000 prisoners that Sunday. 'They didn't want to fight,' Schlieben complained. 'There were signs of cracking up – you could no longer risk sending the men out alone, because it looked as if they were going to make a run for it.' Many of Schlieben's men were enjoying their 'first taste of fighting'; those fleeing to 'Fortress Cherbourg' from the heartland of the Cotentin peninsula were 'utterly exhausted and had been badly affected morally as well as physically' in the preceding battles. And as his troops crumbled physically and morally, so too did von Schlieben. Surrounded by 2,000 wounded men in Cherbourg's historic citadel, the *Generalleutnant* saw no reason for the battle for the port to continue. Despite instructions, Karl-Wilhelm von Schlieben had no intention of fighting to the last man. It was time to surrender, he radioed Rommel: 'The loss of the city in the very near future is inevitable. Given the failure of effective counterattacks, is the destruction of our remaining troops necessary?' To compound the agony, the naval bombardment opened up shortly after midday. Artillery and aircraft were already pounding the city's defenders. Tanks and infantry were moving into the suburbs. When the Americans demanded Cherbourg's surrender, von Schlieben looked to Rommel for guidance. Cherbourg's commandant was all for giving up the struggle. 'It is my duty to report that further sacrifices cannot change anything,' he signalled Rommel. Rommel's reply to Schlieben was unflinching: 'You will continue the fight to the last round in accordance with the Führer's orders.' Schlieben concurred. His domain extended barely beyond a few bunkers, but he would fight on. That evening, he radioed Berlin: 'The final struggle for Cherbourg has begun. The general fights alongside his men. Long live the Führer and Germany!'[36]

The final hours in Cherbourg were hellish. Schlieben and his staff directed the last struggle from an underground shelter on the southern edge of the city. They had little contact with their own men, let alone the outside world. Fighter-bombers ranged overhead as mortars, rockets and artillery shells rained down on the port. Streets were cratered, houses tumbled into rubble and fires raged amid the ruins. A pall of black smoke hung over the city as American tanks trundled into the suburbs. The defenders had now been fighting for nearly three weeks, first in the open terrain of the peninsula, then on the approaches to the fortress, and now in Cherbourg itself. 'There's talk that the particularly bitter resistance by our troops surpasses anything experienced yet in this war,' Joseph Goebbels scribbled in his diary. 'We cannot say how long our men can still hold the fortress. For us every day is a gain.' The Americans had one more savage blow to deal *Kampfgruppe* – battle group – von Schlieben, as it was grandiosely called: a ferocious day-long artillery bombardment on the general's field headquarters in the suburb of St Sauveur. When prisoners told US forces where the commandant of 'fortress' Cherbourg was hiding, they unleashed a ferocious artillery barrage on the bunker which lasted twenty-four hours. It was the final straw for Schlieben. His nerves shattered and unable to command the scattered remnants of his *Kampfgruppe* any longer, the commandant decided it was time to end his personal battle. The airwaves crackled one last time from his command post at 3.06 p.m. on 26 June. 'Documents burned, codes destroyed.' The enemy was now at the gates. The Americans had surrounded the entrances to Schlieben's bunker complex and were preparing to blow it up. And yet still the German general refused to surrender, at least not until a tank had forced him to. Only then could Karl-Wilhelm von Schlieben surrender with honour. The Americans played out the bizarre drama. As a Sherman tank rumbled up to the walls of the citadel, Schlieben gave himself up. Eight hundred men followed their general into captivity. Before the day was out, Allied radio was crowing about the general's surrender. Goebbels was furious. 'Von Schlieben has gone into English captivity,' the propaganda minister recorded bitterly in his diary. 'He has been arrested, so to speak, in a bunker, a repeat of the example of the Field Marshal Paulus.[37] Schlieben gave his soldiers orders to fight to the last breath, and then commit suicide. Our Army generals are for the most part not worth a bean.'[38]

Captive or not, Karl-Wilhelm von Schlieben refused to order a general surrender. The battle for Cherbourg was not over. Rather, fighting for the city continued in isolated pockets, notably the mole in the harbour and the town hall, where 400 men were holed up. The resistance lasted until the morning of 27 June. Convinced the fighting was futile and their general had surrendered, these 400 hung out the white flag. Cherbourg was in Allied hands.

And still the struggle for the Cotentin peninsula was not over. To the west of the port was the tip of the peninsula, the Cap de la Hague and Jobourg where thousands of Germans continued to hold out, led by a determined *Oberstleutnant*, one Günther Keil. 'Keil,' Goebbels noted, 'has earned himself immortality. He has been the true soul of resistance. Had von Schlieben been a man of the same calibre, then perhaps things in Cherbourg might have gone differently.' The defenders were afforded two days of relative calm as US VIII Corps regrouped. The end at Jobourg could not be delayed long. On the morning of 29 June, the Americans jumped off. The struggle was unequal. Keil threw his last reserves into the battle, but he knew the fighting was hopeless. 'The troops are little used to teamwork and have almost no combat experience,' Seventh Army reported. 'They cannot hold out long against an enemy who enjoys material superiority.' Beyond a few strong points, the defenders of the Jobourg peninsula put up little resistance. Instead they climbed out of their foxholes and bunkers to surrender en masse, 6,000 in all. When Keil marched off into captivity at midnight on 30 June, the battle for Cherbourg and the Cotentin peninsula was over.[39]

The Allies had their first prize of the campaign, the Germans their first decisive defeat. The fall of Cherbourg was hard to bear especially as Nazi propaganda had trumpeted the importance of any port falling into enemy hands. 'The loss of Cherbourg is a major disappointment for the

German people – a grave setback for us not merely in terms of prestige, but also militarily,' Joseph Goebbels conceded. But the propaganda minister tried to put a brave face on the city's surrender. 'The shining heroism shown by our soldiers in Cherbourg provides some hope for the future course of the invasion.' The enemy now had his hands on a port. But a port in name only. 'The demolition of Cherbourg is a masterful job, beyond a doubt the most complete, intensive and best-planned demolition in history,' the American engineer charged with bringing the harbour back into use complained. The outer breakwater was partially blown up, the harbour was filled with mines, block ships were sunk in the basins, quaysides demolished, every crane wrecked and 20,000 cubic yards of rubble had been tossed into one of the large basins to prevent its use. A content Goebbels noted: 'Cherbourg and above all its harbour have been destroyed so badly that we can assume that the enemy will need several weeks to be able to use this port as a harbour.' [40] The Americans had once intended to use Cherbourg as a port three days after its capture; by the end of July they hoped to offload 150,000 tons of material in the harbour. In reality, barely one tenth of that amount was disembarked in Cherbourg and it would be September before any vessel entered harbour.

Cherbourg joined the ranks of heroic last stands in Nazi folklore alongside Stalingrad and Tunisia. The defenders had not fought in vain, the Party newspaper, the *Völkischer Beobachter*, proclaimed:

The German soldier fought unshakeably, even when he could no longer hope for localized success, and frequently defended himself in pockets of resistance with his weapons exhausted. His heroism has been denied the crowning achievement of victory laurels, but let no man be in any doubt about this: the day will come when the fruits of this struggle will ripen. Courage is not for nothing, no sacrifice wasted.[41]

Two days later,*Völkischer Beobachter* reporter Klaus Dörner elevated 'the men of Cherbourg' to almost mythical status:

We should remember the example of the soldiers in Cherbourg. The names of the pockets of resistance should be indelibly in our memory. Cherbourg is not Europe, but the example of the men who were still fighting in the outer mole on 29 June may give those from the other side of the Pond an idea of the spirit which the old continent is defended in. They will never understand us, but the thoughtful among them may perhaps ask the question whether they would be prepared to do the same in the same situation.[42]

According to Allied accounts, the defenders of Cherbourg fought 'against all logic'. The *Völkischer Beobachter* provided the answer:

> The enemy soldier in the West does not really know what he's fighting for. But the German soldier knows that he is fighting for the livelihood of his people and for the future of the entire continent. Faced by enemies in the east and west, there is only one choice: victory or destruction! This gives the German soldier in all three branches of the *Wehrmacht* unparalleled inner strength, which that Englishman described as 'against all logic', because he cannot understand it with his outdated way of thinking.[43]

Whatever gloss the Nazi propaganda machine put on it, the loss of Cherbourg was a bitter loss for Germany's cause. The German public regarded the port's fall as 'the beginning of the end, irreplaceable, proof of our advancing weakness'. The monitors of public opinion noted with concern: 'A moral decline is noticeable, one that can only be arrested by an uninterrupted string of German successes.' People asked themselves: 'If we couldn't succeed in stopping the invasion up to now, how can it be possible if our enemies have a large harbour?' Cherbourg, many argued, was the first milestone on the road to defeat in France. 'People's great fear,' the *Sicherheitsdienst* warned, 'is that after the fall of Cherbourg the enemy's superiority will become crushing and they already believe an [enemy] occupation of Paris is all but certain.'[44]

The defenders of Cherbourg were now being led into captivity. As he was led away through Allied lines, one flak regiment commander realized that the game was up for Germany. 'What we saw on the main roads in the way of troops, assault guns and tanks – we said to ourselves: "My God! If it goes on like that, they will destroy us just with their weight of material."'[45]

Notes

1. Rommel to his wife, 14-15/6/44. Rommel, pp.491-2.
2. Bericht Major iG von Ekesparre, 17/6/44. Nachlass Rommel. BA/MA ; KTB Ruge, 17/6/44. Ruge, p.190; TB Jünger, 24/6/44; Rommel to his wife, 18/6/44. Irving, *Trail of the Fox*, p.353.
3. TB Goebbels, 14/6/44; KTB AOK7, 16/6/44; Rommel memorandum, 3/7/44. Rommel, pp.481-4.
4. Goebbels, Joseph, 'Die Hintergründe der Invasion', Das Reich, 18/6/44.
5. SD Meldung, 25/6/44; TB Goebbels, 16/6/44.
6. KTB Pöppel, 13/6/44. Pöppel, p.209.
7. Klapdor, p.219.
8. OB West, NSFO, Nr.5/44, 23/6/44. RH 19 IV/149. Cited in Wegmüller, p.250.
9. Caldwell, pp.236-7.
10. KTB Oqu AOK15, 20/6/44. NA CAB 146/338; Appendices, KTB OQu, AOK7, 13/6/44. Harrison, *Cross Channel Attack*, p.408.
11. Wegmüller, p.237.

12. KTB Flak Regiment 155(W), 6/6/44. IWM MI14/1038/1-2.
13. Milch, 27/4/43. Irving, *Mare's Nest*, p.30.
14. Trevor-Roper, *Hitler's War Directives*, pp.239-40; KTB Flak Regiment 155(W), 2/6/44. IWM MI14/1038/1-2.
15. Irving, p.213.
16. Tagesbefehl Flak Regiment 155, 12/6/44. IWM MI14/1038/1-2.
17. Guderian, *From Normandy to the Ruhr*, pp.42-3; Irving, p.236.
18. OKW Communiqué, 16/6/44; Berliner Nachtsausgabe, 16/6/44; Fritzsche broadcast, 1945 Hours, 17/6/44. BBC Daily Monitoring Report of Foreign Broadcasts, 17/6/44. IWM; TB Goebbels, 17/6/44.
19. KTB Flak Regiment 155, 20/6/44, 4/7/44. IWM MI14/1038/1-2.
20. TB Goebbels, 18/6/44.
21. *Völkischer Beobachter*, 19/6/44, 20/6/44.
22. RSHA to Partei Kanzlei, Ref: Berichte aus den SD Abschnittsbereichen, 27/6/44. Serrano, p.167; Letter *Gefreiter* K.L, staff of 90th Panzer Grenadier Division, June 1944. Buchbender, p.136.
23. Williams, p.157; OB West, NSFO, Nr.5/44, 23/6/44. RH 19 IV/149. Cited in Wegmüller, p.250.
24. McKee, *Caen: Anvil of Victory*, p.132.
25. KTB Pöppel, 17/6/44. Pöppel, p.210.
26. Rommel to his wife, 23/6/44. Rommel, p.492.
27. HGrB Ia Nr.3650/44, 17/6/44. Ose, p.140. See also KTB AOK7, 1035 Hours, 17/6/44. IWM AL 528.
28. KTB AGp.B, 1045 Hours, 10/6/44; KTB AOK7, 2345 Hours, 22/6/44. IWM AL 528; MS B-845.
29. KTB AOK7, 0835 Hours, 14/6/44. IWM AL528; Evening Situation Report, 18/6/44. Heiber and Glantz (eds), *Hitler and his Generals*, p.437.
30. CSDIC GRGG Series. Record of conversations, 30/6/44. NA WO 208/4363.
31. CSDIC GRGG Series. Record of conversations, 30/6/44, 16-17/7/44. NA WO 208/4363; Schlieben an HGrB, 22/6/44. Ose, p.143.
32. Irving, p.356; OKW/WFSt/Op.Nr 772015/44, 21/6/44. Cited in KTB Skl, 22/6/44.
33. Bericht *Oberstleutnant* Hoffmann, III/919th Grenadier Regiment, KTB AOK7, 1830-1950 Hours, 24/6/44. IWM AL528.
34. Dollinger, *Kain, wo ist dein Bruder?* p.261.
35. Schlieben an HGrB, 22/6/44. Ose, p.143; KTB AOK7, 23/6/44. IWM AL 528; KTB Skl, 24/6/44.
36. TB Goebbels, 30/6/44; CSDIC GRGG Series. Record of conversations, 16-17/7/44. NA WO 208/4363; KTB Mar.Grp.Kdo West, 25/6/44. NHB; KTB Skl, 25/6/44; KTB OB West, 1530 Hours, 25/6/44; KTB AGp.B, 1932 Hours, 25/6/44. IWM AL 1531/3.
37. Paulus had surrendered his Sixth Army at Stalingrad in 1943, rather than commit suicide as Hitler had hoped he would.
38. TB Goebbels, 25/6/44, 30/6/44; KTB AOK7, 1506 Hours, 26/6/44. IWM AL974/2; SHAEF Weekly Intelligence Report, No.16, 8/7/44. NA WO219/1921.
39. TB Goebbels, 1/7/44; KTB AOK7, 29/6/44. IWM AL974/2.
40. TB Goebbels, 27/6/44, 30/6/44; Harrison, *Cross Channel Attack*, p.441.
41. *Völkischer Beobachter*, 29/6/44.
42. *Kriegsberichter* Klaus Dörner, 'Die Männer von Cherbourg', *Völkischer Beobachter*, 1/7/44.
43. 'Gegen alle Logik', *Völkischer Beobachter*, 1/7/44.
44. SD Schwerin, 27/6/44. Cited in Steinert, *Hitler's War and the Germans*, p.261; SD Meldung, 28/6/44.
45. CSDIC GRGG Series. Record of conversations, 30/6/44. NA WO

Chapter 7

The Unequal Struggle

The entire battle is a terrible bloodbath as never before seen.
Dietrich von Choltitz

The Western Front in late June 1944 wended its way for eighty miles from the Atlantic coast of the Cotentin peninsula to the north of St Lô, south of Bayeux then past Caen to the shores of the Seine Bay, to the east of the Orne estuary near Ouistreham. In places the Allied beachhead was barely five miles deep, but the *Wehrmacht* could still not drive the enemy back into the sea. In less than a fortnight, the Allies had put ashore in excess of 600,000 men, 81,000 vehicles and 183,000 tons of equipment. And yet for all their superiority on the ground and in the skies, the enemy could not force a decisive breakthrough in the German lines. Even the lowliest soldier realized that there was stalemate in the west in late June 1944. 'Something dreadful seemed to have happened in terms of the overall plan,' one American corporal recalled. 'Things had gone awry.'[1]

British Field Marshal Bernard Law Montgomery had the plan to break the deadlock: Operation Epsom, the capture of Caen and the destruction of the German forces defending it. The salient around the city of the Norman dukes bulged into British and Canadian lines. It invited being cut off; eliminated. Epsom would do just that. The plan was to strike either side of Caen with Montgomery's two pincers meeting south of the city, snaring its German defenders. This would be an all-out effort by the British general, committing all the forces of his Second Army to crush the enemy in the Caen bulge; two corps would strike west of the city, the third from the north-east, no less than 60,000 men and more than 600 tanks. After more than a fortnight of relative stalemate in Normandy, it was time for action. 'We are now ready to pass on to other things,' Montgomery wrote, 'and to reap the harvest.' The British general impressed on his commanders the importance of the coming battle. 'We have now reached the "show down" stage. The first rush inland is over.

We must have no set-backs. What we take we must hold.' Epsom oozed confidence. Around Caen the British outnumbered their enemy six to one in men, seven to one in tanks, and twenty-one to one in artillery – not even counting the Allies' superiority in the air. 'The enemy divisions are weak and there are no reserves,' Montgomery wrote. 'I hope to see Caen and Cherbourg in our hands on June 24th.'[2] Cherbourg fell on 26th. Would Caen fall late too? Would Caen fall at all?

For more than a week there had been an uneasy calm along the front of the *Hitlerjugend* to the west of Caen. The SS unit had spent the lull reinforcing its lines to ward off an enemy attack. But the *Hitlerjugend* had no idea when that attack might come. As Saturday, 24 June, drew to a close, the division's new, youthful commander Kurt Meyer sent off his daily report to his superiors. There were no signs of an impending enemy attack, Meyer reported. The tense calm lasted until daybreak. Through the fog of Sunday, 25 June, the gods of war opened fire. 'We had dug into the ground so deep that we felt safe from any artillery fire,' SS *Panzerobergrenadier* Hans Kempel recalled. 'It had been quiet for days. Such weird calm could not last very long. And so it was. The barrages set in. It could drive you to despair. Tommy had fired smoke. You could not see your own hand in front of your eyes.' This was only the preliminary to the main event.

'The whole terrain was covered by explosions,' anti-tank commander *Oberscharführer* Erich Wohlgemuth remembered. 'Behind the moving wall of fire came tanks and infantry.' In the midst of the artillery inferno, the 'horizon turned black and red'. The barrage was ceaseless.[3]

The horrors of the fighting on 25 June made a deep impression on a man as battle-hardened as Kurt Meyer, the *Hitlerjugend*'s youthful commander. His adjutant Bernhard Meitzel watched the *Standartenführer*'s reaction as British tanks rolled over a reconnaissance company of teenagers. 'The commander knew every one of these seventeen to eighteen year old soldiers who were fighting their last battle in front of us now. When I looked at the *Standartenführer*, I saw tears in his eyes.'[4]

By the day's end, Meyer had lost more than 700 comrades killed, wounded or missing. The British had driven a wedge three miles wide and one mile deep in the German lines. And Epsom was only just beginning.

The *Hitlerjugend* enjoyed the grace of a night of peace. It did not last long. At 7.30 a.m. on Monday, 26 June, the muzzles of 644 artillery pieces flashed, unleashing a barrage on the German lines around Caen. Under dark, overcast skies British troops moved up towards their jump-off positions with a sense of foreboding. One recalled:

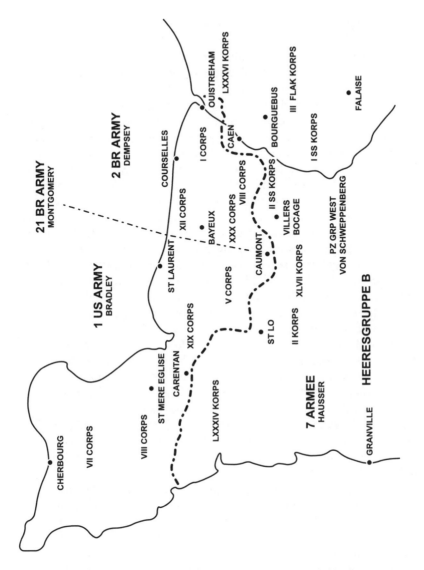

The front line in Normandy at the beginning of July 1944

The horizon was trembling and a thousand eerie lightnings criss-crossed the night sky. For a long time we watched in silence. Then someone said what we were all thinking. 'We have to go into that!' Our breathing became a little harder. Those eighteen year olds of the *Hitlerjugend* Division, strong in their youthful trustfulness and youthful fire, were selling their lives at a high price.[5]

The rain did not lift all day. Its one benefit was that it curtailed Allied air attacks. Instead, the attackers relied on the artillery barrage which crept slowly down the Odon valley. The defenders dug in. 'We had gone to ground,' one prisoner told his British captors, 'and had emerged only to find ourselves surrounded by tanks or furious Scotsmen throwing grenades.' The British objectives were the bridges over the River Odon, but in the rain-drenched cornfields, hedges and meadows which lined the valley, the *Hitlerjugend* sniped at the oncoming attackers, or dug in amongst the rubble of the devastated hamlets scattered along the valley floor. The farthest the British advanced that day was four miles; the advance fell far short of the Odon crossings. Kurt Meyer's men had blunted the enemy attack; fifty shot-up British tanks littered the valley floor. But as Meyer's superior, I SS Panzer Corps' battle-hardened commander Sepp Dietrich, pored over the balance sheet that night, he looked to the future with growing concern. The enemy attacks were sapping his fighting strength. As night fell on the battlefield, the SS commander called Rommel. He needed men and equipment, especially men: '...panzer grenadiers in particular. The *Panzer Lehr* has virtually none left,' then added hopefully: 'The troops are in good heart.' [6]

The wave of British troops moved off again the following morning, determined to seize a bridge over the Odon. Again the *Hitlerjugend* barred their progress. At times, the fighting was hand-to-hand. No quarter was given by either side as *Oberscharführer* August Zinssmeister, defending the village of Tourville on the main road running south-west from Caen, noted in his diary: 'We fire everything we have, with devastating effect, from close distance at the infantry. The Tommies send up smoke signals and hammer us with heavy calibre shells. The bushes and hedges are full of English infantry and the fire fight continues without pause.'[7]

But after two days of relentless fighting, the Germans could no longer hold back the enemy tide. Zinssmeister and his comrades began to fall back – beyond the Odon. By nightfall, the British had a tenuous foothold on the southern bank of the river. The prospect of a break-through beckoned, and with it the threat of encircling Caen. Far from the fighting front at Seventh Army's headquarters in Le Mans, Friedrich Dollmann began to lose his nerve. The reports arriving at his desk looked increasingly pessimistic. It was, Dollmann decided, time to play the last card.

South-west of Caen, II SS Panzer Corps – 9th and 10th SS Panzer Divisions, sent from the Eastern Front on Hitler's orders – was regrouping ready for its first action in the battle for Normandy. Dollmann had already called on the corps to intervene once, then changed his mind. Now the Seventh Army commander wavered again, and ordered Paul

Hausser, II SS Panzer Corps' gruff, ruthless commander, to attack – even though Hausser was not ready. It was Dollmann's final act in a battle increasingly slipping from his grasp. At 10 a.m. on 28 June, Seventh Army's commander committed suicide. 'Dollmann's burden of anxiety grew worse and worse,' his chief-of-staff Max Pemsel wrote decades later. 'His protests to his superiors were ignored, and he learned that his army would not be getting any outside assistance during its desperate defensive actions.'[8] Command of the ill-fated Seventh Army fell to Paul Hausser. Aged fifty-four, and retired from the Army, Hausser had been called upon in 1934 by Heinrich Himmler to train the embryonic *Waffen SS*, which he then led in France in 1940 and then into Russia, where he lost his left eye. Paul Hausser was a soldier's soldier. His men simply called him 'Papa'. At the end of 1943 Papa Hausser found himself in France in charge of II SS Panzer Corps, preparing to defeat the invader. Now Paul Hausser, unblooded in the west, his corps still not ready for battle, suddenly found himself in charge of Seventh Army.

On the road to Caen, *Sturmmann* Herbert Fürbringer and his comrades in 9th SS Panzer Division *Hohenstaufen* noticed 'rumbling and rolling' as they moved up to their jump-off positions ready to deliver Eugen Dollmann's ill-planned counter-attack. It was, Fürbringer noted, 'the matériel battle at Caen and with every kilometre this rumbling became ever clearer, until it rose to a continuous thunder'. Fürbringer's company ground to a halt and watched the spectacle:

> The guns continued to thunder in the distance, the horizon burned ceaselessly. One thousand flashes of lightning flashed, eerily illuminating the night sky. *Sturmmann* Haering said what most of his comrades were thinking. 'We must go there!' Such words went down like a ton of lead and you felt it was hard to breathe, as if someone was lying on your chest, and your heart beat more rapidly. For the first time, the men got an idea of the concept of 'barrages'. It showed beyond doubt our future enemy's overwhelming material superiority. At the front there was death and ruin, and what seemed to the resting column like some phenomenal spectacle was actually the gravest bloodbath just kilometres away. We instinctively thought about our comrades, who had to endure thousands of artillery shells in this chaos.[9]

A few miles to the east of the *Hohenstaufen*, 10th SS Panzer Division *Frundsberg* moved towards the front south-west of Caen. Like Fürbringer, *Hauptsturmführer* Ewald Klapdor was 'spellbound' by the glow on the horizon. He continued:

109

The earth is thumped and shaken by enormous fists. In the distance, I can hear the fire of very heavy guns. This endless flashing, the glow on the horizon is a fascinating sight. The crashes of heavy naval gunfire mingle with the rumble of guns firing and explosions, which rise and then fade away. The land seems like a roaring hurricane. It's as if a mighty hammer wants to crush it. Bewitched, I stare at this inferno. Our attack would be led into this, an attack by our brave young regiments into the destructive fire of an enemy with equipment coming out of his ears.[10]

After a three-week march from southern France, the lead units of the 2nd SS Panzer Division *Das Reich* were reaching the front in dribs and drabs. A combination of uprisings by the French resistance and disruption to France's road and rail network meant that the SS division's move from southern France took at least twice, if not three times longer than expected. By the time it reached Normandy, it was no longer a coherent division. 'Unserviceability among tanks is 60 per cent,' *Das Reich*'s ruthless commander Heinz Lammerding complained. 'The lack of adequate transport, the substantial distances to be covered in unfavourable terrain, the dispersal of units over 300 kilometres and the lack of advance preparations for operational and supply measures has weakened the strength of the division out of all proportion.' Lammerding was enraged at having to use a first-rate armoured division to quell uprisings in the heart of France, which it did most ruthlessly in the village of Oradour-sur-Glane. 'Panzer divisions in the fifth year of the war are too good for this.'[11] The first elements of *Das Reich* to reach the battlefield were the men of the regiment *Der Führer* who arrived at the lines south-west of Caen around 15 June. Its commander, Otto Weidinger, was filled with a sense of foreboding. 'The victory fanfares had long since faded away,' he wrote. 'The war had become more pitiless and cruel. We were no longer fighting to win.'[12]

The *Hohenstaufen, Frundsberg* and *Das Reich* rumbling hesitantly towards Caen were to thrust into the flank of the British corps tearing southwards across the Odon. The two sides would clash on the approaches to, and slopes of, a nondescript height: Hill 112. The men who fought there came to know it as the Hill of Calvary. And around and about it the most bitter of all the fighting in Normandy would rage.

Hill 112 rose out of the low-lying terrain of the Odon valley barely five miles south-west of Caen. It dominated the landscape and – more importantly – the approaches to Caen. Spirited German counter-attacks throughout 28 June thwarted British attempts to seize the height, as an ad hoc force of *Hitlerjugend* and remnants of 21st Panzer Division struck into the British east flank north of the river. The Germans smashed into the village of Mouen, on the main railway line leading from Caen 'advancing through a wilderness of abandoned equipment and dead British soldiers' panzer radio operator Werner Kortenhaus recalled. The next day, British forces swept back into Mouen. 'It must have been some battle,' one Briton wrote later. 'The orchard and the railway and the fields around were a real charnel house. The embankment was littered with German dead.'[13]

As the battle on the approaches to Hill 112 swayed to and fro, the counter-offensive Dollmann had ordered before committing suicide was still not ready. II SS Panzer Corps, under its newly-appointed commander Wilhelm Bittrich, was struggling to move into position. Come daylight on 29 June, he was confident he could throw his panzers into the battle raging south-west of Caen.

So much for confidence. Long after daybreak on that Thursday, the panzers of the II SS Corps were still heading for their jump-off positions, mauled on the way in, under constant aerial and artillery bombardment. As 9th and 10th SS Divisions regrouped, the British wasted no time in driving on Hill 112. The struggle on the hill was ferocious. The Germans did not cede the high ground without a bitter fight. One British officer recalled the hailstorm of *Nebelwerfer* fire which plunged on Allied troops forcing their way up Hill 112:

A howling and wailing grew until it filled the sky, rising in pitch as it approached, and ending in a series of shattering explosions all round us. Then more squeals, the same horrible wail, and another batch of 36 bombs exploded astride us, so that the pressure came first from one side, then from the other, then both at once.[14]

Obergruppenführer Paul Hausser was still waiting for his panzer divisions to assemble. Kurt Meyer held out little hope for the long-awaited counter-attack. It was, he rued, 'bound to fail because of the impossibility of the demands and the insufficient means at our disposal'. Kurt Meyer was right. The counter-offensive was due to begin at 7 a.m. on 29 June, but Allied air power smashed the preparations. 'This disrupted the troops so much that the attack did not start again until 2.30 in the afternoon,' Hausser complained. 'Even then it could not get going. The murderous fire from naval guns in the Channel and the terrible British artillery destroyed the bulk of our attacking force in its assembly area.' Otto Weidinger bore witness to the tragedy. His *Der Führer* regiment moved off with the men of the *Frundsberg* under a ceaseless enemy artillery barrage. The shells blasted all telephone lines apart. Runners dashed between the hedgerows to re-establish communications with the front as medics and stretcher bearers ran back. A direct hit took out a building next to Weidinger's command post, killing ten men. 'The units were senselessly pounded to pieces before they could employ their infantry forces effectively,' the *Sturmbannführer* complained. 'It was a one-sided battle of matériel on a scale never before experienced.' As night fell on the battlefield, the counter-attack had made almost no ground. But *Panzergruppe West* commander Geyr von Schweppenburg, overseeing the faltering armoured offensive had no intention of abandoning it. He impressed the importance of his counter-stroke on Bittrich: 'This attack is the great opportunity.'[15]

Within twelve hours Geyr von Schweppenburg was living in the realms of reality again. At first light on the last day of June, the Allies opened up a ferocious barrage on II SS Panzer Corps. 'The attack is incredibly difficult and costly,' Geyr reported that morning. 'The enemy's naval artillery is unbelievably heavy. It is bombarding the breakthrough area with a continual barrage.' The barrage proved too much for the panzer divisions to take. One commander in the *Hohenstaufen* signed off his midday report fatalistically: 'Abandon hope all ye who enter here.' The enemy was not giving way; the German armour was not making headway, and the attackers were suffering punishing losses. Paul Hausser called off the attack. He hoped for one last attempt to break through on the Odon that night. 'The preparations were so heavily smashed by the enemy air force and naval artillery,' the Germans conceded, 'that the troops could no longer attack.' The counter-offensive had failed, and Seventh Army went over to the defensive. 'Everything at present depends upon husbanding the resources of the panzer divisions committed in battle so that they can carry out further offensive attacks and form a defensive line in keeping with our infantry forces – and beyond the range of fire from enemy naval forces.'[16]

The counter-offensive had been blunted after just one day. Its one notable achievement was forcing the British off the commanding height of Hill 112; the enemy retreated down the slope as the Germans battered the flanks of the British bulge over the Odon. At dawn on 30 June, Kurt Meyer tentatively advanced to re-take the height. An artillery and rocket barrage 'hammered away' at the British defenders, as Max Wünsche urged the men of his 12th SS Panzer Regiment on. Wünsche climbed down from his tank and through the mist of this late June morning. 'Be careful! Stay back! Crouch down a bit. Wait for a break in the fire.' And then the SS troops swarmed over the height. A British machine-gun company holding the hill top disappeared under the weight of rocket fire. Hill 112 was back in German hands. Meyer surveyed his hard-won prize. 'Burning tanks stand on both sides. There is hardly a square metre of earth on the hill that has not been ploughed up by shells and bombs.'[17] It was not the last fighting Hill 112 would see.

With the failure of both offensives – Epsom ran its course as it blunted Hausser's counter-stroke – both sides took stock of the struggle for Normandy. The casualty rate in some British and Commonwealth divisions surpassed losses a generation earlier on the Somme and at Ypres - some front-line units lost upwards of a third of their men. The *Wehrmacht* suffered no less lightly. The five days of Epsom cost the *Hitlerjugend* alone more than 1,200 men; its losses were typical. June had been a bitter month for the whole *Wehrmacht* in the west. The ground war alone cost more than 62,000 officers and men. The Allies too paid a heavy price for the assault on *Festung Europa*; the Americans lost 11,000 dead, a further 1,000 missing, and 3,400 wounded; the British and Canadians suffered some 23,000 casualties, 3,356 of them dead.

Even before Epsom had run out of steam, Erwin Rommel and Gerd von Rundstedt were racing across France and southern Germany in a staff car. They had been summoned. Barely ten days after his last meeting with his western marshals, Adolf Hitler wanted to confer once more. June was ending badly for the Führer. In the east, the Russians were crushing his Army Group Centre. In the west, all efforts to destroy the Allied beachhead had been thwarted and despite the much-heralded wonder weapon, the V1 had not forced the British to their knees. On the morning of 29 June, Rundstedt and Rommel were ushered into Hitler's mountain retreat, the Berghof, for a council of war, to be joined later in the day by Dönitz, Goering, and his commander in France, Hugo Sperrle. For more than three hours Rommel and Rundstedt argued with Hitler about the course of the struggle in the west. To Rommel, it was clear Germany was losing the battle, and with it the war. For the first time he broached the subject in the presence of the Führer. '*Mein Führer*,' he told his leader, 'the entire world is arrayed now against Germany, and this balance of strength...' Hitler stopped him dead in his tracks. Politics was not the realm of a field marshal. 'You will deal with your military situation, and nothing else.' What followed was a dressing down for the two western marshals. They had allowed Cherbourg to fall and failed to counter-attack; instead, the German Army found itself on the defensive against the British blows around Caen. The British were not supermen, Hitler argued; they relied on aerial and naval supremacy, overwhelming masses of material, they acted rigidly, methodically. They could be beaten. 'Everything depends on confining [the enemy] to his bridgehead by building up a front to block it off and then fighting a war of attrition to wear him down and force him back,' the Führer told his audience. But even Adolf Hitler had to concede that the Allies' material superiority had to be checked. To this end, he promised wonder weapons – 'jet propelled and blitz bombers' – 1,000 new fighters to regain aerial superiority, if only temporarily, and mines to blockade the Seine Bay. Above all, the Führer ordered the German Army in the west to stand fast. 'The principal goal is to stop the enemy attacking in the direction of Paris,' he told his two western commanders. 'Seventh Army must not allow itself to be driven into open ground.'[18]

It was late on the last day of June 1944 when Erwin Rommel arrived back at his headquarters in La Roche-Guyon. Waiting for him was a memorandum by Geyr von Schweppenburg. Defeat at Caen that Friday and the preceding day had made a deep impression on the *Panzergruppe West* commander. His force had been battered ceaselessly for more than three weeks and achieved nothing in return. It was time, the panzer leader said, to pull out of Caen. 'Our panzer formations are disintegrating – or have already disintegrated – and soon they will be completely burned out.' Hans Speidel rubber-stamped Geyr's report and told the panzer general to begin making preparations for evacuation. Rundstedt too agreed. At 3.30 a.m. on 1 July 1944, the teleprinter at OKW clattered. 'I request immediate permission to have a free hand and carry out a planned evacuation of the Caen bridgehead,' the Commander-in-Chief, West, demanded. 'The evacuation will relieve the irreplaceable formations of I SS Panzer from an ever-increasing encirclement and free them for further operations.' The one dissenting view in the west was Erwin Rommel. When he called on Geyr at his forward headquarters at noon on 1 July, the field marshal was horrified at plans to pull out of Caen. 'Caen will be the linchpin of the enemy attack on Paris,' Rommel told the panzer general. 'It's important to send even more forces there.'[19]

Hitler gave his answer to Rundstedt, Rommel and Geyr that evening: there would be no withdrawal from Caen. 'The current positions are to be held,' the Führer ordered. 'Any future breakthrough by the enemy will be prevented by stubborn resistance or localized counter-attacks.' Rundstedt picked up the phone and asked to be patched through to Hitler's headquarters. At the other end, the Führer's supine chief-of-staff, Wilhelm Keitel, answered. The irascible Rundstedt seethed. 'Rescind this order,' he told Keitel. 'If you doubt what we are doing, get up here and take over this shambles yourself.' Keitel advised Hitler that von Rundstedt was 'unable to meet the increasing demands' of the battle in France. The next morning the elderly field marshal was dismissed. His place was to be taken by the adept Günther von Kluge, recently recovered from a serious road accident in Russia.[20]

It was not just Rundstedt who suffered the axe; Geyr's proposal to evacuate Caen had sent Hitler into a rage. Now his tenure as commander of *Panzergruppe West* was over. 'I regard my military career to be at an end,' the general wrote dolefully to Rommel in a valedictory. 'The recent battles in a theatre of war more exacting than any I had hitherto experienced have wrought an inner change in me.'[21] Into his place stepped the younger, battle-hardened Heinrich Eberbach. Eberbach was a solid, if unspectacular, forty-nine year old panzer commander who had led tanks into battle in Poland, Belgium, France and Russia, finally commanding a corps. For the past six months and more, Eberbach had been in Germany overseeing the *Wehrmacht*'s tank arm as its inspector general. Now he was thrust immediately into the thick of struggle for Caen.

Günther von Kluge arrived at his new command, the sumptuous headquarters of *OB West* in a Parisian suburb, on the morning of 3 July. There, he found Gerd von Rundstedt dictating his final order to the armies in the west:

We are still at the beginning of the struggle. We don't know how long it will last and what shape it will take. We only know that the Anglo-Saxons won't spare any means to achieve a decisive success. But we also know that, whatever the extent of the enemy's efforts, the heroic resistance of our troops and our unshakeable belief in the final victory will defeat all the enemy's efforts to achieve operational and war-deciding success.[22]

With that Rundstedt bade farewell first to his staff, then to Rommel and headed off to Germany to probable retirement.

Günther von Kluge set about his new task with energy. That afternoon, the field marshal drove to see Rommel. Kluge greeted his new deputy bluntly. 'Now you too will have to learn to obey orders.' The introduction set the tone for a stormy meeting, less a discussion, Rommel later conceded, than an interrogation. The new Commander-in-Chief, West, blustered in as little more than Hitler's mouthpiece. His maxim was: defence. 'Hold the present line whatever happens.' Rommel snapped back. 'You've never fought the British.' Kluge retorted that the Desert Fox had commanded nothing larger than a division to date. The two field marshals parted with Rommel still seething from his dressing down.[23]

The clash with Rommel was typical of sixty-one year old 'Clever Hans' – *der Kluge Hans*. 'Kluge is a completely different type than Rommel,' Rommel's naval adviser Friedrich Ruge remarked. 'Even more factual, crystal clear, just as courageous, but he lacks Rommel's warmth and respect for humans.'[24]There was no doubting Kluge's ability or courage. Clever Hans had led his armies across Poland, France, and then into Russia. When Hitler needed a general to take a firm grip of the army group outside Moscow in December 1941, the task fell upon von Kluge. He did not disappoint, enforcing the Führer's 'stand fast' orders ruthlessly. But despite his outward loyalty – the Führer trusted Kluge implicitly and never dismissed him from his post – the field marshal dallied with the opposition to the Nazi regime, as he became increasingly concerned that the war was turning against Germany through 1942 and 1943. Despite his sympathies with the small clique of conspirators, Clever Hans could never bring himself to act. In time, Günther von Kluge may have acted against Adolf Hitler. But in October 1943, Kluge's staff car overturned on the Minsk-Smolensk highway, severely injuring the field marshal. By the end of June 1944, Clever Hans was fully recovered – and looking for employment.

For the next two days, Kluge was on the road, visiting his front line in Normandy. First to the west, to Dietrich von Choltitz and his battered LXXXIV Corps, holding back the American tide from the Atlantic coast inland beyond Carentan. He had, Choltitz told Kluge, thrown his final reserves into the fray. 'Leadership is extremely difficult. The men don't know their commanders because of the high officer losses.' Next to Seventh Army's headquarters where its commander Paul Hausser and *General* Eugen Meindl, commanding Choltitz's neighbour, II Fallschirmjäger Corps, painted the picture no less black. Hausser protested at the lack of supplies; Meindl protested at the Allies' material superiority which 'rains down artillery and mortar fire' on the front line.[25] Perhaps the situation in the west was as bleak as Erwin Rommel had warned.

But Rommel was past caring. In the first days of July 1944, the Desert Fox was melancholy, even depressed. No one was listening to him. His warnings were simply brushed off with rhetoric. 'It's scandalous that the true extent of enemy air superiority is still not entirely believed by those "up top"' he complained. The stormy meeting with Kluge had proved the final straw. He poured his heart out to his trusted naval aide. 'He was in a very serious mood because the enemy could presumably no longer be stopped,' Ruge wrote. 'The efforts of the soldiers had been in vain.'[26]

On the other side of the lines in Normandy, Allied leaders viewed the situation no less gloomily. The Normandy front was rapidly resembling the Western Front of the 1914-1918 war. It was now approaching 'D+30' – thirty days since the invasion. On a great map of France in the office of Allied planners, three coloured lines marked out the progress the Anglo-Americans should have made in green, yellow and black. The planners predicted the Allied armies would be tearing through Brittany and central Normandy by early July. The reality was very different.

Caen – which should have been taken on the first day of invasion – remained in German hands. Three battles had raged for the city of the Norman dukes, but the enemy salient continued to bulge into the British and Canadian lines. Failure to capture Caen worried Winston Churchill. The British Premier was convinced the Allies 'were descending into a bitter "trench warfare" situation similar to that of World War I'. Allied supreme commander Dwight Eisenhower was similarly worried. 'We must use all possible energy in a determined effort to prevent a stalemate,' he wrote to the British battlefield commander. Bernard Law Montgomery needed no spurring on. He wanted Caen as badly as Churchill, but all his efforts to seize the city had ended in disappointment. This time there would be no sweeping moves, no grand pincer movements to trap the Germans in an Allied vice. Montgomery would batter and bash his way forward with three divisions, more than 100,000 men in 'a big show'.[27] The Allied steamroller would roll into Caen.

Montgomery's 'big show' was earmarked for first light on Saturday, 8 July. The show began early, at 9.50 p.m. the previous evening. For the first time in Normandy, the British general called in the support of the 'heavies' – the four-engined bomber fleet – to soften up the defenders by pummelling the German lines north of Caen. In an hour, the RAF sent 2,500 tons of high explosive tumbling down on the city. From afar *Frundsberg* supply officer Ewald Klapdor watched transfixed:

The strange spectacle casts its spell along the entire front. A wall of exploding flak lies over the city. The city is nothing more than a mushroom cloud rising into the sky. The most important city in Normandy after Rouen, Caen – city of William the Conqueror – is destroyed. He left there in 1066 to conquer England. Today English bombers wiped out his city.[28]

Feldwebel Edmund Brinke of 21st Panzer Division was driving in a convoy of armoured cars through Caen. The convoy ground to a halt. 'The noise was fantastic and I had a glimpse of everything flying about me – debris and dust and red flashes,' wrote Brinke later. 'One moment I had one foot on the car to scramble up inside, the next I was lying in a pool of blood and debris against the wall of the nearest building.' Half dazed, Brinke watched the world around him turned on its head. A pall of smoke lay over the ground, generated by fires and debris which had tumbled to the earth as Caen fell in ruins. 'When I struggled up I saw the terrible sights of bodies among the debris, the remains of our vehicles and half a German body over one of them,' Brinke recalled. 'Slowly, some signs of life began to appear. Only one of my comrades survived with me.'[29]

Across in the Allied lines 'officers and soldiers were jumping out of their slit trenches and cheering', one British regimental commander wrote. The raid 'improved morale 500 per cent'. Canadian troops looked on in awe at the macabre spectacle. 'Everything to our front seems to be in flames,' one unit reported. 'Wonderful for morale.' Some 400 residents of Caen perished in the bombardment, but the raid did little to weaken German resolve. 'Two thousand five hundred tons of bombs have merely succeeded in overturning a few armoured personnel carriers,' Kurt Meyer wrote scornfully.[30] In their bunkers and foxholes, the *Hitlerjugend* waited for the British to attack. 'Every last grenadier is at the ready,' Panzermeyer noted in his diary. 'We stare tensely out into the night awaiting the enemy's ground force's attack. Minutes pass without the silence being broken.' Meyer was astonished. No one came.[31]

It was another six hours before the Allies launched their drive on Caen. At 4.20 a.m. a ten-minute barrage opened along the front, before the tanks and infantry moved forward. The previous night's air raid proved to be a false dawn. When the British advanced, the men complained 'that not a single dead German or any enemy equipment had been found in the area that had been bombed'. As one senior RAF officer commented: 'The bombing made no material difference to the whole operation.'[32]

It was the artillery barrage and the relentless assault of the Commonwealth forces which did for the defenders of Caen. Three Allied divisions bore down on Caen from the north and north-west. 'The artillery fire is now unbelievable,' one Canadian regimental war diary recorded. 'We have never heard anything like it. The smoke, which is now rising, is so dense that it darkens the sun.'[33]

The onslaught was relentless. 16th *Luftwaffe* Field Division holding the line north of Caen simply caved in under the weight of attack from the air and on the ground. Its infantry, Eberbach reported that evening, 'suffered 75 per cent casualties'.[34] The ring of villages circling Caen began to fall one by one, but only after a bitter fight. 'The enemy expenditure of men and material in capturing the town is scarcely credible,' Kurt Meyer wrote. 'The Gods only know why this unoccupied town is being razed to the ground. Caen is enveloped in flames, smoke and ashes.' It was clear to Panzermeyer that his *Hitlerjugend* could not hold Caen much longer. 16th *Luftwaffe* Field Division had been 'swept off the face of the earth'; the Allied steamroller trundled onwards, regiments, battalions, companies, had been crushed. What was left of 12th SS fought 'like crabs' in a battlefield 'turned into a cratered landscape'. Meyer complained. 'The division's front is stretched to breaking, reserves are no longer available. I cannot stand this any more. We can hold out for perhaps a couple of hours longer, but there won't be any survivors from the divisions.' Orders or no orders, Kurt Meyer decided it was time to leave the rubble of Caen to the enemy.[35]

To the citizens of Caen, it was clear the Germans were about to pull out. Madame Luce Tribulet looked out on to her street after the bitterest day of fighting yet for her city. 'The road was sinister, just one German soldier looking at the horizon, his rifle on his shoulder,' she wrote.[36]

In the small hours of 9 July, Kurt Meyer visited his men. One month in Normandy had destroyed the *Hitlerjugend*. Even for a battle-hardened warrior like Meyer, the sight of his troops that night was shocking: 'They went to war weeks ago with fresh, blooming cases. Today, camouflaged, muddy steel helmets shade emaciated faces whose eyes have, all too often, looked into another world. The men present a picture of deep human misery.'[37]

Far behind the front, Erwin Rommel and Günther von Kluge toyed with the fate of Caen – and the fate of the men defending the city. 'Our troops must hold on,' Kluge told his deputy. 'There must be no withdrawal. The enemy must be stopped somehow.' Rommel had visited the front the previous day and watched the bitter battle for Caen. Now he buckled. Later that morning, the Desert Fox ordered Caen held 'at all costs'.[38]

The orders came too late. All through the morning of 9 July, the *Hitlerjugend* had been withdrawing south through Caen and across the Orne. As the final SS man crossed the river, the last bridge on the Orne was blown up. Two days later the *Hitlerjugend* was pulled out of the line to recuperate. Since 6 June it had lost nearly 5,000 men.

It took the Allies until well into the evening of 9 July to realize that Caen had been evacuated. Tentatively, the British and Canadians moved in as dusk fell upon the ruins of the city. Caen was theirs. But at what price, Briton Alexander McKee asked himself. The city was:

...just a waste of brick and stone, like a field of corn that has been ploughed. The people gazed at us without emotion of any kind; one could hardly look them in the face, knowing who had done this. These were the people we came to free, and this is the price that freedom cost.[39]

As the battle for Caen ended, so the battle for Hill 112 to the south-west of the city flared up after a ten-day hiatus, this time between the men of 9th and 10th SS Panzer Divisions and the British. The battle was no less hellish than it had been at the end of June. The Allies recognized its importance. So too did the Germans. There could be no breakout from

Caen – and no drive on Paris – if this height was still in Germany's hands. 'The division's grenadiers and panzer troops knew all too well how important Height 112 was to the enemy,' recalled Heinz Harmel, the *Frundsberg*'s commander. 'From the high ground there, they could, of course, follow the course of the battle on the right bank of the Orne, just as from there they could see the barrage balloons of the Anglo-American invasion fleet swaying in the breeze. The men knew how much depended on occupying or losing Height 112.'[40] The Allies would learn with bitter losses what the hill meant to the German *Landser*.

Before dawn on 10 July, the Allied fleet in the Seine Bay opened fire on the German front line. In two and a half hours 10,000 shells fell upon the 10th SS Panzer Division *Frundsberg*, holding Hill 112 and its approaches. 'The heavy naval gunfire howls and whistles above us and past, deep into the interior,' wrote Ewald Klapdor. 'At the front death leaps from shelter to shelter. It tears across the land. This Stygian darkness, this howling, hissing, crashing of exploding shells! A hurricane of iron transforms the terrain into a land of corpses and ruins.' One panzer regiment simply disappeared amid the maelstrom. 'Panzers, guns and heavy vehicles have been turned over like toys or tossed into craters,' Klapdor noted. Artilleryman Heinz Trautmann added: 'The howling of the shells and the whistle of the bullets had become for us familiar music; wherever we turned up with our tanks, there we would leave behind nothing but ruins and rubble. Every day our reserves grow less. Boys of seventeen are in the line, and grey old men, grandfathers. The homeland is sucked dry; there is nothing more to give.' Even by night the British came on. In the smouldering remains of a small copse of chestnut trees, Hans Greisinger waited for the onslaught. 'Tommy came twice in the darkness with shock troops, but we were able to drive him off,' he remembered. 'One of the attackers was hit and burned to death before he could get his flamethrower going.' Hill 112 did not fall to the British on 10 July. The slopes were a charnel house of British tanks. 'There were dead and wounded men lying all over the ground in the long grass, rifles stuck in the ground marking the positions of their own – a gruesome sight,' one British officer recalled. 'Tank crews who had managed to escape from their flaming vehicles were crawling back, their clothing and exposed parts of their bodies burnt, black all over from smoke, oil and cordite fumes.'[41]

The next day, a wave of Tigers swept inexorably across the cratered hillock. 'The Tigers rolled on, getting ever closer to the crest of the height,' wrote panzer grenadier Herbert Fürbringer, his head buried in the earth to shelter from the Allied counter-barrage. The panzers fell upon enemy Churchill tanks and an infantry battalion defending the hilltop, then fought out a brief, one-sided battle. Fürbringer continued:

The Tigers soon shot up several enemy tanks, one after the other, rolled over ditches and embankments. Some infantry fearlessly got an anti-tank gun into position on the left corner of the southern slope, furiously separating its supports. But one of the Tigers was faster. Before the enemy could aim his anti-tank gun, they were victims of the panzer's gun. The remainder saw all too clearly that there was nothing to be done and laid down a wall of thick smoke between them and the attacking panzer. The Tigers, however, rapidly drove through this pea-souper and came upon a scene every panzer crew could only dream of. Barely 100m from them was the enemy in position. Vehicles careered around wildly, crew and equipment loaded. Two Churchills were shot up in flames before they could direct their guns at the Tigers.

The mist faded again. The fighting this day swung to and fro. Attack, counter-attack, and attack again. That was the situation. Only when the barrage eased and the enemy artillery only shot off disruptive fire could one talk of relative calm. Material stood against men. And repeatedly it was men who were victim to this unequal struggle. It was men too who created this material and set it off, with the sole aim of destroying the other men, whom we called our enemies or opponents. What madness![42]

Panzergruppe West commander Heinrich Eberbach witnessed the ferocity of the battle in person when he visited Hill 112 on 13 June. His munitions officer noted in his diary, 'The landscape gives the impression of having been pulverized by hundreds upon hundreds of shells and churned up by a huge plough. In woods and on raised ground lie destroyed German and enemy armour, guns, anti-tank weapons and their trucks, smashed.'[43]

In this one height, barely rising out of the Orne valley, the struggle for Normandy was encapsulated. Blow. Counter-blow. Another counter-blow. And another, until one side or the other was worn out. And then in a few days it would flare up again. When the fighting lessened somewhat on 16 July, Herbert Fürbringer surveyed the scene:

The face of the hill had changed completely in a few days. Trees and bushes had been destroyed – all that was left was firewood – the ground had been upturned, the grass looked like it had been taken off by a hail storm. Next to the young soldiers lay *Panzerfaust*, *Panzerschreck*, machine guns, machine pistols and pistols. But also close to them lay the corpses of their fallen comrades. The few still alive on this height were merely waiting tensely for the next wave of the enemy. The living waited at their posts under the barrages which repeatedly came in. They knew that they would then fight back with the last ounce of strength.[44]

Amid the carnage of battle south-west of Caen, few *Landsers* found time to reflect upon the enormity of the struggle they had been sucked into. *Hauptscharführer* Ernst Streng drove through St Martin, 'a dreamy little pleasant village on the north-east slope of Hill 112'. By the time the *Waffen SS* and British had finished tussling over St Martin the village 'consisted of nothing but ruins' and 'broken stones'. St Martin and other towns and villages around Caen were subjected to destruction reminiscent of the great battles of matériel of a generation earlier on the Somme, at Passchendaele, at Verdun. In these towns and villages lay burned out armour, their dead crews still inside in most cases. Clouds of thick black smoke tumbled skywards above the burning houses and vehicles. Where once great forests and woods stood, there were merely the blackened stumps of the trunks left. This was the reality of the *Materialschlacht*, the battle of material, the battle of attrition, the weight of Allied firepower pitted against the German soldier. 'Every moment I expected deadly shrapnel,' read an unfinished letter on the body of a *Fallschirmjäger* at St Lô. 'When one hears for hours the whining, whistling and bursting of the shells and moaning and groaning of the wounded, one does not feel too well. I almost lost my mind. I chewed up a cigarette, bit into the ground. The others acted just like me. Altogether, it was hell.'[45] Across the battlefield drifted 'the sickly smell of corpses', recalled Erich Werkmeister, of the 10th SS. The troops ate 'sweet, hot peach soup'. The smell of the dead did not allow them to eat anything else. Panzer commander Willi Fey watched as his comrade Günther Hensel was killed in front of him. His lifeless body toppled into a flowerbed. 'A piece of shrapnel had taken off the back of his head,' wrote Fey. 'Poor Günther, who had looked forward with such impatience to his first battle. Now he was dead.' Another *Landser* stepped into his place.

At the base of the Cotentin peninsula, artilleryman Helmut Hörner cowered in a trench under the latest American shell and mortar bombardment alongside his *Feldwebel* when a round landed in the ditch. 'My comrade collapses next to me, his eyes still wide open,' he wrote in his diary. 'A grenade splinter pierced his steel helmet and tore a fist-sized hole in the back of his head. During the past few days, death has had a rich harvest.' The next day, 3 July, Hörner accompanied his 77th Panzer Grenadier Division in a counter-attack against US lines near La Haye-du-Puits between Carentan and the Atlantic coast. The death wrought upon his comrades the previous day was now repaid in full. 'My eyes witness the usual picture of devastation as we breach the enemy without much resistance,' he observed. 'A machine-gun nest with its dead, there a soldier lies who took a splinter while already in retreat. Two US tanks are now smoking ruins on the landscape. A dead American bends out of the turret tower. This day has cost the enemy considerably in men and matériel.' The following day Hörner himself was wounded by a mine.[46]

The sight of friends being killed, maimed, torn apart each day was as much as most men could bear. 'This terrible slaughter is truly horrendous,' one teenage *Gefreiter* wrote home. He continued:

It affects me deep down inside and it becomes ever harder for me psychologically when you've talked with a dear comrade and half an hour later all you can see of him are a few scraps of flesh – as if he never existed – or when comrades who lie badly wounded in front of you in a large puddle of their own blood, ask you for help with pleading eyes because usually they can no longer speak or it hurts to talk.

We are taken away as young men and return as old men. But we firmly hope for a better time after the war when at least we will have forgotten some of the bitter struggles and terrible memories of this war.

Grenadier Herbert Fürbringer of the 9th SS began smoking. He was soon getting through thirty cigarettes each day. 'My nerves were always on edge,' he recalled 'The dreadful sights I kept running into on the battlefield were having their effect.' Despite the cigarettes, his nerves did not improve especially.[47] *Frundsberg* staff officer Ewald Klapdor marvelled that men could endure this infernal, modern battlefield:

This unimaginable, mad barrage of fire paralyses all life in the area affected. For hours on end there's this dull rumble – monotonous – and the howl and bursting of heavy shells. The earth trembles for many kilometres. And then these gentlemen attack, thinking that our destruction is complete. They break in, or rather break through at one spot, but then the journey to the afterlife begins for them. An unbelievable quantity of ammunition, enormous losses, not the least gain. The moral strain on our men is very great and yet they have chased the English back. They achieve the unbelievable. [48]

Most *Landsers* put their faith in their Führer, their leaders and their comrades. 'There's no reason to paint too black a picture,' one soldier wrote home. 'There are so many good and elite divisions that we must get through somehow. It must turn out all right in the end.' The German soldier endured because he had to, because he did not know any differently. 'It was a situation for despair,' 116th Panzer Division's operations officer Heinz Günther Guderian explained, 'but there was no alternative but to keep one's nerve.' Some men were motivated to endure. SS battalion adjutant *Untersturmführer* Eduard Kalinowsky was convinced of the justness of the Nazi cause. He believed the propaganda of 'wonder weapons' and a change in Germany's fortune. 'We simply must stick it out,' he wrote to his wife. 'It is very hard for the soldiers here, for the English and Americans employ an enormous quantity of material, there is almost no end to their air attacks. But these too have abated in recent days and now it's our turn to give them proper hell.'[49] Kalinowsky's comrade *Untersturmführer* Fritz Stamm was similarly convinced of victory. He wrote home: 'When I see how they are working here at home and with what composure development of wonderful new weapons is being pursued, then my confidence is strengthened. With its accomplishments, such a nation has no need to be ashamed before the front. Who could conquer such a people may not depend on his guns and tanks alone, but the enemy does nothing else.'[50]

Kalinowsky and Stamm were the exception rather than the rule. Most German soldiers believed in the cause, possibly even in victory, but what drove them on was not ideology or propaganda, but what the Nazis called *Volksgemeinschaft* – spirit of community – that indefinable bond between soldiers in battle. Most evenings, the men drank and sang songs together to keep their spirits up, but they could never erase the backdrop of battle. 'We had a little "soldier's hour" and sang our soldiers' and folk songs into the night,' one *Landser* wrote to his wife. 'The evening sky glowed with fire and explosions. One always thinks the earth brings forth new life, but now it is death. What new order will emerge from this devil's symphony?' Company commander Emil Ebner found it increasingly difficult to justify counter-attack after counter counter-attack against an enemy superior in men and material. He watched in silence as his friend, one *Leutnant* Roeder, led a flamethrower assault towards American lines north of St Lô:

We made this flamethrower company move to the spearhead of the attack. All that it produced was a ghostly image and I asked the battalion chief why he made such soldiers advance like this in the dark, without preparations. He told me that it had been ordered this way by division. As I had feared, it was a failure. After roughly ten minutes, you could hear the fire of tanks coming from the direction where our flamethrower section was supposed to be. Then there was a deathly silence. We no longer heard the clatter of battle, even where our grenadiers had made progress in attacking. *Leutnant* Roeder did not return with his flamethrowers. He was killed. His was probably the first vehicle destroyed. The manner in which we attacked there was irresponsible and I feel angry when I think of it.[51]

The simplest way to survive, one *Oberscharführer* recalled, was to ignore the hell raging around you:

> The worst thing which could happen to a soldier was to wait for an attack – if you had time to think about imminent events and become aware of your situation and the consequences. Worse still is if you were surrendered to your fate, helpless, without any chance of being able to do something to counter it. As long as you are geared towards reacting in battle and immerse yourself in it, then you have no time to think about the situation. Our nerves could hardly cope with what was demanded of us during these days.[52]

Courage, comradeship and understanding on their own could not defeat the enemy. The *Wehrmacht* lacked men, but above all it lacked equipment. The battered *Panzergruppe West* was losing twenty-five vehicles every day to enemy air power, or from exhausted drivers crashing their wagons by night as they ran the gauntlet to the Normandy front. After one month in Normandy, the *Frundsberg* and *Hohenstaufen* had lost fifty-eight panzers and 216 trucks; heavy artillery had to be abandoned because of the lack of vehicles to haul them; more cars and wagons were out of action because spare parts were no longer reaching the front in sufficient numbers.

There was no antidote to the Allies' unsurpassed material supremacy; material supremacy which bred anger, discontent, and above all a feeling of helplessness. Alfred Gause, Rommel's chief-of-staff in North Africa and now chief-of-staff to *Panzergruppe West*, protested to the field marshal that the tide was turning against Germany: 'The enemy seemingly has an unlimited supply of ammunition. He fires twenty times more than we can. Against 80,000 rounds of ammunition, we were able to reply with just 4,500. The morale of our troops is good, but they cannot cope with courage alone against the enemy's use of material. The enemy substitutes artillery and bombs for courage and a lack of morale.'[53]

The enemy, 2nd Panzer Division's aristocratic commander *Freiherr* von Luttwitz complained, waged war 'regardless of expense'. Every day the Allies fired off 4,000 artillery rounds, even when there was no offensive or attack. The barrage rose to a crescendo when the enemy launched a major assault. 'We are losing one and a half to two battalions daily,' LXXXIV Corps commander Dietrich von Choltitz protested. 'After an artillery barrage lasting two to three hours, the enemy finds nothing but empty fox holes where there should be resistance.' The barrages were not unaccompanied. For in the sky, the birds of prey sought their next victim. The *Landser* called them *Jabos* – *Jäger* Bomber, or fighter-bombers, 'a burden on our souls' *Gefreiter* Helmut Hesse recalled. 'Unless a man has been through these fighter-bomber attacks, he cannot know what the invasion meant,' wrote Alexander Hartdegen, adjutant of the *Panzer Lehr* Division's commander. He continued:

> You lie there, helpless, in a roadside ditch, in a furrow on a field, or under a hedge, pressed to the ground, your face in the dirt – and there it comes towards you, roaring. There it is. Diving at you. Now you hear the whine of the bullets. Now you are for it.
>
> You feel like crawling under the ground. Then the bird has gone. But it comes back. Twice. Three times. Not till they think they've wiped out everything do they leave. Until then, you are helpless. Like a man facing a firing squad. Even if you survive, it's no more than a temporary reprieve. Ten such attacks in succession are a real foretaste of hell.[54]

Ernst Streng shook his fist at the spotter aircraft circling over his lines, all the more so because he knew he was powerless. 'Nothing stirs in our front line,' he observed. 'The infantryman knows that the slightest sign of life will bring down the shells from the enemy batteries – and they will be bang on target. Throughout the intense heat of the July afternoon our infantry lie motionless in their holes in the ground, following with their eyes every movement in the sky above.' In the skies of Normandy, the Allies had 'set a new standard in the art of war,' one newly-arrived *Fallschirmjäger* commented.[55] But, as Dietrich von Choltitz warned, unless there was some remedy to the crushing aerial superiority, the German Army in the west would 'simply be slaughtered':

> The enemy's fighter-bombers have achieved such air superiority that any movement on the roads is no longer possible. Aerial activity has become almost unbearable since it hinders any organized leadership. Even our artillery cannot fire any more as enemy fighter bombers cover them completely. [56]

Von Luttwitz was even more scathing of the *Luftwaffe*'s absence. The Allies' aerial supremacy was destroying the morale of his division. The Allies, the 2nd Panzer Division commander protested, enjoyed:

> ...complete mastery in the air. They bomb and strafe every movement, even single vehicles and individuals...Against this, the *Luftwaffe* is conspicuous by its absence. During the last four weeks the total number of German aircraft over the division's area was six...

Our soldiers enter battle low in spirits at the thought of the enemy's enormous material superiority. They are always asking: 'Where is the *Luftwaffe*?' The feeling of helplessness against enemy aircraft operating without any hindrance has a paralysing effect, and during the barrage this effect on the inexperienced troops is literally soul destroying – and it must be borne in mind that four-engined bombers have not yet taken part in attacking ground targets in the division's area.[57]

For all the enemy's material supremacy, he had failed to overcome the *Wehrmacht*. Outnumbered the *Landser* always was in Normandy, but never outfought. The enemy, many German soldiers observed, substituted material for courage and bravery on the battlefield. The Anglo-Americans waged war, *Major* Gerhard Lemcke of the *Hitlerjugend* complained, 'the way a rich man fights a war'. Rich, the Allies were, but tank for tank and gun for gun, the *Wehrmacht* was more than a match for its enemies. The 88-mm flak and anti-tank gun had no equal, the standard German machine gun, the MG42, fired faster than the Allied BAR or Bren guns – and the standard German infantry company carried more of them; the Allies had no answer to the *Nebelwerfer* rocket launchers; the Germans in return had no reply to the Allies' air power and heavy artillery. But what the invading armies lacked most was a tank the equal to the Panthers and Tigers. The most common German tank in Normandy was still the veteran Panzer IV, which at best was slightly superior to the Americans' standard armour, the Sherman. The Sherman was reliable, dependable, manoeuvrable. But it was outgunned by the much heavier Panthers and Tigers; in a head-to-head battle their main cannon could maul a Sherman. And a Sherman burned. It burned badly. Crew only had a fifty-fifty chance of escaping a blazing Sherman. The British relied on the Churchill and the Cromwell, reliable but lacking armour and firepower. In North Africa the British had complained their main battle tanks were outgunned by the Panthers and Tigers; the standard armament in Normandy was still the 75-mm gun, which had proved so ineffective eighteen months earlier. It was hardly surprising the Allied soldier began to develop 'a Tiger and Panther complex'.[58]

The *Landser* held a begrudging respect for the 'Tommy' and the 'Ami'. 'We felt they overestimated us,' one German soldier wrote. 'We could not understand why they did not break through. The Allied soldier never seemed to be trained as we were.' An order by a regimental commander in 2nd SS Panzer Division *Das Reich* captured the attitude of the *Landser* towards his opponent perfectly: 'We shall exploit the inferior quality of the enemy soldier as a fighting man. The enemy tanks are timid. If we tackle them energetically, we shall make them run and soon destroy them.' To the German soldier, the Tommy was dogged, determined, but he lacked initiative, as one report commented: 'The British infantryman is distinguished more by physical endurance than by special bravery.' *Panzer Lehr* commander Fritz Bayerlein was more scathing. 'The fighting morale of the British infantry is not very high – the enemy is extraordinarily nervous of close combat. He strives to occupy ground rather than to fight over it.' The most commonly heard comment among German soldiers in Normandy was 'Tommy is no soldier'.[59] After just six days of battle in Normandy, one grenadier battalion felt it has the measure of its English foe:

> The average German infantryman is at least equal to the finest English soldier in terms of attacking spirit. When it comes to enduring psychological burdens, then the German soldier is far superior to the English. The English avoid hand-to-hand combat and all-out infantry attacks, they believe the terrain is just far too good for concealed bocage fighting. In defence they are remarkably tough and show great courage. Their armoured forces possess little attacking spirit or skill.[60]

The Americans, by comparison, were predictable. You could set your watch by them, said panzer battalion commander Helmut Ritgen. 'Normally, the Americans were very aggressive in the morning, but at night they were tired and stopped fighting. From 7 p.m. till morning there was absolute peace.' The American stopped fighting at 7 p.m. or, 3rd *Fallschirmjäger* Division reported, 'at the smallest resistance'. In turn, to the ordinary Tommy or Ami, it seemed every *Landser*, every *Sturmmann* was a fanatical Nazi. The German soldier displayed 'brash arrogance, forlorn hope and outright despair'; he clung to 'the white hope' of the V1 and the rebirth of the *Luftwaffe*. But the Briton, Canadian and American never underestimated his enemy. 'If these soldiers that we're fighting here are demoralized German troops exhausted by years of war,' one British officer wrote to his brother, 'then I wouldn't have like to have faced the fresh-faced German soldiers of 1940.' The *Fallschirmjäger* in particular impressed the Americans – 'the best soldiers I ever saw' one battalion commander observed. 'They're smart and don't know what the word 'fear' means. They come in and keep coming until they get their job done or you kill 'em all.' That was hardly surprising. The ranks of 3rd *Fallschirmjäger* Division looked upon their commander, Richard Schimpf, 'as a god'; Schimpf, for his part, expected his men to live by his motto: a paratrooper dies in his foxhole. They were as good as his word.[61]

If the *Landser* cursed the enemy's material superiority, the *Luftwaffe* was simply overwhelmed by the Allies' aerial might. As June drew to a close, the German air force in the west was outnumbered fifteen to one. The rate of attrition was simply staggering. For every Allied aircraft downed, one German fighter was lost – a loss ratio the *Luftwaffe* simply could not sustain. Berlin had sent 1,000 new machines to the west since the beginning of June; by the end of the month, half had already been destroyed in battle or on the ground. On paper, *Jagdkorps II* should have been able to throw 1,300 fighters into the fray. In reality, it had barely 230 aircraft and 419 pilots available for operations. The task of defending the west was a daunting prospect. The day began at dawn and ended at nightfall; at the height of summer it meant sixteen and seventeen hours daily either on standby or in the air. At least two sorties were expected of the men each day, sometimes more. On the field, the men lived in tents close to their aircraft, ate their principal meal at midday – mainly goulash with potatoes – and slept, if possible, during the brief rests between sorties. After nearly a month of battle, the *Luftwaffe* crews had reached the limits of endurance, as *Leutnant* Gerhard Hanf noticed when he arrived at *Jagdgeschwader 1* late on 5 July. 'The three *Staffel*[62] which made up the *Gruppe* had been engaged on the invasion front since the first day and had suffered heavy losses and could no longer use some aircraft. To us, from a new, intact, fourth *Staffel*, it was clear that we were going to have to do our utmost in the operations to come.'

Oberleutnant Willi Heilmann, a *Staffel* commander in *Jagdgeschwader 54*, the *Grünherz* – Green Hearts – had arrived in France in mid-June, one of the pilots rushed to the west as the *Luftwaffe* had planned in the event of an invasion. But the plan had gone awry. 'Wherever we appear we find an oppressive enemy superiority,' he recorded in his diary on 20 July. 'For eight days now I've been leading the *Staffel*. During this time we have lost 50 per cent of our aircraft and every fifth pilot is a casualty – burns, broken limbs, dead.' The mood in the *Geschwader*[63] mess was grim.

The life expectancy of a pilot in France in the summer of 1944 was less than a month, and his aircraft would remain operational for just five hours. Fresh faces arrived to replace the pilots lost over Normandy. 'All of them were mere boys,' Heilmann observed, 'and their pale faces betrayed that they knew what lay ahead of them.'[64]

Death in the skies was compounded by death on the ground as the *Jabos* ranged across Normandy and north-west France searching out the *Luftwaffe*'s forward air bases. *Gruppe* commander Karl-Heinz Langer complained: 'Our aircraft can only take off the moment 'the sky is clear', so they do not risk an immediate aerial attack and do not reveal their airfield, which would otherwise spark carpet bombing raids and low-level attacks in the next few hours.' Heilmann's airfield at Villacoublay, on the south-eastern edge of Paris, was also singled out by the Allied air forces:

Thirty Mustangs suddenly roared over the airfield like a poisonous swarm of angry hornets.

Low-level attacks. A quick rush for cover. A Focke crashed in flames into the deep narrow valleys to the west of the airfield.

A wild rush began. Men tumbled head over heels into the dugouts which had been built into the walls behind the hangar. The last mechanics and pilots jostled each other in twos and threes to get into the small foxholes between the pens.

And then infernal thunder and explosion. The earth shook beneath the hammer blows. Flames, smoke, the sharp whistle of shrapnel. Whole aircraft wings, undercarriages and tail units were flung into the air and a rain of smashed fragments was strewn over the tortured ground. The earth quaked beneath an apocalyptic flail.

This hellish storm, which lasted a bare quarter of an hour, seemed like an eternity. The whole northern edge of the airfield had changed its face – ploughed up and smashed to pieces. Where once green pines had invited one to a summer siesta there was now an impassable jungle of torn and splintered tree trunks, with the green foliage dripping an oily black. Destroyed aircraft, burning oil, blazing petrol stores and broken human bodies.

When *Luftwaffe* units did get into the air, frequently they did not give battle because they could either not penetrate the Allied fighter screen, or because an attack would achieve nothing more than a pyrrhic victory. 'No one can judge what it meant to be airborne in a few minutes, a futile and hopeless mission against overwhelming odds,' Willi Heilmann noted. 'A short dogfight and then a rapid scramble for home because the enemy came in from every quarter to the help of their friends and neither the finest flying technique nor the craziest bravery was of any avail.' The *Luftwaffe* wasn't fighting. More often than not it was evading battle. 'You had to disappear from the scene of your fight,' wrote Heilmann. 'To remain in the battle was suicide.'[65] The 6 July was a prime example; *Luftflotte 3* sent 450 aircraft into the Normandy skies. They got nowhere near the front. The Allied air umbrella simply brushed them away. The *Luftwaffe* could not return to the skies the next day because its losses that day were simply too heavy. Goebbels bitterly commented:

The enemy air force has achieved victory over the *Luftwaffe*. It's just too humiliating and depressing that we were not once able to achieve a noticeable victory in the air by employing strong fighter forces. You can well imagine what effect this has on the German people, because it cannot be hidden from them. The *Luftwaffe*, and above all its Supreme Command, no longer has a good reputation among the German public.[66]

The sight of German fighters could do wonders for morale. Heinz Harmel, commanding the SS *Frundsberg*, recalled the sight of twenty-five to thirty Me109s roaring over his men one evening in June. 'Because such a sight was so rare, the troops spontaneously celebrated and got excited. "Finally our fighters are here!" A wave of relief passed through the ranks.' The radio reports talked merely of *Luftwaffe* victories and successes in the west; but the *Landser* saw for himself the unfettered might of the enemy air forces and the wealth of war material pouring ashore on to the Normandy beaches. The campaign of 'revenge' was also proving to be a false dawn. Despite more than 2,000 V1s hurled at southern England – mainly London – the British had not thrown in the towel. Of course, German agents and newspapers continued to report the devastating effect of the reprisal weapons. 'Entire rows of houses collapsed like a pack of cards,' one report stated. Goering publicly praised his flak men. After all, they were doing what the *Luftwaffe* was not – bombarding London. The V1 was 'meting out terrible retribution for the crime of the terror raids'. Hitler was delighted by the V1's effects. The flying bomb was bringing relief to the home and western fronts alike. 'We are saving men and aircraft,' the Führer told officers launching the wonder weapon. 'The V1 is both a machine and a bomb, and it does not need any fuel for the return flight.'[67] The German public was spoon-fed similar stories, stories of a wonder weapon wreaking havoc in the British capital. And the V1, the Nazi Party organ *Völkischer Beobachter* proclaimed, was 'merely the beginning'. Other weapons would follow. And then the enemy's storm would finally break:

> When it does, we will enjoy the moral high ground, an eagerness in our hearts, a strength of will, and also a strength of belief which will be equal to the sternest tests until the sun shines once more upon the German people, who are fighting for victory, for their lives and for freedom against a world full of enemies.[68]

The ordinary German was also impressed, as the *Sicherheitsdienst* monitors reported from the city of Schwerin:

> The destruction cannot be too great; hatred for England is finally finding an outlet yearned for, for so long, a revenge without mercy

or compassion. If one action of the Führer ever found an unqualified response, it is this vengeance. The only regret is 'that we cannot get even with the Americans'.[69]

In July 1944, the V1 was Germany's sole 'trump card'. For the first time since the days of Blitz in the winter of 1940 and 1941, the English capital was 'in the line of fire', Joseph Goebbels celebrated. 'Theatres and cinemas are for the most part closed. Life in London has been badly disrupted by our new weapon. We hope that it will be disrupted even more in the future.'[70]

The problem was that the British had the measure of the Germans' 'trump card'. The majority of Allied fighters could out run the 'doodlebug', as the British public nicknamed the flying bomb for its distinctive sound, but shooting the V1 down remained a challenge. The interceptors had barely seven minutes to destroy the missiles over the Channel and southern England before the V1 entered London's twenty-mile deep defensive belt of barrage balloons and anti-aircraft guns. But shoot the V1 down the British did. And in great numbers. In the first month of the flying bomb offensive, 1,240 V1s were destroyed by the defenders. Of the 4,361 flying bombs launched at London and the south-east, barely three in ten reached the target area. The *Engländer* bore the vengeance stoically. In London, British officials noticed 'strain, weariness, fear and despondency' among the capital's inhabitants: 'Many think these raids worse than the Blitz.' The flying bomb offensive was the main topic of conversation in London for more than a month, but for all the destruction, the Briton saw the V1 for what it was: a nuisance. 'These raids are extremely unpleasant,' the monitors of opinion noted, 'but will make no difference to the outcome of the war.'[71]

It didn't take long for the mood in Britain to filter back to the German public. Even before June was out, some sections of the populace were becoming disillusioned with the V1. It simply had not lived up to the hype. 'People expected the retaliation would be sudden and destructive based on earlier propaganda,' the opinion monitors in the *Sicherheitsdienst* reported; now the newspapers were talking about *Störungsfeuer* – disruptive fire – not destruction. Still, after months of promises, the 'revenge weapons' were about all the public had to believe in. The SD observed: 'Faith in the overall "revenge action" is nevertheless undiminished, especially because people are confident that the German leadership has even more "unknown trump cards".' The German people 'have high hopes it will bring about a fundamental change in the course of the war in our favour'.[72]

A fundamental change in the course of the war was a hope which dominated the thoughts of every soldier in Normandy, German and Allied. As the senior National Socialist Leadership Officer in the west wrote, the question the *Landser* asked most frequently was: How can we win the war? He reported the views of the troops frankly:

> The German soldier asks where the *Luftwaffe* is, if we are really fighting for the final decision in the western theatre.
>
> All conversations and talk have once again confirmed that the German soldier regards himself a superior warrior to the Englishman and American. But what use is this feeling of superiority if the enemy's use of material and men is so great that even the strongest determination to fight can no longer bring success?
>
> We must not paint the picture of a crisis, but things must be seen as they are. The men don't want words, they want action.[73]

Above all, the men wanted success. They wanted victories. All they experienced were defeats. 'The lack of any success at all affected the men very badly,' *Gefreiter* Adolf Hohenstein of 276th Infantry Division recalled. 'You could feel the sheer fear growing. We would throw ourselves to the ground at the slightest sound, and many men were saying that we should never leave Normandy alive.' Heinz Harmel watched as the discipline of his men declined in the *Frundsberg*. Some skulked off to repair panzers, others behind the front lay idle rather than round up cattle to feed the division. Harmel acted: 'If you neglect appearance, attitude and discipline it has an adverse impact on the fighting front.' 276th Infantry Division's Curt Badinksi was appalled by the lack of discipline behind the front line in Normandy. 'One man I encountered in Mons was dodging the column and taking part in looting,' he informed his ranks in an order of the day. 'When challenged, he declared he had come out of hospital. He had thrown away his weapons in a weapons dump. He was having a rest period on the way to the front. In reality, he was a malingerer of the worst kind who was too much of a coward to go to the front.'[74]

The decline in morale and discipline did not go unnoticed in the Allied camp. 'Only the true fanatic remains convinced of a German victory,' Eisenhower's intelligence chiefs noted after interrogating prisoners of war.

The balance of Germans can be divided into three classes: those who realized the inevitability of Germany's defeat, but who still retained some faith in the Führer, those who did not think at all (a very high percentage) and those who realized their betrayal.

Whichever 'class' a *Landser* belonged to, he continued to fight on. Even after six weeks of interrupted fighting, of enemy supremacy in the sky and on the ground, the Allies conceded that the will of the German soldier was not broken.[75]

Of course, it could not go on like this, Erwin Rommel knew. The enemy's material superiority had to take its toll eventually. In thirty-three days of battle, his armies had accounted for 1,300 enemy tanks and armoured vehicles and 266 aircraft. But, as the field marshal was forced to concede, 'our own losses are also considerable'. In the *Panzer Lehr* Division only two in every five panzers were still running. Its losses were not untypical. 3rd *Fallschirmjäger* Division was down to just one third of its original strength. In all, the German Army in the west had lost more than 80,000 men since 6 June. Replacements totalled just 10,670. Rommel's commanders screamed for fresh blood. 'If no more reserves are provided, the corps will be annihilated, because it will not retreat,' Choltitz warned. 'The entire battle is a terrible bloodbath as never before seen in eleven [sic] years of war.' Paul Hausser's plea was identical. His Seventh Army was being bled white. 'Strength has sunk to such an extent that commanders no longer guarantee resistance against major enemy attacks,' Hausser warned. What replacements were arriving in the west were merely cannon fodder. Two out of three replacements sent to *II Fallschirmjäger* Corps alone became casualties of war. 'Lack of experience is the chief reason,' Hausser commented bluntly.[76]

Berlin could offer nothing, as one of Hitler's staff officers explained. 'We are no longer in a position to offer much, since all theatres of war are making the same demands.' Heinrich Himmler pleaded to the head of the country's labour service, the *Reichsarbeitsdienst*, Konstantin Hierl, to spare men and boys from construction tasks and repairs in the wake of bombing raids to feed his *Waffen SS* divisions in Normandy. 'If there were not six SS divisions there,' he told Hierl, 'we wouldn't be able to hold the front.' A combing out of the labour service should provide 6,000 fresh soldiers, the SS leader suggested. 'We must ensure that these divisions are not bled white for they are – and I use this word very rarely – decisive for the outcome of the war in the truest sense of the word.'[77]

Six thousand men when the Army in Normandy had suffered more than 80,000 casualties. The cupboard was bare – and there was no hiding it, as Frenchman Albert Pipet observed in mid-July watching German replacements – 'just kids' – moving up to the front:

Bent, exhausted, heavily weighed down by packs of ammunition, one youth headed for the front groaning. A lot cried, I felt sorry for them. 'To the front... How many kilometres?' one young paratroop-er asked me. 'Water! Water! Please!' another asked. Officers called out, pushing ahead through this mass of helmets and guns.[78]

In mid-July 1944 the battle for Normandy was turning against Germany. Rommel knew it. Kluge knew it. There was nothing to counter the Allies' unprecedented use of material. The troops were worn out. The equipment was worn out. There were no reserves to throw at the front. All that came from Berlin was the same old order: Hold the line at all costs. 'Those in high places thoroughly misjudge things,' Kluge complained. 'From the course of the battle during the past few days I have the impression that something has constantly been eating away at our front. Things have gone downhill.'[79]

Field Marshal Erwin Rommel said what Günther von Kluge could not, would not. It was time for politics to come into play. The war in the west was lost. On 15 July he set down his plea for his Führer:

> The position on the Normandy front is becoming more difficult by the day and is approaching a grave crisis.
>
> Our losses are so high that the fighting power of the divisions is rapidly sinking. The freshly-arrived divisions are inexperienced in battle and because of the lack of artillery, anti-tank guns and close-combat anti-tank weapons in sufficient numbers, they are not in a position to thwart major enemy offensives launched after hours of heavy bombing and barrages. The fighting has shown that even the bravest unit is gradually worn out by the enemy's material. As a result, they lose men, weapons and ground...
>
> On the enemy's side, fresh forces and masses of material flow to the front every day. The enemy's reinforcements are not disrupted by the *Luftwaffe*. The enemy's pressure continues to get stronger. Under these circumstances, we must expect the enemy to break through our thinly-held front and thrust into the heart of France...
>
> Everywhere, the troops fight heroically, but the unequal battle is nearing its end. In my opinion, it is necessary to draw the appropriate conclusions from the situation. It is my duty as the Commander-in-Chief of the Army Group to express my views unequivocally.[80]

Fate would intervene before Adolf Hitler cast his eyes on Erwin Rommel's report.

Notes
1. Ambrose, *Citizen Soldiers*, p.56.
2. Hamilton, ii, pp. 677, 684-8.
3. Meyer, Hubert, *12 SS Panzer Division Hitlerjugend*, pp.97, 104.
4. ibid., p.108.
5. *Western Mail*, 27/6/81.

6. Ellis, i, p.278; KTB AGp.B, 26/6/44.
7. Meyer, Hubert, op. cit., p.117.
8. Irving, *Trail of the Fox*, pp.359-60.
9. Fürbringer, Herbert, *9 SS Panzer Division Hohenstaufen*, pp.274-6.
10. Klapdor, p.231.
11. Cited in Hastings, *Das Reich*, pp.163-4.
12. Weidinger, *Comrades to the End*, p.301.
13. McKee, *Caen: Anvil of Victory*, pp.167, 171.
14. Belfield and Essame, *The Battle for Normandy*, p114.
15. Meyer, Kurt, *Grenadiers*, p.141; Shulman, p.156; Weidinger, *Comrades to the End*, pp.307-08; KTB PzGp West, 2145 Hours, 29/6/44. IWM AL1901/1.
16. KTB AOK7, 30/6/44. IWM AL528; KTB PzGp West Appendices, 30/6/44. IWM AL1412/15-16; Tagesmeldung AGp.B, 1/7/44. IWM AL1531/3.
17. Emde, Joachim, *Die Nebelwerfer*, p.155; Meyer, Kurt, op. cit., p.141.
18. Irving, op. cit., p.363; KTB Jodl, 29/6/44. IWM AL930/4/2; FCNA, p.398; Wolfram Bericht, 29/6/44. NA CAB146/338.
19. PzGp West, Ia Nr.116/44, 30/6/44; KTB OB West, Hours, 1/7/44; KTB PzGp West Appendices, 1/7/44. IWM AL1901/2.
20. KTB OB West, 1740 Hours, 1/7/44. IWM AL785/1/1; Rundstedt interrogation, NA WO205/1022; Messenger, *Last Prussian*, pp.197-8; KTB Schmundt, 1/7/44.
21. Geyr to Rommel, 6/7/44. Rommel, p.467n.
22. Tagesbefehl OB West, 3/7/44. Messenger, op. cit., p.199.
23. Rommel, p.499; KTB OB West, 3/7/44; KTB Ruge, 3/7/44, 4/7/44. Ruge, pp.205, 207
24. KTB Ruge, 28/7/44. Ruge, p.239.
25. Report on a trip to the front by von Kluge, 4-5/7/44. KTB OB West Appendices, 5/7/44. IWM AL785/1/1.
26. KTB AGp.B, 5/7/44; KTB Ruge, 4/7/44. Ruge, p.207.
27. D'Este, Carlo, *Decision in Normandy*, p.302; Eisenhower-Montgomery, 7/7/44. Eisenhower Papers, p.1982; Montgomery to Eisenhower, 8/7/44. Pogue, p.186.
28. Klapdor, p.265.
29. Blandford, p.159.
30. D'Este, Carlo, op. cit., p.316; Stacey, p.158; Meyer, Kurt, op. cit., p.145.
31. Meyer, ibid., p.145.
32. D'Este, Carlo, op. cit., p.316.
33. Cited in Meyer, Hubert, op. cit. p.145.
34. KTB PzGp West, 8/7/44. IWM AL1901/1.
35. Meyer, Kurt, op. cit., pp.146-8.
36. McKee, op. cit., p.220.
37. Meyer, Kurt, op. cit., p.150.
38. Telecon Rommel-Kluge, 0655-0715 Hours, 9/7/44. KTB OB West Appendices. IWM AL785/1/1; KTB PzGp West, 1150 Hours, 9/7/44. IWM AL 1901/1.
39. McKee, op. cit., p.207.
40. Fürbringer, Herbert, op. cit., p.311.
41. Klapdor, p.275; McKee, op. cit., pp.235-6; How, *Hill 112*, p.192; Carver, *Second to None*, p.115.
42. Fürbringer, Herbert, op. cit., p.315.
43. Leleu, Jean-Luc, *10 SS Panzer Division Frundsberg*, p.98.
44. Fürbringer, Herbert, op. cit., pp.324-5.
45. Balkoski, p.222.
46. Leleu, Jean-Luc, op. cit., p.101; How, op. cit., p.155; KTB Hörner, 2-3/7/44. Horner, Helmut, *A German Odyssey*, Fulcrum, Golden, Colorado, 1991.
47. Letter from *Gefreiter* Karl B, 20/7/44. Jahnke, Karl Heinz, *Hitlers letztes Aufgebot: Deutsche Jugend im sechsten Kriegsjahr 1944-45*, pp.57-8; How, op. cit., p.152.
48. Klapdor letter, 11/7/44. Klapdor, p.282.

49. Hastings, *Overlord*, pp.212, 259; Agte, p.402.

50. Agte, p.458.

51. Hastings, op. cit., p.260; Perrigault, Jean-Claude, *La Panzer Lehr Division*, pp.257-8.

52. Report by SS-Oscha Stettner, 9/7/44. Stöber, Hans, *Die Sturmflut und das Ende: Geschichte der 17 SS Panzergrenadier Division Götz von Berlichingen*, Band I, p.165.

53. Besprechung OB HGrB mit Chef des Gen.Stabes PzGr West, 10/7/44. Bericht *Hauptmann* Lang, 10/7/44. N117/23. Cited in Klapdor, p.296.

54. Extract from battle experiences from recent operations by 2nd Panzer Division, 17/7/44. SHAEF Intelligence Notes, No.23, 17/8/44. NA WO219/1908; KTB AOK7, 6/7/44. IWM AL973/2; Ambrose, op. cit., p.48; Carell, *Invasion – They're Coming*, p.124

55. How, op. cit., p.203; Stimpel, ii, p.206.

56. KTB AOK7, 6/7/44. IWM AL973/2.

57. Extract from battle experiences from recent operations by 2nd Panzer Division, 17/7/44. SHAEF Intelligence Notes, No.23, 17/8/44. NA WO219/1908.

58. Ambrose, op. cit., p.488; NA WO205/5b.

59. Fritz, p.61; Jentz, ii, p.186; NA WO208/393; *Panzer Lehr* Division-Inspector General of Panzertruppen, 22/6/44. Cited in Wilmot, p.477; NA WO219/1908.

60. Bericht III/858 Grenadier Regiment, 10-12/6/44. IWM AL1697/3.

61. Ambrose, *Citizen Soldiers*, pp.488-9; NA WO219/1908; *Völkischer Beobachter*, 1/7/44; Ambrose, *The Victors*, p.194; G-2 Section, US First Army, '3rd Fallschirmjäger Division in the recollections of POWs, Evaluation by US First Army, December 1944', cited in Stimpel, ii, pp.144-6.

62. The basic Luftwaffe formation of up to a dozen aircraft.

63. A squadron of around 12 Staffel.

64. Caldwell, pp.242-3; Heilmann, pp.21, 37, 42; Frappé, op. cit., p.94.

65. Frappé, ibid., p.148; Heilmann, pp.21-2, 39.

66. KTB AOK7, 6/7/44. IWM AL973/2; TB Goebbels, 27/6/44.

67. N756/162. Harmel: Additifs à l'étude P163, p.4. Leleu, p.168; KTB Flak Regiment 155, 20/6/44, 3/7/44, 5/7/44. IWM MI14/1038/1-2 .

68. *Völkischer Beobachter*, 29/6/44.

69. SD Schwerin, 30/6/44. Steinert, *Hitler's War and the Germans*, p.260.

70. TB Goebbels, 10/7/44.

71. British Ministry of Information Home Intelligence reports 27/6/44-4/7/44 and 11/7/44-18/7/44. NA INF1/292.

72. SD Meldung, 28/6/44.

73. OB West, NSFO, Nr.5/44, 23/6/44. RH 19 IV/149. Cited in Wegmüller, p.250.

74. Emphasis in the original. Hastings, op. cit., p.216; Divisions Sonderbefehl, 21/7/44. RS3-10/4. Leleu, Jean-Luc, op. cit., p.189; Tagesbefehl 276 Infanterie Division, 27/7/44. SHAEF Weekly Intelligence Notes, No.27, 14/9/44. September 14th 1944. NA WO219/1909.

75. SHAEF Weekly Intelligence Summary No.17, 15/7/44. NA WO219/1921.

76. KTB AOK7, 2350 Hours, 15/7/44. IWM AL973/2; Appendix to OB West, Ia Nr.58955/44, 22/7/44. IWM AL510/1/2.

77. Telecon von Buttlar, OKW/WFSt, and Ia OB West, 0830 Hours, 13/7/44. KTB OB West Appendices, 13/7/44. IWM AL785/1/2; Himmler to Kierl, 21/7/44. Jahnke, Karl Heinz, op. cit., pp.58-9.

78. Perrigault, Jean-Claude, *La Panzer Lehr Division*, p.263.

79. Telecon Kluge-Rommel, 2037-2045 Hours, 16/7/44. KTB OB West Appendices, 16/7/44. IWM AL785/1/2.

80. Annex to OB West Ia Nr 5895/44, 21/7/44. 'Observations on the Situation', OB HGr.B, 15/7/44. IWM AL785/1/3.

Chapter 8

The Blackest Day in German History

We General Staff officers must all accept our share of the responsibility.

Count Claus von Stauffenberg

The black Horch staff car tore down the Norman lanes at speed, leaving a trail of dust clouds in its wake. Its passenger was becoming increasingly restless. For two hours now Erwin Rommel had looked out of his vehicle upon a succession of blazing German vehicles. Overhead, marauding enemy fighter-bombers waited to pounce on any traffic they sighted. Barely hours earlier, the field marshal had attended a gloomy briefing with the commanders of I and II SS Panzer Corps and the fiery leader of the *Hitlerjugend*, Kurt Meyer. A fresh British offensive at Caen was imminent. The four officers agreed its outcome was not in doubt; it would be an enemy victory. 'The division will fight and the grenadiers will die in their positions, but they will not prevent the British tanks from rolling over their bodies and marching on Paris,' Meyer told Rommel curtly. The field marshal nodded. 'Something has to happen!' he said frankly. 'The war in the west has to end! But what will happen in the east?'[1]

The staff car continued its tortuous journey eastwards, back to the château at La Roche-Guyon which was the field marshal's headquarters. Around 6 p.m. on this bright July evening, Monday 17th, the Horch neared the village of Livarot. The road, one of Rommel's staff noted, was littered with German vehicles 'recently set on fire – there had to be a strong enemy low-level fighter unit at work here'. The field marshal ordered his driver, *Oberfeldwebel* Daniel, to take a secluded side-road. The Horch rejoined the main road just outside the town of Vimoutiers. And there the field marshal's luck ran out. Rommel's look out screamed: 'Spitfire!' as two enemy fighters bore down on the staff car flat out, just a few feet off the ground. The field marshal glanced behind to see the wings of the enemy aircraft belching fire. Seconds later shells tore down the left-hand side of the Horch. Rommel's face was struck by shards of glass, shrapnel fractured his skull and cheekbone. He lost consciousness immediately. Daniel's left shoulder and arm disintegrated. He lost control of the staff car, which bounced off a tree stump then careered across the lane, throwing Rommel into the middle of the road, before ending up buried in a ditch at the roadside. 'Field Marshal Rommel lay spattered with blood and unconscious on the ground,' his staff noted. 'Blood was pouring from the many wounds on his face, especially his eye and mouth.' One of the fighters returned to fire at the wounded as they lay on the Normandy earth. The French doctor who treated the field marshal within the hour did not expect him to survive his injuries. Erwin Rommel would play no more part in the battle for Normandy. For the time being Günther von Kluge would take over Rommel's duties, but the German public would not be told. To them, Erwin Rommel still commanded 'Army Group Rommel'.[2]

As Erwin Rommel languished in a *Luftwaffe* hospital far behind the front line, his long-time adversary unleashed the offensive he believed would finally achieve a breakthrough in Normandy. Bernard Law Montgomery had Caen. What he wanted was to finally destroy the German Army in the west. 'We want to engage the enemy in battle, to write off his troops and generally to kill Germans,' he wrote to Eisenhower. 'Exactly where we do this does not matter.' The battle-ground Montgomery chose once again was the Orne valley south-east of Caen, the latest plan to deliver victory was codenamed Goodwood, a thrust by hundreds of tanks through the German lines to gain open ground. When Goodwood began, Montgomery promised, the front would 'burst into flames'. The general was confident. 'The time has come to have a real show down,' Montgomery told his superiors in London. 'The possibilities are immense: with 700 tanks loosed to the south-east of Caen, anything may happen.'[3]

The British preparations had not gone unnoticed. On the eve of Goodwood, Heinrich Eberbach demanded fresh forces to bolster his lines. The enemy offensive would begin the following day, the *Panzergruppe West* commander warned on 17 July. Kluge could spare him nothing. Heinrich Eberbach would have to make do with what he already had. He had at least learned from the bitter fighting for Caen not to pack his front line with his best troops. Hastily, the Germans had formed a ten-mile deep defensive belt in the Caen bulge; infantry divisions – the battered 16th *Luftwaffe* Field Division – at the front, panzer grenadiers in the second line and the armoured blade of the *Hitlerjugend* and *Leibstandarte* in the rear. But by 17 July 1944, that blade was blunt. The *Leibstandarte* could muster just 1,440 men, the *Hitlerjugend* 6,000, and between them there were just eighty panzers fit for action.[4]

Dawn was slowly shedding light on the Norman landscape when the first sound of impending battle arrived. It was around 5.30 a.m. on Tuesday, 18 July 1944, six weeks to the day since Allied troops set foot in France. Around Colombelles, just east of Caen, Werner Kortenhaus and his comrades in 21st Panzer Division watched the Allied bombardment with morbid fascination: 'We saw little dots detach themselves from the planes. Then began the most terrifying hours of our lives. It was a bomb carpet, regularly ploughing up the ground. Among the thunder of the explosions we could hear the wounded scream and the insane howling of men who had been driven mad.'

21st Panzer company commander Gerhard Bandomir added: 'The initiative of each of us withered. We just sat and waited to die, unable to do anything.'[5]

For four hours, the bombers came; 4,500 of them. The first wave alone released 6,000 tons of explosives; two more waves followed them. And then the artillery barrage – from land and sea, a quarter of a million rounds in all. The men in the front lines were buried. The bombs turned over the earth, filled in fox holes, covered weapons. Telephone lines were cut, radio trucks smashed, guns and panzers disappeared beneath piles of mud or were covered with soil. When the enemy attack came, they were not ready for battle. 'The bombardment of 18 July was the worst we had ever experienced in the war,' Tiger company commander *Leutnant Freiherr* von Rosen recalled. 'Some of the 62-ton machines lay upside down in bomb craters, thirty feet across. They had been spun through the air like playing cards. Two of my men committed suicide; they weren't up to the psychological effect. Of my fourteen Tigers, not one was operational.' His colleague Gerhard Bandomir wrote ominously: 'I came to the conclusion that a new era of warfare had begun – a preview of the nuclear age.'[6]

The barrage and bombardment were at their height when the Allied armour rolled across the Orne around 7.30 a.m., herded via the six bridges which spanned the river. The *Hitlerjugend*'s youthful commander, Kurt Meyer, ordered his men forward to bar the enemy advance alongside 21st Panzer Division. Meyer was not optimistic about their chances. 'We have no illusions,' he wrote. 'Officers and men know the futility of the battle. They await operational orders in silence but with a will to fulfil their duty to the bitter end.'[7]

Major Hans von Luck was fresh back from a brief spell of leave in Paris. The night before he had been sipping champagne by the Seine. Now Luck jumped into a Panzer Mark IV and rolled towards the front. He got as far as the village of Cagny, three miles south-east of central Caen. The enemy front line at dawn that Tuesday had weaved through the city and in places jutted across the Orne. Now, by mid-morning, enemy tanks were rolling southwards, bypassing Cagny. The village was all but deserted, save for four 88-mm flak guns pointed skywards and their crew waiting for the next air raid. Luck ordered the *Luftwaffe* crew to turn their guns at the advancing tanks. The flak commander refused to help. Hans von Luck was in no mood for inter-service rivalries. 'I drew my pistol and levelled it at him and said: "Either you're a dead man or you can earn yourself a medal."' The guns of Cagny turned the British advance into a rout. The 21st Panzer Division regimental commander returned to the village that afternoon. 'An almost indescribable sight met my eyes,' Luck later wrote. 'The cannons were firing one salvo after the other. One could see the shots flying through the corn like torpedoes. In the extensive cornfields to the north of the village stood at least forty British tanks, on fire or shot up.'[8]

The same sight greeted German commanders wherever they looked upon the Goodwood battlefield: shot-up Allied tanks. Goodwood stalled on the slopes rising east of the Orne in the late afternoon of 18 July, as one British officer lamented: 'Everywhere wounded or burning figures ran or struggled painfully for cover, while a remorseless rain of armour-piercing shot riddled the already-helpless Shermans.' The cost of blunting Goodwood was high. Gerhard Bandomir was one of its early victims. He marched into English captivity shortly after midday. '18 July was a hot and sunny day in Normandy,' he remembered decades later. 'However, for all of us it was a most dismal and depressing day. We were powerless to do anything.' Sepp Dietrich was more hopeful. 'We have maintained our overall cohesion in the face of unprecedented air attack and mass tank formations,' he reported of I SS Panzer Corps' performance in halting Goodwood. 'Yet I must say that the position has inevitably deteriorated, as we have lost a good deal of ground, and this can only be to the enemy's advantage. I see their next effort as being the most crucial for both them and us.' That night, Heinrich Eberbach too submitted a report to his superiors: 'The day's losses were very heavy. Of what was 16th *Luftwaffe* Field Division, there is effectively just the staff and some of the rear services left.' Meyer's *Hitlerjugend* struggled to make its way to the front line in the face of the Allied armour. By the day's end it was down to just fifteen operational panzers.[9]

It wasn't the enemy advance which was killing the German Army in the west. It was the constant attrition. At no point during 18 July had men like Heinrich Eberbach or Sepp Dietrich expected the German front to collapse. But they knew what would happen if their lines did break. Richard Dischen, a staff officer in 1st SS Panzer Division, overheard

Dietrich say 'that only a miracle could hold us together if they did get through'. As it was, 'the British had greatly extended their salient into our territory and we had no chance to erase it'. Dischen himself visited the men holding the line that July afternoon. 'Even though they had suffered greatly from various privations, their morale remained amazingly good,' he observed. Yet the *Landser* was reaching the limit of endurance, as Eberbach warned: 'Daily losses by the divisions in a struggle which is terrible all the time are so great that in a short time their strength will be used up, and it will be no longer possible to make good that strength.'[10]

Heinrich Eberbach was becoming increasingly frustrated. No one was listening to his warnings. And no one in Berlin or East Prussia had any inkling of the gravity of the situation. On 19 July he snapped. The phone at the offices of the Inspector General of Panzer Troops rang dead on 6 p.m. The *Panzergruppe* commander was losing patience with the High Command. 'We need more men and material,' Eberbach protested. 'Dietrich and Bittrich are shocked that the SS offers so little in the way of replacement troops.' The panzer general demanded one of Hitler's senior staff visit the front at last. In more than six weeks of fighting neither the Führer nor any of his officers had been anywhere near the Normandy battlefield. 'The front,' Eberbach signed off, 'feels it has been left in the lurch,' then slammed the phone down.[11] Seventh Army's commander Paul Hausser also protested to Berlin, but not quite so bluntly:

Our forces have been severely depleted by the heavy losses suffered in defensive fighting. Enemy artillery and mortar fire caused the fighting strength of our infantry to fall continuously. The enemy fires off a tremendous amount of ammunition – twenty to one in his favour – and for major attacks it increases to a barrage sometimes lasting for thirty hours. In a lengthy battle, this causes the strength of our infantry to drop from regiment to company strength. Losses from previous battles have thinned out the troops in the main line of resistance so much in many places that the only result must be penetrations. The psychological pressure on troops exposed to such material superiority is particularly felt when commanders are lost.[12]

Against such a gloomy backdrop, Günther von Kluge arrived outside the village of St Pierre-sur-Dives, far to the east of the front line to confer with his battlefield generals. Hausser, Eberbach, I SS Panzer Corps' commander Sepp Dietrich and LXXXVI Corps' leader Hans von Obstfelder gathered in dense woodland away from the prying eyes of Allied aerial reconnaissance for a discussion which dragged on for more than four hours. The generals agreed: the battle could not go on as it was doing. 'Experience in the last few days has taught us that the present conduct of battle will only lead to unbearable losses and therefore the loss of everything,' Kluge balefully concluded.[13] With the conference over, Günther von Kluge began the tortuous journey back to his château on the Seine at La Roche-Guyon. It was now mid-afternoon on Thursday, 20 July 1944. When he reached his headquarters in the early evening, he would find the world changed.

Shortly after 3 p.m. a young *Oberst* had strolled into Günther Blumentritt's office at *OB West* headquarters in St Germain. Eberhard Finckh, in charge of overseeing supplies for the entire Western Front, delivered a thunderbolt. 'I have to report, sir, that there has been a Gestapo putsch in Berlin,' Finckh told his superior. 'The Führer has been assassinated.'[14] Suddenly, the fighting at the front didn't seem to matter any more.

For more than a year discontent had been festering in the ranks of many senior generals and staff officers. Adolf Hitler was leading Germany to destruction. Most had sided with the Führer while the war went well. But defeats in Russia at Stalingrad, Kursk and the Ukraine, in North Africa, then Sicily, then Italy convinced many officers that the war was lost. Rommel, Rundstedt and Kluge were among their ranks. But they could not bring themselves to act against Hitler and his regime, for ten years earlier they had sworn an oath of allegiance to defend it to their dying breath:

> I swear by God this holy oath that I will show unconditional obedience to Adolf Hitler, leader of the German nation and people, Supreme Commander of the *Wehrmacht*, and I am ready as a brave soldier to lay down my life at any time for this oath.

Some men, like Rundstedt, hid behind the oath; he would never act against the regime. Nor too his chief-of-staff, Günther Blumentritt, who spoke for many of his fellow generals. 'An oath is an oath and remains an oath, particularly in "impossible" or "hopeless" situations – that's when the oath is needed most,' he said later. 'Troops fighting for their lives have a basic right to expect their commanders to be loyal, even when the going gets too rough.'[15] Some like Rommel and Kluge wrestled with their conscience: to act or not to act. But in the spring of 1944, a handful of officers were prepared to break their sacred oaths. Their efforts revolved around one man, a young *Oberstleutnant* named Claus von Stauffenberg.

A career soldier, born in 1907, Stauffenberg had served with distinction as a panzer division supply officer in France and Poland, then as a staff officer with the Army High Command. His attitude to the Nazi regime verged between indifference and disgust, but the longer he spent at OKH, the more he became convinced the war was lost – and only Hitler's removal could spare Germany disaster. In February 1943, Stauffenberg returned to the front, as the operations officer of 10th Panzer Division in North Africa. His tenure lasted less than two months; he fell victim to an air attack on 7 April, an attack which cost him his right arm, two fingers on his left hand and his left eye. But the young officer was not placed on the reserve list, despite his terrible injuries. In October 1943, he was recalled to duty. His post: a staff officer in the offices of the *Ersatzheer*, the Replacement Army which provided fresh blood for the fighting fronts, in Berlin's Bendlerstrasse. 'You know, I feel I must do something now to save Germany,' he told his wife. 'We General Staff officers must all accept our share of the responsibility.'[16] Stauffenberg had come to the right place; the headquarters of the *Ersatzheer* was the seat of revolution.

The putsch, as the conspirators in the Bendlerstrasse quickly realized, was more than a mere assassination. The entire Nazi Party apparatus – the propaganda machine, the police and security services, the SS – had to be stifled or eliminated, even if Hitler himself were killed. In the autumn of 1943 and opening months of 1944, the grand plan for the coup, *Walküre* – Valkyrie – began to take shape. The moment the attempt was made, orders would emanate from the offices of the *Ersatzheer* to units throughout occupied Europe to impose martial law, to dissolve the Nazi Party and arrest its instruments of power, to seal off Berlin. A new government would be formed with *General* Ludwig Beck, Chief of the General Staff until 1938 when he had clashed with Hitler over the invasion of Czechoslovakia, at its head and Field Marshal Erwin von Witzleben, the retired former commander of *OB West*, as the Supreme Commander of the *Wehrmacht*. By June 1944 the plans were ready; what the conspirators needed now was opportunity.

The German Army in the west was also infested with conspirators: at Rommel's headquarters, at Kluge's headquarters, at *Luftflotte 3*, from France's military governor Karl-Heinrich von Stülpnagel to Rommel's chief-of-staff Hans Speidel. They were in the know – and willing to act if Hitler was removed. But what of the two field marshals? Their support was crucial; it was not guaranteed. For two years, Günther von Kluge's staff at Army Group Centre on the Eastern Front had sought the field marshal's support. Kluge vacillated. At times he supported a coup, at others he refused to participate. In the autumn of 1943, Clever Hans finally agreed to back a putsch – but only if the Führer was dead. Days later he was wounded in a serious car accident. By the time he was recalled to service in July 1944, the field marshal had changed his tune

1. 'Waiting for Tommy' - the eternal *Wacht am Kanal* (watch on the Channel).

2 and 3: A wall 'built with fanatical zeal' to stand firm 'under all circumstances'. The propaganda image of Hitler's vaunted *Atlantikwall*. (*Author's collection*)

4. 'Rommel set an example in the *West*' – the field marshal and his staff inspect the Channel defences, January 1944.   (*Author's collection*)

5. The fruit of Rommel's tour - wooden ramps intended to flip over an incoming landing craft and send its occupants tumbling into the sea. (Author's collection)

6. The Desert Fox and the Old Hand... Rommel confers with his superior Field Marshal Gerd von Rundstedt, *Oberbefehlshaber West*. *(Author's collection)*

7. A formal portrait of the icy *Grossadmiral* Karl Dönitz, Commander-in-Chief of the *Kriegsmarine*. Dönitz demanded his men 'prepare a bloody welcome for our enemies and bar their entry to Europe'. *(Author's collection)*

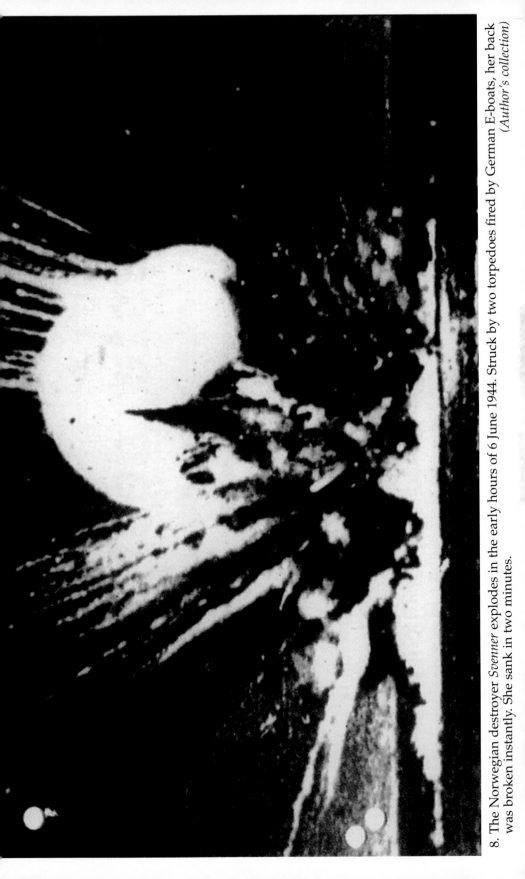

8. The Norwegian destroyer *Svenner* explodes in the early hours of 6 June 1944. Struck by two torpedoes fired by German E-boats, her back was broken instantly. She sank in two minutes. *(Author's collection)*

9 and 10. Death in the *Atlantikwall* – German soldiers killed in the fighting for the beach defences on 6 June, 1944.   *(Author's collection)*

r Ausgabe
„Freiheit und Brot"
Berliner Ausgabe

/ 57. Jahrg. / Einzelpr. 15 Pf. / Auswärts 20 Pf.
Berlin, Mittwoch, 7. Juni 19

ÖLKISCHER BEOBACHTER

Kampfblatt der nationalsozialistischen Bewegung
Großdeutschlands

Überfall auf Europa setzte zwischen Le Havre und Cherbourg ein

oskaus Vasallen mußten Invasion beginner

Der mit aller Energie sofort aufgenommene Kampf
nserer Wehrmacht gegen die Aggressoren ist in vollem Gange

die Entscheidung

VB. Berlin, 6. Juni.

Berlin, 6. Juni

Der seit langem erwartete Angriff der Briten und Nordamerikaner gegen die nordfranzösische Küste hat in der letzten Nacht begonnen. Wenige Minuten nach Mitternacht setzte die Seine-Bucht unter gleichzeitigen heftigen Bombenangriffen im Gebiet der Seine-Bucht starke Luftlandeverbände ab. Kurze Zeit später schoben sich, geschützt durch schwere und leichte Kriegsschiffeinheiten, zahlreiche feindliche Landungsboote auf gegen andere Abschnitte der Küste vor. Die Abwehr ließ sich an keiner Stelle überraschen. Sie nahm den Kampf sofort mit aller Energie auf.

Die Luftlandetruppen wurden zum Teil schon beim Absprung erfaßt und die feindlichen Schiffe bereits auf hoher See wirksam unter Feuer genommen. Viele Fallschirmeinheiten wurden aufgerieben oder gefangen, andere von hochgehenden Minen zerrissen. Trotz fortgesetzter heftiger Luftangriffe und schweren Beschusses durch die feindliche Schiffsartillerie griffen die Geschütze des Atlantikwalls ebenfalls sofort in den Kampf ein. Sie erzielten Treffer auf Schlachteinheiten und den sich einschebenden Landungsbooten. Der Kampf gegen die Invasionstruppen ist in vollem Gange.

Die Sowjetoffensive im Westen

Von
Helmut Sündermann

Auf Befehl Moskaus haben sich nun die Briten und Amerikaner entschließen müssen, das unabsehbare Risiko so lange hinausgezögerten Invasion auf sich zu nehmen. Damit setzt eine ungeheure Kraftprobe an, für die der Feind seine seit Jahren gesammelten und aufgesparten Reserven in breitester Front einsetzen wird. Die deutsche Führung ist auf diesen Waffengang vorbereitet, in dem es um die Verteidigung Europas, seiner Freiheit und ewigen Größe geht. Das deutsche Volk ist sich bewußt, daß es eine ganze soeft bewährte Seelenkraft aufzubieten hat, um diese sieghafte Entscheidung, die nicht nur ein Kampf der Waffen ist, herbeizuzwingen. Es tritt in diesen neuen Abschnitt des Krieges mit dem unerschütterlichen Mut und Vertrauen ein, die es in nun fast fünf Jahren eines harten und opfervollen Ringens stets beseelt haben, in ihm große Erfolge schenkten und ihm die Kraft

gegeben haben, auch allen Wechselfällen gegenüber, in Ehren zu bestehen und nur unerschlossenen alle Energien anzuspannen, um seine Zukunft zu sichern.

In dieser Stunde wächst es erst recht an den Anforderungen, die der Generalangriff des Feindes an uns stellt, an der Größe der geschichtlichen Aufgabe, deren Bewältigung in unsere Hand gegeben wird. Wir gehen in diesen Kampf mit der leidenschaftlichen Entschlossenheit, ihn nicht früher zu beenden, bis der Sieg unser ist und damit Leben, Ehre und Freiheit unseres Volkes auf Generationen hin gesichert sind. Das deutsche Volk schart sich in dieser schicksalsschweren Stunde in festem Glauben an den Triumph ihrer gerechten Sache um den Führer, den Garanten des Sieges und einer Zukunft, der unserer Nation würdig ist und den Sinn unserer Geschichte erfüllt.
VB.

Die ersten Stunden
Von Kriegsberichter Adolbert Schwarz

Panzerkampf bei Caën

USA.-Flugzeugträger im Atlantik versenkt

Stockholm, 6. Juni.

11. 'The attack on Europe begins between Le Havre and Cherbourg - Moscow's vassals have to launch the invasion.' – The battle in the West dominates the official Nazi Party organ on 7 June, 1944 . *(Author's collection)*

13. *Panzergrenadiers* leap out of half-track to avoid incoming *Jabos* – Allied fighter-bombers. (*History in the Making Archive*)

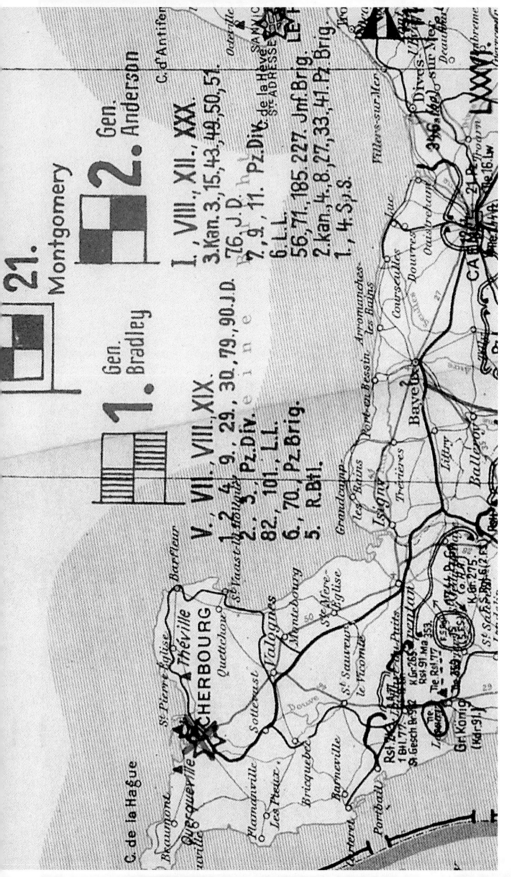

14. *Lage West – Situation West* – as recorded by the staff officers in the German High Command on July 3, 1944. The stars over Cherbourg

15. The armour of *Schwere Panzer Abteilung 503* – Heavy Tank Detachment 503 – takes cover from Allied air power in a wood south-east of Caen, July 1944. *(History in the Making Archive)*

17 and 18. Too late to save the day... *Panzer Brigade 111* rushes through Lorraine in
September 1944 as the Western Front caves in.

(History in the Making Archive)

again. His meeting with Hitler before taking up his appointment in France fired him up again; at the beginning of July 1944 Günther von Kluge was in no mood for talk of a putsch.

Erwin Rommel on the other hand appeared ripe for conversion to the plotters' cause. Since mid-April, his chief-of-staff had been gnawing away at the Desert Fox. Hans Speidel had arrived in the west fresh from the Eastern Front with a warning from Jodl ringing in his ears: beware Rommel's *afrikanische Krankheit* – his African sickness, or pessimism. Speidel did nothing of the sort.

With his round face, spectacles and calm bearing, Hans Speidel seemed more like a doctor or professor. The forty-six year old *Generalmajor* had fought with distinction, most recently in the Ukraine, extricating his troops from Russian encirclement in the vast Cherkassy pocket. And yet for more than a year, Hans Speidel had been party to the plans for a putsch. He openly referred to Hitler as 'that asshole at the Berghof' – except in Rommel's presence – and introduced a succession of figures to the field marshal's La Roche-Guyon headquarters. The problem was that Erwin Rommel was not for turning. The melancholy and depression which had beset the field marshal through 1943 evaporated in the spring of 1944 as Rommel became convinced his defensive measures would thwart the invasion. But when they failed, Erwin Rommel realized only politics could save the day. 'It's high time for the politicians to act as long as we still hold any kind of a trump,' he confided in his naval adviser Friedrich Ruge, who added cryptically in his diary. 'He had to lend his name, but a name alone did not yet mean success.'[17]

But when it came to the crunch, Erwin Rommel would not lend his name to any military revolt. When *Luftwaffe Oberst* Caesar von Hofacker, adjutant of the military governor in France, called on the field marshal in early July to suggest 'coercing' Hitler, Rommel refused to partake in any action. It was not the impression Hofacker took away from his meeting. That night, 9 July, the *Luftwaffe* officer told his fellow plotters that the Desert Fox could 'scarcely be restrained' from taking part in the coup.[18] Hofacker's words would seal the fate of the Desert Fox.

In those bitter days of mid-July, with Caen gone, with his forces being bled white daily, Erwin Rommel was convinced disaster was staring Germany in the face. But the field marshal could not bring himself to act against Hitler. He still believed in the Führer; it was Hitler's advisers who were at fault for the present crisis, for misleading, for failing to put him in the picture about the true gravity of the situation. No, Erwin Rommel would not rise up against his leader.

Instead, he drafted a memorandum, more accurately an ultimatum.

145

'Military leaders in responsible positions should express their opinions openly,' he told Ruge. It was as close to revolt that Erwin Rommel came: 'Everywhere, the troops fight heroically, but the unequal battle is nearing its end. In my opinion, it is necessary to draw the necessary political conclusions from the situation. It is my duty as the Commander-in-Chief of the Army Group to express my views unequivocally.'[19]

The word 'political' was stricken from the final draft, but Erwin Rommel had burned his bridges.

Opportunity and necessity in equal measure forced the plans for a putsch ahead in July 1944. Opportunity in the form of a promotion for Claus von Stauffenberg which gave him personal access to the Führer, reporting on the progress of forming new divisions; necessity in the form of the Gestapo net closing on the conspirators' circle. Arrests at the beginning of the month of outlying supporters of the coup gave greater impetus to the plotters. Stauffenberg's chosen method of assassination was a time bomb, 2lbs of explosives hidden inside a briefcase. He aborted one attempt on 11 July at Hitler's mountain retreat near Berchtesgaden – Himmler and Goering were not present. Four days later, the Führer was back at the Wolf's Lair in East Prussia when Stauffenberg reported again; again Himmler was absent, and the *Oberst* called off the coup for a second time. The tension among the plotters was unbearable; they had all been ready to go on 15 July. Finally, on 19 July Stauffenberg received a third summons from Hitler's headquarters. The Führer wanted to hear about the new divisions being raised. The *Oberst* was to report to the Wolf's Lair for the midday conference the following day, Thursday, 20 July 1944. Stauffenberg was resolved to act once and for all.

Word passed down through the plotters' intricate web. They realized the stakes. 'We have only a five to ten per cent chance of success,' Caesar von Hofacker, the officer who had told his fellow conspirators Rommel was behind them, admitted to a comrade. 'If the affair miscarries, it is the hangman who will get us.'[20]

Claus von Stauffenberg's Ju52 transport aircraft touched down at Rastenburg airfield around 10.15 on Thursday morning. From there he faced a four-mile journey by staff car to the Wolf's Lair, then a two-hour wait before the conference began in a wooden briefing hut. The discussion – focused on developments on the Eastern Front – was under way when the *Oberst*, the time fuse in his briefcase bomb already running, was ushered in. It was a little after 12.30 p.m. The officer placed his briefcase under the large oak table where the Führer was studying the latest situation maps. Then almost as quickly as he entered, Stauffenberg left the briefing room 'to make an urgent phone call'. He had no intention of returning.

The conference continued in his absence. Army staff officer Adolf Heusinger resumed his depressing assessment of the situation in the east. 'Unless at long last the army group is withdrawn from Peipus, a catastrophe...' Heusinger's words ceased at 12.42 p.m. There was a blinding yellow flash and loud crack as 2lbs of explosives went off. The briefcase vaporized, leaving an 18in crater in the briefing room's floor. The blast blew out the windows, panels and beams came down, and a dust cloud filled the shattered room. Of the twenty-four people in it, four were mortally wounded, but none of them was Hitler. The bomb exploded less than six feet from the Führer, yet he came around to find himself lying on the floor, close to a door, covered with debris. His hair was burned but beyond minor cuts and bruises and two burst eardrums, the Führer was relatively unharmed.

The dust was still clearing as Stauffenberg left Wolf's Lair bound for the nearby airfield. Thirty minutes later he was in the air on his way back to Berlin.

What Stauffenberg did not know as his Heinkel He111 aircraft crossed East Prussia heading west to Rangsdorf airbase was that the bomb had failed. At his headquarters in Benderstrasse, a drab thirty year old office block in Berlin's western heart, the telephone rang shortly after 1 p.m. 'Something fearful has happened,' a voice from the Wolf's Lair reported. 'The Führer's alive.'[21] And yet for the conspirators there was no thought now of going back. For better or worse, the putsch would proceed.

One man stood in the plotters' way: *Generaloberst* Fritz Fromm, commander of the *Ersatzheer*. Only Fromm could give the *Walküre* signal, the order for internal unrest to the scattered commands of the German Army within occupied Europe. And Fromm was not convinced there was internal unrest. There were rumours, but nothing more. At 4.10 p.m., the *Generaloberst* was put through to Field Marshal Keitel, Hitler's Chief-of-Staff, at the Wolf's Lair. 'What the hell is going at the Führer's headquarters?' Fromm demanded. 'The wildest rumours are buzzing around in Berlin.' Keitel calmed him down. 'Everything's fine.' Fromm persisted. 'I've just received a report that the Führer has been assassinated.' The OKW Chief-of-Staff put him straight. 'Rubbish. There was an attempt but thankfully it failed.' Fritz Fromm put the telephone down. He refused to issue the *Walküre* orders.

Events were already beyond Fromm's control. The conspirators had seen to that. While Fromm talked with Keitel, the men of the *Grossdeutschland* guards battalion began mobilizing, ordered to seal off the governmental heart of the German capital.

147

Back at the Benderstrasse, Claus von Stauffenberg had finally arrived, full of confidence and aghast at the indecision among his fellow conspirators. 'He is dead,' he announced breathlessly. 'I saw the whole thing from outside. The explosion was as if the hut had been hit by a 6-in shell. It is hardly possible that anyone could be alive.' When Stauffenberg was told Fromm was blocking *Walküre*, the *Oberst* stormed into his superior's office. Fromm refused to act; Keitel had assured him that the Führer was alive. Stauffenberg cut him off: 'Field Marshal Keitel's lying as usual. I personally saw Hitler being carried out dead.' When told some *Walküre* orders had already been issued, the *Ersatzheer* commander exploded and demanded the conspirators be arrested for treason. But it was Stauffenberg's comrades who drew their pistols. Fritz Fromm was ushered into a side room under arrest. 'There's never been anything like it,' he raged. 'An officer acting against his Supreme Commander. The German uniform is besmirched for eternity. Never again can we wear this tunic with honour. My officers are traitors.'[22] Now the coup could proceed. The teleprinters began whirring frantically.

By now it was past 5 p.m. – more than four hours since the failed explosion and only now was *Walküre* beginning to take shape. Tension and anxious waiting at Bendlerstrasse were replaced by frenetic activity. In the late afternoon, a string of senior conspirators started to arrive at the *Ersatzheer's* headquarters. First came Ludwig Beck, then panzer general Erich Hoepner, earmarked to take over as commander of the *Ersatzheer*. By 6.30 p.m. the government quarter of Berlin was cordoned off. Apart from the failure to kill Hitler, *Walküre* was running smoothly.

It was coming up to 5 p.m. when the first news of the coup began to filter through to Paris. The news came from Stauffenberg. 'The coup d'etat is in full swing,' he told Caesar von Hofacker. 'We're now occupying the government quarter of the city.' Hofacker was ecstatic. 'Hitler is dead,' he excitedly told his fellow conspirators. 'Perhaps Himmler and Goering as well. It was a terrible explosion.'[23]

The news was exactly what Hofacker's superior Karl-Heinrich von Stülpnagel wanted to hear. It was time to set his plans in train. The organs of Nazi rule in Paris – the SS and the *Sicherheitsdienst* – had to be eliminated. He summoned two trusted officers into his office. 'There's been a Gestapo putsch in Berlin and an attempt on the Führer,' he declared. 'The SD must be arrested and senior SS officers with them. If they show fight, you can shoot.' The wheels were in motion, the military governor told Ludwig Beck minutes later. Beck nodded with satisfaction. But the former Chief of the General Staff warned Stülpnagel there was a long and difficult road ahead of them. 'Whatever happens, the die is cast. We can do nothing else but go ahead,' Beck urged. Stülpnagel reassured him. 'We'll go ahead. I'll see to that.'[24]

Whatever Karl-Heinrich von Stülpnagel did, only the acts of one man alone in the west on Thursday, 20 July, made any difference. But Günther von Kluge knew nothing of the burgeoning coup. The Commander-in-Chief, West, had spent the day, as was his custom, visiting the front. It was shortly after 6 p.m. when his staff car finally pulled into the grounds of the château at La Roche-Guyon which was home to Army Group B's headquarters. He found the army group's chief-of-staff, the wily, bespectacled Hans Speidel, waiting for him. There had been an attempt on the Führer's life. Clever Hans' face barely flickered. It barely flickered again when Beck was patched through to him around 6.30 p.m. The retired general was convinced he could persuade Kluge to join the conspiracy. 'Herr Kluge, the fate of Germany is at stake!' Beck begged. But the field marshal held a transcript of a radio bulletin in his hand. 'Today an attempt was made on the Führer's life,' he read. 'The Führer himself suffered no injuries beyond light burns and bruises. He resumed his work immediately...'[25] He refused to commit himself to the coup.

But now the teleprinter in the castle clicked, bearing orders in the name of Field Marshal von Witzleben. Hitler was dead it proclaimed. The field marshal was Germany's new supreme authority. 'The German soldier is confronted with a historic task,' the proclamation concluded. 'The salvation of Germany will depend on his energy and morale.' The printer had barely finished when it whirred into life again. 'Broadcast communiqué not correct. The Führer is dead. Measures ordered to be carried out with utmost despatch.' The two teletypes had a profound effect upon Günther von Kluge. For a moment he believed Hitler was dead. 'A historic hour has arrived,' he told his chief-of-staff Günther Blumentritt, then began plans for a ceasefire on the Western Front. The field marshal was resolved to support the coup.[26]

His resolve lasted no more than minutes. The teleprinter which had brought news of the Führer's death now brought a contradictory order from Keitel at Hitler's East Prussian headquarters. 'The Führer is alive! In perfect health! *Reichsführer* SS C.-in-C. *Ersatzheer*. Only his orders valid.' Walter Warlimont, a senior staff officer at the Wolf's Lair, confirmed Kluge's now growing doubts. 'The Führer is in full health,' Warlimont, himself injured by the bomb blast, told the field marshal. 'Lying officers have formed a new regime and declared a state of emergency.' The coup had failed. The Führer was alive – and if he was, then Günther von Kluge could no longer support any putsch.[27]

In such an atmosphere did Karl-Heinrich von Stülpnagel and Caesar von Hofacker arrive at Kluge's sumptuous headquarters with darkness

149

falling across north-west France. Beck had hoped Stülpnagel's personal intervention would sway Kluge, but it was Hofacker who spoke most eloquently. 'The Army and the nation will thank you,' he begged Kluge. 'Put an end in the west to bloody murder. Prevent a still more terrible end and avert the most terrible catastrophe in German history.' The field marshal was not for turning. He would not throw his hand in with 'just a bungled affair'. Stülpnagel was surprised. 'I thought, field marshal, you knew about it,' he told Kluge. 'Not in the slightest.'[28]

So Günther von Kluge would not act. But what if the field marshal's hand was forced? Now Stülpnagel informed him he had already ordered the arrest of the Party apparatus in Paris. Kluge exploded. 'Such indiscipline I never heard of.' He immediately demanded the order rescinded. It was too late. The troops were already on the streets rounding up the SS and SD. Stülpnagel would have to resolve matters himself. 'You must get back to Paris and release the arrested men,' he ordered the military governor, adding coldly: 'The responsibility is wholly yours.'[29]

As their staff cars were summoned, Stülpnagel and Hofacker urged Kluge to reconsider. 'It is your honour that is at stake and the honour of the Army,' Hofacker implored him. 'The fate of the nation is in your hands.' The field marshal brushed him aside. 'No', said Kluge. 'Regard yourself as suspended from duty.'[30] The pair drove off into the night.

Major Otto Ernst Remer was beginning to have his doubts about the coup. The commander of the *Grossdeutschland* guards battalion had carried out his orders for the past two hours and more: seal off the government quarter of Berlin. But the major was becoming increasingly convinced it was not the Party revolting, rather the military. Disobeying orders, Remer answered a summons from propaganda minister Joseph Goebbels to meet him in his study in Hermann Göring Strasse. Remer had instructions to arrest Goebbels, but the major decided to hear the minister out. The Führer was alive, Goebbels assured him; he had spoken to him minutes earlier on the telephone. 'I promised that as an honest National Socialist officer I was willing under all circumstances to do my duty, true to my oath to the Führer,' Remer told him. Next, Goebbels called the Wolf's Lair and passed the receiver over to the young officer. '*Major* Remer. Do you recognize my voice?' Adolf Hitler asked. 'They tried to kill me but I'm alive. You are to restore order in Berlin for me. Use whatever force you consider necessary.'[31] Remer was promoted *Oberst* on the spot, then left Goebbels' residence to begin recalling his men; instead of sealing off the capital's government quarter, they would defend it.

The conspirators in the Bendlerstrasse had no idea of Remer's defection yet. But it was clear to Field Marshal Erwin von Witzleben, the

150

Supreme Commander of the *Wehrmacht* in a post-Hitler Reich, that the putsch had miscarried. He reached the Bendlerstrasse around 8 p.m. in a fury. 'This is a fine mess,' he blustered, before tearing a strip off Stauffenberg and Beck. The latter tried to assuage the field marshal, assuring him that the putsch was in full swing, but Witzleben would have none of it. 'Everything you are all doing is nonsense,' he told the conspirators bluntly, then left the Bendlerstrasse in a huff. He wanted nothing to do with the bungled coup.[32]

Only Claus von Stauffenberg seemed not to lose hope. On the telephone he continued to reassure outlying commands, notably France, that the putsch was proceeding. 'It's very likely that counter-orders will be given by Führer HQ,' he warned. 'Don't believe them. The Reich is in danger and as always in times of danger, the soldiers take charge.'[33]

But the radio continued to report otherwise. At 10 p.m., the national service gave a fuller account of the failed coup:

Providence protected the man who holds the destiny of the German people in his hands. The fact that the Führer is alive is crucial for us. The overriding emotion of every German is the feeling of gratitude for his salvation. 'With the Führer to victory' – that is the slogan of the German people. All the more so now.

To most conspirators in the Bendlerstrase, it was clear the game was up. Remer's men were congregating outside the *Ersatzheer* offices, not to defend the building but to seal it off; the major was determined to crush the coup. In the Bendler building, Friedrich Olbricht, one of the leading putschists, gathered his staff. 'Gentlemen, for a long time we have been anxiously watching the way things were going. There is no doubt. We're heading for disaster.'[34]

In the minutes following Olbricht's announcement, the headquarters of the *Ersatzheer* descended into civil war as officers declared their support either for Beck or Hitler. The Führer's loyalists grabbed their guns and began marching through the Bendler block asking: 'For or against the Führer?' In the mêlée which followed, Stauffenberg was shot – but not fatally – and Fromm released from his temporary custody. Determined to regain authority, Fromm rounded up the conspirators and arrested them.[35] The putsch was over.

In Paris, Theodor Krancke was baffled. The *Vizeadmiral* had been reading the teletypes coming off the printers at *Marinegruppe West*'s headquarters. First Witzleben's orders had arrived, followed minutes later by an order of the day from Karl Dönitz:

Men of the *Kriegsmarine*. The treacherous assassination attempt on the Führer fills each one of us with righteous anger and bitter fury at our criminal enemies and their hired henchmen. Providence spared the German people and their *Wehrmacht* from unimaginable misfortune. In the Führer's salvation we can see renewed proof of the justness of our struggle. Now we shall rally even more closely around the Führer, we will fight even harder until victory is ours.

The *Vizeadmiral* needed clarification. He picked up the telephone and called Dönitz at Hitler's headquarters in East Prussia, where he had hurried after being summoned. The grand admiral calmed down his western commander. The Führer was indeed alive and orders bearing Witzleben's signature should be dismissed. Krancke agreed. The *Kriegsmarine* would play no part in the coup unfolding in Paris.[36]

Instead, Krancke watched as the symbols of Nazi power in the French capital were rounded up by the army. This was a bloodless coup. The ranks of the SS and SD, 1,200 strong, put up no resistance. They were herded off meekly into captivity by truck to military prisons around Paris.

But as the coup made progress, so the plot also began to unravel. First came news from Berlin. The putsch had failed. The wolves were at the door, Stauffenberg reported. 'It's all over in Berlin. All's lost,' one of Stülpnagel's staff lamented.[37] The military governor himself arrived with news of Kluge's vacillation. Then, at one minute before 1 a.m., the martial music on German national radio ceased. In its place, a forty-minute speech by Hitler recorded an hour and a half earlier 'so that you can hear my voice'. The Führer continued:

A tiny clique of ambitious, unscrupulous and criminally insane officers plotted to kill me and at the same time wipe out the command of the German *Wehrmacht*. The bomb was planted by *Oberst* Graf von Stauffenberg and exploded six feet to my right. Several of my closest comrades were seriously injured, one has died. I am uninjured, save for minor superficial burns and bruises. I regard this as confirmation of the mission assigned me by Providence to continue towards my goal.

At a time when Germany's armies find themselves in the most difficult struggle, a tiny clique has arisen which believed that today, as in 1918, it could drive a dagger into our back. They have made a very grave mistake this time...

It is impossible, for hundreds of thousands, millions of brave men give their all at the front, while at home a small group of ambitious, miserable wretches try to undo this self-sacrifice. This time we are going to settle accounts in the manner we know best as National

Socialists. I am convinced that every good officer and every brave soldier will realize this in this hour.

What Germany's fate would have been had this plot succeeded is something very few people can imagine. I thank Providence and my Creator not for sparing my life – my life is one long struggle for my people – rather I thank Him because he has given me the opportunity to continue my job.

To those listening in Paris there was finally no doubt: Hitler was alive. There was equally bad news for Stülpnagel closer to home. Civil war between the army and navy was imminent on the streets of the French capital. For more than an hour now, Theodor Krancke had stood his 1,000-strong ranks on alert. The *Vizeadmiral* had watched the Army round up the SD and SS with growing concern. All the orders from Germany pointed to a failed putsch, yet here on the streets of Paris the security services were being arrested. Krancke listened first to Hitler's radio speech, then a short address by Dönitz promising 'we will get even with these traitors'. Unable to obtain any satisfactory explanation from any of the senior army officers in Paris, Krancke, a convinced Nazi, took matters into his own hands. Shortly after 1.30 a.m. he threatened to liberate the incarcerated SD and SS officials – by force if necessary.[38] Within minutes, the prisoners were freed. The coup in France was at an end. Almost.

Its final scene was an act of sycophancy. 'I would suggest the field marshal sends a letter of congratulations and loyalty to the Führer,' Günther Blumentritt suggested. Kluge agreed. Just hours earlier, Günther von Kluge had briefly been prepared to throw his weight behind a coup d'etat. Now he grovelled to his Führer:

The coup against you life, carried out by the hands of ruthless assassins, has, *mein Führer*, failed, thanks to the gracious will of Providence. At this moment, may I congratulate you and assure you, *mein Führer*, of our unflinching loyalty, whatever may happen.[39]

The following morning, Karl-Heinrich von Stülpnagel was ordered to report to Berlin and account for his actions the previous day. He knew what the summons meant. On the road back to Germany, the military governor of France paused from the lengthy car journey to walk around the former Verdun battlefield on the Meuse. As he did, he shot himself twice in the head, but succeeded only in blinding himself in one eye, and leaving gaping holes in his temple and throat. The *Generaloberst* survived to face trial with his adjutant Hofacker on 29 August. The trial was a formality. Stülpnagel was hanged the following day, Hofacker five days before Christmas.

In Berlin, Fritz Fromm began restoring order. He started with a summary court-martial. The verdict was pre-ordained: death by firing squad. Beck and Hoepner were given the option of taking their own lives. Beck shot himself in the head twice, but neither was fatal; it was left to a senior non-commissioned officer to finish him off. Hoepner preferred to face trial and was sent to military prison. But for Stauffenberg, Olbricht and two fellow officers there would be no show trial. Around 12.30 a.m. on Friday, 21 July, they were marched into the courtyard of the Bendler block and despatched by the loyal troops of the *Grossdeutschland* guards battalion. Fromm announced the end of the putsch to all the authorities in Germany:

Attempted putsch by irresponsible generals suppressed with bloodshed.

All leaders shot.

Orders from Field Marshal Witzleben, *Generaloberst* Hoepner, *General* Beck and *General* Olbricht not to be obeyed.

I have resumed command after being temporarily held at gunpoint.[40]

It was beginning to get light that Friday when Joseph Goebbels sat himself down at a table in his offices in Hermann Goering Strasse. There was an air of self-satisfaction in his voice. 'It's been like a thunderstorm that's cleared the air.' It was time to settle an old account with the General Staff and impose Nazi authority on the armed forces once and for all. 'I'm going to make an example of them that will make anybody else think twice about betraying the German people,' Hitler railed. Goebbels recorded the Führer's contempt for the Officer Corps:

The Führer is particularly incensed by the generals, especially the General Staff. He is determined to now set a bloody example and to wipe out this Masonic lodge which has always been hostile towards us and merely waited for the moment to thrust a dagger into our back at the most critical hour for the Reich.[41]

The authority of the General Staff and Officer Corps evaporated as Adolf Hitler imposed his authority on the *Wehrmacht*. He began while the coup was still in progress in Berlin, giving his trusted SS leader Heinrich Himmler charge of the *Ersatzheer*. Next came a new Chief of the General Staff – the most important post in the army. It had lain vacant for three weeks; the previous occupant, Kurt Zeitzler, had reported sick on 30 June, unable to cope with the demands of a war on two fronts any more.

Less than twenty-four hours after the bomb blast, a staff car pulled into the Wolf's Lair carrying one of the forgotten doyens of the German Army. Father figure of Germany's panzer arm and the man at the spearhead of the Army's thrusts across Poland and France and to the gates of Moscow, for more than two years *Generaloberst* Heinz Guderian had played a peripheral role after falling out with his Führer in the shadow of Christmas 1941. Guderian, never a 'Nazi general' – but never an 'anti-Nazi' either, had been rehabilitated as the Inspector General of armoured troops. And now, on Friday, 21 July, his Führer needed him again. Guderian's loyalty had never been in doubt. Guderian had no time for the conspiracy or the conspirators. He was an archetypal *nur Soldat* – pure soldier. After the war, the general justified his attitude:

> At that time the people, the great proportion of the German people, still believed in Adolf Hitler. The people's hatred and contempt would have turned against the soldiers who, in the midst of a struggle for national existence, had broken their oath, murdered the head of the government, and left the storm-wracked ship of state without a captain at the helm.[42]

Guderian had a point. The assassination attempt provoked 'sudden dismay, emotional shock, deep indignation and anger' throughout the Reich according to the security service, which was on the streets within hours to record the public's reaction. The Germans heaved a sigh of relief: 'Thank God, the Führer is alive.' The reaction went beyond relief, the *Sicherheitsdienst* observed: 'Almost everywhere, the people's bond with the Führer has been strengthened as has faith in the leadership, which has shown it has mastered the situation.'[43]

Joseph Goebbels and the Nazi propaganda machine seized upon the failed putsch and the Führer's 'miraculous' escape to mobilize the German public. The Nazi Party organ, *Völkischer Beobachter*, not surprisingly responded. It proclaimed on 22 July: 'Answer of the nation: unconditional loyalty.' The newspaper eulogized over the Führer's deliverance which 'borders on a miracle'. He had been saved by 'a superior force holding a protective hand over the Führer's life'. The article continued:

> Our fate lies in his hands. His belief steels our resistance, his will overcomes difficulties, his knowledge points the way to the turn of the tide. Maybe we would have won the war without him. With him, we will win it for sure, something which the enemy too is in no doubt about. Whoever attacks the Führer attacks a German victory.[44]

And after relief came anger; anger directed at the army and the Officer Corps in particular. The German public was clamouring for blood. They hoped 'that now for once everything will be "cleared out"; there is a demand for a general purge'. The German people wanted a clean sweep of all Germany, as the *Sicherheitsdienst* reported public opinion: 'Now, it's all or nothing. If there are no total measures this time, then the war will finally be lost.' They hoped Goebbels would 'get down to business' in invigorating the Reich's war effort. The propaganda minister had 'awakened large – and justifiable – hopes'.[45]

The reaction of the ordinary *Landser* was no different. Barely one in every thousand soldiers supported the putsch according to the censors who monitored troops' letters from the front. Most regarded the failed assassination attempt as 'a stroke of good fortune for the German nation'. In letters home, soldiers reaffirmed their 'love for and loyalty towards the Führer' and 'their firm determination to fight in his way and to win'.[46] Recovering in hospital from wounds suffered a fortnight earlier, artilleryman Helmut Hörner wrote in his diary: 'It has come this far: now the Germans are eating each other. That is what all those strange decisions add up to since the invasion. Sold and betrayed, all the brave German soldiers stand on the fronts and fight in hopeless combat.' The words of one senior NCO with a naval flak battery were typical: 'Thank God he came through it again. You would not have thought such a crime possible. Among us there is the strongest indignation at this crime. Hopefully the ringleaders will all be punished as bitterly as they deserve. No punishment is too great for them.'[47]

Beyond outrage, the failure of the putsch filled *Landser* and civilian alike with renewed belief in the Führer and in victory. 'Adolf Hitler is the man who wants to bring a new order to Europe and above all the freedom of all nations,' one *Obergefreiter* wrote home. 'His death would have been a body blow for Europe's freedom, for he is the one who will lead us to ultimate victory.' Engineer Richard Wolff-Boenisch, preparing to go into battle with 116th Panzer Division in Normandy wrote indignantly: 'One is outraged by this act, which will only lead us deeper into misery. High officers committing a murderous attack against their highest commander. Now more than ever, we must continue the fight.'[48] The *Völkischer Beobachter* promised vengeful retribution:

No trace of this insane act will be left in the wheels of history. Its effects are in inverse proportion to its importance. Where silent disgust gave way to an understanding of the situation, indignation everywhere was wiped out by a determined will to act with all our authority and powers against such criminals and protect us. No appeal, no rally could have affected the morale of the troops at the front and workers at home more. New weapons will emerge – and with them victories which will lead the way to ultimate victory...

We lament the embarrassing fact that treason thrived among the German people and in our Officer Corps. But we welcome the fact that these selfish individuals are not worthy of the language in which they spoke, nor the uniforms they wore.[49]

The purge of the *Wehrmacht* began immediately. On 22 July, centuries of tradition were brushed aside. The military salute was abolished, replaced by the *deutsche Gruss* – the Hitler salute – 'as an outward token of gratitude for his miraculous escape'. The following day, Heinz Guderian broadcast to the nation:

A few officers lost courage and preferred the path of disgrace to the only path befitting an honest soldier – the path of duty and honour. The people and the army stand firmly united behind the Führer. I guarantee to the Führer and to the German people the close unity of the generals, the Officer Corps and the men of the army with the sole aim of fighting for victory and with the motto so often impressed upon us by the venerable Field Marshal von Hindenburg: "Loyalty is the mark of honour." Long live Germany and our Führer Adolf Hitler. And now: Nation to arms![50]

Alfred Jodl, still bandaged by the wounds he suffered in the bomb blast, addressed his staff in a similar vein:

20 July was the blackest day that German history has seen up to now and perhaps will remain so. Previously it had been 9 November 1918. But compared with what happened just now, 9 November was almost a day of honour. The deed of 20 July... was carried out by officers who were bound by their oath of allegiance, who went in and out of the Führer headquarters constantly, were permitted to shake hands with the Führer, and had been promoted by him...

We have learned from 1918 what happens if one hopes for a cheap peace by getting rid of the regime.

Now a general accounting will be made and carried through one hundred per cent. This is not the time for mercy, and the time for lukewarm followers is past. Hatred for all those who resist! That is what I myself feel...

Thus we grow stronger and dare hope that we will weather this crisis, a worse one than this cannot be imagined. I am convinced we will get through this situation. But even if luck should be against us, then we would have to determine to gather around the Führer with our weapons at the last...We must acquit ourselves with honour before the eyes of posterity.[51]

And then came the final act of surrender. On 29 July, Heinz Guderian abandoned centuries of impartiality at a stroke. The German Army would no longer remain aloof from politics. In future, the German Army would be Hitler's Army. That day he ordered:

> Every General Staff officer must be a National Socialist Leadership Officer, namely he must demonstrate that he is one of the 'best of the best' not merely in the realms of strategy and tactics, but also in the political realm through his exemplary attitude and active guidance and instruction of younger comrades in the Führer's ideas.
>
> I expect every General Staff officer to accept and convert to my views immediately – and to do so publicly. Anyone who cannot do so should ask to leave the General Staff.[52]

The humiliation continued. Staff officers attending situation conferences before Hitler were forcibly searched to see if they were carrying weapons or explosives. Political commissars – National Socialist Leadership Officers – began appearing at front-line units in increasing numbers to imbue the German Army with the spirit of National Socialism. 'If a commander failed to follow orders to fight to the last man, his political officer would report this to the Nazi Party,' infantry officer Siegfried Knappe wrote. The Party, in turn, 'would take action to have the commander relieved of his command'. On 1 August, Himmler introduced the *Sippenhaftung* – the arrest not merely of all the suspected conspirators, but their entire families, their homes, all their worldly possessions. 'This man is a traitor, the blood is bad,' the *Reichsführer* SS declared, 'there is bad blood in them, that will be eradicated.' The Stauffenberg family would be eliminated 'to the last member'.[53] Three days later, a specially convened 'Court of Honour' was set up to expel members of the *Wehrmacht* from military service so they could be tried in civilian courts for their involvement in the putsch. It was a formality. Each man was dismissed in 'only a few minutes'. Gerd von Rundstedt was wheeled out of retirement to preside over affairs. The elderly field marshal had his doubts, but passed judgment anyway. The leading conspirators, including Hoepner and Witzleben, were led before the People's Court set up to try them on 7 August. The verdict was swiftly delivered: guilty; the penalty, death by hanging the following day at Plötzensee prison in Berlin's north-western suburbs.

The *Luftwaffe* and *Kriegsmarine* fared no better as a National Socialist broom swept through all three branches of the *Wehrmacht* in the aftermath of 20 July. Goering ordered any participants of the putsch in his *Luftwaffe* 'arrested and shot'. The *Reichsmarschall* continued:

'Officers who took part in this crime place themselves outside their *Volk*, outside the *Wehrmacht*, outside every concept of soldierly honour, outside oath and loyalty. Their extermination will give us new strength.' Karl Dönitz was no less ruthless in his determination to root out any conspirators. 'We will deal with these traitors appropriately,' he warned. 'The Navy stands true to its oath, in proven loyalty to the Führer, unconditional in readiness for battle. Destroy ruthlessly anyone who reveals himself as a traitor.'[54]

And yet even Hitler realized that the purge could go too far. He needed the Officer Corps. However infested with doubters it was, whatever its failings, the General Staff was the backbone of the *Wehrmacht*. Without it, military discipline and military action would collapse.

> The Führer wants no one to allow himself to be carried away so as to criticize or offend the Officer Corps, the generals, the aristocracy, or military services. Instead, it must be emphasized repeatedly that we are dealing with a well-defined, relatively small officer clique which participated in the putsch.[55]

Unfortunately for Adolf Hitler, the Gestapo continued to uncover fresh evidence against the Officer Corps. The tentacles of the conspiracy seem to extend into every facet, every office, every department of the General Staff, from the head of the intelligence service, *Admiral* Wilhelm Canaris, to the army's chief quartermaster, Eduard Wagner. Then, on 1 August 1944, came the bitterest blow of all. Hitler was handed the interrogation report of one Caesar von Hofacker. Hofacker, it seemed, had discussed the putsch with the Führer's two western marshals. Hitler pondered their fate: Kluge would be dismissed, but Rommel would be summoned to answer questions from his Führer, then dismissed from military service. 'The Führer believes that Rommel was clearly not involved in the preparations for the coup, but that he clearly knew about it,' Goebbels recorded. 'But I must admit that I knew a long time ago that Rommel was no stayer. Politically, his ideas are mere fantasy. When he's advancing, he's outstandingly useful, but as soon as there's a grave crisis, Rommel lacks any inner resolve. It doesn't surprise me that Kluge is a member of the opposition. I've never really trusted him.'

Rommel's involvement in the coup was a body blow for Hitler. 'He did the worst that could be done in such a case for a soldier: he looked for non-military solutions,' he complained to his entourage. 'I consider Rommel in certain circumstances to be an extraordinarily bold and also clever leader. But I don't consider him tenacious.'[56]

Just hours after he had reaffirmed his loyalty to the Führer – and long before his complicity had been uncovered – Günther von Kluge sat behind his desk at La Roche-Guyon and began drafting a letter for Hitler. Clever Hans had arrived in France full of bluster, determined to stem the Allied tide. But three weeks of fighting had convinced him that Erwin Rommel was right; the Western Front could not hold. Kluge dictated:

There is no way in which we can find a strategy which can counterbalance the destructive effect of the enemy's dominance of the skies, without abandoning the battlefield. Entire armoured formations allocated for counter-attacks have been caught in the heaviest air raids – the only way the panzers could be dragged out of the churned-up ground after them was to pull them out with armoured recovery vehicles.

The psychological effect on the fighting troops, the infantry especially, of such a mass of bombs raining down with all the force of nature is something which must be given particularly serious consideration. The troops are more or less wiped out and their equipment in particular is beyond repair. They see themselves pitted against a relentless force which cannot be overcome by force of arms and so lose faith.

I arrived here determined of imposing your 'stand fast' order at all costs. But when you see for yourself that such a strategy can only lead to the slow but sure destruction of the forces, when you see that the material supplies arriving in almost all areas are utterly inadequate, and that our weapons, especially artillery and anti-tank weapons and ammunition, for the most part are not up to the task at hand – with the result that the burden of defending falls upon the will of the brave troops – then anxiety about the immediate future of the front is thoroughly justified.

As a result of the outstanding bravery of the men and the strength of will of the leaders here, the front has held to date, although it loses ground almost every day. Despite the strenuous efforts, the moment is approaching when this front will break. And once the enemy reaches open ground, unified command will hardly be possible because my troops lack mobility. I regard it as my duty as the responsible commander of this front to bring these conclusions to your attention, *mein Führer*, in good time. My final words at the conference with the commanders south of Caen were: We will hold out and if our position does not fundamentally improve, we will die honourably on the battlefield.[57]

As Kluge's gloomy letter headed east, the Commonwealth offensive around Caen ground to a halt no more than five miles outside the southern and eastern outskirts of the city. There was no breakthrough. Once again the German lines had bent and buckled, but they never broke. Montgomery now had all of Caen in his hands; the Orne and Odon rivers were finally behind his front and the enemy had been driven back to positions overlooking Caen he could scarcely hold in the long-term. But at what price? The four-day battle had cost the Anglo-Canadian armies more than 6,000 men and 400 tanks. One British officer walked over the Goodwood battlefield and surveyed not a beaten German army, but a smashed Allied force. He recalled:

It was a scene of utter desolation. Trees were uprooted, roads were impassable. There were bodies in half; crumpled men. A tank lay upside down, another was still burning with a row of feet sticking out from underneath. In one crater a man's head and shoulders appeared sticking out from the side. The place stank. [58]

The Allies could at least take heart that the German Army was wracked by inner conflict. 'That a "military clique", as Hitler calls them, should have been plotting to liquidate him is encouraging; that they should have chosen this moment is exhilarating,' Eisenhower's intelligence officers wrote. 'It is only to be regretted that it wasn't a bigger and better bomb. It is hardly surprising that generals with little else but Hitler's intuition to serve should be despondent.' But the ordinary *Landser* fought on, Eisenhower's staff lamented. 'As long as the battle continues, the miracle may still take place. The German soldier is still on the Party's side.'[59]

The German soldier was indeed still fighting for Hitler. For six weeks he had fought the invader and denied him the breakthrough he desired. He fought out of necessity. He knew the stakes. The Nazi propaganda machine no longer painted a rosy picture of the war. The soldiers' newspaper *Front und Heimat* – Front and Home – reported at the end of July:

The Soviets are at the gates of East Prussia! An attempt to murder the Führer! Large-scale attacks in Normandy! Increased enemy pressure on Turkey, hitherto neutral! It would be a crime to deny that the situation has become serious, very serious indeed... The time is finally past when there still existed in Germany incorrigible dreamers who imagined that we could give up this war, like a 10,000m runner who may repeat his attempt after some weeks... Our last but at the same time greatest chance lies in victory.

The *Wehrmacht*'s commanders placed their faith in the steadfastness of the *Landser*. There was nothing else left to believe in. There was no

Luftwaffe in the west. There was no hope of fresh blood from the Reich. There was no hope of the Allies letting up. 'The heroism of the individual German fighter will counterbalance material superiority,' I SS Panzer Corps' commander Sepp Dietrich told his men. The ranks of the SS had blunted Goodwood, Epsom, Charnwood; in short every onslaught the Allies had thrown at them. In coming battles too, his men would stand 'like a bronze wall'. Dietrich continued:

> The divisions, proven on the battlefields of Europe and welded into a sworn community, will stand fast.
> Each officer, non-commissioned officer, and man must be aware that this is a struggle for the fate of Germany. Each must be willing to fight at the most decisive sector of the front. We will prove ourselves worthy of our comrades who have fallen for the greatness of our *Volk*.[60]

Sepp Dietrich would quickly learn that words alone would not be enough.

Notes
1. Meyer, Kurt, *Grenadiers*, pp.152-3.
2. Bericht über die Verwundung des Oberbefehlshabers der Heeresgruppe B, Generalfeldmarschall Rommel, durch Tiefffliegerangriff am 17/7/44, 21/8/44. NA CAB146/434.
3. Montgomery to Eisenhower, 8/7/44. Pogue, p.186; Montgomery-Eisenhower, 12/7/44. Montgomery-Chief of the Imperial General Staff, 14/7/44. Stacey, p.167.
4. Leleu, Jean-Luc, *10 SS Panzer Division Frundsberg*, p.108.
5. McKee, *Caen: Anvil of Victory*, pp.259-60; Luck, p.346.
6. Conference between Kluge, Eberbach, Hausser, Obstfelder, Dietrich, 20/7/44. KTB PzGp West Appendices, 20/7/44. IWM AL1901/2; Luck, pp.199, 346.
7. Meyer, op. cit., p.154.
8. Luck, pp.193, 197.
9. *The Story of the 23rd Hussars 1940-1946*; Luck, p.347; Blandford, p.214; Tagesmeldung, 18/7/44. KTB PzGp West, 18/7/44. IWM AL1901/2; Telecon Eberbach-Speidel, 2120 Hours, 18/7/44. KTB AGp.B, 18/7/44.
10. Blandford, p.213; PzGp West Ia Nr.480/44, gKdos 20/7/44. Leleu, op.cit., p.108.
11. KTB PzGp West, 1800 Hours, 19/7/44. IWM AL1901/1.
12. KTB AOK7, 20/7/44. IWM AL974/2.
13. Besprechung OB West und OBs, AOK7, PzGp West, I SS Pz Korps, LXXXVI Korps, 20/7/44. KTB PzGp West Appendices, 20/7/44. IWM AL1901/2.
14. Schramm, p.27.
15. Irving, *Trail of the Fox*, p.409.
16. Manvell and Fraenkel, July Plot, p.56.
17. Irving, op. cit., pp.309-10, 318; KTB Ruge, 2/7/44, 3/7/44. Ruge, p.205.
18. Irving, ibid., p.372.
19. KTB Ruge, 13/7/44. Ruge, p.222; Annex to OB West Ia Nr 58955/44, 21/7/44. Observations on the Situation, OB HGr.B, 15/7/44. IWM AL785/1/3.
20. Schramm, p.37.
21. Hoffmann, p.412.
22. Hoffmann, p.422; Bernhard Kroener, *Der starke Mann im Heimatkriegsgebiet:*

Generaloberst Friedrich Fromm, pp.686, 689.
23. Schramm, p. 38.
24. ibid., pp. 39-40.
25. Hoffmann, p.472; Manvell and Fraenkel, op. cit., p.124.
26. Hoffmann, pp. 473, 755-8.
27. Cited in Hoffmann, p.757; Telecon Warlimont-Kluge, 2040 Hours, 20/7/44. KTB AGp.B, 20/7/44. IWM AL1710/6.
28. Schramm, pp. 59-60.
29. ibid., pp. 63-4.
30. ibid., p.64.
31. Irving, *Hitler's War*, 1st Edition, p.668.
32. Reynolds, *Treason Was No Crime*, p.267.
33. Zeller, *Flame of Freedom*, p.314.
34. ibid., pp. 314-15.
35. ibid., pp. 316-17.
36. KTB Mar.Grp.Kdo West, 20/7/44. NHB 508.
37. Schramm, p.72.
38. KTB Mar.Grp.Kdo West, 21/7/44. NHB 508.
39. KTB OB West Appendices, 21/7/44. IWM AL785/1/2.
40. Cited in Hoffmann, p.760.
41. Manvell and Fraenkel, op. cit., p.148; Irving, *Hitler's War*, 1st Edition, p.669; TB Goebbels, 23/7/44.
42. Guderian, p.349.
43. 'Erste stimmungsmäßige Auswirkungen des Anschlags auf den Führer,' 21/7/44. Cited in Steinert, *Hitler's War and the Germans*, p.267; SD Meldung, 28/7/44.
44. 'Antwort der Nation: bedingungslose Treue – Die Folgen des 20 Juli', *Völkischer Beobachter*, 22/7/44.
45. Cited in Padfield, Himmler, p.529; SD Meldung, 28/7/44.
46. Report of the censor of Third Panzer Army, 2/9/44. Buchbender, pp.20-4.
47. KTB Hörner, 20/7/44; Letter, *Obergefreiter* W.H, Staff Marine Flak Abteilung 708, 21/7/44. Buchbender, p.141.
48. Letter, *Obergefreiter* A.K, Staff Sicherheits Battalion 772, 21/7/44. Buchbender, p.143; Guderian, *From Normandy to the Ruhr*, p.53.
49. 'Antwort der Nation: bedingungslose Treue – Die Folgen des 20 Juli,' *Völkischer Beobachter*, 22/7/44.
50. Irving, *Hitler's War*, 1st Edition, p.677; Guderian order of the day, 23/7/44. Cited in *Nazism*, iv, p.628.
51. Jacobsen, Hans-Adolf, *Germans Against Hitler*, Press and Information Office of the Federal Government of Germany, Bonn, 1969, pp.186-8.
52. Guderian Tagesbefehl, 29/7/44. Cited in Messerschmidt, p.435
53. TB Goebbels, 3/8/44; Knappe, p.291; Cited in Padfield, *Himmler*, p.528.
54. Cited in Padfield, ibid., p.515 and Padfield, *Dönitz*, p.373.
55. Instructions by Martin Bormann, No.170/44, 24/7/44. Cited in Steinert, *Hitler's War and the Germans*, p.272.
56. TB Goebbels, 3/8/44; Führer conference, 31/8/44. Heiber and Glantz, pp.465-6.
57. OB West Ia Nr.58955/44, 21/7/44. OB West Appendices, 22/7/44. IWM AL785/1/3
58. Belfield and Essame, p.145.
59. SHAEF Weekly Intelligence Summary No.18, 22/7/44. NA WO218/1921.
60. Tagesbefehl I SS Pz Corps, 24/7/44. Cited in Weingartner, pp.106-7.

Chapter 9

Only the Dead Can Now Hold the Line

The time has come when Normandy can no longer be held. All that's left for the grenadiers is to lie down and sacrifice their lives. It's heart-breaking to have to stand by and watch.

General Eugen Meindl

A little after 11 a.m. on Tuesday, 25 July 1944, company commander Emil Ebner scrambled out of his ditch. He had been there for the past hour or more. Ebner had hurried forward from his command post as soon as the aerial bombardment was unleashed on the German lines, six miles west of St Lô. The front had been obliterated, first by fighter-bombers, then by those four-engined monsters. It took an hour for the Flying Fortresses, Liberators and Marauders to pass, all 1,800 of them, dropping their payloads on the Norman countryside. Throughout this infernal barrage, Emil Ebner and his radioman had buried themselves at the foot of a ditch. Now it was past, Ebner dashed to the front. He was horrified by the sights before him. 'We could no longer see any grenadiers alive,' he recalled. 'Everywhere, there was nothing but horror.'[1] Cobra had been unleashed upon Emil Ebner and his comrades. Within seven days, the German front in Normandy would collapse.

In the first two weeks of July 1944, Omar Nelson Bradley looked up and down the front of his US First Army from Lessay on the Atlantic coast to his boundary with the British near Caumont thirty miles inland, for a suitable place to strike. Since the fall of Cherbourg, the focus of attention had been fixed on British efforts to breakthrough around Caen. All had failed, save for seizing Caen itself. But in these efforts, it had not gone unnoticed to Bradley that the German *Schwerpunkt*, their point of main effort, was focused on Caen. The road and rail network in the Seine Bay converged on the city, not to mention the fact that the ground of the Orne valley was the best suited for deploying German

164

armour. At the end of July 1944, four panzer divisions were arrayed around Caen. But what the Allies really needed was good ground to fight over, ground not dissected by hedgerows, not cratered by shellfire and bombing, not turned into a quagmire by a combination of armour and the rain. The ground 'Brad' chose for his fresh onslaught was a ten-mile stretch of front running west from the town of St Lô at the base of the Cotentin peninsula. St Lô had finally fallen to the Americans on 18 July. 'Few towns in all of Europe suffered such devastation,' one war reporter touring the town noted.[2] Now it would serve as the spring-board for the offensive, codenamed Cobra, a thrust southwards along the Atlantic coast. Cobra was not meant to deliver the decisive blow in Normandy; it was aimed at finally breaking the shackles imposed on the Allies by fighting in the bocage. 'If this thing goes as it should,' Bradley declared, 'we ought to be in Avranches in a week.' The coastal town of Avranches, gateway to Brittany, was about as far as Omar Bradley expected Cobra to reach before it ran out of steam. Cobra would begin with an aerial onslaught, followed immediately by an armoured steam-roller on the ground. Bradley summed it up succinctly: 'First smash a division from the air, and then tramp right on through it.'[3]

Two German corps were unfortunate enough to hold the line earmarked for Cobra's spearhead, upwards of 30,000 troops, including the shattered ranks of the once elite *Panzer Lehr* Division. *Panzer Lehr* was not the unit it had been on 6 June. There were fewer than 2,500 men in its ranks now, and fewer than fifty tanks. Kurt Kauffmann, *Panzer Lehr*'s operations officer, faced the coming battle with foreboding. 'I realized the situation was hopeless with more than forty per cent of our infantry gone and the tremendous Allied shelling and air activity,' he said. Reinforcements, such as the men of the 2nd SS Panzer Division, moved towards the Normandy front with a sense of trepidation. The *Das Reich* had faced an arduous march from southern France to the bat-tlefront; some of it had been committed piecemeal around Caen at the end of June and mauled; now the core of the division was being deployed in western Normandy. As his division approached the front line, *Standartenführer* Karl Kreutz watched in awe at a night-time barrage rippling across the Normandy sky like lightning. 'Look at that,' he elbowed a comrade. Kreutz kept his thoughts to himself. 'For the first time,' he conceded, 'I knew that we had lost.'[4]

As with all the Allies' attempts at a breakthrough in Normandy, the build-up around St Lô did not go unnoticed in the days leading up to Tuesday, 25 July. There was talk of 800 to 1,000 American tanks massing opposite the German lines; enemy air activity reached unprece-dented levels. By dusk on 24th it was clear that an attack was imminent. Günther von Kluge was not confident. 'Only weak German forces can oppose it,' he warned Alfred Jodl at Hitler's headquarters.[5]

Cobra began with 550 P47 Thunderbolts attacking the German lines in waves, dropping bombs and napalm. The *Jabos* arrived punctually at 9.38 a.m., as American war reporter Ernie Pyle watched in awe: 'They came in groups, diving from every direction, perfectly timed, one right after another. Everywhere you looked separate groups of planes were on the way down, or on the way back up, or slanting over for a dive.'

It went on like this for twenty minutes, but the *Jabos* were merely the precursor to the main event. At 10 a.m. precisely, the wail of the fighter-bombers was replaced by the low drone, the growl of 1,800 heavy and medium bombers. 'Their march across the sky was slow and studied,' Pyle noted. 'I've never known anything that had about it the aura of such ghastly relentlessness.'[6]

The grenadiers of the *Panzer Lehr* Division simply disappeared under the carpet of bombs. *Landser* Werner Laska leapt from foxhole to foxhole with two comrades. He recorded his impressions in his diary:

> While the earth trembles and shakes, and bombs explode with a hellish noise, I feel the breath of my comrade on my ear. Soil falls on top of us and I feel that the ground is going to crack. I think that this must be the end – either we'll take a direct hit or I'll be buried alive. I shout and stand upright, shaking myself, but my comrade no longer moves. He is surely dead, hit by shrapnel. My comrade falls to the bottom of the foxhole. He has been hit once or twice in the back and is covered in blood. He is dead. I can see it in his eyes. My uniform and I myself are covered with his blood. Quickly scanning my surroundings, I no longer recognize this landscape: hedges and bushes are no more than smoking remnants, there are no longer any trees standing. I want to go back into my foxhole and simply stay there. There are craters on all sides, everywhere, at least one every four metres. Around our foxhole, they merge with each other. Once again I've been lucky: it's almost 'painful' to have survived again. Many of my comrades have been buried or hit.[7]

Near Marigny, six miles west of St Lô, medical orderly Walter Klein watched in horror as the ranks of 5th *Fallschirmjäger* Division were decimated. 'When a wave of aircraft passed, you could hear the cries of the wounded,' he remembered. 'As long as the attack lasted, any help was impossible.' The once proud paratroop division melted away. 'The view of my comrades was: 'The next attack will be our end.' We no longer had any heavy weapons. We still had a rifle, but only six rounds of ammunition.' As Klein stumbled towards his command post, a wounded paratrooper, a veteran of almost every campaign, buttonholed the young orderly. 'Don't you know it's no longer a battle here in Normandy?' he told Klein. 'We're led like lambs to the slaughter. Our supreme command has left us in the lurch.'[8]

Across the confined Cobra battlefield, men everywhere were emerging from makeshift bunkers, ditches, foxholes where they had spent the past hour cowering, sheltering, clinging on to life. The sight which greeted all was the same: 'the landscape of the moon'. One *Oberleutnant* wrote: 'The entire sector is nothing but a cloud of dust and smoke. One bomb crater touches the next.' Joachim Barth, commanding an anti-tank battalion, did not recognize the landscape before his eyes. 'The world had changed. There were no leaves on the trees.'[9]

The aerial barrage killed perhaps 1,000 men and wiped out all but a dozen or so panzers. At the divisional command post a mile behind the front line, Fritz Bayerlein was desperate. His division was melting away in front of his eyes. It was now midday, more than two hours after the battle had begun. Bayerlein had heard nothing from his men holding the main line of resistance. He stepped out on to the battlefield to gain a first-hand picture of the fighting. 'I saw nothing but smoke and dust,' he recalled. 'My positions looked like the landscape of the moon, and at least seventy per cent of my men were out of action, dead, wounded, stunned, or unfit for battle. All my panzers had been put out of action. The roads were practically impassable.' Bayerlein climbed on to a motor-cycle and headed for the battle headquarters of the 901st Panzer Grenadiers. He needed to know what was happening to his men. As the general arrived, a breathless *Leutnant* returned from the front line. 'The main line has vanished,' the officer reported. 'Where it used to be is now a zone of death.'[10]

As Fritz Bayerlein struggled to piece together what was happening at the front, three American divisions were rolling across his lines. Overhead, the *Jabos* continued to prowl as German reserves were thrown into the fray to halt the American advance. The fighter-bombers pounced. One infantry regiment moving up towards St Lô counted fewer than 200 men by the day's end. One company of paratroopers which had begun the day with thirty-five men ended it with just five. The rest had become victims of enemy air power. And yet the *Landser* hung on. Men disorientated and shaken by the bombardment began to re-occupy their positions and fight back. The American attackers at best advanced little more than three miles through the German lines. They had expected much more from Cobra.

At his headquarters on the Seine, Günther von Kluge studied the day's reports and radio messages pouring in from west of St Lô. They were not encouraging. The Americans had punched a hole three miles wide and three miles deep in his lines. 'As of this moment,' the field marshal bluntly reported to Berlin, 'the front has burst.'[11]

Wednesday, 26 July, dawned brightly. It would be another hot, sunny day in Normandy. And it would be another day of stemming the American tide. It began on the German left flank, along the Atlantic coastline. The Americans threw another corps into the attack, two divisions, to batter the German line anchored on the Atlantic shore. The ranks of the 17th SS Panzer Grenadiers bore the brunt of the onslaught near the town of Périers. For once, panic struck the usually reliable ranks of the *Waffen SS*. 'Battery crews came back from the front and reported: "There's nothing more at the front," ' gunner Hans Weidner of the 17th SS Panzer Grenadiers remembered. The men of *Götz von Berlichingen* streamed to the rear in flight. Weidner continued:

> A destroyed bridge over a river with swampy banks, which was the only link with the rear still open, forced a halt. After a short discussion and under the weight of the *Jabos* still operating above us, the gun barrels were rendered useless; the breechblocks sank into the swamp.
>
> Barely had the scattered battery assembled in the rear area than the order reached us that we were to be used as infantry. In platoon strength, under the command of *Obersturmführer* Prinz we marched to the planned area of the front, which was not continuous. For us artilleryman, not trained as infantry, this was action which caused us extremely bloody losses. After a number of days, when we were almost half wiped out, we were pulled out and sent on our way far to the rear to re-form and re-arm.[12]

To the east, somehow the *Panzer Lehr* held on. For three hours fighter-bombers pounded the division's crumbling front, before the Americans jumped off, again supported by a rolling air assault. Weakened by two days of fighting and two days of bombing, the panzer grenadiers fell back. And all the time, the *Jabos* circled hoping to pick off the retreating Germans. *Major* Helmut Ritgen waited for the American steamroller with his panzer regiment on the outskirts of the small town of St Gilles, a few miles west of St Lô, mostly turned to rubble by the air raids of the previous day. 'Every road to my panzers was monitored by the murderous circling Thunderbolts,' he wrote. 'One had to play Russian roulette by trying to outwit the pilots while they rose back into the air after descending to attack. It took an entirety to move along any road.'[13] The fighters-bombers ranged deep into the interior, far behind *Panzer Lehr*'s lines. It was impossible to send reinforcements to the front. All roads leading to the line were blocked by air attacks. No vehicles could move. No men could move. The defenders were on their own. The

Panzer Lehr's front buckled. By the day's end, the enemy penetration was four miles deep.

Panzer Lehr still had a front. But for how much longer, Fritz Bayerlein asked himself. The forty-five year old general was becoming increasingly war weary, despondent, irascible. Bayerlein was a rarity in the *Wehrmacht*: an officer who had served in all theatres of war – Poland, North Africa, Russia, and twice in France. But after six weeks in Normandy, *Panzer Lehr*'s operations officer Kurt Kauffmann was beginning to question his commander's leadership. 'He was a very good soldier, but he was worn out,' Kauffmann commented. 'In Normandy he showed himself nervous and weak.' Günther von Kluge was also beginning to have doubts about Bayerlein's state of mind. On 26 July, an emissary from the field marshal's staff arrived at *Panzer Lehr*'s forward headquarters near the village of Dangy. The officer, an *Oberstleutnant*, brought personal orders from Kluge. 'You've got to hold out,' the officer told Bayerlein. 'Not a single man is to leave his position.' Bayerlein was enraged. 'Out in front everyone is holding out. Everyone,' he told the emissary. 'My grenadiers and my engineers and my tank crews – they're all holding their ground. Not a single man is leaving his post. Not one. They're lying in their foxholes mute and silent, for they are dead. Dead. You may report to the field marshal that the *Panzer Lehr* Division is annihilated. Only the dead can now hold the line.'[14] To reinforce his point, the *Panzer Lehr* commander sent a report to Kluge's headquarters which pulled no punches:

> The forces are so weak, however, that we fear a breakthrough at any time. The division's losses in panzers, *panzerjäger*,[15] and 5,000 men in forty-eight days of continuous heavy fighting are so great, and the poorly-trained replacements who lack battle experience so inadequate, that the division no longer has any substantial infantry or armoured forces.
>
> In previous reports, I have already pointed out that we can calculate the precise moment when we will have no more panzer grenadiers or engineers left as a result of the unavoidable losses of a material battle waged with such unequal forces. That moment has now come, unless the division is provided with forces immediately.[16]

The thin veneer of the German front along the Atlantic coast disintegrated the next day. The house of cards collapsed. American armour rolled all night, bypassing the German defenders. In the small hours of 27 July, the US 2nd Armored Division reached its first objective – a road junction far behind the *Panzer Lehr*'s lines. The Americans were all but in open ground. For once, the Allied attack did not lose momentum. The

American armour did not pause for the infantry. It kept on rolling. To the south, to the south-east, to the south-west. It kept on rolling. The Americans had learned the art of Blitzkrieg, Hans Stober of the 17th SS Panzer Grenadiers astutely observed. 'We could see that the Americans had learned how to break through, ignoring their flanks and pushing on. We lost vast quantities of matériel.'[17]

Throughout the base of the Cotentin peninsula, isolated pockets of German troops – *Fallschirmjäger*, infantry, panzer grenadiers, *Waffen SS*, regular Army – were left behind, encircled, cut off. Their comrades ran. 'Everything was chaos,' grenadier Walter Padberg recalled. 'Allied artillery and aeroplanes were everywhere. I did not know any of the people around me.' The temporary commander of 2nd SS Panzer Division *Das Reich*, one *Obersturmbannführer* Christian Tychsen, tried to rally his men. 'I am a veteran panzer commander,' he urged them on. 'If the enemy succeeds with this breakthrough, then the war in France for us is over.' Tyschen lasted two days in command of *Das Reich*; he died of wounds suffered in an air attack on 28 July. His rallying cry fell on deaf ears. The German Army was breaking apart. It was a sight few, if any, *Landsers* had witnessed. 'I had seen the first retreat from Moscow which was terrible enough, but at least units were still intact,' *Sturmmann* Helmut Gunther of the 17th SS recalled. 'Here, we had become a cluster of individuals. We were not a battle-worthy company any longer. All that we had going for us was that we knew each other very well.'[18]

Fritz Bayerlein could see the writing was on the wall. He had no front. He had no division. That evening, he reported bitterly: 'After forty-nine days of fierce combat, the *Panzer Lehr* Division is finally annihilated. The enemy is now rolling through all sectors. All calls for help have gone unanswered, because no one believes how serious the situation is.'[19]

At the day's end, the splintered groups of the *Panzer Lehr* just about linked up with grenadiers of the 17th SS in the west, but in the east there was a gaping hole, a six-mile gap in the front before there was any sign of men of the 352nd Infantry Division and II *Fallschirmjäger* Corps. At his headquarters near the village of St Vigor des Monts, the corps' commander, the uncompromising Eugen Meindl, pondered over the task of sealing the gap. Meindl was a battlefield general. He had little time for theory. The soldier, he said, learned his trade on the field of battle. 'Do not hesitate,' he told them. Defence was an anathema to him, the very opposite of what the paratrooper trained for. 'Our task must change rapidly from defence to attack.' Now Meindl himself hesitated. He had been ordered to throw two panzer divisions into the fray – the veteran 2nd, the untried 116th – and halt the breakthrough. But the paratroop general had seen for himself Allied air supremacy at work

170

that very day; it had taken him four hours to drive nine miles. And now, the high command wanted to commit two armoured divisions under skies which the enemy ruled. Meindl would have none of it. When Kluge's son, a staff officer at *OB West*, arrived at the paratroopers' headquarters to pass on his father's orders, Meindl was blunt. 'Tomorrow's attack is going to be a failure. Those tanks are destined to be smashed,' he told the young Kluge. 'The time has come when Normandy can no longer be held. It cannot be held because the troops are exhausted. All that's left for the grenadiers to do is to lie down and sacrifice their lives. It's heartbreaking to have to stand by and watch.'[20]

The American advance was now rolling at fifty miles per hour, tearing south-westwards down the Norman lanes. In doing so, they were shredding five German divisions, including two *Waffen SS* units. The scattered remnants of these divisions were either left where they stood and held out to the last, or fled southwards, disorganized. The German Army streamed back across the foot of the Cotentin peninsula. Time and again the German soldier found the 'Ami' had already beaten him to his objective. 'The roads were crowded with American vehicles, and all that we could do was to take to the fields on foot,' Helmut Günther of the *Götz von Berlichingen* recalled. 'We were losing stragglers all the time. We were not a battle worthy company any longer.'[21] This was a new experience for the German soldier in Normandy: encirclement. Those who did not fall victim to the American armour, fell victim to the fighter-bombers. 'Wild confusion in all units,' the operations officer of a flak unit in the 17th SS wrote in his diary. 'Roads clogged with vehicles. Heavy losses caused by *Jabo* attacks, since we have to move by daylight to escape encirclement.' He continued:

> The entire valley we are in seems to be on fire. Thick columns of smoke rise from the shot-up vehicles. Amongst them ammunition shoots upwards. In the evening we are again attacked with bombs, and before it is pitch black, they also fire at us with artillery. It's barely dark when the streets are again clogged with vehicles. A blood-curdling picture. Everywhere there are blazing vehicles, exploding ammunition, burning fuel and supply trucks...Everyone streams to the rear. If the Americans used paratroops here now, the chaos would be complete – or it would be the end. We go past numerous blazing wrecks.[22]

The retreat was desperate, one SS *Untersturmführer*, recalled. The German Army had been driven back so far that maps, given to front-line commanders before the battle, ran out. The men followed their instincts and headed south. 'We were unable to tell whether the US army had stretched this far already with its feelers,' the officer wrote. 'There was no sound of battle, no German soldiers, but also no Americans in the land. Weary, hungry and at the end of our strength we marched south. My men could hardly stay on their feet. I too was tired, but the uncertainty about how everything would progress did not allow me to sleep.'[23]

The rout had begun. It would not end. Omar Bradley saw to that. The US First Army commander was determined to press home his advantage. 'We shall continue attacking, never give him a chance to rest, never give him a chance to give in. We shall never stop until the [German] Army is beaten and until the [German] Army knows it is beaten.' Late on 28 July, he wrote to Allied Supreme Commander Eisenhower. 'To say that we are riding high tonight is putting it mildly. Things on our front really look good.'[24]

The attack which Eugen Meindl feared would fail stuttered forwards at first light on 29 July. 'Fate did not smile on the 116th Panzer Division,' its operations officer Heinz Günther Guderian later wrote. Forged from a worn-out division of grenadiers and a partially-formed armoured unit, the 'Greyhound' Division – named after the divisional badge – was poorly-equipped and barely ready for battle. What it lacked in material, its aristocratic commander *Generalleutnant* Graf von Schwerin believed would be made good by its fighting spirit. Schwerin yearned to 'fight the English and Americans. We will take great pleasure in soundly beating the hell out of those fellows in every way we can.'[25] Instead, the Greyhounds ran headlong into the US 2nd Armoured. Almost immediately, the battalion commander leading the assault was mown down. The leaderless German panzer assault faltered before midday, while the supporting panzer grenadiers cowered in a nearby forest, pinned down by Allied fighter power. 'Any vehicle breaking cover,' the infantry complained, 'is fired upon.' All the Greyhounds heard were recriminations. XLVII Panzer Corps' commander, the pompous aristocrat *Freiherr* von Funck, was furious with the division's failure that morning. Funck was not an easy man to get along with at the best of times. His subordinates described him as 'brutal and ruthless'; he was 'much disliked by officers and men'; he never visited the front line and barked at his subordinates if they failed to accomplish a task.[26] Funck's anger boiled over when 116th Panzer did not resume the assault that afternoon as it struggled to regroup with Allied aircraft bearing down on every movement. 'This looks to me like pure obstruction,' Funck roared down the telephone. 'I am quite sure that 116th Panzer Division does not want to attack today. I will not be afraid of changing the leadership of the division so that my instructions will be carried out.'[27]

At sunrise on the penultimate day of July, the Greyhounds set off again into the flank of the enemy rolling southwards to the east of the small town of Percy. But this was bocage country. The panzers and Panthers rumbled down lanes lined with hedgerows where their effect was limited. The *Jabos* appeared overhead immediately and began to pick off the attackers as American resistance on the ground stiffened. The assault got no further than it did the day before. That afternoon, the attack was called off, and with it the last hope of halting the American break-through died.

To the west of the failed thrust into the American flank, the *Landser* was fighting for his very survival across 250 square miles of Norman terrain. In four days, the German front line had been driven back fifteen miles. Worse still, more than 10,000 men had been left behind, out run by the American advance dashing southwards. Cut off, the flotsam of six divisions tried to batter their way back to their own lines. Some succeeded. Most did not. Near the village of Roncey, the advancing Americans found nearly 400 abandoned vehicles – guns, panzers, trucks – spread out in a three-mile-long column, either burned out or damaged, savaged by fighter-bombers. A couple of miles further south 1,200 *Waffen SS* of the *Das Reich* and *Götz von Berlichingen*, aided by ninety panzers and the cover of darkness, struggled to batter their way out of Cobra's pocket early on 30 July. They ran headlong into two American groups before finally joining forces with their comrades, with at least 700 fewer men than they had begun their breakout. A mile to the west, near Lengronne, 2,500 more Germans struck through the night and were slaughtered by the enemy troops they ran into. No more than half got through, the rest lay strewn across the bocage. An American officer visiting the carnage outside Lengronne described it as 'the most Godless sight I have ever witnessed on any battlefield'. The Americans' official historian wrote: 'As day broke, hundreds of destroyed vehicles and wagons, innumerable dead horses and the miscellaneous wreckage of defeat lay scattered over the countryside, grim testimony to the extent of the debacle suffered by the Germans in the Cotentin.'[28]

And still the Americans rolled south. This was now becoming a road march. The tanks were covering as many as twenty miles a day. US First Army was all but in open ground. As darkness began to fall that Sunday, 30 July, American troops moved across the River Sée – so hasty had been the German evacuation that two bridges still stood – and into the town of Avranches, 'the symbolic entrance into Brittany'. The next day, the armour advanced another five miles, crossed the River Selune, and rumbled into the town of Pontaubault. The road to Brittany was wide open.

173

As July 1944 turned to August it was clear to commanders in France, Allied and Axis alike, that the fate of the Western Front hung in the balance. The Allies could sense victory. 'It is doubtful that the German forces in Normandy can continue for more than four to eight weeks as a military machine,' American intelligence chiefs proclaimed. 'One more heavy defeat such as the recent breakthrough battle will most probably result in the collapse of the forces now at the base of the Cherbourg peninsula. Surrender or a disastrous retreat will be the alternative for the German forces. In the next four to eight weeks, the current situation may change with dramatic suddenness into a race to reach a chaotic Germany.'[29] Günther von Kluge had pored over the balance sheet for days now and reached a similar conclusion. The field marshal was beginning to think the unthinkable: a separate peace on the Western Front. The events of 20 July had shattered Kluge. Torn between suicide, betrayal and loyalty to the Führer, the field marshal mulled over the fate of the German Army in the West with *Oberst* Rudolf von Gersdorff, whom he had just appointed as chief-of-staff of Seventh Army. Gersdorff had served under Kluge on the Eastern Front – and been at the heart of the anti-Hitler conspiracy on his staff. Now he urged Clever Hans to make contact with Omar Bradley. But Kluge displayed the same indecisiveness he had shown on 20 July. 'Gersdorff, if it goes wrong then Field Marshal von Kluge will be the greatest swine in history,' he told the young officer. '*Herr* field marshal, all the great men of the world have faced a decision by which they will be condemned by history or be regarded as the saviour at the hour of supreme need,' Gersdorff implored him. The field marshal put his hand on the staff officer's shoulder. 'Gersdorff, Field Marshal von Kluge is no great man.'[30]

And so Günther von Kluge continued the unequal struggle in Normandy. Almost daily he warned Hitler's staff that his men had reached the limit of endurance, that the front was on the verge of caving in. After seven weeks' continuous fighting, Seventh Army was 'exhausted and worn out'. The fighting in the final days of July had done for it. Neither its men nor equipment were in a position to thwart an enemy attack any longer. The enemy's air force dominated the skies, hounded every movement. Supplies were sent on lengthy detours to reach the front; they were simply not arriving quickly enough in sufficient quantities. But did Hitler and his staff officers, shut off from the world in their headquarters in East Prussia, have any grasp of the fighting in the west? In fact, Kluge wondered, did his own staff? 'You have no idea what it's like here,' the field marshal told his chief-of-staff bluntly on a visit to the front on 31 July. He vented his frustrations on the hapless Blumentritt:

The men are utterly exhausted. It's a madhouse. All you can do is laugh out loud. Don't they read our reports? They still seem to be living in a dream world. The Führer must be told that if the enemy breaks through here at Avranches, he is in open ground and can act as he pleases. The infantry has been completely shattered. The men no longer fight. Their mood is miserable. Conditions here are crazy.[31]

Minutes later the *Oberbefehlshaber West* was patched through to the Wolf's Lair in East Prussia. 'It's doubtful the enemy can be stopped,' Kluge warned staff officer Walter Warlimont. 'Enemy air superiority is enormous and restricts almost all movement. Losses of men and material are particularly heavy. The troops' morale is suffering badly under the constant enemy fire. The front line cannot be re-formed with the forces we have at present.'[32]

Three days later Walter Warlimont was in France in person to inspect the front of *Panzergruppe West* for himself. The staff officer listened to Heinrich Eberbach's arguments and protests, then brushed them aside. There would be no retreat in Normandy. 'If a front eighty miles long cannot be held, one further back certainly cannot,' Warlimont told the *Panzergruppe* commander bluntly. Besides, 1,000 new fighters would be in action in the west 'by the second half of August' to turn the tide. 'If we can last another one or two months, then this summer's battle will not have been lost,' he reassured Eberbach. 'The British have been promised the war would end this year. If it doesn't, then there's a great opportunity.'[33]

Adolf Hitler was beginning to think the unthinkable. Maybe France would be lost after all. Even before Cobra opened up the Western Front, the Führer had ordered the West Wall, Germany's untested Maginot Line, prepared for the defence of the Fatherland. Yet Hitler could not bring himself to order a retreat. Now was not the time. Nor could his generals know he was toying with retreat. 'Tell Field Marshal von Kluge that he should keep his eyes riveted to the front and on the enemy, without ever looking backward,' he insisted. To lose France, the Führer knew, was to lose the war. 'It's the fate of Germany,' Hitler told his entourage. But did Günther von Kluge realize the stakes? 'He must know that he must fight here in all circumstances, that this battle is decisive and that the idea of operating freely in the open is nonsense,' the Führer railed. After less than a month in command in France, Hitler contemplated replacing the field marshal. 'I cannot leave the campaign in the west to Kluge,' he continued. 'The troops wouldn't understand if we sat here in East Prussia while the decisive struggle was taking place

175

there.'34

The Führer chose not to replace his western field marshal. He instead chose to attack in the west. He chose to gamble, to cut off the head of the American advance. Shortly before midnight on 2 August, the orders for Operation *Lüttich* – Liege – rolled off the teletype at St Germain. It was time, Hitler ordered, to strip the front of its panzer divisions and send them west to drive into the flank of the Americans pouring into the heart of France. German armour would smash its way through to the Atlantic coast at Avranches, sealing off the breakthrough. The Americans' head would then wither and die. The more the Führer thought about *Lüttich*, the more he became excited. 'We must strike like lightning,' he told his staff. 'When we reach the sea, the American spearheads will be cut off. The more troops they squeeze through the gap, and the better they are, the better for us when we reach the sea and cut them off! We might even be able to eliminate their whole beachhead.'35

In France, Kluge passed on Hitler's instructions in emphatic terms. 'I must draw every commander's attention to the fact that the decision in the decisive battle for Normandy depends on this attack being success-fully carried out.' Günther von Kluge did indeed understand the stakes. His diary recorded: 'The attack represents the decisive attempt to restore the situation in Normandy. If it succeeds, the enemy who has advanced into Brittany will be cut off. But if it fails, then we must expect more developments.'36

The grand plan for *Lüttich* was a three-pronged thrust to drive a wedge ten miles wide westwards to the Atlantic coast at Avranches, a lunge by four panzer divisions – from north to south 116th, 2nd, 1st SS and 2nd SS – and the motorized ranks of the 17th SS on the southern flank. But the German Army simply could not mass five divisions under the Allies' noses without enemy air power intervening. By 6 August – three days after ordering his commanders to deliver the counter-stroke – Kluge's divisions were still not ready. Moving into position east of the small town of Mortain, twenty miles from the shore of the Atlantic, was proving a time-consuming affair, and each day *Lüttich* was delayed, the American spearheads fanned out further across Normandy and Brittany, while the German Army was punished by Allied fighter-bombers. With his divisions still forming, his panzers still moving up, his troops exhausted, late in the afternoon of Sunday, 6 August 1944, Günther von Kluge made a momentous decision. Now was the time to strike. The Americans were racing through Brittany; Le Mans was within striking distance, and with it the soft underbelly of Seventh Army's southern flank would be exposed. 'I must attack as soon as possible,' the field marshal told Hitler's headquarters in East Prussia. 'The attack will roll

176

this evening! If we wait any longer, we will gravely threaten our situation. Of course, we could wait another twenty-four hours, but then there is the danger that our preparations will be wrecked. The longer we wait, the more difficult things will become.' The *Oberbefehlshaber West* realized the gravity of the hour. 'If this attack fails,' he confided in Heinrich Eberbach, 'it could lead to a collapse of the entire front in Normandy.' This was the last chance to restore the Western Front. The order to execute *Lüttich* stood. Hans *Freiherr* von Funck immediately complained. The irascible XLVII Panzer Corps commander was not ready. All day long Allied aircraft had hounded Funck's efforts to move his panzers into position for *Lüttich*. As night fell on the battlefield, the general demanded his attack be postponed. Paul Hausser was in no mood for an argument. '*Lüttich* will be carried out as planned,' the Seventh Army commander told Funck. 'I have to admit that this is a poor start. Let's hope tonight's loss of time will be made good by fog tomorrow morning.'[37] That evening, Hausser passed the word down to the front line. *Lüttich* would roll:

> The outcome of the war in the west – and perhaps with it the outcome of the entire war – depends on the successful execution of this operation which the Führer has ordered.
> Only one thing matters. Unflagging dedication and a firm will to win! For Führer, Volk and Reich!

It was 2 a.m. on Monday, 7 August, when the final roll of the dice for the German Army in the west began. It was maybe twenty miles to the coast from the eastern tip of the front in Normandy. In his eagerness to unleash *Lüttich* before enemy air power smashed it in its infancy, Günther von Kluge had blunted Germany's best sword. Barely half the 150 panzers the field marshal hoped to commit were ready as the great counter-stroke opened.

Few divisions were less ready to begin the attack than 116th Panzer, the Greyhound division. *Lüttich* was the acid test for a unit which had so far experienced only defeat. Still bloodied from its failed attempts to halt Cobra a week earlier, now it was to guard the counter-offensive's northern flank. Except that it was not ready. Most of its panzers were still moving into place when the offensive rolled forward. 'To begin an attack with the idea that it is without hope is not a good idea,' the division's operations officer Heinz-Günther Guderian bitterly observed. 'We did not have this hope.' The grenadiers and what armour could be thrown into the attack made good progress. The dagger sliced nine miles into Allied lines. Then the Americans struck back. 116th Panzer Division fell back. Funck was livid at the failure of the Greyhounds. If they 'had one spark of honour left, something like this could not have happened,' he berated the division's aristocratic commander Graf von Schwerin. 'When can I count on your division to somehow execute one of my orders?' Schwerin was affronted. '*General*, I will not allow myself or my division to be insulted.' Two days later, 116th Panzer's commander was dismissed.[38]

In the centre of the great offensive to save France, the 2nd Panzers and *Leibstandarte* had advanced, its panzers massed as they had done on the Russian steppe. Fog was their guardian. But then it cleared, *Oberscharführer* Jupp Steinbüchel with the *Leibstandarte*'s reconnaissance unit recalled. 'The fine weather invited heavy enemy air activity. It was so great, we didn't know if we were coming or going. Although *Luftwaffe* support had been promised – there should have been 100 of our fighters attack – we saw none of our aircraft on this fine summer's day.' Instead, the *Jabos* pounced. Steinbüchel's half-track and the unit's armoured radio trucks were wrecked. After the fighter-bombers had passed, he and his comrades tried to salvage what was left. 'It was sheer hell,' he wrote. 'The radiomen had been badly wounded by rockets which gave off a lot of shrapnel. We pulled Walter Hofbauer from the half-track and immediately packed him off to the first-aid post. Although the left side of his body was badly wounded, we thought there would be a happy ending and one day he would again be with the company, but Fate decided otherwise.'[39] *Sturmmann* Walter Hofbauer, aged barely nineteen, died the following day.

The *Leibstandarte* advanced no more than five miles on the first day of the great counter-stroke. Its advance ground to a halt in the small town of Le Mesnil-Tôve. There were still another fifteen miles to cover to the Atlantic coastline.

The Panthers of 2nd Panzer had rolled into the village of St Barthelemy, just north of Mortain, in mid-morning. It proved to be an ambush, as a two-hour firefight erupted between the lead German panzers and American anti-tank guns and bazookas in and around St Barthelemy. Rather than bypass the resistance, 2nd Panzer's commander, Hans von Lüttwitz, was determined to bludgeon his way through the village. Finally, shortly after midday, his spearhead began to edge nervously out of St Barthelemy, heading for the small town of Juvigny le Tertre, three miles to the west. If Avranches was to be recaptured, Juvigny had to fall. But as the Panthers fanned out beyond St Barthelemy, two dozen Typhoon fighter-bombers armed with rockets pounced on the concentration of armour. Juvigny would not fall that day.

A few miles to the south, the *Das Reich* and *Götz von Berlichingen* battered their way towards the town of Mortain on the southern wing

178

of *Lüttich*'s fist. The southern flank had been the first to unleash *Lüttich*, shortly after midnight on 7 August. The onslaught opened hopefully, as one *Oberscharführer* from the 17th SS recalled:

The Americans left parts of the town in a hurry. Everywhere a lot of weapons, ammunition and food were captured; jeeps and supplies of fuel were particularly welcome for us.

The street and house-to-house fighting continued throughout the night, but by around 11 a.m. the only fighting still going on was for the church and the outskirts. Fire was directed against us from an observation post in a tall steeple. From the catacombs of the church, individual riflemen offered furious resistance, which cost us numerous dead and wounded. An *Unterscharführer* then dived in through a cellar window with his machine gun firing, and it was thanks to him that we could then move through open space to the church. The fighting inside the church was of course no longer a major operation, but it still lasted a few hours.

The houses had been abandoned by the people. Around 300 old people were gathered in a retirement home. The town's inhabitants had celebrated their liberation with the Americans that evening – food and drink was still on the tables. Some comrades feasted on it, before they thought about further searches through homes. Individual Americans, who had slept through the attack, were still being flushed out.

All houses were covered in flags. The flags were makeshift, some colours did not actually match the shades of the national colours. Nobody had expected our attack. The town was abandoned in panic and fear, a result of our air attack.[40]

The Germans were made to fight for every street, every block in Mortain. But the American defenders could not stem the SS tide. Only a mile outside the town did the offensive by the *Götz von Berlichingen* run out of steam, blunted by determined American resistance bolstered by air power. On its right, the men of the 2nd SS Panzer Division too had hoped to slice through the flank of US VII Corps. The advance began promisingly, but the US 30th Infantry which the SS men had expected to crumble stood firm. First the infantry, then the *Jabos* stopped the *Das Reich* in its tracks. The mist which had offered a protective blanket to the attackers at dawn evaporated under the August sun. The clear skies revealed targets on an unprecedented scale to the Allied airmen. North of Mortain, RAF crews sighted 250 armoured vehicles. Before the afternoon was out nearly ninety pieces of armour were burned out wrecks, another fifty were damaged and more than 100 trucks and vehicles were scattered across the terrain. The Allies dominated the skies. Seventh Army's new chief-of-staff, Rudolf Gersdorff, was furious. 'Not one of the announced 300 German fighters appeared. Afterwards, the *Luftwaffe* declared that the fighters had started but had either been contained by the enemy air force at their bases or during the approach flight.' The enemy aircraft attacked at will, 'plunging like vultures on the attacking columns,' regimental commander Otto Weidinger complained. At midday *Lüttich*'s three prongs had ground to a halt. The farthest the attack extended on its first day was within ten miles of Avranches.[41]

At his headquarters, Günther von Kluge was faced with a dilemma. His great counter-stroke had failed. His divisions had been mauled. And the Americans were still racing through the heart of Normandy and Brittany. They had to be stopped, but the forces assembled for *Lüttich* could clearly not deliver victory. What now?

Adolf Hitler provided the answer. The Führer was furious his great counter-stroke had gone off half cocked. 'It would have been much better if the attack had been delayed until all the troops had been assembled and the weather had been more favourable,' he complained.[42] But now battle had been joined, it had to continue. In the mid-afternoon of 7 August, a new message flashed on the teleprinter at *OB West*. The teletype from Hitler's headquarters began ominously: The decision in the battle of France depends on the success of the attack. The Führer continued: 'A one-off opportunity, which will never be repeated, presents itself to thrust into territory all but empty of the enemy, so we can turn the situation around.' Adolf Hitler tried to rally his troops: 'The utmost boldness, determination and imagination must inspire commanders from the highest to the lowest ranks. Every man must believe in victory.'[43]

For better or worse, *Lüttich* would continue. The troops had spirit. One prisoner told his American captors that evening that Allied air power 'disrupted our plans for attacking today, but my comrades would be ready to renew the attack either tonight or tomorrow'.[44] German commanders did not share his optimism. 'All the divisions have suffered extremely heavy losses,' Eberbach warned his commander-in-chief with night falling on the battlefield. The field marshal was implacable. The attack would continue 'regardless of risk', Kluge told the *Panzergruppe West* commander. 'I am aware that if this attack fails it could lead to a collapse of the whole Normandy front but the order is so unequivocal that it must be carried out at all costs.' Within ten minutes, Paul Hausser was also on the phone. He pulled no punches. 'Our panzer losses have been considerable. There have been extremely severe fighter-bomber attacks.' Kluge had heard all this before. 'There's not the slightest doubt that each commander knows how high the stakes are,' he told Hausser.

'Each man must do his utmost to carry out the mission. If we don't make considerable progress tonight or tomorrow, the plan will fail.'[45]

The 7 August was hurtling towards midnight when the telephone jangled at Kluge's headquarters on the edge of Paris. It was Alfred Jodl. The Führer wanted to know of *Lüttich*'s progress. Kluge was still at the front; his able chief-of-staff, Günther Blumentritt, took the call. *Lüttich* had not gone as well as hoped for, Blumentritt told Jodl. The enemy air force had hounded the attacking panzers 'on an unprecedented scale – not carpet bombing, but fighter-bombers which swooped down from the heavens for hours on end'; the *Luftwaffe* 'simply cannot get near'. Blumentritt continued gloomily: 'If we have not reached our goals by tomorrow night, then we will have to take a fresh decision.'[46]

In a hamlet north-west of Mortain, Otto Weidinger and his staff huddled in a row of houses under American mortar fire. With each incoming round, the men took shelter under tables. And then, through this 'hellish din', Weidinger could hear the strains of music. 'Someone suddenly began playing a folksong on a harmonica,' he remembered. 'In a display of gallows humour everyone joined in the melody, singing.'[47] Thus did Monday, 7 August, end.

While *Lüttich* stuttered, the American army raced through open ground. By midday on 8 August, Le Mans had fallen. Omar Bradley could see a great prize tantalizingly within his grasp: the encirclement of the German Army in the west:

This is an opportunity which comes to a commander not more than once in a century. We are about to destroy an entire German army. If the other fellow will only press his attack here at Mortain for another twenty-eight hours, he'll give us time to close at Argentan and there completely destroy him. And when he loses his Seventh Army in this bag, he'll have nothing left with which to oppose us.[48]

Throughout 8 August the Americans tried to force their way back into Mortain. Each armoured thrust down the roads running into the town from the west were thwarted by the panzer grenadiers of the 17th SS. From the hills surrounding Mortain, the enemy directed artillery fire against the SS troops. By nightfall, the town was in ruins. The August night was lit up by 'the flickering embers of fires from ruined houses'. The Norman countryside around Mortain glowed a dull red as 8 August turned to 9 August, lit up by the remnants of *Lüttich*'s armoured fist burning across the land. The great counter-stroke was being massacred by Allied artillery and air power. It was simply overwhelming. On the ground, Eberbach's panzers were mauled by enemy aircraft; in the air, the *Luftwaffe* was warded off by an impenetrable screen of fighters which sealed off the battlefield. Hitler immediately ordered four *Geschwader* sent west. Four *Geschwader*. Fewer than 200 aircraft, to turn the tide of victory. The *Luftwaffe*'s new chief-of-staff Werner Kreipe was horrified. 'They're not ready,' he complained. 'They will flounder in the chaos in the west, and the homeland will miss them.'[49]

Lüttich got nowhere that Tuesday. So badly had the attack been battered on 8 August, there could be no thought of resuming the 'advance' on 9 August. 'We must make preparations to continue the attack,' Kluge told Hausser in the late afternoon. 'We won't continue tomorrow, but we will prepare to attack on the following day.' The Commander-in-Chief, West, was gambling with the fate of the German Army in the west to carry out Hitler's orders. 'The field marshal is determined to do all he can and to run any risk to force the attack through,' Blumentritt told Jodl that night. And there were risks. Kluge knew it, as his chief-of-staff warned Hitler's headquarters. 'Attacking step-by-step is something which the English will merely want in their drive from Caen to Falaise. The more we fight metre for metre, the easier the English breakthrough becomes.'[50]

Frustration on land was mirrored by frustration at sea and in the skies. Across France in the first week of August there was a growing realization in the mind of the *Landser, Matrose* and *Flieger* that the house of cards was about to collapse, that the efforts of the summer of 1944 had been in vain. The *Kriegsmarine*'s campaign against the invasion armada had been an unmitigated disaster, despite Karl Dönitz's attempt to hide the fact with his continued exhortations:

> Two years ago it was fair to say that Norway had to be defended in American waters where we could sink the most shipping. Such a concept is no longer applicable. Today it is more important to sink one landing ship in the invasion area than it is to sink one Liberty ship in the Atlantic, for example.[51]

The problem was that Dönitz's U-boats could get nowhere near the invasion fleet. The Allied defensive blockade was impenetrable. 'The very strong defences encountered in the Seine Bay are striking,' the admiral complained. 'U309 had to return after only six days' operations in the invasion area because of the utter exhaustion of her crew.' Herbert Werner's U415 too lasted just six days, another victim of enemy counter-measures – an aerial mine dropped outside the imposing U-boat pens at Brest. Werner had sunk no enemy vessels. In return, he lost his boat and two of his crew. Its loss, Werner bemoaned, 'became just another statistic in the dismal obliteration of our U-boat force'. In the first fortnight of July, thirteen U-boats had been lost, leaving just six submarines to challenge the invasion fleet. 'During these disastrous two weeks, no more than three or four U-boats at a time were attacking the convoys ferrying invasion supplies,' Werner wrote. 'New Allied divisions, fully equipped and with thousands of tanks and vehicles, poured ashore.' As he buried his dead in the cemetery of a Brest suburb, Werner found himself pondering his fate. 'What could I say to parents who, if their sons must die, wanted them to die as heroes in combat?' he asked himself. 'I was still struggling with my sentences long after midnight.'[52]

Karl Dönitz had made no rash promises on behalf of his navy in the event of invasion. His men would do their duty, but he had never assured Hitler they could halt an enemy armada. Hermann Goering, on the other hand, had pledged his *Luftwaffe* would give its all, that it would fight itself to death in achieving victory in the west. And now, two months after the invasion, the Allies had a firm foothold on French soil while the German air force was heading for oblivion. It could not make good its leader's promises.

It was too much for Adolf Hitler. In the summer of 1944, he began to vent his anger at the *Luftwaffe* for its failures from the Battle of Britain to Stalingrad and now Normandy. 'Goering! The *Luftwaffe*'s doing nothing,' he railed at the *Reichsmarschall* during one conference. 'It's no longer worthy to be an independent service. And that's your fault. You're lazy.' Tears rolled down the *Reichsmarschall*'s cheeks. He reported himself 'sick' for future conferences and ordered his generals to deputize. The tirades did not abate. 'At every conference the Führer rants on for hours about the *Luftwaffe*,' Karl Koller, head of the *Luftwaffe*'s operations department, complained. 'He levels the meanest accusations about our meagre aircraft figures, our technical blunders.' Werner Kreipe, the *Luftwaffe*'s youthful new chief-of-staff – his predecessor had been fatally wounded by the 20 July bomb blast – was introduced to this world on 11 August. The Führer gave him a lesson in the 'collapse' – as he called it – 'and failures of the *Luftwaffe*'. Hitler condemned Goering's 'technical advisers, who influenced him with rash promises about the quality and numbers of new models. The General Staff, too, had possibly been deceived and had – either unconsciously or carelessly – given him [Hitler] false reports, which he had unfortunately partially used as the basis for his decisions.'[53]

And yet the men of *Luftflotte 3* were giving their all in the west. At the beginning of August, the ranks of *Jagdkorps II* mounted their most concerted effort to strike back against Allied air superiority. The American drive down the Atlantic coast did at least present the *Luftwaffe* with inviting targets – traffic jams of armour struggling to funnel their way south over a handful of bridges and suitable roads. In that first week of August, the Messerschmitts and Focke-Wulfs of *Jagdkorps II* were flying more than 200 sorties per day against the American armoured concentrations around Avranches, not merely by night but also by day, bombing bridges, strafing columns of troops.

In the great panorama of the Normandy battlefield the strikes by the fighter corps against Cobra were little more than pin pricks, the last hurrah of the *Luftwaffe* in the battle for France. 'Never before did we have to fight in such desperate conditions,' wrote *General* Adolf Galland, visiting his fighter crews in the first fortnight of August 1944. 'And the orders were to fight with increased vigour.' Galland continued:

> My impressions were shattering. In addition to the appalling conditions, there was a far-reaching decline in morale. This feeling of irrevocable inferiority, the heavy losses, the hopelessness of the fighting, the reproaches from above, the disrepute into which the *Luftwaffe* had fallen among the other arms of the forces from no fault of the individual, together with all the other burdens that the war at this stage had brought to every German, were the most severe test ever experienced by the *Luftwaffe*.[54]

Even the wonder weapon, the V1, no longer appeared to offer salvation. On 3 August, 316 rockets left their launch ramps in north-west France. Their crews were convinced Londoners were fleeing their city in their droves, that British morale was collapsing. 'Day after day the missiles crash into the heart of the Empire causing enormous devastation,' Flak Regiment 155's diarist gloated. 'The morale of the people is suffering considerably. The population is leading a hellish existence.'[55]

The German people were not convinced. For nearly two months now they had listened to or read reports of the V1's devastating impact in Britain – 22,000 homes in Plymouth 'damaged', three out of four homes in Croydon razed to the ground – and yet the invasion had not faltered. The public renamed the flying bomb *Versager 1* – Failure No. 1. It had not lived up to the expectations which the propaganda machine had fostered. As one senior Party official observed, given such 'exaggerated expectations the V1 itself was bound to disappoint' in the long run.[56]

And so after the initial euphoria following the Führer's 'miraculous' escape on 20 July, morale throughout the Reich declined steadily as the summer of 1944 drew on. One official report in early August warned:

> At the moment, the issue being discussed is not whether we can win the war – the vast majority are convinced the enemy powers will win – rather how long this war will go on...Nobody believes in victory apart from a very small number of compatriots and Party comrades,

unless a miracle happens and people no longer believe in miracles.[57]

It was well into the afternoon of 9 August when Günther von Kluge picked up the telephone to call Heinrich Eberbach. For two days, *Panzergruppe West* – now renamed Fifth Panzer Army – had tried to batter its way to the Atlantic coast. It was getting nowhere. But Clever Hans was not willing to give up yet. There was still time for one last push, the field marshal told his panzer general. Besides, the Führer insisted upon it. Eberbach was to command the attack personally, leading the thrust from the front. The fate of the Reich was in his hands. 'Success could bring a change in the situation,' Kluge impressed on his army commander. 'Failure on the other hand could lead to a collapse of the entire front.' And so the general took command of *Panzergruppe Eberbach*, the armoured divisions on the western extremities of the Western Front, handing over the rest of his army to Sepp Dietrich to ward off the British and Canadians in the north. Eberbach did not relish his new mission. 'There are just six hours every day when we can attack – between 3 a.m. and 9 a.m. – and then only with ground fog after dawn,' he noted glumly. 'An attack by any major force during the day is impossible because of enemy air superiority.'[58]

There was still hope on 9 August that somehow the attack on Avranches might be carried, that the Western Front might yet be restored. On 10 August all hope evaporated. In the week since *Lüttich* had first been mooted, then poorly executed, George Patton's US Third Army had driven ever deeper into the heart of France: Nancy, Rennes, Nantes had all fallen; the ports of Brittany were being invested; the American spearheads were little more than eighty miles from Paris. All von Kluge heard from Berlin was: attack, attack, attack. All he heard from his front-line commanders were lamentations and protestations. The German hammer was becoming the Allied anvil. Paul Hausser was brutally honest with his field marshal: the drive to the sea was impossible. The enemy was too strong, Seventh Army too weak. 'The drive to the sea cannot be rushed. It will be a long, hard battle, which the panzer troops are no longer equal to,' he told Kluge. The field marshal agreed. That night, Kluge signalled Berlin: 'Because of weather conditions which suit the enemy and the time needed to bring up troops, I do not expect the attack on Avranches can be resumed before 20 August.'[59] *Lüttich* was dead.

Hitler never forgave Kluge for unleashing his great counter-stroke early; the field marshal never forgave the Führer for forcing an impossible attack upon him. Kluge 'twice pointed at the map lying in front of him,' Blumentritt reported to Hitler's staff a few days later, 'and said: "Avranches, Avranches. This place has cost me my reputation as a soldier. History will know me as the Benedeck of the Western Front.[60] I have done all that was humanly possible. Ah well, that is fate." '[61]

By 11 August, the leading American unit, XV Corps had taken Le Mans, just eighty miles from Paris. Now it turned north towards the city of Alençon. A giant noose was forming around the German front in France; the German divisions were caught in a huge 'sack' seventy miles wide and thirty miles across from Mortain in the west to Argentan in the east. A great victory was now tantalizingly within the Allies' grasp – the encirclement of the German Army in the west. 'We have a great opportunity for victory which if fairly complete will allow us complete freedom of action in France and will have incalculable results,' Eisenhower wrote excitedly. 'The enemy's bitter resistance and counter-attacks in the area between Mortain and south of Caen make it appear that we have a good chance to encircle and destroy a lot of his forces.' The threat to the German front was obvious, but US First Army commander Omar Bradley was baffled by 'the failure of the Germans to grasp [the] seriousness of the situation and feels they are either dumb or thoroughly oblivious to our intentions'. Two days later, the Americans rolled into the town of Argentan, twenty miles north of Alençon. There they halted and waited for the British and Canadians to come from the north. The gap between the Allied armies was maybe twenty miles. George Patton was furious. Here was the opportunity to trap the German Army in France and destroy it. Instead, his armour was stuck in Argentan when it could 'completely close the gap. I am sure that this halt is a great mistake, as I am certain that the British will not close.'[62] The next day Montgomery opened his attack to seal the gap. His objective was the historic city of Falaise.

Notes
1. Perrigault, Jean-Claude, *La Panzer Lehr Division*, p.276.
2. Balkoski, p.275.
3. Blumenson, *The Duel for France*, p.73; Bradley, p.330.
4. Hastings, *Overlord*, p.212; Hastings, *Das Reich*, p.237-8.
5. Tagesmeldung PzGp West, 21/7/44. KTB PzGp West Appendices, 21/7/44. IWM AL1901/2; Telecon Kluge-Hausser, 1800-1811 Hours, 24/7/44. KTB OB West Appendices, 24/7/44. IWM AL785/1/3; Telecon Kluge-Jodl, 1830 Hours, 22/7/44. KTB OB West, 22/7/44. IWM AL785/1.
6. Cited in Ambrose, *Citizen Soldiers*, p.82.
7. Perrigault, op. cit., pp. 274-76.
8. Stimpel, ii, p.210.
9. Perrigault, op. cit., p.276; Cited in Ambrose, op. cit., p.84.
10. Cited in Klapdor, p.313; Carell, op. cit., p.266.
11. Cited in Blumenson, *Breakout and Pursuit*, p.240.
12. Stöber, Hans, *Die Sturmflut und das Ende: Geschichte der 17 SS Panzergrenadier Division Götz von Berlichingen*, Band I, p.236.
13. Ritgen, p.114.
14. Hastings, *Overlord*, p.80; Carell, op. cit., pp. 267-8.

15. Tank destroyers.

16. Tagesmeldung, Panzer Lehr Division, 26/7/44. Stöber, Hans, *Die Sturmflut und das Ende: Geschichte der 17 SS Panzergrenadier Division Götz von Berlichingen*, Band I, pp.234-5.

17. Hastings, *Overlord*, p.303.

18. Ambrose, op. cit., pp. 87, 88; Stöber, op. cit., p.237.

19. Ritgen, p.110.

20. II Fallschirmjäger Korps Ia Nr.604/44, 11/5/44. Wegmüller, p.288; Stimpel, ii, p.142; Carell, op. cit., pp. 270-1.

21. Hastings, *Overlord*, pp.304-5.

22. KTB Ia, Flak Abteilung 17, 28/7/44. Cited in Stöber, op. cit., p.259.

23. Bericht Ustuf Günther. Stöber, ibid., p.247.

24. D'Este, Carlo, *Decision in Normandy*, p.405; Blumenson, *Duel for France*, p.127.

25. Cited in Guderian, *From Normandy to the Ruhr*, p.2.

26. Annex No.1 to 12th Army Group G-2 Periodic Report No.71, 16/8/44. Cited in Reardon, p.51.

27. Guderian, op. cit., pp. 57-60.

28. Weigley, p.160; Blumenson, op. cit., p.124.

29. FUSA Intelligence Report, 1/8/44. Cited in Blumenson, *Breakout and Pursuit*, p. 442

30. Gersdorff, pp. 151-2.

31. Telecon Kluge-Blumentritt, 1023-1028 Hours, 31/7/44. KTB OB West Appendices, 31/7/44. IWM AL785/1/3.

32. Telecon Kluge-Warlimont, 1045 Hours, 31/7/44. KTB AOK7, 31/7/44. IWM AL976.

33. Discussion between the Commanders-in-Chief of Panzergruppe West and I SS Panzer Corps with Warlimont, 3/8/44. KTB PzGp West Appendices, 3/8/44. IWM AL1901/2.

34. Führer conference, 31/7/44. IWM AL998.

35. OKW/WFSt/Op (H) West Nr.772703/44, 2315 Hours, 2/8/44. KTB OB West Appendices, 2/8/44. IWM AL785/2/1; Irving, *Hitler's War*, 1st Edition, pp.683-4.

36. HGrB Ia Nr.5517/44, 1745 Hours, 3/8/44. KTB OB West Appendices, 3/8/44. IWM AL785/2/1; KTB OB West, 4/8/44. IWM AL785/2.

37. Telecon Kluge-Buttlar, 1625 Hours, 6/8/44. KTB OB West Appendices, 6/8/44. IWM AL785/2/1; Telecon Kluge-Eberbach, 2140 Hours, 7/8/44. KTB PzAOK5, 7/8/44. IWM AL1901/1; Telecon Funck-Hausser, 2200 Hours, 6/8/44. KTB AOK7, 6/8/44. IWM AL976.

38. Ambrose, op. cit., p.92; Guderian, op. cit., p.71.

39. Steinbüchel memoirs. Author's Papers.

40. Bericht Oscha Webersberger re: Attack on Mortain, 7/8/44. Stöber, op. cit., pp.287-9.

41. MS A-921; Weidinger, *Comrades to the End*, p.324; Telecon Funck-Hausser, 2035 Hours, 7/8/44. KTB AOK7, 7/8/44. IWM AL976; IWM AL974/2.

42. KTB OKW, 12/8/44.

43. OKW Ia Nr.772774/44, 1500 Hours, 7/8/44. KTB OB West Appendices, 7/8/44. IWM AL785/2/1.

44. US 117th Infantry Regiment S-3 Journal entry, 2150 Hours, 7/8/44. Cited in Reardon, p.150.

45. Telecons Kluge-Eberbach, 2120 and 2140 Hours, 7/8/44. KTB PzAOK5, 7/8/44. IWM AL1901/1; Telecon Kluge-Hausser, 2150 Hours, 7/8/44. KTB AOK7, 7/8/44. IWM AL976.

46. Telecon Blumentritt-Jodl, 2320 Hours, 7/8/44. KTB OB West Appendices, 7/8/44. IWM AL785/2/1.

47. Weidinger, op. cit., p.325.

48. Bradley, p.367; Weigley, p.200.

49. Stöber, op. cit., p.296; KTB Kreipe, 8/8/44. Jung, *Hermann, Die Ardennen Offensive 1944-1945*, p.208.

50. Telecon Kluge-Hausser, 1845 Hours, 8/8/44. KTB AOK7, 8/8/44. IWM AL976;

Telecon Blumentritt-Jodl, 2300 Hours, 8/8/44. KTB OB West Anlagen, 8/8/44. IWM AL785/2/1.

51. KTB BdU, 10/8/44.

52. KTB BdU, 15/8/44; Werner, pp.245-6.

53. Guderian, p.445; Cited in Forsyth, p.34; KTB Kreipe, 11/8/44. Jung, p.209.

54. Galland, pp.290, 300.

55. KTB Flak Regiment 155 (W), 3/8/44. IWM MI14/1038/1-2.

56. Kershaw, *Hitler Myth*, p.214; Generalstaatsanwalt Naumburg, 27/9/44. BA R22/3380. Cited in Serrano, p.173.

57. SD Stuttgart report, 8/8/44. Cited in Nazism, iv, p.578.

58. Telecon Kluge-Eberbach, 1520 Hours, 9/8/44. KTB PzAOK5, 9/8/44. IWM AL1901/3; KTB OB West, 10/8/44. IWM AL785/2.

59. OB West Ia Nr.5835/44 gKdos, 0045 Hours, 11/8/44. IWM AL510/1/2; OB West Ia Nr.5834/44 gKdos, 10/8/44. IWM AL510/1/2.

60. Commander of the Austrian forces crushed by the Prussians in the Austro-Prussian war of 1866.

61. Letter Blumentritt-Jodl, 19/8/44. Ose, Dieter: Entscheidung im Westen 1944, p.247.

62. Eisenhower to Marshall, Cable S57189, 9/8/44. Eisenhower Papers, p.2062; Diary of Chester B Hansen, 11/8/44. Cited in Reardon, p.239; Irving, *War Between the Generals*, p.244.

Chapter 10

Death has Reaped a Terrible Harvest

I don't want to fight anyone, it is so useless. God grant that we get out of this alive.
German Medic, Falaise, 20 August 1944

On a high rock in the heart of a historic town on the River Ante, a tributary of the Dives, stood an imposing castle, dating back to the eleventh century, crowned by a 115ft round tower added two centuries later. Near its main gate stood an imposing bronze statue of a king riding his rearing horse, a spear clasped in his hand, his name William – Duke of Normandy, conqueror of England. This was Falaise, a town of fewer than 10,000 people. For a millennium Falaise had been known as William's birthplace. After August 1944 it would be indelibly linked with the destruction of the German Army in the west.

For a good fortnight the front south of Caen, the focal point of six weeks of fighting, had lain silent. An ominous lull had fallen over the eastern wing of the Western Front after the failure of Goodwood in mid-July. But with the Americans racing across France, General Montgomery seized the opportunity of a great battle of encirclement in the west. His grandiose plan, dubbed Totalize, was to send the newly-activated Canadian First Army down the Caen-Falaise highway, then turn to the east towards the Seine to trap the German forces in a sweeping battle of encirclement. The historic town of Falaise would be the pivot around which the entire operation would swing. It would begin close to midnight on 7-8 August, be preceded by heavy bombers pounding the German lines, and lead to success, Canadian First Army commander Harry Crerar predicted. 'I have no doubt that we shall make 8 August 1944 an even blacker day for the German armies than is recorded against that same date 26 years ago.'[1]

The exhausted ranks of the *Hitlerjugend* holding a stretch of the line between Falaise and Caen knew the uneasy peace could not last. The

189

Canadians would come again. 'It was made known to us that we would have to fight as we had not fought before,' one panzer grenadier recalled. 'We felt that we had the measure of the Canadians and that their armoured effort would be as slow and ponderous as usual. We knew that we could hold.'[2]

As dusk began to shroud the lower Normandy landscape in darkness on Monday, 7 August, Canadian troops enjoyed a few moments' peace. 'It was a perfect evening,' one wrote. 'Warm and clear. We stood about near our tanks while the long summer twilight gradually turned to dusk. Some smoked; few talked.'[3] Around 11 p.m. they mounted their tanks and waited for the aircraft to come.

The rumble came from the north. It was more of a drone, a low hum from 1,000 medium and heavy bombers, followed by a rolling artillery barrage from 400 guns, churning up the German front line. The storm of wrath and steel fell upon two poorly trained, inexperienced divisions, as yet untested in battle. 89th Infantry had been in Normandy just a matter of days; its neighbour, 271st Infantry, was 12,500 men strong, but one in twelve was a 'volunteer' from the east, and not one was fully trained. From his command post in the historic town of Falaise, fifteen miles south of the front line, 12th SS Panzers' commander Kurt Meyer lifted his eyes northwards and pitied the men being subjected to this infernal barrage. 'Air attacks hammer the 89th Infantry Division's positions and create a fiery glow in the sky,' Meyer noted in his diary. 'The front is burning. The rumbling battle sounds like a dull roaring of the drums of destruction. There are no blaring victory fanfares to be heard.'[4]

Thirty minutes after the bombardment began, seven British and Canadian divisions – 1,400 tanks, half-tracks and vehicles in all – moved off through the night. As they rolled forwards, the armoured convoys threw up a wall of dust on the dirt tracks baked by the August sun. 'The columns soon disintegrated into utter chaos,' one Allied officer remembered. 'The confusion was indescribable. Everyone had been told to keep closed up and follow the tank in front, but it was soon apparent that it was the blind leading the blind. Great shapes of tanks loomed up out of the fog and asked who you were.' The advance continued nevertheless. It was gone midnight – a good half hour after the Allied troops jumped off – before the first German infantry, a mix of *Hitlerjugend* and regular soldiers from 89th Infantry Division, offered any fight back in earnest. Flashes from *Panzerfaust* pierced the night, then 'showers of molten sparks' drifted to the ground as the rockets exploded against the brittle shell of the Canadian tanks. 'At first everything peaceful, then in a moment death, destruction, and fire,' one Canadian officer recalled. 'As the flames leapt from the turret of the tank the eerie light illuminat-

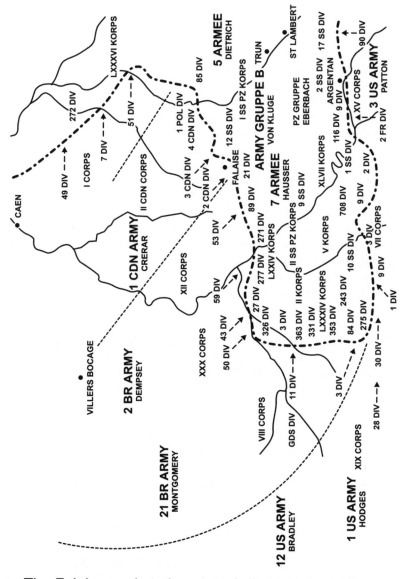

The Falaise pocket almost sealed, 15 August 1944

ed the railway hut and shadowy figures could be seen running for shelter. Watched from a distance of less than a hundred yards one had a sense of unreality, as if it were some macabre scene at the theatre.'[5]

By first light, the Canadians and Poles were filtering into the small villages which straddled the Caen-Falaise highway, as the untested

Landsers turned and fled. 89th Infantry Division simply melted away. 'I cannot believe my eyes,' Kurt Meyer wrote. 'I am seeing German soldiers running away for the first time during these long, gruesome, murderous years.' Meyer tried to rally the 89th, but the men continued to stream to the rear.[6] To the advancing British and Canadians, it seemed as if for the first time they had achieved a true breakthrough, like the Americans on the west coast one week earlier. 'Out of all the chaos and anxiety of the night had come success and the reassuring sunlight,' one tank commander wrote. 'Our weariness gave way to a feeling of exhilaration. It was a glorious morning and the fresh, unscarred countryside for a few brief hours belonged to us.'[7]

Panzermeyer scratched together some makeshift groups of his *Hitlerjugend* and tried to rally on the Caen-Falaise highway. Shortly after midday the Tigers rolled northwards astride the main road. The legendary Michael Wittmann led the way. But after 130 kills to his credit, Wittmann was becoming cocky, almost complacent, confident his legendary reputation could stem the Allied tide. As Wittmann edged out of the hamlet of Gaumesnil, he noticed a wood 800 yards away on his right flank. Amid the trees, Captain Tom Boardman waited with the Sherman tanks of the 1st Northamptonshire Yeomanry. Normally, Boardman would never confront Tigers; but this was a shooting gallery. Crossing Boardman's line of sight was a squadron of Tigers, their less-heavily armoured sides presenting the perfect target. *Hauptscharführer* Hans Höflinger, followed Wittmann's lead Tiger when the panzer column came under attack. Rocked by a direct hit, Höflinger and his crew fled their blazing tank. As he clambered out, the senior NCO surveyed the battlefield: five German panzers were ablaze or knocked out. 'The turret of Michael's tank was displaced to the right and tilted down to the front somewhat. None of his crew had got out,' he observed.

Thus at the age of thirty died Michael Wittmann, Germany's leading panzer ace. His burned out Tiger was abandoned on the battlefield, alongside four more panzers. His comrades withdrew from the battlefield. 'It was the most difficult battle,' one SS NCO lamented. 'We had to pull back somewhat, but the tank of our dear *Hauptsturmführer* could not. We had to withdraw, not knowing what had become of the crew. We couldn't comprehend that our Michael Wittmann was no longer with us.'[8]

As Michael Wittmann met his fate, another armoured lunge by a separate makeshift *Kampfgruppe* blunted the first blooding of the Polish tanks in Normandy, before being forced to withdraw as the Canadians roared past on its left, crushing the 89th Infantry. 'It is almost fantastic that the overwhelming superiority has not swamped us,' Kurt Meyer wrote. But Meyer's energetic defence and his battle-weary *Hitlerjugend* ensured that the Germans still held the line on 8 August. That night, in his forward headquarters near the village of Potigny, Kurt Meyer found time to write a birthday card for his daughter under the light of a candle. He also found time to contemplate his future. His men were exhausted; they had been in action continuously since the Allied invasion. Once fine soldiers were now 'emaciated bodies' snatching whatever sleep they could get between the barrages. Why did his men still fight, Panzermeyer asked himself, then he answered his own question. 'We continue the fight in the just belief that in this futile situation we also have to fulfil our duty to the homeland.'[9] The *Hitlerjugend*, Meyer concluded, would hold the line again on 9 August.

In his command post, Heinrich Eberbach grappled with the news that his north flank was on the verge of collapse. The Canadians and British had broken through 'at many places'. There could be no hope of plugging the gaps, the panzer commander gloomily concluded. As the day drew on, the telephone conversations between von Kluge and Eberbach became increasingly despondent. 'The enemy penetrated the main defence line with a large number of tanks, roughly 500,' Eberbach told his field marshal. Kluge shook his head. 'What, 500?' Eberbach confirmed the figure, then added ominously: 'I must admit that I await tomorrow with anxiety.' So too did Günther von Kluge. 'I understand that. We must be clear that tomorrow or the day after will bring a decision here.' Matters in Normandy were spiralling out of control for the Commander-in-Chief, West. 'We did not expect everything to happen so quickly,' the field marshal told Eberbach, 'but I have the feeling that this didn't come as much of a surprise for you.' Eberbach agreed. 'I always expected this and looked to each new day with a very heavy heart.' It was 11.30 p.m. when Kluge made his final call of the day. 'Has the situation got worse or improved?' the field marshal asked impatiently. Eberbach sighed. 'I can't say it's got better.' The Allies seemed to be massing their forces for a counter-stroke. The situation appeared ominous. 'I have no more forces,' Kluge signed off resignedly. 'If it continues like this tomorrow, we won't be able to hold it.'[10] At that very moment, the enemy was one third of the way towards Falaise.

Before dawn on 9 August, Kurt Meyer climbed to high ground north of Falaise to survey the ground where his men would fight and die this day, scanning the heights facing him with his binoculars. The world was at peace, the battle-hardened commander observed:

Slim spruces wave in the first beams of sunlight on the hill tops. Even the glittering dew on the grass shines in such a wonderful way as to make me forget the war for a few moments. The sun breaks through and the first morning greeting comes from thousands of little birds' throats. The silence is misleading. I know that Tigers and Panthers are in position to destroy young human lives with a deadly swipe from their paws. Yes, the silence is misleading: the dance of death will soon start.

Wednesday, 9 August would turn out to be a good day for the *Hitlerjugend* and a bad one for Canada. When the enemy blundered on to high ground in front of the SS Panthers and Tigers without any support, Meyer seized his chance and counter-attacked. The oncoming Shermans 'brewed up' in the face of ferocious fire from the Germans' 88-mm, leaving the ground littered with burned-out Allied armour. 'Smoke cloud after smoke cloud,' the *Hitlerjugend*'s commander wrote. 'We can hardly believe it, each cloud is another tank's grave.'[11]

The Canadians tried again on 10 August, this time trying to drive Meyer's men from a height west of the main Caen-Falaise highway in the small hours of the morning. The Argyll and Sutherland Highlanders swarmed over Hill 195. With the high ground about to fall into enemy hands, the grenadiers of the 12th SS struck back under cover of a wall of panzer fire and halted the Allied drive. Later in the day, the Poles attempted to take the same high ground. Again, the enemy attack came within a whisker of success. Nine Polish tanks were shot up before Meyer lost his last anti-tank gun. 'The way was open for the Polish division,' Meyer noted. 'There were simply no more troops available.' But the Poles did not come. The tenacious German defence of Hill 195 forced the Polish leaders to attempt to outflank the height in the dark that night. Burning tanks and blazing villages and hamlets lit the way of the Polish advance. Forty enemy tanks were knocked out before the Poles finally made a small breach in the SS lines. It was as far as they would go. Totalize had breathed its last breath. It died on the hills, in the woods and villages north of Falaise. Both sides were exhausted by the three-day struggle. And still there were six miles to go to Falaise.[12]

Meyer's grenadiers – there were now no more than 1,000 men in the front line of a division 18,000-strong on 6 June – dug in on the high ground astride the Caen-Falaise highway. This could not go on much longer, Panzermeyer knew. 'Further Canadian attacks will inevitably lead to a catastrophe,' he noted in his diary. 'We are at the end of our tether. The last ten weeks have sucked the marrow from our bones.' The *Hitlerjugend* held out for relief. It began to arrive on 11 August, in the shape of the 85th Infantry. Here was yet another untested, under-strength division thrown into the Normandy mincing machine. After a forced march across the Seine from Fifteenth Army, 85th Infantry Division was in no condition to hold the line. 'The units had all suffered from air attacks,' one infantryman remembered. 'We had had to march a great part of the way on paths parallel to the road and this cross-country marching was very tiring. We were worn out.'[13] The men of the 85th infantry would be allowed just three days' peace.

It was now clear to any *Landser* in Normandy that the enemy was trying to encircle the German Army in the west. The armour began to roll east, not west. The German soldier was trying to escape from his foe, not attack him. It had to be this way, as Fifth Panzer Army's new commander Sepp Dietrich warned. 'Unless every effort is made to withdraw the forces eastwards and out of the threatened encirclement, the army group will have to write off both armies,' the SS *Oberstgruppenführer* complained to Hans Speidel, Army Group B's chief-of-staff. Dietrich's views were gaining credence among the German commanders in the west. Late on 14 August, Günther von Kluge arrived at Dietrich's forward headquarters. Kluge was not a general who led from the rear. He led from the front. He wanted to see the men at the coal face. His staff tried to dissuade him. But Kluge could not be dissuaded. He had to go into the witch's cauldron of Falaise. It was gone midnight when a call was patched through to the field marshal's head-quarters in Paris. It was time, Kluge had decided, to be blunt. 'Unless a far-reaching decision is taken immediately, the entire Army Group will be lost.' The front was breaking. His panzers were being mauled. He had no fuel. His men were being hounded from the air. There was no chance of resuming the attack on Avranches. There was only one chance: to break out of the pocket. The next morning, Günther Blumentritt sent Kluge's plea to Hitler's headquarters. Blumentritt did not mince his words. 'A decision must be taken immediately. Any delay will threaten all our forces.'[14]

As Günther von Kluge demanded a withdrawal from the pocket developing around his armies, his divisions were already on the move eastwards. After dark on 14 August, the 10th SS Panzers, the *Frundsberg*, headed off. 'The night is eerily lively,' supply officer Ewald Klapdor noted in his diary. 'Endless columns rush eastwards and block the roads. Fuel dumps go up in flames, ammunition depots fly through the air. Villages burn and turn to dust. Huge pylons light the roads of the retreat, the collapse of an Army. Shells tear into the columns which are driven on top of each other and next to one another. Screams pierce the night. The columns rattle along to the next stop.' The withdrawal was hellish. 'The enemy is hot on our heels,' Klapdor recorded. 'The same picture greets us on the roads. Lined by burned out vehicles, in places there's a horrible sickly sweet smell of decomposition in the air.' There was a growing sense of urgency – and a growing sense of impending doom. There was a single will in the Falaise pocket – to escape. All roads led east. 'The gap which is still left must be used,' wrote Klapdor. 'It is the last major opportunity to escape this witch's cauldron, where for days there has been no sleep, only inadequate food, fighter-bombers and shells falling from all directions.'15

As the first strains of light were cast upon the battlefield of Normandy on Tuesday, 15 August, Kluge climbed into his staff car to drive into the pocket and confer with Hausser and Eberbach, with his staff in tow. The command column moved by the back roads, against the tide of two German armies pouring eastwards. Almost immediately enemy aircraft appeared, hounding any movement, knocking out Kluge's radio truck. Out of contact with his commanders, the field marshal decided to plough on. But as 15 August passed, so too did the hour for the marshal's meeting with his generals. Kluge's car spent most of the afternoon camouflaged by corn, parked up at the side of a country lane.

At St Germain, hub of the German defence of the west, Günther Blumentritt was becoming increasingly desperate. For nine hours Kluge's chief-of-staff had heard nothing from his commander. He had heard nothing from Hitler's headquarters. A decision was needed. The jaws of a great pincer movement were to close on two armies. It was 6.30 p.m. when he picked up the telephone and called Alfred Jodl. And Jodl was in no mood to be reasonable. He simply would not accept the gravity of the German Army's position in Normandy. 'There's no other option than to attack in the direction of the sea,' Hitler's operations chief insisted. Blumentritt shook his head. 'We must talk frankly,' he told Jodl. 'If the general intends to carry out that operation, it's no longer possible.' The battle in the west was rapidly slipping out of Günther Blumentritt's grasp. 'The Führer must pick someone at all costs if the field marshal doesn't reappear,' he insisted. A new Commander-in-Chief, West, was needed. And his first duty, Blumentritt pleaded, would be to order a withdrawal 'otherwise we'll lose our best divisions. It's five minutes to midnight.'16

Kluge's disappearance alarmed Adolf Hitler. For four weeks now the case against the field marshal had been growing. In the Führer's mind, there was no doubt that Kluge had conspired in the failed putsch; his name kept cropping up in interrogations and Gestapo reports. There was, Hitler concluded, something sinister about the field marshal's disappearance on the battlefield. '15 August was the worst day of my life,' the Führer admitted a fortnight later. He had convinced himself that Kluge intended 'to lead the entire Western Army to capitulation and go over to the enemy. The idea was what we would surrender to the British and then join with them against Russia – a totally idiotic concept.' Hitler had no qualms about replacing Kluge. At 7.30 p.m. on 15 August 1944, the encircled Paul Hausser became Germany's supreme commander in the west temporarily. The next day, Adolf Hitler confirmed his decision. Günther von Kluge was to report in person to his headquarters. Field Marshal Walter Model, rock of the Eastern Front, would head west to take over in France.[17]

By the time the order arrived, the Commander-in-Chief, West, was no longer missing. Darkness had long since fallen on the maelstrom of the pocket on 15 August when Kluge's battered staff car pulled up outside Eberbach's makeshift headquarters near the village of Briance, a few miles south-east of Falaise. It had taken Kluge and his staff sixteen hours to cover fifty miles, at a cost of one staff car and four men. He had learned nothing from his sally to the front.

The pocket was rapidly closing. Two German armies were about to be caught in a trap. Kluge resolved to share their fate. He had led his men into this predicament. He would stay with them. Heinrich Eberbach convinced him otherwise. The field marshal owed it to the German Army in the west to try to save as many troops as possible from encirclement. The next morning Kluge began his journey back out of the pocket to direct the battle from the outside.

It was mid-day on 16 August before Günther von Kluge could be patched through to his headquarters in a Parisian suburb. The field marshal had stopped briefly at Sepp Dietrich's headquarters. 'We are glad you're back safely,' Blumentritt reassured him. 'There was a lot of concern at the top.' In his hands, Kluge held Hitler's order relieving him of command. Clever Hans was defiant. 'Tell those at the top that I'm back and that I never once let command slip from my grasp.' Fifty minutes later, the field marshal was on the line to Alfred Jodl, Hitler's most trusted military adviser. Kluge was blunt:

A real thrust as ordered in the last directive from the Führer is not possible. The best you can hope for from these forces is that they attack, and you can order what you like but they won't accomplish it – they cannot accomplish it. It would be a fateful error to cherish hopes today which we cannot fulfil – in fact which no power in the world can do, not even if it is ordered to do it. That's the situation![18]

Jodl nodded in agreement, but Adolf Hitler was still not ready to abandon Normandy. That afternoon he ordered Eberbach and Hausser to begin moving eastwards. But only so far. The German dictator still clung to the dream of holding Normandy – and defeating the invasion. The German Army would stand fast around 'fortress Falaise', regroup then deliver a fresh blow to the enemy. Nor was the Führer willing to rescind his decision to sack von Kluge. Walter Model was already on his way to Hitler's headquarters to receive a personal briefing from Hitler. The next afternoon confirmation arrived at La Roche-Guyon; Günther von Kluge was placed on the inactive list. An hour later his successor arrived.

General Bernard Law Montgomery was beginning to sense victory. It was time, Montgomery decided, to seal what would become known as the Falaise pocket. The latest master plan was dubbed Tractable, a thrust into and around Falaise and on to Argentan, fourteen miles to the south-east, closing the pocket. Canadian First Army would strike east of the main Caen-Falaise road, except this time the troops would strike not by night, but by day. The troops went into battle clutching an order of the day from Eisenhower: 'We can make this week a momentous one in the history of this war – a brilliant and fruitful week for us, a fateful one for the ambitions of the Nazi tyrants.'[19]

At twenty minutes before midday on 14 August Allied bombers appeared over the German lines six miles north of Falaise, accompanied by an artillery barrage laying down smoke shells. The Canadian and Polish armour moved off as infantry swarmed forward. This time, the enemy front collapsed, ten miles of it. *Feldwebel* Heinrich Laser, serving with 85th Infantry Division, was surprised to find his opponents were Poles. There was no love lost between the two nationalities. 'One of the men yelled "*Polen!*" and I believe the fighting became even fiercer. There was real hatred on both sides and not one prisoner was taken by us,' Laser recalled. 'It was a very hard fight and I'm sorry to say a bitter one, beyond our norms to that time.' However fiercely the men of the 85th fought, they were still pushed back. 'Their tanks simply ran over us – and I mean that literally; some wounded Germans would have survived.' By nightfall, the most advanced Allied troops had moved more than five miles. Dietrich pointedly told his superiors his men had been so weakened 'by the major attack under way that a breakthrough to Falaise can hardly be prevented any more'. The enemy was at the gates of Falaise, but Tractable was more than an attack to simply seize Falaise; it was the final push to close the jaws of the pocket and encircle two German armies. By nightfall on 14 August, the spectre of encirclement loomed ever larger. The gap leading east for the troops to squeeze through was now just eleven miles wide.[20]

As dawn shed light on the Falaise battlefield on 15 August, the German front line bent around little more than a couple of miles from the birthplace of William the Conqueror. The *Hitlerjugend*, pulled out of the fight on 11 August and thrown back in three days later, found itself defending two hills just north of the town which blocked the enemy advance into Falaise – Hills 159 and 168. 'Within a short time,

Hill 159 is a boiling mountain,' Kurt Meyer wrote in his diary. 'Shell after shell explodes around our tanks standing in ambush in loose formation.' The *Hitlerjugend* waited for the moment to strike; as the first enemy armour came within range, the guns of the 12th SS barked. The Allied tanks burned; the infantry accompanying them pinned down by machine-gun fire.[21]

The 12th SS successfully defended Hill 159, but not 168. Canadian infantry forced off a makeshift *Hitlerjugend Kampfgruppe* holding the height after bitter fighting. The road to Falaise was open and the Allies were determined to use it. Yet the Canadians did not enter Falaise on 15 August. They stopped a good two miles from the historic town. The attackers that day, one Canadian diarist commented bitterly, 'paved the way with blood for the liberation of Falaise by other Canadian troops'.[22]

It was well into the afternoon of 16 August before the Canadians stormed Falaise itself, and nearing midnight before they were on its streets as the Germans withdrew to a line south of the town. Just a few score stragglers from the *Hitlerjugend* held out. Falaise had been flattened by a bombing raid four days earlier. Now householder Paul German watched as Canadian and German troops grappled for his town. He recorded in his diary:

> Night was slowly falling on the ruins of Falaise. The skeletons of what used to be our houses at one time stretched black into the sky, illuminated by the red glow of the fires which had been started by the fighting. What valour did these Canadians show who had come across the ocean to defend freedom, advancing down our streets, knowing that any piece of broken wall could hide one of those excellent riflemen who rarely missed his target. Did we not equally have to admire the valour of the eighteen year old, young Germans who remained quietly in their positions until the Canadian tanks and infantry advanced – at a ratio of thirty to one – waiting for the most promising moment to fire. They knew well that such delay increased the uncertainty of their survival and they accepted death in the defence of their Fatherland.

As other Allied troops swept past Falaise, encircling it from all sides, the remnants of the 12th SS stood firm in the town's principal high school. It was 2 a.m. on 18 August before the battle for Falaise ended. The *Hitlerjugend* fought to the last man, all forty of them. Not one surrendered. All the Allied soldiers found were 'several piles of dead Germans' around the school and 'burnt corpses inside'.[23] Falaise had fallen, but at what cost the Canadian official historian Charles Stacey asked himself:

The destruction in Falaise had been appalling. In some parts of the town it was difficult even to tell where the streets had run, and our bulldozers had much difficulty in opening routes. The castle where William the Conqueror was born, on the high rock or falaise that gives the place its name, was little damaged, save for the marks of a few shots fired at it in the process of clearing out snipers; the Conqueror's statue in the square below was untouched; but as a whole, the ancient town that had been our objective for so long was little more than a shambles.[24]

By Wednesday, 16 August 1944, the German Army in Normandy was squeezed inside a pocket with a seventy-mile perimeter. The Western Front ran along the valley of the Dives, westwards past Falaise as far as the small town of Condé, then curved southwards past Flers and bent eastwards once more to Argentan, where the American tanks had halted three days earlier. Across, it was maybe twenty miles, north to south roughly a dozen – and it was shrinking day by day.

Inside the pocket, the *Landser* wearily trudged eastwards. He had given his all in the two-month battle for Normandy and it had not been enough. Now he sought salvation. 'Vast columns clog the roads, two, three columns side-by-side,' Ewald Klapdor observed. 'Heavy trucks, cars, carts and horses form a tangled mess which can barely be separated. The carts are pushed aside, some lie in the ditch at the foot of the embankment; there's swearing, screaming. Entire groups make their way robot-like, tiredness shows in their deep eyes. Others sleep as if sleep has overcome them.' 85th Infantry Division's forty-nine year old commander Kurt Chill 'craved sleep'. His men hallucinated, too tired to sleep, too tired to eat. His division was no longer fit for battle. 'I began remembering almost with nostalgia the long march to the Seine,' he recalled. 'How long ago it seemed and yet it had been less than two weeks.'[25]

There was now a growing sense of despondency and defeatism. The *Landser* saw a defeated army wearily marching eastwards. He saw men who had not slept or eaten properly in days, who had fought every day for the past two months or more. He saw them grab lifts on any vehicle still fit for the road, huddled with comrades on the back of half-tracks or struggling for space on panzers. 'I am wondering how the war will end,' one medic scribbled in his diary on 17 August. 'Nobody believes in a turn for the better. No rest or sleep by day or night.' One *Landser* was even more pessimistic. 'Our future looks hopeless. Most likely we will be taken prisoner.' Leaders like Heinrich Eberbach noticed the declining morale of the men. The German soldier 'had not time for thinking, but his feeling told him that this war could no longer be won.

He felt himself betrayed. He no longer fought with a belief in victory, only from a soldier's pride and fear of defeat.' The odd German soldier found hope. 'I wonder what will become of us,' one *Gefreiter* wrote home. 'The pocket is nearly closed. I don't think I shall ever see my home again. However, we are fighting for Germany and our children and what happens to us matters not. I close with the hope that a miracle will happen soon and that I shall see my home again.'[26]

What demoralized the German soldier most was that in the air he saw only Allied aircraft, rarely – normally never – the *Luftwaffe*. The enemy air forces had the run of the Normandy skies. And they enjoyed an unparalleled number of targets on the ground, at least 2,200 stuttering to the east. The British and American air forces took full advantage, aided by 'clear, sunny weather which dominated for days', Eberbach lamented. By day, the panzer general complained, movement was impossible. Bomber and fighter-bomber attacks hounded the encircled forces, 'even individual men on foot'. This Allied air power was simply not challenged. The *Luftwaffe* simply did not exist as a fighting force any more. The plight of 2nd *Fliegerdivision* was typical; by mid-August it could offer just a single fighter for battle in the skies of France.[27]

The *Landser* suffered for the *Luftwaffe*'s absence daily. Few things could cause such disorder, such panic so suddenly, then disappear in a matter of seconds. 'The *Jabos* shot out of the clouds and fired right into the middle of the horse-drawn wagons,' nineteen year old *Fallschirmjäger* Karl Max Wietzorek remembered. 'Panic broke out. The horses broke loose and plunged into a ravine, the petrol tanks of the motor vehicles were blazing, soldiers were trampled to death by the stampeding horses. And into all this, the rockets screamed, hitting men and animals alike; a gigantic fireball of charred horses and charred soldiers.'[28]

It was worst for the panzer crews. Their tanks attracted swarms of fighter-bombers, and there was little hope of escaping a blazing Tiger or Panther. *Sturmmann* Ernst Kufner, of the *Leibstandarte*, remembered: 'With the arrival of dawn, the tank had to be camouflaged at the side of the road. Combat vehicles which thought they could continue driving down the road became easy prey for the fighter-bombers. The enemy aircraft were in the air from dawn until late in the evening and kept the road under constant surveillance. They never failed to find badly-camouflaged vehicles beside the road.[29]

Supply officer Ewald Klapdor was forging his way across the River Orne, one of two natural barriers to the *Wehrmacht*'s progress eastwards. Near the village of Mesnil-Jean, the *Hauptsturmführer* found a crossing still intact, as he describes in his diary:

It is night. The sky is fiery red. All around the flickering light of the flares lights up the ground. Our column drives as quietly as possible towards the bridge. Two half-tracks now rattle in front of us in the same direction. The crunch of the tracks can be heard far and wide. Perhaps both are lost. It doesn't take long. The howling shells explode on the road. Hit, the half-tracks burn. After we have taken cover for a while, we take advantage of a break in the shooting and push past the blazing vehicles.

And then Ewald Klapdor was across the Orne. 'I take one more look at what is now behind us,' he noted in his diary. 'The land is lit up by a red flame.'[30]

In Berlin, propaganda minister Joseph Goebbels watched events in Normandy from afar with growing concern. For days now there had been nothing but gloomy reports from France. 'Our situation in the west is anything but encouraging,' he recorded in his diary on 17 August. 'Having fortunately overcome the crisis in the east in part, now we have this mess in the west. We have no more reserves available to offer determined resistance anywhere.'[31]

The Allies' prognosis was as bright as Goebbels' had been depressing. Eisenhower's staff rubbed their hands at the prospect of as many as 'six or seven' panzer and ten infantry divisions being destroyed in the Falaise pocket. In their weekly review of the situation, Allied heads of intelligence declared:

> The bulk of Seventh Army and *Panzergruppe West* is in the melting pot, fighting desperately hard with little chance of escape and faced either with running the gauntlet through a narrow, but closing neck, annihilation or surrender. To be a member of the German forces in Normandy held little future for any soldier from the day the Allies assaulted, but the end for most of them looks as though it is going to be more sudden than we ourselves dared to hope. The major portion of the enemy forces in northern France is completely disorganized and stands a very good chance of being eliminated for the enemy will find it extremely difficult to get his forces that do escape from the cauldron across the Seine.[32]

The German Army's one hope was that its new commander in the west could arrest the collapse of the front. The monocled Walter Model came to France full of bluster. Like von Kluge and Rommel before him, he led from the front. But the fifty-three year old field marshal lacked Kluge's civility or Rommel's sense of humour. Walter Model was another *nur Soldat* – pure soldier. His staff hated him 'because he demands as much from them as from himself', one SS officer told a colleague. 'He is exceptionally cold-blooded, extraordinarily popular with the men because he has a certain amount of feeling for them and doesn't push himself forward in any theatrical sort of way.' Model's methods would be different from Rommel's and Kluge's, as *Panzer Lehr* commander Fritz Bayerlein found out when he asked for his division to be pulled out of the line to re-form. 'My dear Bayerlein! In the east, divisions are refreshed at the front. It will be that way here too in future. Stay with your units, where they are.' Even Hitler was somewhat intimidated by the blunt, uncompromising field marshal. 'I trust that man,' he told his staff. 'But I would not want to serve under him.' Model had progressed from a corps chief-of-staff at the war's outbreak to panzer division commander in Russia, then corps commander, before being given charge first of an army then, as 1944 opened, an army group. When the centre of the Eastern Front collapsed in June 1944, it was to Model that the Führer turned. 'When Field Marshal Model came, Army Group Centre was only a hole,' Hitler said later. 'There was more hole than front, and then finally there was more front than hole.' Now there was a crisis in the west with more hole than front again, it was to Walter Model that Hitler turned again.[33]

The field marshal arrived in Normandy determined to enforce the Führer's orders. His first task was to impose his will upon his front-line commanders. The day after he arrived in France, Model drove to Seventh Army's forward headquarters. 'We must form a continuous front again at all costs,' he told the gathered generals and staff officers. 'Whether it is in front of, or behind the Seine depends on how the situation develops. Behind the Seine would be the worst solution.' Heinrich Eberbach listened to the field marshal's grand plan disinterestedly. The time for great plans had passed. 'We are waging a poor man's war,' he told Model bluntly. 'The morale of the troops has collapsed. The German soldier has witnessed the arrival of hundreds of enemy ships, has fought hundreds of air squadrons on their way to a completely bewildered Germany who return as if on a fly past – and apparently without loss. The mail which reaches the German soldier brings him nothing but news of cities in ruins.' The field marshal interrupted brusquely: 'These are opinions, not facts.' But Model quickly realized that the situation in the west was grave, bordering on the catastrophic. He did not mince his words with Hitler's staff. 'The troops have been decimated. If the minimum requirements for replacements are not met, no achievements can be expected of them.'[34]

After more than four decades in the service of his country, Field Marshal Günther von Kluge sat at his desk contemplating the end of his military career. Walter Model had arrived at his headquarters bearing a hand-written note from the Führer, who was convinced Kluge had 'undertaken too much and was in need of a rest'. Dismissed from his post, summoned to Germany to report to Hitler, Kluge had no intention of sharing the fate of fellow officers executed in the wake of 20 July. He would go on his own terms and he would go down fighting. He would address the Führer 'without mincing words. Something has to happen. I owe this to the troops and to the German people.'35 This was his testament to the German people; to history:

When you receive these lines, I shall be no more. I cannot bear the criticism that I have sealed the fate of the west through faulty strategy; and I have no means of defending myself. I have drawn my conclusions from that and am sending myself where thousands of my comrades already lie. I have never feared death. Life has no more meaning for me.

When I read your decisive order, I immediately had the impression that here something was being asked of me which would go down in history as an outstandingly daring operation. In practice, it was unfortunately impossible to carry out.

I did all that I could to carry out your orders. I admit that it would have been better to have waited another day to begin the attack. That would have changed nothing fundamentally, however. That is an unshakeable belief which I will take to the grave...

There was no chance of success. On the contrary, the attacks ordered were bound to make the army group's position decisively worse. And that's precisely what has happened.

Mein Führer, I think I can say that I did everything I could to keep on top of the situation. Rommel, myself and probably all the commanders in the west, who know what it is to fight the Anglo-Americans with their overwhelming material superiority, foresaw current developments. No one listened to us. Our appreciations were not dictated by pessimism, rather from a sober assessment of the situation. I do not know whether Field Marshal Model will be able to master the situation. In my heart, I hope he will. But if he cannot, and your new weapons are unsuccessful, then, *mein Führer*, then make up your mind to end the war. The German people have borne untold suffering; it is time to put an end to this misery. There must be ways to achieve this goal and prevent the Reich from falling prey to the Bolshevik yoke.

Mein Führer, I have always admired your greatness, your bearing in this titanic struggle and your iron will to uphold National Socialism. If fate is stronger than your will and genius, then such is

Providence. You have fought an honourable and great fight. History will show you that. Now also show that you are great enough to put an end to this hopeless struggle.

I leave you, *mein Führer*, as someone who was closer to you than you may have realized, and I do so knowing I did my duty to the best of my ability.[36]

As his letter made its way to the Führer's headquarters, Kluge drove eastward with his aide to report to Hitler in person. It was shortly after midday on 19 August when the staff car stopped a few miles outside Verdun, scene of the bitterest fighting a generation earlier. There died Field Marshal Günther von Kluge in a matter of seconds after swallowing a cyanide capsule.

A few hours before Günther von Kluge took his own life in the Meuse valley, Ewald Klapdor and his comrades in the *Frundsberg* were trying to save theirs. Shortly after dawn on 19 August, the remnants of the 10th SS crossed the main Falaise road three miles north-west of Argentan. The highway was jammed with an endless column of vehicles trying to thread their way eastwards through a pocket only a handful of miles wide. The Allied air forces had taken a terrible toll of the lethargic Germanic exodus. 'There are terrible scenes,' Klapdor wrote in his diary. 'Masses of dead men, the bodies of dead horses torn apart, smashed vehicles litter the road. The wounded trudge onwards. Vehicles pass them without a thought. In some cases they have to be forced to take their unlucky comrades aboard.'

The *Waffen SS* moved on under the relentless August sun. As the *Frundsberg* filtered through a forest, Allied artillery pieces opened up. 'We can't find even half an hour's peace and quiet anywhere. There's always the howling and crashing of exploding shells.' For the first time Klapdor and his comrades began to lose hope:

The questions 'what will happen?', 'where is there still a front?', 'is it still possible to link up in the east?', 'how have things come to such a pass?' grow louder.

It continues in the afternoon. The same picture on the roads and streets, an army rolling endlessly eastwards. The front lines become ever thinner, they are close to breaking. Thousands try to escape again. No one wants to be subjected to authority any more. The law of the jungle rules on the road. Eastwards! Eastwards![37]

Leaderless, without communications, without food, the German Army at Falaise wandered around almost aimlessly. Each man followed the next robotically. Few knew where they were heading, except somewhere to the east. This was the reality of the *Kesselschlact* – the battle of the cauldron, the battle of encirclement – as the *Landser* called it. Wherever he found himself, the same sights greeted him. Burned out panzers and half-tracks. Dead men. Dead horses. Mangled limbs. Body parts. Charred cadavers. The German soldier became insensitive to death. The experience of Falaise numbed the soul, *Oberfeldwebel* Hans Erich Braun recalled. 'Forward through hell, but also towards the enemy, past the dead and the wounded. We were alive, but inside we were dead, numbed by watching the horrible scenes which rolled past on both sides, just like a film.' Braun was a veteran, but even he found it hard to reconcile the sights he witnessed at Falaise:

> The dead, their faces screwed up still in agony. Huddled everywhere in trenches and shelters, the officers and men who had lost their nerve. Burning vehicles from which piercing screams could be heard. A soldier stumbling, holding back the intestines which were oozing from his abdomen. Soldiers lying in their own blood. Arms and legs torn off. The horses, some still harnessed to the shafts of their ruined wagons, appearing and disappearing in clouds of smoke and dust like ghosts. There were civilians lying by the roadside, loaded with personal belongings, often of no value at all, and stilling clinging to them in death. Close by a crossroads, caught by gunfire, lay a group of men, women and children. Unforgettable, the staring gaze of their broken eyes and the grimaces of their pain-distorted faces. Destroyed prams and discarded dolls littered the terrible scene.[38]

Allied artillery and aircraft turned the cauldron of Falaise into a shooting gallery. The enemy held most of the high ground overlooking the valley of the River Dives and brought his guns to bear. It was too easy. 'Targets appeared one after another,' one Canadian artillery officer recalled. 'Roads and fields were full of Germans moving eastward, seeking a way out of the trap. The resulting carnage was terrible.' By night, and especially by day, the Dives valley was 'a gunner's paradise', one Allied gunner observed, 'and everybody took advantage'. When the Allied artillery found its mark, it was lethal. Confined to the narrow, sunken lanes, the retreating German Army was cut to pieces, as *Sturmmann* Leo Knebelsberger recalled:

> Shells hit the low-lying road and there was nothing left there. The head of the panzer and half-track column slowly set off. In the hollow road lay the dead and wounded. No one dragged them aside. Nobody felt responsibility for them. Everyone merely thought of himself. Leaving everything behind, the beaten army continued its march. One thing obsessed every man: 'To get out of there. The next shell will get me!'[39]

The infantry divisions suffered the most. The horse remained their main form of transport. Their endless columns blocked the narrow lanes. Under the artillery and aerial bombardment, the animals reared up and panicked. They tried to shake off the sluggish carts they drew, turned over limbers and threw off their riders. 'Appalling scenes took place: the tanks, armoured elements and motorized supply units ruthlessly forced their way through to the east,' panzer commander Hans von Luck wrote. 'On and beside every road and track leading east, shot-up vehicles had broken down; the cadavers of horses lay around. Even ambulances, packed with wounded, stood burning by the side of the road.'[40]

Rudolf von Gersdorff, Seventh Army's chief-of-staff, struggled against this tide of soldiers trudging wearily eastwards, to find his master, Paul Hausser. 'The scenes I saw were horrendous,' he recalled. 'I encountered thousands of German soldiers in utter disarray, without weapons. The seriously wounded lay covered in blood by the roadside; no one was concerned for them.' Gersdorff finally found Hausser and his staff at dusk on 18 August, sheltering in a quarry which was bombarded by Allied aircraft and artillery fire. 'No one slept, with one exception,' the chief-of-staff recalled. 'That old veteran Hausser slept despite the hard rocks and artillery fire as if he was in a four-poster bed.'[41]

In this chaos the discipline of the German Army began to break down. There was little semblance of order. Men seized any vehicle, any car, any truck, to escape a pocket growing narrower by the hour. They were determined to escape the cauldron. A *Gefreiter* riding one of 21st Panzer Division's few remaining tanks recalled: 'At the sight of naked, half-burned tank men we promised ourselves that we would not let ourselves be finished off in the pocket. It was a hellish journey.' *Sturmmann* Leo Knebelsberger joined a column of armour which no longer had any guns to pull. They had been lost in the chaotic retreat. 'The eighteen-ton half-tracks were filled to the brim with all available ammunition and men,' he remembered. 'In an endless file of vehicles loaded in such a strange fashion, our unit moved to the south-east, passing high hedges. The column remained stuck endlessly and often spent hours in the same place.' Some men showed signs of delirium, others melancholy – the *Landser* called it *Kesselfieber*, pocket fever. All men showed signs of exhaustion from the endless marching eastwards, continually harassed by the Allied artillery and *Jabos*. 'Fighting through waves of exhaustion, we would find ourselves still marching, still putting one foot in front of the other and still keeping touch with the man in front and the man behind,' one survivor recalled. Simply resting against a tree, a wall was enough for a *Landser* to fall asleep.[42]

Officers tried to direct traffic at choked junctions. They were simply disobeyed. The trucks and armour rolled past. They did not stop even to pick up the wounded. Ewald Klapdor watched as the *Frundsberg*'s commander dragged a driver out of his vehicle and beat him when he refused to take casualties with him. 3rd *Fallschirmjäger* Division's commander *Generalleutnant* Richard Schimpf felt it necessary to re-impose discipline on his men:

> There is no reason for concern about the situation. It is rumoured that the division is encircled by the enemy. All rumours of this kind are false.
>
> The army, British or American, which can encircle or capture our division does not exist...It is certain that we will finish this war victoriously. And it is just as certain that the glorious 3rd *Fallschirmjäger* Division will never cease to fight and will do its duty unvanquished to the end of the war.
>
> Whoever thinks or speaks differently will be slapped across the face.[43]

There was no reason for concern, Richard Schimpf insisted. There was every reason for concern. At 7.20 p.m. on the evening of 19 August, American and Canadian troops finally joined forces near Chambois. 'The cauldron is closed,' panzer man Heinz Trautmann noted bitterly. 'Everybody is depressed.'[44]

Salvation came at different times on different days to different men. The core of the *Hitlerjugend* bolted eastwards in the small hours of 20 August. The division's commander, Kurt Meyer, had spent most of the preceding day struggling to find the command post of Seventh Army. The journey was infernal. 'The misery around us screams to high heaven,' Meyer recorded in his diary. 'Refugees and soldiers from the broken German armies look helplessly at the bombers flying continuously overhead.' Forests and copses were littered with the cadavers of horses or wounded soldiers, abandoned by their comrades to an uncertain fate. Meyer eventually found Paul Hausser and his staff in their 'command post' – a ditch next to a farm. It was time, Hausser told the young commander, to break out. Seventh Army's chief-of-staff had convinced him of the need to break out that morning to save what was left of his Army. Meyer ran the Allied gauntlet back to his men 'crowded together in the shadow of the steep walls, waiting for the protection of night to jump off '.[45] In those final minutes before the breakout, staff burnt what papers they could, then seized weapons to fight their way out alongside their men. At the stroke of midnight, the remnants of the *Hitlerjugend*, *Leibstandarte* and 3rd *Fallschirmjäger* Division struck out into the night. Kurt Meyer led from the front. He no longer had a division to command, only the remnants of a once great panzer division. He could no longer command either. He could not communicate with his men; all his radios were gone, telephone links simply did not exist. The best Panzermeyer could do now was to will his troops on. Through the dark and drizzle – it was raining now – this makeshift group of *Waffen SS* men headed off, bound for the village of Chambois – outside the *Kessel*. 'The mist stank of death and gunpowder,' *Fallschirmjäger* Johann Bornert remembered. 'We were still being shelled and my ears could no longer bear the screams and the misery of the wounded, calling for stretcher bearers. I knew that there weren't any left.' The banks of the River Dives, an insignificant obstacle ordinarily – barely a dozen feet wide near Chambois – were stained with blood. Kurt Meyer watched as teams of horses galloping down the west bank, hauling their wagons, tumbled. The carts toppled over, and a hideous entanglement of man and beast struggled through the mud to climb the opposite bank, only to be cut down by enemy artillery. From the high ground on the west bank of the Dives, Panzermeyer surveyed a battlefield 'covered with dead and dying German soldiers'. He continued: 'The enemy stands on the hilltops firing relentlessly into the pocket. Most of the victims belong to the infantry support units who remain in the pocket with their horse-drawn transport. Leaderless, they run for their lives.' Meyer and his band of 200 officers and men spent the morning running between hedges and ditches north-east of Chambois, before finally running into a reconnaissance party of the SS *Das Reich* trying to break into the pocket from the outside.[46]

Panzer Lehr company commander Josef Graf and his men spent the night of 19-20 August resting next to the blackened remnants of Fifth Panzer Army: burned out panzers, wrecked half-tracks, trucks, smashed artillery pieces. Here, in the fields south of Trun, what was left of the German Army in the west assembled for one final onslaught – the breakout, under the ever-present eyes of the Allied air forces. How, Graf asked himself, had it come to this? 'A distressing scene unfolds before our eyes – the end of two armies.' Dawn brought hope. The battlefield stretched out in front of a motley assortment of German troops, SS and *Wehrmacht*:

Panzers roll forwards, personnel carriers follow on a wide front, followed by numerous vehicles – artillery, trucks. The infantry walks on the pavement trying to find cover. We're right in the middle of the move when the enemy tanks and anti-tank guns open fire on the panzer spearhead. Motorized units nervously turn about and look for cover in the meadows. With some officers and soldiers, I drive

209

into a pasture meadow with a personnel carrier. I then realize we're being fired at from all sides. Where are our friends? Where is the enemy?... Everything's on the road to ruin on the battlefield. While panzers continue to struggle to advance to free the road for other vehicles and for the infantry, a lot of the others roll down neighbouring lanes to break through independently. Our personnel carrier crosses a brook. There, there is a general with his adjutant who wants to stop all vehicles. He threatens a court-martial, waving his pistol. But in the face of this will to escape, he's powerless. We continue to roll with the personnel carrier and other vehicles and look to save ourselves on side roads. Now, my personnel carrier is on its own. At that moment, near a junction, we come across a German car whose driver calls to us that the road is occupied by the enemy: a breakthrough is impossible. Then we take the secondary road and tear along at top speed. Suddenly an enemy anti-tank gun fires at us. We are on our own in a huge field and at 9 a.m. we reach the assembly point in the German line. The breakthrough has succeeded.[47]

The majority of the 2nd and 9th SS Panzers also broke out on 20 August. By now, the two divisions could muster little more than twenty tanks between them. But fate smiled on them on 20 August. The skies were overcast, the *Landser*'s best shield from Allied air power. The breakout succeeded somehow. Two thousand German soldiers rejoined their comrades, with a motley assortment of maybe seventy-five tanks and vehicles, all that was left of two *Waffen SS* panzer divisions.

For at least 20,000 men the ordeal was still not over. They were still pushing, stumbling, in some cases riding, in rare cases driving, eastwards. The encircled men were being funnelled towards the neck of the pocket, barely three miles wide, centred on the small town of St Lambert, on the east bank of the River Dives. The Falaise pocket was now nowhere near Falaise. It was barely a pocket, more a bubble running from St Lambert in the east to the fields north of Argentan. It was no more than seven miles long, no wider than maybe two miles. Around St Lambert it was barely a few hundred metres across, and there it ended.

St Lambert was the gateway to freedom. The road to St Lambert became the corridor of death. 'The closer we got to the breakout point the more ghastly was the scene that met our eyes,' a *Leutnant* in 21st Panzer Division wrote. 'The roads were blocked by two or three shot-up, burnt-out vehicles standing alongside each other, ammunition was exploding, tanks were burning and horses lay struggling on their backs until they were eventually released. In the fields far and wide was the same chaos. The enemy artillery fired into the turmoil from all sides; everything was pressing east.'[48]

In Seventh Army's command wagon, chief-of-staff Rudolf von Gersdorff headed a long column of vehicles which ground to a halt on the edge of St Lambert shortly after dawn on 20 August, when Allied anti-tank guns opened fire. Gersdorff commandeered two partially combat-worthy panzers to knock out the guns. He wrote later:

Our action was the signal for all the panzers, half-tracks, artillery vehicles, self-propelled guns, cars and trucks to break from cover and join us in a great mass. There may have been more than 100 vehicles which clusters of men were clinging to. We crossed a small river, the Dives, without encountering any resistance, and passed St Lambert. Then our enemy seemed to have recovered from his surprise, for there was suddenly strong defensive fire. We were already in the midst of the front lines of a Canadian brigade. Hundreds, with their arms raised, surrendered to us. Since we could not do anything with them, we disarmed them and left them.

When Gersdorff's command truck could go no further, he moved to a Tiger of the *Leibstandarte* and began to coordinate the final stages of the breakout:

There were about 100 vehicles and roughly 1,500 men, members of almost every division in the pocket [Gersdorff recalled]. I formed an armoured group from the combat vehicles and split the motley assortment of troops – infantrymen, panzer crew, artillerymen and members of supply units – into companies of about 100 men each, placed under the officers present – even veterinary officers and pay-masters. Enemy fire in the meantime had become stronger. Even during the briefing several officers and men had been wounded. After thorough reconnaissance the attack continued. We soon encountered British armoured forces. After destroying about a dozen Churchill tanks the attack continued unimpeded. Finally we ran into II SS Panzer Corps which was coming to meet us. We were through![49]

Supply officer Ewald Klapdor had yet to reach the Dives valley. As dawn broke on 20 August revealing a light mist shrouding the Norman landscape, the stragglers of the *Frundsberg* were forcing their way up a small hill near the village of Aubry, thirteen miles south-east of Falaise. As they reached the wooded summit, the Dives valley stretched out before them to the east and with it the way home. The terrain was littered with panzers, armoured vehicles, horses with and without their carts, with and without their riders, and weary grenadiers, pioneers, infantrymen, *Landsers* looking for a way out of encirclement. And then the mist began to lift, revealing the exodus to Allied observers. The enemy artillery quickly found its range, Ewald Klapdor noticed:

Shells crash nearby, causing unease in the mass of vehicles. On the surrounding slopes the flash of barrels can clearly be seen. We have no doubt that all hell will be let loose here and run back to our vehicles. We must reach the other side of the wood with them so we are at least partially out of sight.

While we force our way through the halted, helpless columns, the first shells howl close by and hit the column. Salvoes of twenty and thirty shells follow one after the other. Panic seizes men and animals. They wander around all over the place. They only want to evade death, which is unpredictable and leaping around like a lunatic.

I watch this chaos spellbound. The vehicles have orders to drive into the valley and wait. Shells whistle past from all sides. The ring must already be very tight.

An officer, *Major* Prince Holstein, comes up to me to ask about the situation. That's obvious. We only have to look around for ourselves. We both stare at the flashing red fountains of earth going past. 'No orders can help here any more,' he says. 'Let's hope the bulk of the army can still get out in time.' He shakes his head resignedly and heads off.

I now run to the vehicles which are right under a hedge. The fire increases, it rains shells. The valley and the slopes are strewn with destroyed material and vehicles. The dead stare into the gleaming sun. The bloated bodies of horses, collapsed in their harnesses, ammunition and weapons covered with earth.[50]

Another caught in the Allied barrage on the Dives valley that morning was Heinrich von Lüttwitz, 2nd Panzer Division's commander. The Allies had come to regard Lüttwitz as a worthy adversary, his division as an equal to the very best of the *Waffen SS* armoured units. Now the general had little to do but survey the carnage:

Numerous trains of vehicles ran into direct enemy fire of every description, turned back, and in some cases drove round in a circle until they were shot up and blocked the road. Towering pillars of smoke rose incessantly from petrol tanks as they were hit, ammunition exploded, riderless horses stampeded, some of them badly wounded.[51]

Ewald Klapdor and his men dashed down the gentle slopes towards the valley floor. With each salvo from Allied artillery, the *Waffen SS* men buried themselves in the ground as best they could. The staff car suffered a direct hit and blazed uncontrollably, its dead driver behind the wheel. To stay in open ground was to court death. The remnants of the *Frundsberg* headed for the Dives. But not all of them. By now many men were resigned to their fate. Death or captivity. 'For several days now we have been inside the pocket,' one forlorn medic jotted in his diary. 'We are supposed to fight our way out. Our comrades of the infantry fall like flies. There is no leadership left. I don't want to fight anyone, it is so useless. God grant that we get out of this alive.' Near the eastern edge of the pocket, Klapdor came upon a sunken road. Salvation was maybe a few miles away, but many men refused to accept it:

> There's a scene of devastation – all manner of burned and wrecked vehicles. Soldiers have dug into the slope's sides so deeply that you fear the holes will collapse. Some have been killed in their foxholes by splinters from trees; others crawl into the holes and shelter next to the dead. The floor of the hollow is littered with the dead. No one buries them. We have to clamber our way over the corpses of horses, which already smell.
>
> We order individual soldiers to come with us. But they merely stare at us not understanding, fear and terror written all over their exhausted faces. They are simply waiting for the moment that they are led away into captivity – the moment of salvation.[52]

It was early afternoon when von Lüttwitz reached the River Dives before the village of St Lambert, a few miles upstream from Trun. The Dives was the last major natural obstacle barring the Germans' exit from the Falaise pocket, a few feet deep, a few feet wide. But almost every bridge over the Dives had been destroyed. At St Lambert, one still stood. Here was the exit from the Falaise pocket. 'The crossing of the Dives was particularly grim,' Lüttwitz recalled. 'Men, horses, various equipment was thrown from the bridge into the Dives where they formed a macabre mess.' The bridge running into St Lambert was proving to be a bottleneck, as Ewald Klapdor noted:

> A vast cemetery of vehicles spreads out in front of the bridge. Blackened, burned out wrecks, overturned horse-drawn carts, the corpses of horses all over the place and on top of each other. Leaning against a burned-out heavy truck there's a motorcycle, its burned rider still sitting on it. Terrible! Here in front of the Dives bridge, death has reaped a terrible harvest.
>
> Things are no different on the road to the village. Slowly we make

our way. Everywhere there is this sweet smell mixed with the smell of something still burning.[53]

The encircled troops set up a temporary command post opposite the village church, a few hundred yards from the last major obstacle, the River Dives. *Frundsberg, Hitlerjugend, Panzer Lehr*, 2nd Panzer. It seemed as if the remnants of every German division in Normandy had converged on this hamlet hoping for salvation. They were tired, hungry, often unarmed. They had seen their comrades mauled by enemy air power or artillery. They had abandoned their panzers, their half-tracks, their staff cars. They came mostly on foot. They came mostly without their leaders. St Lambert sur Dives was 'burning fiercely' when Hans Erich Braun rolled into the village in his battered half-track. The scenes which greeted him were appalling:

> Torn-off arms and legs still clad in jackboots, bodies covered in rags of uniform, these were lying in a doorway. And, standing in a side road, burning fiercely, dozens of motorcycles and sidecars of a motorcycle unit, the drivers still sitting in their saddles, being roasted by the flames. Torn bodies, men and horses, hit a hundred times over by bullets, lying both sides of the road. [54]

In a house opposite the village church, Heinz Harmel gathered what men of his 10th SS Panzer Division were still left. 'The last windows have been smashed, the door is blown in, the walls tremble,' Klapdor observed. 'A bizarre briefing in a divisional command post, where among the commanders, soldiers of all ranks and even civilians cower. After dark, the stragglers still stuck in the Falaise pocket would make one last desperate lunge to join German lines. From the east, their comrades would attack westwards to keep the neck of the pocket open. 'The break out is this evening,' Heinz Harmel told his men. It was now or never.

The waiting during those final hours before the breakout was intolerable. 'The mood is depressed,' wrote Klapdor. 'The fate of this heroic division rests on these final hours. The thoughts in this room are dictated by the uncertainty of the coming night. Will the breakout be successful?'

A light drizzle filled the air. The troops caught a few hours' sleep if they could. Most could not. And then out of the darkness, the incoming howl of shells. The damp night was lit up by the fiery yellow-red flames of artillery rounds impacting on the streets of St Lambert. 'The enemy seems to have realized our intentions, or suspected them,' Klapdor recorded with concern. 'Wild fire destroys almost the entire place. The walls of our house tremble, too, but still stand.'[55]

And then came the signal to move. 'We gripped our weapons tighter,' one survivor of the breakout recalled. 'We may have been tired, even exhausted, but the chance of escape gave us new speed and inspiration.' Among bushes, undergrowth, under the shadow of trees, German soldiers had waited anxiously for the final chance to escape encirclement. The trapped *Landsers* were breathing down the necks of their jailors. One soldier recollected:

> We were so close to the enemy we were not troubled by his artillery fire. I think that perhaps he did not know that we were so near to him for much of the barrage fell a long way behind us and upon a countryside now almost deserted for, remember, we were among the last units to leave.[56]

It was the small hours of 21 August before the *Frundsberg* moved off, almost in silence. Ewald Klapdor described the breakout:

> It's difficult getting past the ruins blocking the road. Without a sound we go over fences, through hedges, across meadows and then again on the dirt tracks. The rain, which is falling more heavily, has already soaked us to the skin. We barely feel it any more. On a heavy truck I find a coat and sling it around me.
>
> Eyes pierce the black night and ears listen tensely to every sound. Hand grenades are clasped in our hands, ready to be thrown. Everyone is determined to get out of here. Repeatedly the marching stops when dark shadows rise from the earth and whisper. But they are our comrades, with the same goal – they all want to go through the forest in front of us and reach freedom. [57]

As the *Frundsberg* moved out of St Lambert, Canadian troops moved in. The last Germans leaving the village were caught in a wild firefight with the Allies. Hans Erich Braun's half-track ran into Canadians furiously holding out in a farmhouse which blocked the German rush to the east. 'Every gun opened up at them,' the senior NCO remembered. 'Their bodies were instantly and unrecognizably torn to shreds, leaving two lone steel helmets bowling along still in the escape direction, spinning like mad as the bullets kicked them.' Elsewhere, it was the escaping Germans who were mown down, as one Canadian officer observed:

> There was no cover at hand for them. Those who were not hit ran towards the dead ground in the draw to their right, through which a stream runs. The attack was completely disrupted.
>
> The gun numbers had been presented with just such a target as they had often wished for. Until about 0800 hours the machine-

gunners fired at whatever they could see. During this time a host of white flags appeared and hundreds of the enemy crowded in to surrender.[58]

Corporal Dick Raymond watched in awe as the flotsam of a once mighty army ran, rather than fought. 'It was the first time we had ever seen the German Army out in the open,' the Canadian recalled. 'We would see a group trying to run across a field from one wood to another, and watch some fall, some run on, some lie moaning in front of us. It was more of an execution than a battle.'[59]

Three miles to the south, the final stragglers of the *Hitlerjugend* were forcing their way out of the pocket around the village of Chambois. The enemy was waiting for them, unleashing a fearsome artillery barrage as Kurt Misch bitterly recalled:

Nearly all tree bursts, dreadful wounds, men rolling, screaming, with torn stomachs. With gruesome irony, I recalled the words of that song which begins: 'No better death in the world than by an enemy's hand.' Traction engines rolled over bodies. The sight of squashed flesh in the caterpillar tracks was unbearable. All order was gone. Panic triumphed.[60]

Amid this panic there was no time to help fallen comrades. The wounded and dead were left where they fell. The rolling terrain of the Dives valley became a graveyard for Seventh and Fifth Panzer Armies, as one *Landser* observed:

Wherever one looked there were bodies. The stench was appalling for the fields were filled also with the bodies of artillery horses and civilian cattle. There were columns of burnt out trucks and in the cabs of some the incinerated bodies of the drivers. There were corpses along the roads, in the ditches, some of them blown into the tree tops. Along some stretches of the road whole blocks of lorries formed a dam and had to be pushed to one side by pairs of tanks working together. There could be, under such conditions, no great respect shown to the dead and bodies lying in the roads were often rolled over by the tanks and crushed under the tracks. It was not lack of feeling, but it was more important to save the living than to respect the corpses.[61]

The Canadian troops following on the Germans' heels were astonished by the scenes which greeted them:

The road – as were all the roads in the area – was lined and in places practically blocked by destroyed German vehicles of every description. Horses and men lay rotting in every ditch and hedge and the air was rank with the odour of putrefaction. Unburied dead and parts of them were strewn about by the score.[62]

Under the first strains of light on 21 August Ewald Klapdor and his comrades climbed the slopes on the right bank of the Dives. The momentum of the exodus could not be stopped. The German soldier swarmed eastwards:

> This morning, hundreds upon hundreds are pouring through the gap kept open for them here. Despite the days they have endured, they are nevertheless somehow happy and brave.
>
> This scene on the road cannot be described. Officers and soldiers march in confusion, without a unit, all merely happy to have escaped. The road is lined with abandoned or destroyed vehicles and all manner of military equipment.[63]

Outside the pocket, the *Das Reich* Division struck westwards in a bid to join forces with their comrades. The SS thrust quickly cut through the encircling forces, and men breaking out fell into their arms. 'They had obviously been through a tremendous mental and physical ordeal,' regimental commander Otto Weidinger recalled. 'The tension of the past hours was visible in the faces of these men, and they were proud to have brought their weapons and equipment out of the hellish pocket.'[64] The men reaching him, Weidinger remembered, talked of a 'Stalingrad in Normandy'.

It was nearing 9 a.m. on 21 August when Kurt Misch's comrade Leo Freund closed in on German lines. The final few hundred yards were the worst. 'One of our comrades was ripped apart and almost all of us were splattered with blood and pieces of flesh,' he wrote years later. 'Many of our comrades stayed behind in that pasture.'[65]

Ewald Klapdor was still making his way eastwards. The panzer which he and his comrades clung to finally stuttered to a halt maybe ten miles from the village of Chaumont, the rallying point. Those final miles were covered on foot. It was well into the afternoon when the last of the *Frundsberg* reached German lines in Chaumont, no more than sixteen miles from St Lambert where Monday, 21 August, had begun. The sole inn was swamped with exhausted, thirsty *Landsers*, guzzling cider.[66]

The men of the *Das Reich* held open the path to freedom until 4 p.m. 'No more stragglers were going to arrive,' Otto Weidinger gloomily concluded. The *Das Reich* moved out to the east. As they did, the jaws of the Falaise pocket snapped shut. They would not re-open. The breakout was over. Panzer grenadier Walter Padberg spoke for every man who had escaped. 'We were of the opinion,' he said decades later, 'we had left hell behind us.'[67]

At Army Group B's headquarters in La Roche-Guyon there was optimism. The breakout had succeeded. Maybe 'forty to fifty per cent of the encircled units succeeded in breaking through to the east and north-east' its new leader Walter Model reported to Berlin. Men had been saved, but not their equipment. 'Material losses were very high,' the field marshal conceded. One American division alone counted 220 destroyed panzers, another 160 self-propelled guns, 700 artillery pieces, 130 flak guns, 130 half-tracks, 5,000 vehicles and 2,000 wagons smashed.[68]

Yet somehow the remnants of Seventh and Fifth Panzer Armies had escaped. 'Who can describe our surprise over the numbers who have already found their way here and keep on coming,' Ewald Klapdor noted in his diary on the evening of 21 August, his first night outside the pocket. How many escaped? Maybe 20,000, maybe 40,000. But Seventh and Fifth Panzer Armies existed in name only. In the days after the break out, the German Army tallied its losses at Falaise, or rather counted what was left of two once great armies. The *Frundsberg* consisted of four weak infantry battalions, no panzers, no artillery; the *Hitlerjugend*, down to just 300 men and ten panzers; the *Hohenstaufen*, just 460 men and two dozen panzers; the *Leibstandarte* was no longer a panzer division, it was no longer a division, just a collection of shattered infantry; *Das Reich* could muster 450 men and maybe fifteen panzers. The regular army divisions fared no better. 2nd Panzer had no panzers just an infantry battalion; 21st Panzer comprised four weak infantry battalions and the Greyhound division, 116th Panzer, brought just twelve tanks across the Seine. The encircling Allied armies simply lost count of the number of prisoners they were taking. The best estimates suggest 50,000 Germans fell into Allied hands in the week-long battle. The bodies of at least another 10,000 men littered the Norman countryside, its towns and villages scarred by a fortnight of ferocious fighting. Now a lugubrious silence fell across the Falaise pocket. And numbers tell only half the story. The men who escaped the inferno of Falaise were never the same again. When Eugen Meindl staggered back to *Fallschirmjäger* headquarters in Nancy, his staff noticed their leader had changed. Gone was the 'well-known iron discipline', in its place 'loud emotional outbursts' aimed at the 'impossible demands of the supreme command'. Meindl would fight on to the war's end, but never again with the same ferocity. He was not alone.[69]

In Mont Ormel on the eastern edge of the pocket, the French mayor surveyed what was left of his village. 'It was a horrible sight. The road was jammed for more than 300 yards with burnt-out trucks and shattered vehicles of all types. The houses were flat. The apple trees uprooted. And German corpses were everywhere. There were about 200 dead Germans. All the farms were damaged, the cattle killed or wounded, the trees smashed and the fences broken down.'[70] The scene was the same throughout the Dives valley. Village after village, town after town had been all but razed to the ground. Two out of three homes in Trun alone were in ruins. The fields were littered with discarded rifles, boots, tunics and empty steel helmets, their owner's fate unknown. This was a charnel house unsurpassed in the west. The Allied soldier entering the pocket on 22 August found every lane, every path, every road littered with the detritus of a beaten army.

Group Captain Desmond Scott and his comrades in their Typhoon fighter-bombers had sowed the battlefield of Falaise with iron. Now, touring the pocket, Scott found himself pitying his foe. 'Bits of uniform were plastered to shattered tanks and trucks and human remains hung in grotesque shapes on the blackened hedgerows,' he recalled four decades later. 'Corpses lay in pools of dried blood, staring into space as if their eyes were being forced from their sockets.' Here on the lanes, roads, paths, and byways of lower Normandy two armies had tried to escape. Not just with panzers and trucks, guns and ammunition, but with everything which a modern army needed to survive. Field canteens, mobile workshops, spare parts, uniforms, helmets, and sacks of mail bound for the front line or heading for loved ones in the Fatherland. Desmond Scott found the contents of one torn bag scattered on the roadside. 'I picked up a photograph of a smiling young German recruit standing between his parents, two solemn parents who stared back at me in accusation,' he wrote.[71] Even Allied supreme commander Dwight Eisenhower, who visited the Dives four days later with a party of press, was moved by the sight before him. It was a scene which 'could only be described by Dante. It was literally possible to walk for hundreds of yards at a time, stepping on nothing but dead and decaying flesh.'[72] His staff showed more relish for the destruction wrought at Falaise, as Bradley's First Army commented:

> The carnage wrought during the final days as the artillery of two Allied armies and the massed air forces pounded the ever-shrinking pocket was perhaps the greatest of the war. The roads and fields were littered with thousands of enemy dead and wounded, wrecked and burning vehicles, smashed artillery pieces, carts laden with the loot of France overturned and smouldering, dead horses and cattle swelling in the summer's heat.[73]

219

The Allied soldier had encountered nothing like it. Death had indeed reaped a terrible harvest. Death was everywhere. In every town. In every village. On every bridge. On every road. Especially on every road. One British soldier tried to advance eastwards from Falaise in the wake of the retreating *Wehrmacht*. He wrote home:

> After we left Falaise behind, all the roads were so choked with burnt-out German equipment that it was quite impossible to continue the journey. The bloated corpses of unfortunate domestic animals also lay in our path, so we took to the fields and tried to make some progress across country. Each spinney and copse contained its dreadful quota of dead Germans lying beside their wrecked vehicles, and once we came across the body of what had been a beautiful woman lying sprawled across the back seat of a staff car.[74]

Bulldozers and tractors were driven down roads to clear a path, piling cadavers four deep by the wayside. In the late August heat, the corpses of men and horses decomposed. 'The bodies crawled with blue-grey maggots,' English private Alfred Lee remembered. 'The spectacle was unspeakable when tanks drove over them. Many men had to put on gas masks to endure getting through it.'[75] The stench was so all-embracing, so overpowering that Allied soldiers clearing out the pocket made no tally of the booty or the burnt-out and wrecked vehicles and armour. Tally, or no tally, Falaise was a vast graveyard. On the last day of the month, an American officer, veteran of the battles of the Western Front from a generation earlier, toured the battlefield near Trun and recorded his impressions:

> The grass and trees were vividly green as in all Normandy and a surprising number of houses [were] untouched. That rather peaceful setting framed a picture of destruction so great that it cannot be described. It was as if an avenging angel had swept the entire area bent on destroying all things German.
>
> I stood on a lane surrounded by twenty or thirty dead horses or parts of horses, most them still hitched to their wagons and carts. As far as my eye could reach, on every line of sight, there were vehicles, wagons, tanks, guns, prime movers, sedans, rolling kitchens, in various stages of destruction...
>
> I saw no foxholes or any other type of shelter or field fortifications. The Germans were trying to run and had no place to run. They were probably too exhausted to dig. They were probably too tired even to surrender.
>
> I left this area rather regretting I'd seen it. [76]

Notes

1. Stacey, p.216.
2. Lucas and Barker, *The Killing Ground*, p.105.
3. Belfield and Essame, p.213.
4. Meyer, Kurt, *Grenadiers*, p.157.
5. Belfield and Essame, pp. 214-15.
6. Meyer, op. cit., pp. 157-8.
7. Belfield and Essame, p.217.
8. Agte, pp.424, 430.
9. Meyer, Kurt, op. cit., pp. 160-1.
10. Telecons Kluge-Eberbach, 2100 and 2330 Hours, 8/8/44. KTB PzAOK5, 8/8/44. IWM AL1901/1.
11. Meyer, Kurt, op. cit., pp. 161-2.
12. Meyer, ibid., p.164; Lucas and Barker, op. cit., pp. 110-12.
13. Meyer, ibid., p.164; Lucas and Barker, ibid., p.112.
14. Telecon Dietrich-Speidel, 1035 Hours, 13/8/44. KTB PzAOK5 Anlagen, 13/8/44. IWM AL1901/4; KTB Pz.AOK 5, 14/8/44. IWM AL1901/3; KTB OB West, 0045 Hours, 15/8/44. IWM AL785/2; OB West Ia Nr.717/44, 15/8/4/44. IWM AL785/2/2.
15. Klapdor, p.377.
16. Telecon Jodl-Blumentritt, 1830 Hours, 15/8/44. KTB OB West Anlagen, 15/8/44. IWM AL785/2/2.
17. Meeting of the Führer with Generalleutnant Westphal and Generalleutnant Krebs, 31/8/44. Conferences, pp.465, 468; OKW WFSt Nr.772887/44, 1930 Hours, 15/8/44. KTB OB West Anlagen, 15/8/44. IWM AL785/2/2.
18. Telecon Kluge-Blumentritt, 1155 Hours, 16/8/44. Telecon Kluge-Jodl, 1245 Hours, 16/8/44. KTB OB West, Anlagen, 16/8/44. IWM AL785/2/2.
19. Eisenhower order of the day, 14/8/44. Eisenhower Papers, p.2068.
20. Blandford, p.248; KTB PzAOK5, 14/8/44. IWM AL1901/3; Stacey, pp.240-3; Tagesmeldung AGp.B, 14/8/44. IWM AL1531/3.
21. Meyer, op. cit., p.167.
22. Cited in Reynolds, *Steel Inferno*, p.254.
23. Cited in Meyer, Hubert , *12 SS Panzer Division Hitlerjugend*, pp.190-1.
24. Stacey, pp.250-1.
25. Klapdor, p.378; Lucas and Barker, op. cit., p.122.
26. Shulman, pp.211-13; 'Panzergruppe Eberbach and the Falaise Encirclement', MS A-922. Cited in Reardon, p.277.
27. KTB PzAOK5, 17/8/44. IWM AL1901/3; Tagesmeldung PzAOK5, 18/8/44. KTB PzAOK5 Anlagen, 18/8/44. IWM AL1901/4; XL 6875, 0545 Hours, 18/8/44. NA DEFE3/121.
28. McKee, p.378.
29. Agte, p.456.
30. Klapdor, p.379.
31. TB Goebbels, 17/8/44.
32. SHAEF Weekly Intelligence Summary No.22, 19/8/44. NA WO219/1922.
33. Standartenführer Lingner, 17th SS Panzer Grenadier Division, CSDIC Reports, SRM 1206, 11/2/45. NA WO208/4140; Görlitz, Model, pp.124, 197; Meeting of the Führer with Generalleutnant Westphal and Generalleutnant Krebs, 31/8/44. Conferences, p.466.
34. KTB PzAOK5, 18/8/44 and Anlagen, KTB PzAOK5, 18/8/44. IWM AL1901/3; IWM AL1901/4; Tagesmeldung OB West, 18/8/44. KTB OB West Anlagen, 18/8/44. IWM AL785/2/2. Florentin, p.183.
35. *OB West: A Study in Command*, pp.152-3; MS B-807.
36. Kluge letter, 18/8/44. Author's papers. Various translations, including Shulman, pp.202-05.
37. Klapdor, pp.379-80.

38. McKee, p.377.
39. Stacey, p.260; Belfield and Essame, p.209; Leleu, *10 SS Panzer Division 'Frundsberg'*, p.147.
40. Luck, p.204.
41. Gersdorff, pp. 158-9.
42. Luck, p.205; Leleu, op. cit., p.146; Lucas and Barker, op. cit., pp.151-2.
43. Tagesbefehl 3 Fallschirmjäger Division, 14/8/44. Cited in Shulman, pp.207-8.
44. McKee, p.375.
45. Meyer, Kurt, op. cit., p.169.
46. Florentin, p.236; Meyer, ibid., p.170.
47. KTB Josef Graf, 20/8/44. Cited in Perrigault, *La Panzer Lehr Division*, p.312.
48. Luck, pp. 205-6.
49. Gersdorff, pp. 159-60.
50. Klapdor, p.381.
51. Shulman, p.210.
52. Shulman, p.211; Klapdor, p.385.
53. ZA1-157. *Témoignage du Generalleutnant von Lüttwitz*, p.20. Leleu, op. cit., p.149; Klapdor, p.385.
54. McKee, p.382.
55. Klapdor, pp.386-7.
56. Lucas and Barker, op. cit., p.154.
57. Klapdor, pp. 387-8.
58. McKee, pp. 383-4; Stacey, p.263.
59. Hastings, *Overlord*, p.358.
60. McKee, p.380.
61. Lucas and Barker, op. cit., pp.152-3.
62. Stacey, p.264.
63. Klapdor, p.388.
64. Weidinger, *Comrades to the End*, pp. 328-9.
65. Meyer, Hubert, op. cit., p.200.
66. Klapdor, p.389.
67. Weidinger, op. cit., p.332; Ambrose, op. cit., pp. 103-4.
68. Tagesmeldung AGp.B, 20/8/44. IWM AL1531/3; Blumenson, *Breakout and Pursuit*, p.558.
69. Klapdor, p.389; OB West Tagesmeldung, 31/8/44. Cited in Canadian Report No.50: The Campaign in Northwest Europe – Information from German Sources, Part II: *Invasion and Battle of Normandy*, p.284; Stimpel, ii, p.204.
70. Florentin, pp.294-5.
71. Hastings, op. cit., p.365.
72. Eisenhower, p.306.
73. Blumenson, op. cit., p.557.
74. Belfield and Essame, p.238.
75. Hastings, op. cit., p.365.
76. Blumenson, op. cit., p.558.

Chapter 11

Out-Generalled and Out-Fought

History has shown that the loss of Paris always means the fall of the whole of France.

Adolf Hitler

The army retreating in 1918 after the revolution looked like guards compared with the scores of fleeing troops today.

General Georg Ritter von Hengl

Paris. City of light. City of darkness. The swastika still fluttered atop the Eiffel Tower, along the Tuilieries, from the Chamber of Deputies, above the Arc de Triomphe. Unfamiliar signposts in a foreign language littered familiar landmarks and road junctions. Each day a military band strutted past the Arc de Triomphe and down the Champs Elysées, just as it had done for more than four years. Since shortly after dawn on 14 June 1940, the French capital had been the jewel of Hitler's Reich, enjoyed by German soldiers, endured by Frenchmen. 'It is wonderful to stroll through the streets like this and take in the fine sights of a city – and all that is sad and sordid too,' *Landser* Heinrich Böll observed as he soaked up Paris. There were historical sights: Notre Dame, the Eiffel Tower, the great military academy, the École Militaire, whose sprawling Champs de Mars parade ground 'where Bonaparte drilled with his comrades', Böll observed, was now 'completely silent', as was the Quai d'Orsay, once home to the French Foreign Ministry. And there was the nightlife. The clubs, the bars, the theatre, the Folies. Some *Landsers* succumbed to temptation. 'To be on the safe side send me fifty Reichsmarks – that's a month's wages,' one begged his family so he could enjoy the city of light.[1] Even the Allied landings in Normandy had failed to overtly disrupt life in Paris for occupier and occupied, at least not initially. Captured Allied soldiers were paraded through the streets, proof of German 'victory' on the invasion front, reinforced by the *Pariser Zeitung*, the capital's German-language newspaper.

But since the middle of August there had been a noticeable anxiety among the occupiers. The theatres, cinemas and dance halls were closed, or their shows severely curtailed by power cuts. Crowds of Parisians gathered outsides hotels where German troops were billeted as trucks waited for the men and their kit. 'For the first time the fist of war is banging at the gates of the city,' artillery officer Hans Blöthner, a para-trooper, wrote in his diary on 13 August. 'That frivolous lifestyle we've enjoyed for so long, rotting away in the rear area, is drawing to a close. We laugh, nod our heads. We want to go to the front.' French journal-ist Jean Galtier-Boissière wandered through the French capital, from the Sorbonne to the great railway termini of the Gare du Nord and de l'Est. 'On every thoroughfare,' he observed, 'scores, hundreds of trucks, loaded cars, mounted artillery, ambulances full of wounded on stretch-ers, were in file or overtaking and criss-crossing one another.' Parisians called it 'the great flight of the Fritzes'. To Parisians, as well as the German public, it was obvious now that 'the Anglo-Americans' capture of Paris is merely a question of time'.[2]

Paris did not occupy the thoughts of most *Landsers* in the third and fourth weeks of August 1944, but the river that was its lifeblood did. The Seine was another obstacle the German soldier had to overcome as the remnants of fourteen divisions streamed towards the right bank in the hope that resistance might be offered there. British commander Bernard Montgomery was determined not to give his enemy such an opportunity. He urged his troops on:

> The Allied victory in north-west Europe will have immense reper-cussions; it will lead to the end of the German military domination of France; it is the beginning of the end of the war.
> We must hurl ourselves on the enemy while he is still reeling from the blow; we must deal him more blows and ever more blows; he must be allowed no time to recover.
> This is no time to relax or to sit back and congratulate ourselves. I call on all commanders for a great effort. Let us finish off the business in record time.

It was now a straight race between the Allies and Germans for the Seine crossings downstream of Paris – principally ferries, as bombing had destroyed almost every bridge. The Allied commanders could sense victory. 'We have the greatest chance to win the war ever presented,' US Third Army leader George S. Patton noted in his diary on 21 August as his divisions raced for the Seine. 'We can be in Germany in ten days.' His British rival, Bernard Montgomery, was equally brimming with optimism. 'The German armies in north-west Europe have ceased to exist as effective fighting formations,' Monty wrote. 'We could capture

Paris any time we like. I do not see what there is to oppose us.'3

To protect the crossing points, Model began stripping the still unused Fifteenth Army, sending divisions south over the river. Among those sent was the unfortunate 344th Infantry. Hitherto untried in battle, the division set out for the left bank of the Seine with 8,000 men. As it reached the great river, it fell apart, as its rotund commander, Eugen-Felix Schwalbe, complained. 'Air attacks were so bad, it was only possible to move my formation piece by piece over the river.' 344th Infantry was never an integral division again. By the time it began to deploy on the left bank of the Seine, the Allied armies were upon it. 'We attempted to withdraw, but chaos resulted,' Schwalbe lamented. 'Vehicles jammed every road in all directions and planes attacked us constantly. In a little over a week, my division ceased to exist as a fighting formation. I lost three-fifths of my men and two-thirds of the weapons had to be abandoned.' The general was bitter at the handling his men received. 'I had untried troops under my command and my orders were vague and impossible. I never knew exactly where my division was, what its task was supposed to be and what was taking place all about me.'4

The horrific scenes of the Falaise pocket one week earlier were repeated on the banks of the Seine. Only the weather was on the *Landser*'s side. Rain and cloud persisted as the German Army traipsed across the river. It merely added to the misery. Stragglers from the 10th SS Panzer Division reached the artery of France at Elbeuf, on the great bend of the Seine south of Rouen, on 25 August. The bridge had been destroyed the day before, now the town itself was coming under artillery fire. The SS troops hotfooted six miles downstream to the village of Oissel. Its railway bridge had fallen victim to Allied air attacks, but German engineers had thrown a makeshift wooden structure across the Seine. Vehicles faced a two-day wait to cross the Seine at Oissel. Men filtered across the wooden bridge; vehicles rolled tentatively across the rail crossing which had temporarily been repaired.

Hans-Ulrich Jägermann, a staff officer in the *Leibstandarte*, had escaped from Falaise and re-established some semblance of order among the men he carried along with him. But at the Seine he found 'absolute chaos'. German soldiers were trying to cross the great river 'by all manner of makeshift craft'. Jägermann commandeered two old rowing boats, lashed them together, loaded the wounded aboard, then pushed off from the west bank. 'The scenes on both sides were awful,' he remembered. 'There were masses of dead horses and corpses and equipment lost through the constant Allied air attacks.'5

The *Hohenstaufen*'s Herbert Fürbringer also arrived at the Seine, a few miles downstream of the *Frundsberg*, at Duclair to the west of

Rouen. There was no bridge here, only a ferry. That was the only difference from Oissel, Fürbringer observed:

Things looked awful on the Seine! Columns, in some cases disintegrating, streamed en masse towards the Seine. They were mainly supply and medical columns, but there were also some units among them which would have been better at the front.

One thing was certain – the decision by the supreme command to change banks came too late. In particular it jammed road and side-roads, bombed or shot-up columns, which driving together formed an almost inextricable mess. In the midst of them field police and officers despairingly tried to bring order to this chaos. Where was the once so famous iron discipline of the German soldier? This mass was a popular target for the enemy's fighter-bombers, which fired at will at everything which raised its head.[6]

Somehow, despite the makeshift bridges, the pontoons and the over-worked ferries, around 25,000 vehicles were ferried across the Seine in five days of frenetic activity. But the figure was misleading; what vehicles crossed the Seine were not the panzers and half-tracks, but the rearward services, the supply trains, not the fighting punch of the German Army. In the words of I SS Panzer Corps' commander Sepp Dietrich: 'The Seine crossing was almost as great a disaster as the Falaise pocket.' The *Panzer Lehr* reached the right bank of the river with just twenty panzers, half a dozen guns and five anti-tank destroyers. Its situation was typical. Most panzer divisions reached the right bank of the Seine with, at best, ten tanks still fit for battle and only a handful of artillery pieces. The horse was the most reliable form of transport. Fuel for motor vehicles was at a premium. Fifth Panzer Army no longer merited the word 'panzer'; Heinrich Eberbach could offer just forty-two tanks and self-propelled guns and fewer than 18,000 fighting troops for battle on 25 August. The German Army in the west was in no position to fight a pitched battle. It needed time to re-organize.[7]

Upstream of this tragedy, there was a changing of the guard in the French capital in those depressing mid-August days. Defeat in the west, coupled with mistrust following the 20 July putsch, provoked a wave of dismissals as Adolf Hitler sought to reassert his authority on his crumbling empire. He began with the *Luftwaffe*. *Luftflotte 3* commander, the pompous and ineffective Hugo Sperrle, was sacked and never re-employed. In his place, the Führer picked the uncompromising Otto Dessloch, a man eager to prove his worth to his leader. 'The scapegoat for France has been found,' *Luftwaffe* chief-of-staff Werner Kreipe recorded in his diary. He disagreed with the treatment of Sperrle, but quickly changed his mind when his colleague Karl Koller reported back from an inspection trip of the west. 'Four years as an occupying power and the life of luxury in France is taking its revenge,' Kreipe recorded scathingly, adding: 'The same scandal also afflicts the Army.' Dessloch was appalled by what he found in France. Sperrle's staff were 'completely disorganized, senile and unfit'. To the new arrival the *Luftwaffe* officers guiding the battle in France seemed little more than 'the field marshal's dinner table company'. With Paris threatened, they had quickly fled east to the historic city of Reims, where Dessloch tried to round them up and gain a grip on the situation. The new commander of *Luftflotte 3* quickly showed himself to be ruthless:

> The enemy possesses superiority in both numbers and material. This superiority must and will be equalled and thwarted by determination and bravery. Every commander must act energetically and swiftly. Only the soldier who knows what is at stake knows how to help himself. I have set myself the task of waging a ruthless battle against the enemy forces. All senior and unit commanders who are not involved in actual battle should have one goal – to help the front-line troops...Any complacent spirit will be ruthlessly stamped out. Only the traditional military virtues – discipline, bearing, vigour, toughness, the will to bear responsibility and the joy in bearing it lead to success. Long live the Führer.[8]

Even before Dessloch's order had flashed along the teletype wires in what was left of occupied France, his front-line commanders had begun to break off the battle in the west. South of Paris, Willi Heilmann watched as *Jagdgeschwader 54* abandoned its wrecked airfield at Villacoublay on 19 August. 'Boxes and trunks were packed and loaded on to lorries,' he wrote. 'Any machines that could not be flown had to be scuttled. In sections, the pathetic remains of the once so proud *Gruppe Grünherz* made its way eastward.' Of the eighty men who had served with the *Geschwader* at the beginning of the invasion, just six were still flying. And now the unit was abandoning France. Heilmann concluded glumly: 'We had all flown in vain.'[9]

In his headquarters in the Hotel Meurice, a stone's throw from La Place de la Concorde, Dietrich von Choltitz struggled to get to grips with the task before him. Just a few weeks earlier, he had been commanding LXXXIV Corps on the western flank of the Western Front. But on 3 August had arrived the summons to East Prussia. The Führer wanted to brief him in person on his new assignment: the defence of Paris. The French capital already had a commandant, one Hans von Boineburg-Lengsfeld. But Boineburg was unreliable. He had carried out the arrest of the party organs in Paris on the night of 20 July. Even if he was not a member of the conspiracy, he could not be trusted. Choltitz, on the other hand, could. The stumpy general's chubby face and stocky figure belied his determination and personal bravery. Choltitz had jumped with his men in Rotterdam in May 1940 and led his regiment from the front in the capture of the Crimean fortress of Sevastopol two years later. Dietrich von Choltitz was 'an officer who had never questioned an order no matter how harsh it was'. He was also 'fat, coarse, bemonacled and inflated with a tremendous sense of his own importance'. Now the Führer wanted him to re-impose the rule of German law in the French capital; he would crush any insurrection 'without pity'. As he departed for the west again, Hitler told him: '*General*, you are leaving for Paris. You will receive all the support you need from here. You have the most far-reaching powers a general could be given.' A few days later, at a staff conference, Hitler again asserted his intention to hold the French capital. 'We must hold Paris,' he told his senior planner Alfred Jodl. 'We will hold in front of Paris, we will hold in Paris. We will hold Paris. Paris is to be defended to the last man, without regard to the destruction the fighting may cause.'[10]

The defensive plan Hitler had in mind was throwing up a string of strongpoints on the arterial roads leading into Paris, calling upon the *Luftwaffe* and the security services to man these makeshift barricades. Hitler told von Choltitz to act ruthlessly: 'Scrap all signs of the rear area, get rid of all superfluous agencies and individuals and release all able men to fight at the front; protect the area of greater Paris against stirrings of revolt, and acts of terror and sabotage.' Dietrich von Choltitz was to make the French capital 'the terror of all who are not loyal supporters and servants of the front line'.[11]

Choltitz had arrived in Paris on 9 August and found maybe 25,000 German troops – principally the second-rate 325th Security Division – holding the city. How to defend a city of nearly four million people with such paltry forces? Choltitz asked himself. The enemy was, at least, still eighty miles away. But he was closing almost by the day. His predecessor, von Boineburg-Lengsfeld, had taken some steps to defend the French capital, but only on its approaches. Boineburg-Lengsfeld had no intention of defending Paris street-by-street.

In the second week of August 1944, Choltitz began bolstering his meagre forces. Anti-tank companies were stripped from units in southern France, now streaming north from the Mediterranean coast following Allied landings on 15 August, and an anti-tank specialist was sent from the Reich to train the motley collection of troops in the art of destroying enemy armour. Choltitz ruthlessly emptied headquarters and offices of young officers and thrust light machine guns into their hands and rounded up deserters and stragglers passing through Paris stations. By mid-month, Choltitz had maybe 50,000 men under his command – the remnants of divisions which had escaped the fighting in Normandy and southern France. All but 5,000 of them spread out on the western and south-western approaches to the city along a forty-mile long defensive belt stretched around the city. The remainder, with a handful of artillery pieces and sixty aircraft, would defend the heart of Paris to the last man. A young *Oberst* was given the task of rounding up 'all Germans bearing arms, irrespective of rank, service or branch of the *Wehrmacht*' so they could be trained to become 'determined and ferocious anti-tank fighters' and defend the approaches to Paris. But Dietrich von Choltitz realized he had command of little more than a paper army. 'These emergency units disintegrated with the speed with which they had formed,' he wrote later. 'Conscientious soldiers looked to rejoin their own units, but the bad ones, far from becoming fighters in a Paris becoming uncomfortable, deserted and disappeared.' Nor was the enemy fooled, as one Allied intelligence report's verdict of the defenders of Paris showed: 'No combat troops, a few solid units, lack of commanders and training, inadequate weapons. We should not expect the commander of the *Wehrmacht* in Paris to offer resistance worthy of the name.'[12]

The first American troops crossed the Seine near La Roche-Guyon overnight on 19-20 August. By the following day three US divisions were on the river's right bank. On 23 August, US forces were over the Seine upstream of Paris too. The French capital was being bypassed to the east and west. General Eisenhower was reluctant to send his forces into Paris. He much preferred sweeping past the French capital, into the Pas de Calais to destroy what was left of the German Army in France, rather than slugging it out with the enemy in Paris. In the great American plan, Paris would be encircled and dealt with later on.

Events in the city forced Eisenhower's hand. From 15 August, strikes began to paralyse Paris. The police vanished from the streets. Posters began to appear on walls urging the city's residents to rise up against the Germans. The Parisians responded. On 19th alone, fifty German troops were killed and another 100 wounded by the growing insurrection in the French capital, a revolt fanned by 3,000 gendarmes who had taken over the city's police headquarters on the island which split the Seine and was also home to Notre Dame. It was time, Dietrich von Choltitz decided, to crush the rebellion with 'a bloody gesture'. It was time to send in the panzers and call in the *Luftwaffe*. Before von Choltitz could act, the insurgents in the police prefecture asked for a ceasefire to pick up their dead and wounded. The general agreed. For now, Paris would be spared.[13]

At the Wolf's Lair there was an air of relish at news of the uprising in Paris. Here was the opportunity to raze the French capital to the ground. No longer would Paris be the jewel of Europe. 'If people now try to organize revolts and set up barricades in Paris, then I believe that the fate of the French insurgents will be exactly the same as the Poles in Warsaw,' Joseph Goebbels gloated; the Polish capital was at that very moment being systematically flattened by the SS following a popular uprising. The orders reaching Choltitz from East Prussia were sounding increasingly hysterical. 'Whatever happens, the Führer expects you to carry out the widest destruction possible,' Jodl told him. 'Every measure must be taken for defence.' On the evening of 20 August, the Paris commandant was handed a new instruction: 'If necessary fight in and around Paris and do not worry about the destruction of the city.' Otto Dessloch was eager to prove that after its failure in Normandy, there was one order the *Luftwaffe* in France could carry out. A staff officer rushed to Choltitz's Hotel Meurice offices, offering to lay waste to the north-eastern suburbs in a day of continuous raids. The homes of 800,000 Parisians would be flattened, the major promised Choltitz. It would be 'a little Hamburg'. It would bring an end to the uprising.[14]

Choltitz gave his blessing to the air attack. The uneasy truce between the Germans and French agreed in the early hours of 20 August had done nothing to halt the wave of insurgency sweeping the city. Perhaps an act of terror would work. But Walter Model was becoming increasingly irritated by the commandant's failure to quell the revolt. The field marshal gave the portly general an ultimatum: 'Restore order in the city at any price.' At any price? The general was struggling with his conscience. He had ordered a mass air raid on suburbs clearly of no military value in a bid to stem the uprising. That was a justifiable act, Choltitz reasoned with himself. But how much further could he go? Simply restoring order was beyond *General* Dietrich von Choltitz this Monday evening. He knew it. Model knew it. Maybe even Adolf Hitler knew it. 'The situation in Paris is becoming untenable,' the diarist in Hitler's headquarters recorded tersely that night. 'The 20,000 men stationed there are inadequate.'[15]

For all his ruthless determination, Field Marshal Walter Model was opposed to fighting a pitched battle for the capital of France. It would suck in thousands of men, men which he simply did not have. He warned Hitler's staff:

This city of 3,500,000 people has insufficient power supplies to maintain adequate working or living conditions. Signs of insurrection, limited to localized outbreaks, have been put down by force everywhere, but the alarm units will be inadequate to deal with a larger uprising...

Paris remains a big problem militarily if, with fighting going on around it, a major uprising begins at the same time, it will not be possible to maintain the upper hand with the 20,000 troops at our disposal.[16]

Hitler's reply was uncompromising:

The defence of the Paris bridgehead is of decisive military and political importance. Its loss will tear apart the entire coastal front north of the Seine and deprives us of the base for the long-range war against England.

Moreover, history has shown that the loss of Paris always means the fall of the whole of France.

The Führer therefore repeats his order that Paris must be defended by fortified lines in front of the city and refers to the reinforcements promised by *OB West*.

Inside the city you must take the harshest action at the first sign of rioting, namely demolishing a block of houses, public execution of the ringleaders, evacuation of the area affected, since this is the best way of preventing it spreading.

The Seine bridges are to be prepared for demolition. Paris must not fall into enemy hands or if it does then only as a pile of rubble.[17]

Hitler's instructions were dutifully passed on to Dietrich von Choltitz. The general looked at the order, shook his head, then began implementing the Führer's wishes: three tonnes of high explosive at Notre Dame, two tonnes in Les Invalides, another tonne in the Chamber of Deputies. He was even planning to flatten the Arc de Triomphe to improve his field of fire. And all this he did begrudgingly. 'Thanks for the wonderful order,' he berated Hans Speidel in a telephone conversation. 'What order, *mein general?*' Model's chief-of-staff asked. 'The order for demolition!' Choltitz bellowed. Speidel sighed. 'I've acted correctly, haven't I, my dear Speidel?' the commandant continued. Speidel hesitated: '*Jawohl, mein general,* but it's not us but the Führer who has given the order!' Choltitz had no time for excuses. 'Look, you are the one who passed on the order and you will answer to history!' he told Speidel and slammed the phone down.[18]

But Paris' commandant had even greater concerns than preparing the city for demolition. By 23 August 1944, he could no longer even maintain order in the French capital. The *Luftwaffe* raid which promised to flatten the homes of 800,000 inhabitants had simply not materialized. Instead, the outlying suburbs were sealed off by barricades thrown up by the insurgents. Parisians were hurling Molotov cocktails at armoured cars and taking pot shots at German patrols. 'There is shooting going on everywhere,' Choltitz warned Hans Speidel. 'Public executions and other acts of repression outlined in the Führer's order are no longer possible. Of course, the police are loyal, but they are powerless.' Could the German troops still blow up the Seine bridges? The commandant doubted it. 'To blow up bridges we must fight our way through the bridge approaches first, but that doesn't seem possible when there are seventy-five bridges. Such a step would probably drive the majority of the population, who are still wavering, into the enemy's camp.' The edifice of Nazi rule in France was crumbling. Rear units, supply services, administration staffs panicked and fled for the sanctuary of the Reich. They commandeered passing trucks, loaded personal effects aboard, and disappeared. When one of Choltitz's officers asked him to release his staff so they could leave Paris, the commandant tore a strip off him. 'If we shirked from this final, decisive battle at this hour, we would have lost what soldierly honour still remained,' Choltitz insisted. The general had no intention of abandoning Paris, if only because an evacuation of the city would lead to utter chaos. 'There was no doubt that abandoning Paris at this moment with the roads to the east blocked by the enemy, would have quickly turned into a disorderly flight and would have meant certain death for many soldiers and members of the *Wehrmacht*,' Choltitz reasoned. Instead, the defenders of Paris waited for the inevitable end. Not that the end would be far off. Paris not only lacked the men to defend it to the last man, it lacked the means to. On 21 August the commandant warned bread would run out in two days and his remaining food supplies would not last beyond the end of August'.[19] Whatever the bluster from Jodl, Model, or even Hitler, the defence of Paris was an illusion.

The phone in the OKW bunker at Hitler's East Prussian headquarters rang at ten minutes before midnight that Wednesday evening, 23 August. It was Walter Model. He needed to speak to Jodl. Events in the west were spiralling out of control far too quickly. Orders were becoming outdated even before Hitler was issuing them. 'We must be prepared for things happening differently from how we expected them to,' the field marshal warned. Model wanted guidance. Jodl was merely his master's voice. Paris had to be held 'first and foremost'. The field marshal was exasperated. 'The harshest orders cannot change the fact that the panzer divisions are merely skeletons,' he rasped. OKW promised reinforcements, but Model was not buying it. 'A city of millions cannot be defended from inside or out with a single self-propelled gun unit,' he railed.[20]

When Joseph Goebbels called the field marshal at noon the following day, he found Model in a more optimistic mood. Goebbels liked Model. He was the 'type of general we can rely on'. Goebbels sighed: 'If all our generals were like him, then we would stand more firmly on the other fronts than is the case today.' The field marshal was confident he could arrest the retreat in France, form a new Western Front and hold it into October 'when we will have made thirty divisions available to him,' the minister recorded the conversation.[21]

None of this helped the immediate situation; thirty divisions in October would not save Paris. By midday on 24 August, the leading American and now Free French forces – let off the leash for the honour of liberating their capital – were just ten miles from the city centre. Some enemy troops were already through the blockade line. As Dietrich von Choltitz contemplated the loss of Paris, the telephone rang. It was a *Luftflotte 3* officer who told the commandant it was now time to enact the order the general had approved three days earlier. But three days had changed everything in Paris. The uprising was now so widespread, German troops dealing with the rebellion so dispersed, that to bomb the centres of insurrection was to bomb the *Wehrmacht* too. 'I hope that you're coming in daylight,' Choltitz told him. No, the staff officer informed him, that was not possible. Would it be possible to attack specific targets, the commandant asked. No, the *Luftwaffe* officer replied: the only targets which could be considered were entire city quarters. *Luftflotte 3* had its orders. 'The *Luftwaffe* will annihilate any quarter of the city in which insurrection persists,' they read. The raid would take place. By night. It could not, however, say which night.[22]

It was too late. As darkness shrouded the French capital that Thursday evening, von Choltitz could hear the peal of church bells rippling across the capital. 'A string of thoughts entered my mind, thoughts which didn't have anything to do with my own fate,' the general remembered. 'Failing to carry out the demolition orders, I knew that I had delivered my wife and children into the hands of a regime which threatened their freedom and even their lives. On the other hand, I had preserved the lives of hundreds of women and thousands of children.' For Choltitz, the enemy was at the gates. For Parisians, liberation was a hair's breadth away.[23]

At the same time, Walter Model signalled his masters. 'The Paris problem remains a burning one.' His position was unenviable. His troops were exhausted. They were pouring back across north-west France. No fresh blood would reach the Western Front before the first day in September. Model had to stem the tide. And he had to hold the French capital. But he did not hold out much hope. He was sending reinforcements – one infantry division – into the city itself, but they would not arrive before 26 August at the earliest. 'Even these,' Model warned, 'will probably not be enough given the enemy's pressure from outside and the growing threat from within.'[24]

Daylight on Friday 25 August brought no relief to the defenders of Paris. Instead, the Allies pressed on into the heart of the capital. As Friday morning drew on, Model's staff watched the battle for Paris unfold. 'Throughout the city, there is bitter fighting under way against enemy troops and terrorists,' they recorded in a situation report. 'Numerous fires reported. Elements of the *Panzer Lehr* Division with panzers have the task of forcing their way through to the city centre from the east during the night.'[25]

The faithful *Panzer Lehr* – battered in Normandy to the brink of destruction. Now it was called upon to save Paris. Early on 25 August one of its *Kampfgruppen*, a makeshift assortment of troops, was near the city's Gare du Nord railway station. It was ordered to turn about and head into the heart of Paris to block the enemy advance. 'We were fired upon from windows and we could never see the enemy,' *Panzer Lehr* surgeon Hans Herrmann recorded. 'One would hear a round whistle through the air and not know from where it came.' As French and American forces swarmed into the city, Parisians began to exact revenge for four years of occupation and oppression. 'German prisoners were abused, spat upon, flogged and treated as they were in 1918, perhaps even worse,' an appalled Herrmann observed.[26]

With the battle for Paris at its height, fresh orders from East Prussia landed on Walter Model's desk. 'The Führer stands by his order of 23 August regarding defence to the last.' Model read on: 'In due course the centres of revolt are to be surrounded by bringing up security formations from outside [Paris] and using special tactics. Then the parts of the city in revolt are to be wiped out by the *Luftwaffe*.[27]

Such exhortations meant nothing to Dietrich von Choltitz. The commandant had spent the morning inspecting his defensive positions before returning to his headquarters in the Hotel Meurice. Choltitz had already resolved not to raze Paris to the ground. The chatter of small-arms fire was followed by the crash of shells from enemy tanks, now within sight of the hotel. Communications with the outlying strongpoints were cut off. Choltitz wrote some personal letters, realizing his actions could no longer influence the battle raging through the streets of the French capital, then dined as usual, before sending a quick situation report to his masters:

The strongpoints in the city are being defended. The eastern and northern suburbs of the city are in the hands of the resistance and saboteurs, who fire from houses. Only where all-round defence is possible is everything still clear at present.

The Military Commander of the Greater Paris area controls the area around La Concorde and remains there. The order has been given to defend the Seine bridges with all other forces. They are holding them.[28]

By the time the signal was decoded by Model's staff, Choltitz had already surrendered. When the fighting around his headquarters flared up again around 2 p.m., the general looked into the eyes of his men. They 'merely wanted to give up the struggle,' he remembered. After conferring with his staff, Choltitz reached the only conclusion he could. 'I agreed that we should bring an end to the fighting.' He marched off into captivity convinced of Germany's defeat. 'The collapse will come within the next few weeks.'[29]

It was the early afternoon on 25 August when Adolf Hitler realized the battle for Paris was being lost. 'Jodl!' he yelled at his most senior operations officer. '*Brennt Paris?*' Is Paris burning? Jodl did not answer. Again the Führer asked: 'I want to know is Paris burning? Is Paris burning right now, Jodl?' Hitler demanded that the general speak to Model in person on the telephone. Walter Model was to be left in no doubt as to the French capital's fate. Paris, the Führer insisted yet again, 'must be reduced to a pile of ruins'.[30]

After dark on 26 August – more than a day after Paris had fallen, with the city's inhabitants still celebrating freedom – the drone of some 150 aircraft rumbled through the August night approaching the French capital from the north-west. By the time they had passed over Paris and emptied their payloads, nearly 600 buildings were flattened and more than 200 Parisians dead. It had been the heaviest raid on the city in five years of war. But it would be the *Luftwaffe*'s last hurrah over the skies of France in the summer of 1944. Watching from afar, *Hauptmann* Theo Wulff commented bitterly. 'Never again will we see so many of our planes in the sky at one time.' The same evening, Otto Dessloch reported to Berlin that he no longer had any units he could commit to battle.[31]

The fall of Paris was buried by the Nazi propaganda machine, masked by the 'great victory' on the Seine where the core of Army Group B had escaped the Allied trap and withdrawn eastwards with 'most of its panzers, almost all its guns, all the army group's baggage trains and not least most of the men'. The crossing of the Seine, the *Völkischer Beobachter* declared, was 'one of the most difficult undertakings in military history'. The loss of Paris, on the other hand, was worthy of little more than a footnote in this mighty clash of arms, the newspaper explained:

Sooner or later, Paris would have fallen into the Americans' lap like a ripe fruit. For a long time we have made it clear that it is not our intention to hold Paris in the long run. In the end, from the military viewpoint, the French capital was of insignificant importance compared with the decisive battle of withdrawal...

The old magic of the name 'Paris' has clouded the military calculation of Eisenhower's and Montgomery's staff... Now the enemy will occupy Paris three, five or eight days earlier than events would have allowed anyway. But the enemy's strong, mobile units, whose fighting power during these days has been committed against the weak German defenders of Paris, were not available on the lower Seine – a crime against the spirit of true strategy, which wants to be strong at the decisive point – and only there.[32]

The German people were not fooled. They could see the writing on the wall. The Atlantic Wall had failed. The V1 had failed. The Western Front had collapsed. The Eastern Front had collapsed. In late August 1944, 'dejection and widespread helplessness as never before in five years of war' dogged the German public, monitors of morale noted. 'Although everyone knows that the front-line soldier is fulfilling his duty to the utmost, the public has more and more come to the conclusion that even the greatest bravery cannot compensate for the enemy's numerical and matériel superiority.' The loss of Paris merely added to the German *Volk*'s woes. 'Unless a miracle occurs the war can no longer be won,' the security services reported three days after the city's liberation. 'Even previously optimistic people remarked: "In our hearts, we will continue to believe in victory, but our minds ask, how can the situation improve?"'[33]

To Allied soldiers the dash across France in the dying days of August 1944 was intoxicating. Day and night the armour rolled, as long as there was fuel which had to pass along an ever-lengthening supply chain to reach the front. The only thing faster than the Allied advance was the Germans' efforts to escape to the Reich. Frequently units reported driving into towns and villages to be told by a jubilant civilian population that the Germans had already gone. For many Allied troops this was a *Blumenkrieg*, a 'war of flowers' such as the *Landser* had enjoyed, marching into Austria and the Sudetenland six years earlier. 'This mad chase is getting crazier hour by hour,' British war correspondent Alexander Clifford wrote on 2 September. 'You can't digest it in the least as you go along. It is so big and so swift that you almost feel it is out of control. Our columns just press on and on and on. The atmosphere is heady and intoxicating.' The tank men grabbed the glory. They were 'first into the towns, with first shot at the cheers, the cognac and the kisses'. But after a fortnight of such receptions, it was beginning to become repetitive. As US 3rd Armored Division liberated yet another French town, it laconically reported. 'Once again cognac, champagne and pretty girls.'[34]

The *Landser* streaming back from the Seine and now the Somme, from Paris and north-west France had one thought on his mind as the summer of 1944 turned to autumn: to reach the Reich and the safety of the West Wall, Germany's decrepit, unused and abandoned Maginot Line. He raced back across northern France faster than the blitzkrieg occupation of the country had carried him four years previously. Vehicles, out of petrol, were abandoned along the roads. No man who participated in the great retreat would forget it. 'For stragglers, small groups or single vehicles it was like running the gauntlet through a hate-filled country in an uprising,' regimental commander Helmut Ritgen recalled. Artilleryman Hans Blöthner watched as a nation occupied, oppressed for more than four years sought vengeance. Everywhere bunting hung from buildings, the Tricolore was draped from windows. And here and there 'a *Leutnant* shot in the head, a *Hauptmann* with his throat cut'. It was like 1914 all over again. The population was rising up against the invader. 'The civilian population is armed and shooting from every house,' Blöthner noted in his diary. 'There's machine-gun fire and rifle fire from rooftops, from cellars, from windows, from the church steeple...The population goads us like cattle.' And if these partisans, these *franc-tireurs*, were not enough to contend with, the *Jabos* hounded the retreat. Blöthner's staff car left the main road north-west of Valenciennes to avoid the constant air attacks. When he returned to his artillery unit he found 'only smoking, burning ruins. My wonderful unit has been destroyed in just a few minutes.'[35]

For every man, the retreat was debilitating. 'We had no supplies,' *Landser* Alfred Stoob remembered. 'We had to scavenge for food. Here a dog without a master, there a few eggs in a chicken coop.' An anonymous artilleryman wrote home: 'We have no vehicles or guns left. Whoever is still alive will have to fight as infantrymen. I don't know what we are still fighting for. Very soon I shall run over to the Tommies.' North-east of Paris, artilleryman Helmut Hörner marched on foot towards Soissons. After a long lay-up in hospital, his feet burned 'like the fires of hell'. The prospect of continued marching overwhelmed Hörner and his comrades with fear. He wrote in his diary:

In May 1940 I first set foot on French soil with the best-equipped and best-trained army in the world. Then the German troops overran this land with a victory march without comparison…Today, four years later, I slip out by the dark of night toward the starting point, back in the Reich, with the bitter feeling of shame in my soul at the way the rest of my brave division has dissolved, while troops from a continent 4,000 miles away follow close on our heels.

Before the week was out, Helmut Hörner's war was over. He was taken prisoner near Soissons by the Americans after two days of trying to break out of encirclement. Hörner and his makeshift battalion was on foot; the Americans rolled around in Shermans and jeeps. Now he sat on the bonnet of a jeep and contemplated his fate:

Why didn't I put a bullet into my head? What purpose is there to living without freedom, especially now after the world in which I believed, for which I fought and bled, has collapsed? What will happen to us, what must the homeland face if these Americans are successful in pushing into the Reich?[36]

For others, the seemingly endless trek to the German border continued, for there they would find salvation. *Rottenführer* Wolfgang Dombrowksi of the *Frundsberg* recalled: 'The division was virtually burnt out in the Normandy fighting. We felt that once we got over the German border it would all be over.' The state of 17th *Luftwaffe* Field Division, mauled defending the Seine crossings, was symptomatic of the state of the German Army in the west at the end of August. It was down to just 400 men – 300 infantry, another 100 engineers. Its commander, one Hans-Kurt Höcker, wrote dolefully: 'My few troops have fought valiantly despite everything. I sent *Oberst* Kaestner and *Oberstleutnant Freiherr* von Massenbach home today because of a breakdown. *Oberst* Engelke, whose nerves were similarly shattered, takes note of the stragglers and baggage vehicles which are heading to the rear. Although we have not lost our will to fight, we do not know how we will resist the imminent major offensive given our lack of reserves.' The division's operations officer added: 'The situation is serious and becomes increasingly critical. We have disbanded all our staffs and thrown them into the front line. If the enemy makes a serious attempt, a breakthrough on a broad front is only a question of hours. It would be truly more than we could hope for, if we could at least have a halt.' Frequently the advancing Allies caught up with the retreating *Wehrmacht*; Heinrich Eberbach, commander of the disintegrating Fifth Panzer Army, fell into Canadian hands near Amiens on the last day of the month. Hans Blöthner found himself surrounded on 5 September after evading capture for more than a week. 'We are done for,' he wrote hurriedly in his diary. 'We cannot go on any longer. Partisans are behind us. In front of us are uniformed units. Should we dig in or surrender?' Blöthner surrendered. 'Resistance is pointless.'[37] Eisenhower's intelligence section had come to a similar conclusion:

> The German Army in the west is no longer a cohesive force but a number of fugitive battle groups, disorganized and even demoralized, short of equipment and arms. The enemy has been out-generalled and out-fought and is no longer in position to offer serious resistance on any line short of the West Wall.[38]

Reinforcements arriving from the Reich, Italy and Russia to shore up the crumbling façade in France were shocked by the scenes they encountered. They struggled to make headway against the tide of soldiers heading back to the Reich. 'Germans stream back from all over France in the opposite direction towards home,' Wilhelm Heidtmann, a thirty year old from Germany's North Sea coast, wrote on 29 August. 'Men of the *Organisation Todt*, civilians, soldiers from shattered units, their regiments and divisions are to be re-formed in Germany. Sadly among them are some who travel without legitimate passes. Will we succeed in restoring order in this chaos? We must try!' Regimental commander Fritz Fullriede, arriving with the Hermann Goering Division complained in his diary: 'The whole west front has collapsed. The other side is marching about at will. What a big mouth we had over the Atlantic Wall.' Two days later he added: 'The West Front is finished, the enemy is already in Belgium and on the German frontier. Romania, Bulgaria, Slovakia and Finland are pleading for peace. It is exactly like 1918.' Except that it was not like 1918. It was worse, as fervent Nazi *General* Georg Ritter von Hengl noted on a tour of the Western Front. 'There were scandalous scenes,' he wrote upon his return. 'Experienced and senior commanders confirm irrefutably that the army retreating in 1918 after the revolution was like an army of guards compared with this mass of fleeing troops [today].' Supply dumps were blown up prematurely. Weapons were abandoned by the roadside. 'A feeling of panic', one officer observed had gripped the *Wehrmacht*; it was 'an image which is embarrassing to and unworthy of the German Army'. In Luxembourg, Party officials abandoned their posts and ran for the Reich, taking with them the fuel and trucks needed to move the Army eastwards. As far east as Amsterdam, *Luftwaffe* staff were packing their things and fleeing for the security of the Reich. The dissolution was infectious and reached to the very top of the *Wehrmacht*. When Sepp Dietrich's staff tried to contact the front line to gain a picture of the situation, the SS general told them to give up. 'Stop that. It won't make any difference.' The mood of commanders was not helped by impossible orders from above which bore no relation to the true situation. After one-too-many 'orders straight out of a war diary', Fifth Panzer Army's chief-of-staff, Alfred Gause, flew into a rage. He couldn't issue 'unworkable orders' to his men any more. 'There aren't any troops any more,' he complained. 'There's nothing you could call a front.'[39]

In East Prussia, an increasingly aloof and out-of-touch Adolf Hitler was issuing orders which were being overtaken by the speed of events in the west. At least he was no longer needlessly sending troops to the west to defend indefensible lines. By the end of August, the Führer realized that everything south and west of the River Somme was lost to Germany. But the manner in which he had lost France was angering Hitler. Reports poured into East Prussia of the disintegration of his army. He rebuked Model: 'The troops present a picture of a hurried, panicky, shameful flight, accompanied by shameful baggage trains, which are crammed with German and foreign women and goods collected during the lengthy spell in the rear areas and from the country roads.'[40]

After barely a fortnight in the west, the normally unflappable field marshal had seemingly lost his nerve. 'What can we really do now to master the situation?' Model asked Blumentritt resignedly. On 2 September, he vented his anger at Jodl who was still trying to direct the battle in the west from East Prussia. 'I assume that the view of the situation is different 'above' than it is here,' he complained. 'You seem to believe that we can still carry out attacks here. Haven't my assessments of the situation been passed on to the Führer? I can't go on in command like this.'[41]

Walter Model could do little to halt his armies as they rushed for Belgium, Holland and the West Wall, beyond try to offer his men belief:

> We have lost a battle, but I tell you we will win this war. Despite everything that has happened, do not allow your firm, confident faith in Germany's future to be shaken one bit. Gain the time which the Führer needs to bring into operation new troops and new weapons. They will come.[42]

The *Luftwaffe* too was fleeing east, and only just in time as *Leutnant* Alfred Hammer, *Staffel* commander of 6 *Staffel, Jagdgeschwader 53*, recalled leaving his airfield at Catillon, near Amiens on 28 August. The night before American tanks had closed in on the base. 'We were then very alarmed to see them continue during the night and thus gravely threaten our departure the following morning,' Hammer wrote. 'Some soldiers stationed nearby reassured us, by telling us that the Americans "stopped fighting" every night at 6 p.m. precisely and only resumed it the following morning, having shaved close to hot water.' The following day the few operational Messerschmitt 109s took off. The battle for France had cost the unit nine pilots and thirteen aircraft. It had scored just thirteen victories since 6 June. And yet, the pilots' morale was still high. 'Things were so feverish, so tense,' *Hauptmann* Julius Meimberg recalled. 'We lived only for the moment, and nothing else!'[43]

The morning of Tuesday, 29 August dawned grey. Mist shrouded the rolling landscape of Picardy, north of Paris. On the grass airstrip at Frières, the pilots and crew of *Jagdgeschwader 4* were preparing to return to Germany. The lame ducks, aircraft no longer airworthy, were to be destroyed to prevent them falling into Allied hands. Their pilots and their engineers would head east by road, not by air. At first light, *Staffel* commander Hermann Weber clambered into his Focke-Wulf 190. As he pushed forward the throttle, the fighter lifted into the air. Its undercarriage retracted. 'I immediately headed off in the direction of the Franco-Belgian border at top speed,' the pilot recalled. Below, his colleagues trundled eastwards by truck. The Germans were leaving France.[44]

Notes

1. Böll letter, 16/3/43. Böll, pp.647-9; Letter from a soldier in 6th Panzer Division, 6/8/42. Tewes, p.274.
2. KTB Blöthner, 13/8/44. Cited in Stimpel, ii, p.239; Pryce-Jones, p.199; SD Meldung, 17/8/44.
3. Montgomery directive, 20/8/44, and letter, 21/8/44. Hamilton, ii, pp.802-04; Weigley, p.247.
4. Shulman, p.217.
5. Blandford, p.253.
6. Fürbringer, Herbert, *9 SS Panzer Division Hohenstaufen*, p.393.
7. KTB PzAOK5, 25/8/44. IWM AL1901/3; Weingartner, p.116; Perrigault, La Panzer Lehr Division, p.313; HGrB Ia Nr.6704/44, 29/8/44. IWM AL510/1/2; KTB PzAOK5 Anlagen 50, 25/8/44. IWM AL1901/4.
8. KTB Kreipe, 17/8/44, 23/8/44. Cited in Jung, pp. 211, 212; KTB Dessloch, 19-20/8/44. Cited in Ludewig, p.171; Tagesbefehl Luftflotte 3, 22/8/44. NA DEFE3/573.
9. Heilmann, p.62.
10. Collins, Larry and Lapierre, Dominique, *Is Paris Burning*, pp. 31, 36, 53; Interrogation of General Dietrich von Choltitz, 31/8/44. NA WO208/4363; Choltitz, p.206.
11. KTB OB West, 8/8/44. IWM AL785/2; Hitler-Choltitz, 8/8/44. KTB OB West Anlagen, 8/8/44. IWM AL785/2/1.
12. Choltitz, pp.216-17; Blumenson, *Breakout and Pursuit*, pp. 592-3; KTB OB West Anlage, 12/8/44. Cited in Ludewig, p.110.
13. Collins and Lapierre, op. cit., pp.125-6.
14. TB Goebbels, 21/8/44; Collins, Larry and Lapierre, Dominique, op. cit., pp.141, 164-5; KTB OB West, 20/8/44. IWM AL785/2.
15. Collins and Lapierre, op. cit., pp.168,174-6; KTB OKW, 21/8/44.
16. HGr B Ia Nr.6390/44 gKdos, 1800 Hours, 21/8/44. NA CAB146/343.
17. OKW/WFSt/Op (H) Nr.772989/44, 23/8/44. KTB OB West Anlagen, 23/8/44. IWM AL785/2/3.

18. Choltitz, p.240.
19. Telecon Choltitz-Speidel, 2215 Hours, 23/8/44. KTB AGp.B, 23/8/44; Choltitz, pp.246-7; Bericht über die Ernährungslage von Paris, 23/8/44. Cited in Ludewig, p.165.
20. Telecon Model-Jodl, 2350 Hours, 23/8/44. KTB AGp.B, 23/8/44.
21. TB Goebbels, 25/8/44.
22. Choltitz, p.246; Collins and Lapierre, op. cit., pp.230-1.
23. Choltitz, p.249.
24. HGp B Ia Nr.6360/44 gKdos, 2300 Hours, 24/8/44. IWM AL510/1/2.
25. KTB AGp.B, 25/8/44.
26. Ritgen, p.119.
27. OB West Ia Nr.7330/44, 1400 Hours, 25/8/44. KTB OB West Anlagen, 25/8/44. IWM AL785/2/3.
28. KTB OB West Anlagen, 25/8/44. IWM AL785/2/3.
29. Choltitz, pp.252-3; Interrogation of General Dietrich von Choltitz, 31/8/44. NA WO208/4363.
30. Collins and Lapierre, op. cit., p.284.
31. ibid., p.339. XL 8354, 2044 Hours, 28/8/44. NA DEFE3/127.
32. 'Um die neue Front im Westen,' Völkischer Beobachter, 27/8/44.
33. Weekly activity report by the head of the propaganda division, RMVP, 22/8/44 and 28/8/44. Cited in Steinert, Hitler's War and the Germans, pp.275-6.
34. Cited in D'Este, Eisenhower, p.586; Blumenson, op. cit., pp.673, 695.
35. Ritgen, p.201; KTB Blöthner, 3/9/44. Stimpel, pp.242-3.
36. Ambrose, Citizen Soldiers, p.110; Shulman, p.228; KTB Hörner, 24/8/44, 28/8/44.
37. Kershaw, It Never Snows in September, p.20; Letters from the Commanding Officer and Operations Officer, 17th Luftwaffe Field Division, to LXXXI Corps, 28/8/44. KTB LXXXI Corps, Appendices and Telephone Conversations, 2/8/44-21/10/44. IWM AL1538/1; KTB PzAOK5, 31/8/44. IWM AL1901/3; KTB Blöthner, 5/9/44. Stimpel, ii, p.244.
38. SHAEF Weekly Intelligence Summary, No.24, 2/9/44. NA WO219/1923.
39. Letter Heidtmann an Heimat, 29/8/44. Bahr, p.445; Kershaw, op. cit., pp.19, 56; Chef des NS-Führungstabes im OKW, General der Gebirgstruppen Georg Ritter von Hengl. Kurze Aktennotiz über Frontbesuch im Westen, 22/9/44-3/10/44. BA Koblenz NS19/1858. Müller and Volkmann, Die Wehrmacht: Mythos und Realität, p.380; KTB LXXXIX Corps, 1/9/44. Ludewig, p.224; Ludewig, pp.198, 216, 225; Ferngespräch Gause-Tempelhoff, 2330 Hours, 1/9/44. Cited in Ludewig, p.219.
40. Befehl des OKW/WFSt an HGr.B, 30/8/44.
41. Ludewig, pp.198, 242.
42. To his son, the field marshal was more succinct. 'Right now, we must hold out, then the decision will come. A turbulent period! Nevertheless, we must stick it out!'. Model, Tagesbefehl, 3/9/44. Shulman, pp.229-30.
43. Frappé, op. cit., p.234.
44. ibid., p.290.

Chapter 12

This Cannot be the End

We'll keep fighting this battle at all costs until one of our damned enemies gets tired of fighting.

Adolf Hitler

In the second week of August, British troops swarming across lower Normandy came across the body of a dead *Waffen SS* platoon commander, one *Untersturmführer* Riegamer, killed a few days earlier. The passing Tommies frisked the stiff, cold body and pulled out a small worn diary, its pages scarred by six weeks of fighting. They flicked through the pages, glancing over the entries. The final jottings were entered under Friday, 11 August 1944:

Is everything that we have behind us, is that all for nothing? I cannot believe that this is the end! Believe. Believe – and fight!

Things have become incredibly difficult!

What is the meaning of the quiet from our leaders? Hopefully it is well-founded!

I am hardly afraid of death any more, but I am afraid for my Germany!

How will we go beyond winter?

...and on the radio is light, frivolous music, images of Noyers, Evrecy, May, Vire, Presles, strained faces, the cries of the wounded, dirt, dust of people half-buried, barrages, senseless, bloody attacks, which often seem pointless and futile, constantly appear. It gnaws at your belief! You can forget about a lot with a bottle of wine and joyful music, but not in the long run.

How wonderful, how fanatical, how manly are our young men, the eighteen and nineteen year-olds. A single word spurs them on to make supreme efforts. But they become fewer and fewer. All these terrible, tormenting questions, which can be answered by belief which is almost superhuman.

This cannot be the end! [1]

Riegamer's death was merely a statistic. He was one of 450,000 German victims of the battle for Normandy on land: the dead numbered at least 60,000; the wounded another 180,000, and prisoners totalled around 210,000. Of the 1,500 panzers and self-propelled guns fed into the furnace of the Norman battlefield, just sixty-seven returned. The remainder, plus 20,000 vehicles and 3,500 field guns were left behind. Before his capture, Heinrich Eberbach showed quite bluntly that the German Army had no chance of halting the invaders. On the day his entire army mustered 17,980 men, 314 artillery pieces and forty-two tanks and self-propelled guns, 25 August 1944, the Fifth Panzer Army commander estimated the enemy opposite him could throw more than 110,000 infantry, 1,320 field guns and nearly 1,900 tanks into the fray. Worse still, Eberbach reckoned the Allies still had a further 90,000 men, 1,100 guns and 2,000 tanks in reserve, not yet committed to the battle. The core, the flower of the German field army in the west had been destroyed, arguably the cream of the *Wehrmacht* had been eliminated. In the summer of 1944, the Germans buried their best in the foreign soil of France.

The *Landser* did not need to read the balance sheet to grasp the scale of the German defeat in France in the summer of 1944. He looked at the gaps in his ranks, for the comrades he had lost; he looked at the handful of panzers and guns his division still had. 'After Normandy we had no illusions any more,' wrote Adolf Hohenstein, whose 276th Infantry Division had somehow escaped the inferno of Falaise. 'We knew that we stood with our backs to the wall.'[2]

Defeat in Normandy was catastrophic for Germany. It went beyond the appalling losses of men and material, beyond the loss of U-boat bases and launch sites for the V weapons, beyond the loss of Paris, the Atlantic and Mediterranean coasts, and the whole of France herself. Defeat in Normandy spelled the defeat of Nazi Germany. Hitler's strategy for 1944, indeed for winning the entire war if it were still possible, was wiped out. Germany's great battle plan for the year had been to defeat the invasion in the west, then concentrate on the Eastern Front; the Reich would no longer be fighting a two-front war. Instead, the fronts in the east and west had collapsed and there was little hope of stemming the enemy tide on either. As Rommel put it: 'With the invasion battle we lost the last chance of gaining that strategic vantage point which a victory on the coast would have given us.'[3]

And so public and *Landser* alike placed their faith in the Nazi leadership delivering on its promises. 'The entire nation's hope that 'we will come through after all' is based solely on the most fearsome use of the new weapons,' the security service monitors of public opinion commented. Many Germans were resigned to the Reich's defeat. 'The hope that we can still end the war victoriously has sunk to zero,' a senior party official in Vienna recorded at the beginning of September. People openly commented: 'Even if we lose the war, things won't be so bad!' There was even talk of a repeat of the revolution of 1918. 'It is no wonder that among broad sections of the populace a depression which deepens by the day is visible.' The *Landser* too had given his all in five years of war. It was not enough. 'Whether the new weapons will do it, we shall see,' wrote one Manfred Korbacher, twenty-nine year old artilleryman and veteran of campaigns in the west and east. 'We live and die today with the hope of "revolutionary weapons, which will transform the war in a revolutionary way," as Goebbels says. We must [hope] that these weapons will be used soon and swiftly and have the desired effect.' Radioman Albert Pretzel wrote similarly to his wife: 'When will the new weapons actually be ready so they can be used en masse? Only they can bring us victory. I believe strongly in them. They must and will be a cataclysmic addition to technology and the conduct of war. They will be something utterly new, something which our enemy will have no countermeasure for.'[4]

As the Allies celebrated the capture of Paris, Karl Dönitz took a bitter decision: it was time to call off the battle against the invasion fleet. 'In the end I could no longer match the moral fortitude displayed by the U-boat crews,' he wrote a decade later. 'To continue U-boat operations would be an irresponsible act.' The Commander-in-Chief of the German Navy looked at the tally of his efforts to halt the invasion. In two and a half months, his submarines had sunk twelve escort vessels and twenty ships totalling little more than 110,000 tons for the loss of two out of three U-boats sent into the Channel and, with them, 750 sailors. 'The old fighting spirit of the U-boat arm once again proved itself with distinction,' the *Grossadmiral* convinced himself. 'Despite all our fears beforehand, the operation was right.' His men had suffered 'heavy but bearable losses' in return for 'an important if not decisive impact on enemy supplies, and as a result relieved the troops involved in the fighting on land'. And yet, daily nine convoys had run back and forth across the Channel ferrying war matériel to the Allied invasion forces. Few campaigns have proved more futile than the U-boat's attempt to thwart the invasion of Europe.[5]

The *Luftwaffe* suffered losses on a par with the U-boat arm in its failed efforts to stop Overlord. *Luftflotte 3* simply failed to exist by the end of August 1944. It had fought to the point of extinction. Grappling the invasion armada on land, sea and in the skies of north-west France had cost it more than 2,000 aircraft. The plight of II Gruppe,

Jagdgeschwader 53, since 6 June were typical. Forty-two of its Me109s had been shot down by the enemy, another eighteen destroyed in accidents, twenty were abandoned on its airfields as it fled westwards, and a further twenty were lost to miscellaneous causes.[6]

As August 1944 petered out, Dwight David Eisenhower was taking stock of the catastrophe which had befallen his enemy. 'The German Army in the West has suffered a signal defeat,' he wrote boldly. 'The enemy is being defeated in the East, in the South and in the North; he has experienced internal dissension and signs are not wanting that he is nearing collapse.' By the reckoning of his intelligence chiefs, five panzer divisions had been destroyed, six more mauled; twenty infantry divisions wiped out, another twelve badly depleted; 200,000 dead, another 200,000 prisoners of war; 1,300 panzers smashed on the battlefields of Normandy, alongside 20,000 trucks, 500 self-propelled guns and 1,500 field pieces; more than 3,500 German aircraft destroyed in the air or on the ground; and not least four German armies defeated, depleted, scurrying headlong across France towards the borders of the Reich. Victory in Normandy had not been bought cheaply. The eleven-week battle cost the Allies just short of 210,000 casualties, nearly 40,000 of them dead.[7]

Throughout the Allied high command there was widespread rejoicing as August 1944 drew to a close. The fall of France was within their grasp. The liberation of Europe was finally back on schedule after two months of deadlock. 'The August battles have done it,' the Allied intelligence bureau wrote at the month's end:

> The German Army in the West has had it. Crippled in the northwest by appalling losses, in the southwest by sheer futility and in the south by totally inadequate reserves, the armies are committed willy-nilly to what must shortly be a total surrender of more than two-thirds of France. It is an achievement of which the Allied Armies may well feel enormously proud, and of which the enemy is frankly envious. Two and a half months of bitter fighting, culminating for the Germans in a bloodbath big enough even for their extravagant tastes, have brought the end of the war in Europe within sight, almost within reach. The strength of the German Army in the West has been shattered. Paris belongs to France again, and the Allied Armies are streaming towards the frontiers of the Reich.[8]

One thought dominated the Allies' front-line leaders after Falaise, the Seine and Paris: chase the enemy back to the Reich. Bernard Law Montgomery spurred his men on: 'Every officer and man must understand that by a stupendous effort now we shall hasten the end of the war.' Eisenhower was more sober than many of his field commanders. 'There is still a lot of suffering to go through,' he wrote to his wife. 'God I hate the Germans.'[9]

No soldier who fought for Normandy in the summer of 1944, Axis or Allied, would forget the bitter experience. The Western Front of 1944 often resembled the Western Front of 1916-18. An Allied soldier involved with burial parties in the aftermath of battle recalled:

> There were lots of bodies we never identified. You know what a direct hit by a shell does to a guy. Or a mine, or a solid hit with a grenade, even. Sometimes all we have is a leg or a hunk of arm.
>
> There's only one stink and that's it. You never get used to it, either. As long as you live, you never get used to it.[10]

It took weeks, months, years to clear away the detritus of the battle of Normandy, but the effects of victory and defeat were noticeable instantly. On 2 September 1944, a Canadian officer drove through the ancient Norman city of Rouen on the Seine and recorded his impressions:

> I cannot possibly convey the cumulative effect of passing for hours through a liberated countryside, with the wreckage of the beaten enemy – his tanks and vehicles, his dead horses and the graves of his dead men – littering the roadside ditches, and the population, free once more, welcoming the oncoming troops with smiles and flowers and the V-sign.
>
> The scene in a liberated town is quite extraordinary. Everyone seems to be in the street, and no-one ever seems to tire of waving to the troops passing in their vehicles, who likewise never tire of waving back. The young people wave and laugh and shout; the children yell and wave flags; the mothers hold up their babies to see the troops and wave their little paws too; the old people stand by the roadside and look happy; and the army rolls through.[11]

For the *Landser*, there was the bitter taste of defeat, and yet the German soldier refused to accept he had been beaten. Events had conspired against him, but the *Landser* held his head high. Like *Untersturmführer* Riegamer, he struggled to accept his sacrifices had been in vain. This could not be the end. 'German soldiers have once again acquitted themselves superhumanly in battle,' *Hitlerjugend* commander Kurt Meyer wrote bitterly in his diary. 'They do not deserve the terrible defeat. The defeat cannot be blamed on the front-line soldiers as this bitter cup was served to them by a gambler at the map table. The German soldier's performance in Normandy will forever be immortalized in the history books.'[12] The *Landser*'s foe paid him compliments too. One Canadian observer commented:

> The German soldier and field commanders showed themselves to be excellent practitioners of their trade. The German fighting soldier was courageous, tenacious, and skilful. He was sometimes a fanatic, occasionally a brutal thug; but he was almost always a formidable fighting man who gave a good account of himself, even under conditions as adverse as those in Normandy certainly were.[13]

Defeat was a word Adolf Hitler refused to acknowledge. The Führer quickly forgot about the loss of France and the destruction of his western army. 'We will fight – if necessary even at the Rhine,' he told his staff in one of the monotonous soliloquies which dominated situation conferences. 'That doesn't matter at all. We'll keep fighting this battle at all costs until, like Frederick the Great once said, one of our damned enemies gets tired of fighting.' With the battle for the Falaise pocket at its height, Hitler had summoned his senior military adviser, Alfred Jodl. 'Prepare to take the offensive in November when the enemy's air forces cannot operate,' he ordered the general. 'Main thrust: around twenty-five divisions must be transferred to the West in the next one to two months.'[14] Thus was born the Ardennes offensive, the last German advance in the West. It was as if the battle for Normandy had never happened. On 23 August, Hitler talked at length with Joseph Goebbels. The propaganda minister recorded in his diary:

> Although we are experiencing severe setbacks at present, the Führer still hopes to be able to take the offensive again given favourable weather conditions. He expects that in November roughly. The Führer is proving particularly active in all these plans and measures. It's now important to spare no effort in overcoming the present crisis. We are intending to create precisely the necessary prerequisites for this...
>
> By the autumn we will form seventy new divisions, which for the most part will be sent to the West. For here we want to go over to the offensive again – in fact not only there, but also in the East, as soon as the opportunity presents itself. We must overcome the current military and psychological lethargy at all costs. Now the moment has come when real men must come to the fore – not just in politics but also in the military.[15]

Across the Reich appeals for fresh blood were posted. The 1927 year group was called up – teenagers of sixteen and seventeen – while *Hitlerjugend* leaders were urged to encourage their boys to volunteer for the front with stirring stories of the deeds of the 12th SS division which bore the movement's name. Its bi-monthly magazine, *Der Pimpf* – 'The Young Scamp' – aimed at boys as young as ten, proclaimed that the *Hitlerjugend* made outstanding warriors and 'fanatical supporters of National Socialist spirit. To conquer and die for the Führer's idea is the greatest honour.' The fields of battle in Normandy were littered with the graves of young dead – 'silent witnesses of the selfless willingness and soldierly spirit of our youth. Young hearts carry this belief and this spirit of the immortal battalions onwards.'[16] The ranks of the 12th SS Panzer Division *Hitlerjugend* would swell and join battle in the west once more, before the year was out, in Adolf Hitler's great offensive.

At his home in southern Germany, Field Marshal Erwin Rommel was recovering from the wounds he suffered in that air attack on his Horch staff car six weeks earlier. Since his discharge from hospital in mid-August, the wounded marshal had time to mull over defeat in the west. Rommel never doubted that his strategy in France – to destroy the enemy on the beaches – was the correct one. But he began to realize that whatever strategy Germany had employed against the invader, it would have failed. The argument of the panzer reserve had been a futile one. 'Even if we had had these forces at the scene of the landing, we would still have lost the battle, as our counter-attacks would have been smashed by the Allied naval guns and air force,' the marshal wrote. 'No compromise of any kind can make up for total enemy air and artillery superiority.'[17] Defeat in the west, Erwin Rommel told himself, had been inevitable.

Adolf Hitler had planned to summon his favourite marshal before him once he recovered from his wounds, then dismiss him from the *Wehrmacht* over his links with the 20 July putsch. But the evidence against the Desert Fox was too damning. First, his chief-of-staff Hans Speidel was arrested; Speidel was acquitted, although Hitler was convinced of his guilt. Then the interrogation report of Caesar von Hofacker, adjutant to France's military governor, von Stülpnagel, was placed before the Führer. Hofacker stuck to the line he had taken with his fellow plotters in the days before 20 July: Rommel had given his assurance he would support the uprising.

Erwin Rommel had no intention of going to Berlin to face the music. Hitler had no intention of putting on trial Germany's most respected and popular field marshal; then the German public might indeed believe the war was lost. Instead, the Desert Fox was offered a choice: 'suicide' followed by a state funeral and the promise that his family would be cared for, or trial before the People's Court. Erwin Rommel chose suicide. On 14 October the captor of Tobruk, the scourge of the British

Army for eighteen months in north Africa, took his own life.[18]

The German people and the ordinary soldier were told nothing of Rommel's 'involvement' in the July plot. He had died a hero's death, of wounds he suffered in the air attack on 17 July, as Model told Rommel's former army group in an order of the day: 'We have lost a commander with lightning power of decision, a solider of the greatest bravery and of unexampled dash. He will go down into history as one of the greatest commanders of our nation.'[19]

Erwin Rommel was buried with military honours. Hitler afforded him a state funeral, but did not deign to attend in person. Instead, he sent the field marshal's wife a hollow message of condolence: 'Accept my sincerest sympathy for the heavy loss you have suffered with the death of your husband. The name of Field Marshal Rommel will be forever linked with the heroic battles in north Africa.'[20]

And so it has proved. Six decades on, Erwin Rommel's name is attached not to defeat in Normandy but to his triumphs in Africa. But then, Normandy was not a battle of the *Feldherren*, masters of the battlefield. Erwin Rommel worked wonders in the six months up to 6 June; after the invasion, the Desert Fox's influence was negligible. As one of Montgomery's staff officers remarked: 'In Normandy there was no particular sign of Rommel's presence.'[21] The same could be said of Rundstedt, Kluge, Model, Geyr, Eberbach and Dietrich. The battle for Normandy was won and lost by the ordinary soldier, the *Landser*, the non-commissioned officer, company, battalion and regimental commanders. No German general stamped his mark on the defence of France in 1944.

The German soldier in the west would fight on after Normandy. The Western Front anchored again in September 1944, along the West Wall and through Belgium and Holland. The advancing Allies had exhausted their long lines of supplies; the *Wehrmacht*'s, in turn, shortened dramatically. But just six weeks earlier, the Western Front had been a mere seventy miles long. Now it stretched from the North Sea to the border with Switzerland. Even the lowliest German soldier could see the plight of the Reich was perilous. Infantryman Wilhelm Pruller, recovering from wounds at home in Germany, scribbled in his diary:

> It doesn't look very rosy anywhere you turn. I'm a born optimist, but how shall this end? A world full of enemies. All round us they set out for the death blow, with an enormous superiority of men and material, weapons and munitions and machines; one success after another for them. And we?[22]

Shortly before his death, Erwin Rommel wrote in a similar vein:

My men went to their death in their thousands, without hesitation, in a battle that could not be won. No longer could we carry the burden of three fronts. The Russians broke through our lines in the East, destroyed many of our divisions and are pushing westwards. Only with great difficulty and by using our last reserves have we been able to improvise new fronts, both East and West. The sky over Germany has grown very dark. [23]

Notes

1. Fürbringer, Herbert, 9 SS Panzer Division Hohenstaufen, p.374.
2. Hastings, Overlord, p.365.
3. Rommel, p.511.
4. SD Meldung, 17/8/44; Rauchensteiner, Manfried, Der Krieg in Österreich 45, p.25; Korbacher, 31/8/44 and Pretzel, 31/8/44. Latzel, p.323.
5. Dönitz, p.422; KTB BdU, 28/8/44.
6. Ellis, i, p.491; Murray, Luftwaffe, p.386.
7. Eisenhower directive, 29/8/44. Eisenhower Papers, p.2100; Eisenhower Cable S58760, 30/8/44. Eisenhower Papers, p.2103.
8. SHAEF Weekly Intelligence Report, No.23, 26/8/44. NA WO219/1922.
9. Montgomery directive, 26/8/44. Hamilton, ii, pp.830-1; Ambrose, Eisenhower, p.148
10. Belfield and Essame, p.240.
11. Stacey, p.298.
12. Meyer, Grenadiers, p.171.
13. Carell, Invasion, p.317.
14. Meeting of the Führer with Generalleutnant Westphal and Generalleutnant Krebs, 31/8/44. Conferences, p.468; KTB Jodl, 19/8/44.
15. TB Goebbels, 24/8/44.
16. Jahnke, pp.70-1.
17. Rommel, pp.510-11.
18. KTB Jodl, 1/8/44; Irving, Trail of the Fox, p.399.
19. Model Tagesbefehl, 18/10/44. Cited in Shulman, p.184.
20. Rommel, p.505.
21. Hastings, op.cit., p.209.
22. KTB Priller, 9/8/44. Priller, p.175.
23. Rommel, p.524.

Appendix
Comparative ranks

Heer	Waffen SS	Kriegsmarine	British Army
Generalfeldmarschall	Reichsführer-SS	Grossadmiral	Field Marshal
Generaloberst	SS Oberstgruppenführer	Generaladmiral	General
General	SS Obergruppenführer	Admiral	Lieutenant General
Generalleutnant	SS Gruppenführer	Konteradmiral	Major General
Generalmajor	SS Brigadeführer	Vizeadmiral	Brigadier
Oberst	SS Standartenführer	Kapitän zur See	Colonel
	SS Oberführer		
Oberstleutnant	SS Obersturmbannführer	Fregattankapitän	Lieutenant Colonel
Major	SS Sturmbannführer	Korvettenkapitän	Major
Hauptmann	SS Hauptsturmführer	Kapitänleutnant	Captain
Oberleutnant	SS Obersturmführer	Oberleutnant zur See	Lieutenant
Leutnant	SS Untersturmführer	Leutnant zur See	2nd Lieutenant
		Stabsoberfeldwebel	
Stabsfeldwebel	SS Sturmscharführer	Oberfeldwebel	Sergeant Major
Hauptfeldwebel	SS Stabsscharführer	Stabsfeldwebel	
Oberfeldwebel	SS Hauptscharführer		
Feldwebel	SS Oberscharführer	Feldwebel	Colour Sergeant
Unterfeldwebel	SS Scharführer	Obermaat	Sergeant
Unteroffizier	SS Unterscharführer	Maat	
Stabsgefreiter		Matrosenhauptgefreiter	
Obergefreiter	SS Rottenführer	Matrosenobergefreiter	Corporal
Gefreiter	SS Sturmmann	Matrosengefreiter	Lance Corporal
Oberschutz	SS Oberschutz		
Schutz	SS Schutz	Matrose	Private

Bibliography

Unpublished sources

Imperial War Museum, London

AL 510/1/2   Army Group B weekly reports
AL 528   Seventh Army Telephone Log, June 1944
AL 785/1-3   War Diary and appendices of OB West, July-
              September 1944
AL 930/4/2   Personal diary of Alfred Jodl
AL 973/2   Seventh Army Telephone Log, June 1944
AL 974/2   War Diary of Seventh Army, 6 June-16 August 1944
AL 1412   Appendices to the War Diary of Panzergruppe West
AL 1531/3   Daily Reports, Army Group B, June-August 1944
AL 1538/1   Appendices to the War Diary of LXXXI Corps, 2
              August-21 October 1944
AL 1547/1-2   War Diary of the Quartermaster of Panzer Lehr
              Division, 30 December 1943-31 July 1944
AL 1697/3   Personal papers of Erwin Rommel, March-September
              1944
AL 1901   War Diary of Panzergruppe West, June-September
              1944
Zimmerman, Bodo (et al), OB West: A Study in Command

National Archives, Kew

CAB 106   Files prepared for the British Official Histories
CAB 146   Files prepared for the British Official Histories

Naval Historical Branch, Portsmouth

Diaries of Marinegruppenkommando West and Befehlshaber der U-
Boote

Published sources

Newspapers

Das Reich, 1944
Völkischer Beobachter, Berlin edition, 1944
Deutsche Allgemeine Zeitung, Berlin edition, 1944
The Times, London, 1944

Primary Sources

23rd Hussars, *The Story of the 23rd Hussars 1940-1946*, privately published by the Regiment, 1946

Ambrose, Stephen E., (et al), *The Papers of Dwight David Eisenhower*, eleven volumes, John Hopkins University Press, 1970-1980

Bähr, Hans and Bähr, Walter, *Kriegsbriefe gefallener Studenten*, Wunderlich Verlag, Tübingen, 1952

Boberach, Heinz (ed), *Meldungen aus dem Reich*, Luchterhand, Berlin, 1965

— *Meldungen aus dem Reich. Die geheimen Lageberichte des Sicherheitsdienstes der SS 1938-1945*, seventeen volumes, Manfred Pawlak Verlag, 1984

Böll, Heinrich, *Briefe aus dem Krieg 1939-1945*, Kiepenheuer & Witsch, Köln, 2001

Bradley, Dermot (ed), *Tätigkeitsbericht des Chefs des Heerespersonalamtes General der Infanterie Rudolf Schmundt*, Biblio Verlag, Osnabrück, 1984

Buchbender, Ortwin, *Das Andere Gesicht des Krieges: Deutsche Feldpostbriefe*, C. H. Beck, Munich, 1982

Chandler, Alfred D. Chandler, and Ambrose, Stephen E., (eds), *The papers of Dwight David Eisenhower: The War Years*, five vols, John Hopkins Press, Baltimore, 1970

Choltitz, Dietrich von, *De Sebastopol à Paris*, J'ai Lu, Aubanel, 1964

Cremer, Peter, *U333*, Bodley Head, London, 1984

Dollinger, Hans, (ed), *Kain, wo ist dein Bruder?* Frischer Verlag, Frankfurt am Main, 1987

Dönitz, Karl, *Memoirs: Ten Years and 20 Days*, Weidenfeld & Nicolson, London, 1959

Fey, Willi, *Armor Battles of the Waffen SS*, J. J. Fedorowicz, Winnipeg, 1990

Gersdorff, Rudolph-Christoph Freiherr von, *Soldat im Untergang*, Ullstein, Frankfurt am Main, 1979

Goebbels, Joseph, *Die Tagebücher von Joseph Goebbels*, fifteen volumes, K G Saur, Munich, 1993-1996

Guderian, Heinz, *Panzer Leader*, Michael Joseph, London, 1952

Heiber, Helmut, (ed), *Hitler and his Generals. Military conferences 1942-1945. The First Complete Stenographic Record of the Military Situation Conferences, from Stalingrad to Berlin*, Greenhill, London, 2002

Heilmann, Will, *Alert in the West*, Wrens Park, London, 2003

Heusinger, Adolf, *Befehl in Widerstreit*, Wunderlich Verlag, Tübingen, 1950

Horner, Helmut, *A German Odyssey*, Fulcrum, Golden, Colorado, 1991

Jahnke, Karl Heinz, (ed), *Hitlers letztes Aufgebot: Deutsche Jugend im sechsten Kriegsjahr 1944-45*, Klartext, Koblenz, 1993

Klapdor, Ewald, *Die Entscheidung: Invasion 1944*, Siek, 1984

Knappe, Siegfried, *Soldat: Reflections of a German Soldier 1936-1949*, Dell, New York, 1993

Luck, Hans von, *Panzer Commander*, Dell, New York, 1991

Martienssen, Anthony (ed), *Führer Conferences on Naval Affairs 1939-1945*, Greenhill, London, 1990

Meyer, Kurt, *Grenadiers*, J. J. Fedorowicz, Winnipeg, 1994

Mohrmann, Wolf-Dieter, *Der Krieg hier ist hart und grausam! Feldpostbriefe an den Osnabrücker Regierungspräsidenten 1941-1944*, Wenner, Osnabrück, 1984

Noakes, Jeremy, (ed), *Nazism 1919-1945*, vol. 4, University of Exeter Press, Exeter, 1998

Pimlott, John, (ed), *Rommel in his own Words*, Greenhill, London, 1994

Pöppel, Martin, *Heaven and Hell: The War Diary of a German Paratrooper*, Spellmount, Staplehurst, 1996

Pruller, Wilhelm, *Diary of a German Soldier*, Faber, London, 1963

Ritgen, Helmut, *Western Front 1944-1945*, J. J. Fedorowicz, Winnipeg, 1994

Rommel, Erwin, *The Rommel Papers*, Collins, London, 1953

Ruge, Friedrich, *Rommel in Normandy*, Macdonald & Jane's, London, 1979

Schramm, Percy Ernst, (ed), *Kriegstagebuch des Oberkommando der Wehrmacht*, seven volumes, Bernard & Graefe, Frankfurt, 1961-65

Schramm, Wilhelm Ritter von, *Conspiracy Among Generals*, Allen & Unwin, London, 1956

Severloh, Hein, *WN62*, Hek Creativ Verlag, 2004

Sündermann, Helmut, *Tagesparolen: Deutsche Presseweisungen 1939-1945 – Hitlers Propaganda und Kriegsführung*, Druffel-Verlag, 1973

Trevor-Roper, Hugh, (ed), *Hitler's War Directives*, Pan, London, 1966

— *Hitler's Table Talk*, Oxford University Press, Oxford, 1988

Warlimont, Walter, *Inside Hitler's Headquarters 1939-1945*,
    Weidenfeld & Nicolson, London, 1964

Weidinger, Otto, *Comrades to the End: 4th SS Panzergrenadier
    Regiment 'Der Führer' 1938-1945*, Schiffer, Atglen, 1998

Werner, Herbert, *Iron Coffins*, Pan, London, 1970

Secondary Sources

Agte, Patrick, *Michael Wittman and the Tiger Commanders of the
    Leibstandarte*, J. J. Fedorowicz, Winnipeg, 1996

Ambrose, Stephen E., *Band of Brothers*, Pocket, London, 2001

— *Citizen Soldiers*, Pocket, London, 2002

— *D-Day*, Pocket, London, 1997

— *The Victors*, Pocket, London, 2004

Balkoski, Joseph, *Beyond the Beachhead*, Stackpole, Mechanicsburg,
    1999

Barnett, Correlli, (ed), *Hitler's Generals*, Weidenfeld & Nicolson,
    London, 1989

Bartov, Omer, *Hitler's Army*, Oxford University Press, Oxford, 1991

Belfield, Eversley and Essame, H., *The Battle for Normandy*, Pan,
    London, 1967

Bernage, Georges, *The Panzers in Normandy*, Editions Heimdal,
    Bayeux, n.d

Blair, Clay, *Hitler's U-boat War: The Hunted 1942-1945*, Weidenfeld
    & Nicolson, London, 1999

Blandford, Edmund, *Two Sides of the Beach*, Airlife, Shrewsbury, 1999

Blumenson, Martin, *Breakout and Pursuit*, Office of the Chief of
    Military History, Dept. of the Army, Washington DC, 1961

Boog, Horst, (et al), *Das Deutsche Reich und der Zweite Weltkrieg*,
    Band 7, *Das Deutsche Reich in der Defensive*, Deutsche-Verlag
    Anstalt, 2001

Buchner, Alex, *German Infantry Handbook*, Schiffer, Atglen, 1991

Caldwell, Donald, *JG26: Top Guns of the Luftwaffe*, Ivy, New York,
    1993

Carell, Paul, *Invasion – They're Coming!*, Corgi, London, 1963

Carver, Lieutenant Colonel R., *Second to None: The Royal Scots
    Greys 1919-1945*, McCorquodale & Co., Edinburgh, 1954

Collins, Larry and Lapierre, Dominique, *Is Paris Burning?*, Simon &
    Schuster, New York, 1965

Delaforce, Patrick, *Smashing the Atlantic Wall*, Cassell, London, 2001

D'Este, Carlo, *Decision in Normandy*, Harper Collins, London, 1994

Ellis, Major L. F., *Victory in the West*, two volumes, HMSO, London,
    1962-68

Emde, Joachim, *Die Nebelwerfer*, Podzun-Pallas Verlag, Friedberg, 1979

Fischer, Karl, (ed), *Die Wehrmacht: Das Buch des Kriegs 1941-1942*, Die Wehrmacht Verlag, Berlin, 1942

Florentin, Eddy, *Battle of the Falaise Gap*, Elek, London, 1965

Forsyth, Robert, *JV44: The Galland Circus*, Classic Publications, West Sussex, 1996

Fowler, Will, *The Commandos at Dieppe*, Collins, London, 2002

Frappé, Jean-Bernard, *La Luftwaffe face au débarquement allié*, Editions Heimdal, Bayeux, 1999

Fraser, David, *Knight's Cross: A Life of Field Marshal Erwin Rommel*, Harper Collins, London, 1993

Fritz, Stephen G., *Frontsoldaten*, University Press of Kentucky, Lexington, 1995

Fürbringer, Herbert, *9 SS Panzer Division Hohenstaufen*, Editions Heimdal, Bayeux, 1984

Gawne, Jonathan, *The Americans in Brittany*, Histoire & Collections, Paris, 2002

German Foreign Ministry (ed), *Akten zur deutschen auswärtigen Politik 1918-1945*, Serie E, Volumes 7 and 8, Göttingen, 1969-1979

Görlitz, Walter, *Model*, Ullstein, Frankfurt am Main, 1992

Guderian, Heinz-Günther, *From Normandy to the Ruhr: With the 116th Panzer Division in World War II*, Aberjona Press, Bedford, 2001

Hamilton, Nigel, *Montgomery: Master of the Battlefield 1942-1944*, Hamish Hamilton, London, 1983

Harrison, Gordon, *Cross Channel Attack*, Office of the Chief of Military History, Washington DC, 1951

Hastings, Max, *Das Reich*, Pan, London, 2000

— *Overlord*, Pan, London, 1999

Heber, Thorsten, *Der Atlantikwall 1940-1945: Die Befestigungen der Küsten West- und Nordeuropas im Spannungsfeld Nationalsozialistischer Kriegführung und Ideologie*, Dissertation, Heinrich Heine Universität, Düsseldorf, 2003

Hessler, Günther, *The U-boat War in the Atlantic 1939-1945*, HMSO, London, 1989

Hoffmann, Peter, *The History of the German Resistance*, 3rd Edition, McGill Queen's University Press, Montreal, 1996

How, Major J. J., *Hill 112*, William Kimber, London, 1984

Irving, David, *Goebbels*, Focal Point, London, 1996

— *Hitler's War*, Hodder and Stoughton, London, 1977

— *Trail of the Fox: The Life of Field Marshal Erwin Rommel*, Weidenfeld & Nicolson, London, 1977

— *The War Between the Generals*, Penguin, London, 1982
Jacobsen, Otto, *Erich Marcks, Soldat und Gelehrter*, Musterschmidt Verlag, Göttingen, 1971
Jentz, Thomas, *Panzertruppen*, two volumes, Schiffer, Atglen, 1996
Jung, Hermann, *Ardennenoffensive*, Musterschmidt Verlag, Göttingen, 1971
Kershaw, Ian, *The Hitler Myth*, Oxford University Press, Oxford, 1987
Kershaw, Robert, *D-Day: Piercing the Atlantic Wall*, Ian Allan, London, 1993
— *It Never Snows in September*, Crowood, Marlborough, 1990
Knopp, Guido, *Hitler's Children*, Sutton, Stroud, 2002
Kroener, Bernhard, *Der starke Mann im Heimatkriegsgebiet: Generaloberst Friedrich Fromm*, Ferdinand Schöningh, Paderborn, 2005
Kursietis, Andris, *The Wehrmacht at War*, Aspket, Netherlands, 1999
Latzel, Klaus, *Deutsche Soldaten, nationalsozialistischer Krieg?* Ferdinand Schöningh, Paderborn, 1998
Leleu, Jean-Luc, *10 SS Panzer Division 'Frundsberg'*, Editions Heimdal, Bayeux, 2001
Linderman, Gerald, *The World Within War: America's Combat Experience in World War II*, Harvard University Press, Cambridge, 1999
Lormier, Dominique, *Rommel: La fin d'un mythe*, le cherche midi, Paris, 2003
Lucas, James and Barker, James, *The Killing Ground*, Batsford, London, 1978
Lucas, James, *Das Reich: The Military Role of the 2nd SS Division*, Cassell, London, 1999
Ludewig Joachim, *Der Deutsche Rückzug aus Frankreich*, Verlag Rombach, Freiburg, 1995
Manvell, Roger and Fraenkel, Heinrich, *The July Plot*, Pan, London, 1966
McKee, Alexander, *Caen: Anvil of Victory*, Pan, London, 1972
Messenger, Charles, The Last Prussian, Brassey's, London, 1991
— *Hitler's Gladiator: The Life and Wars of Panzer Army Commander Sepp Dietrich*, Brassey's, Washington DC, 2001
Messerschmidt, Manfred, *Die Wehrmacht im NS-Staat*, R. V. Decker Verlag, Hamburg, 1969
Meyer, Hubert, *The History of the 12 SS Panzer Division Hitlerjugend*, J. J. Fedorowicz, Winnipeg, 1994
Michaelis, Rolf, *Die 10 SS Panzer Division Frundsberg*, Michaelis Verlag, Berlin, 2004

Miller, Russell, *Nothing Less Than Victory*, Penguin, London, 1994

Müller, Rolf-Dieter and Volkmann, Hans-Erich, (eds), *Die Wehrmacht: Mythos und Realität*, Oldenbourg Verlag, Munich, 1999

Murray, Williamson, *Luftwaffe: Strategy for Defeat 1933-45*, Grafton, London, 1988

Neillands, Robin, *D-Day 1944: Voices from Normandy*, Weidenfeld & Nicolson, London, 1993

Ose, Dieter, *Entscheidung im Westen: Der Oberbefehlshaber West und die Abwehr der alliierten Invasion*, Deutsche Verlags-Anstalt, Munich, 1986

Padfield, Peter, *Dönitz: The Last Führer*, revised ed, Cassell, London, 2001

— *Himmler*, Macmillan, London, 1991

— *War Beneath the Sea*, Pimlico, London, 1997

Perrigault, Jean-Claude, *21 Panzer Division*, Editions Heimdal, Bayeux, 2003

— *La Panzer Lehr Division*, Editions Heimdal, Bayeux, 1995

Pogue, Forrest C., *The Supreme Command*, Office of the Chief of Military History, Washington DC, 1954

Price, Alfred, *The Last Year of the Luftwaffe*, Arms & Armour, London, 1993

— *The Luftwaffe Data Book*, Greenhill, London, 1997

Price-Jones, David, *Paris in the Third Reich*, Harper Collins, London, 1981

Rauchensteiner, Manfried, *Der Krieg in Österreich 45*, self-published, Vienna, 1995

Reardon, Mark, *Victory at Mortain: Stopping Hitler's Panzer Counter-Offensive*, University Press of Kansas, Kansas, 2002

Reynolds, Michael, *Steel Inferno: I SS Panzer Corps in Normandy*, Spellmount, Staplehurst, 1997

Ritgen, Helmut, *Das Geschichte der Panzer Lehr Division im Westen 1944-1945*, Motorbuch Verlag, Stuttgart, 1979

Ryan, Cornelius, *The Longest Day*, Wordsworth, London, 1999

Salewski, Michael, *Die deutsche Seekriegsleitung 1935-1945*, three volumes, Bernard & Graefe, Munich, 1973

Schramm, Wilhelm von, *Conspiracy Among Generals*, Allen & Unwin, London, 1956

Seaton, Albert, *The German Army*, Sphere, London, 1982

Seidler, Franz, *Die Organisation Todt*, Bernard & Graefe, Bonn, 1987

Seidler, Franz and Zeigert, Dieter, *Hitler's Secret Headquarters*, Greenhill, London, 2004

Serrano, Andrew Smith, *German Propaganda in Military Decline 1943-1945*, Pentland Press, Edinburgh, 1999

Shulman, Milton, *Defeat in the West*, 2nd Edition, Coronet, London, 1973

Stacey, C. P., *The Victory Campaign*, Queen's Printer and Controller of Stationery, Ottawa, 1960

Steinert, Marlis, *Hitler's War and the Germans*, Ohio University Press, Athens, 1977

Steinhoff, Johannes, *Voices from the Third Reich*, Regnery, Washington DC, 1989

Stimpel, Hans-Martin, *Die deutsche Fallschirmtruppe 1942-1945*, E.S. Mittler & Sohn, Berlin, 2001

Stöber, Hans, *Die Sturmflut und das Ende: Geschichte der 17 SS Panzergrenadier Division Götz von Berlichingen*, vol.1, Schild Verlag, Munich, 2000

Tarrant, V. E., *The Last Year of the Kriegsmarine*, Arms & Armour, London, 1994

Toland, John, *Adolf Hitler*, Ballantine, New York, 1977

Tieke, Wilhelm, *In the Firestorm of the Last Years of the War*, J. J. Fedorowicz, Winnigpeg, 2001

Tiemann, Ralf, *Chronicle of the 7 Panzer Kompanie, 1 SS Panzer Division 'Leibstandarte'*, Schiffer, Atglen, 1998

Wegmüller, Hans, *Die Abwehr der Invasion*, Verlag Rombach, Freiburg,1986

Weigley, Russell, *Eisenhower's Lieutenants*, Indiana University Press, Bloomington, 1990

Weingartner, James, *Hitler's Guard: The Story of the Leibstandarte SS Adolf Hitler*, Battery Press, n.d.

Williams, Andrew, *D-Day to Berlin*, Hodder & Stoughton, London, 2004

Williamson, Gordon, *Loyalty is My Honour*, Motorbooks International, London, 1995

Wilmot, Chester, *The Struggle for Europe*, Collins, London, 1952

Zeller, Eberhard, *The Flame of Freedom*, Westview Press, Boulder, 1994

Zetterling, Niklas, *Normandy 1944*, J. J. Fedorowicz, Winnipeg, 2000

Index

I SS Panzer Corps, 79, 84, 114, 141

II Fallschirmjäger Corps, 68, 116, 170

II SS Panzer Corps, 108, 109, 111, 112, 211

III Gruppe, 71

LXXXIV Corps, 16, 33, 37, 116, 227

1st SS Panzer Division *Leibstandarte*, 15-16, 139, 176, 178, 201, 208, 211, 218, 225

1st U-boat Flotilla, 30, 58

2nd *Fliegerdivision*, 201

2nd SS Panzer Division *Das Reich*, 24, 25, 80, 81, 110, 165, 170, 173, 176, 178-9, 209, 210, 214, 217, 218

3rd *Fallschirmjäger* Division, 26, 68, 134, 208

4th Panzer Grenadier Regiment *Der Führer*, 110, 111

5th *Fallschirmjäger* Division, 166

6th *Fallschirmjäger* Regiment, 41, 78

7th Panzer Division, 9

9th SS Panzer Division *Hohenstaufen*, 15, 77, 108, 109, 112, 119, 125, 210, 218

10th SS Panzer Division

Frundsberg, 15, 77, 89, 108, 109, 111, 117, 119, 120, 125, 195, 205, 211, 213, 214, 215, 217, 225

12th SS Panzer Division *Hitlerjugend*, 15, 17, 42-3, 48, 56, 66, 69, 77, 79, 83, 106, 107-8, 110, 113, 118, 119, 139, 141, 189-90, 192, 193, 194, 198-9, 208, 214, 216, 218, 248-9

16th *Luftwaffe* Field Division, 118, 139, 141

17th *Luftwaffe* Field Division, 238

17th SS Panzer Grenadiers *Götz von Berlichingen*, 16, 17, 42, 68-9, 78, 168, 170, 171, 173, 178-9, 181

21st Panzer Division, 17, 24, 25-6, 55, 62, 69, 70, 77, 79, 81-2, 95, 110, 117, 140, 210-11, 218

22nd Panzer Regiment, 55, 58

25th SS Panzer Grenadier Regiment, 56, 66, 69, 70

77th Infantry Division, 68, 76, 96

77th Panzer Grenadier Division, 122

85th Infantry Division, 194, 198, 200

89th Infantry Division, 190

91st Infantry Division, 96
101st SS Panzer Battalion, 11
116th Panzer Division, 24, 25,
92, 156, 170, 172, 176, 177-8,
218
243rd Infantry Division, 96
271st Infantry Division, 190
276th Infantry Division, 244
302nd Infantry Division, 4
319th Infantry Division, 16
325th Security Division, 228
331st Infantry Division, 26
344th Infantry Division, 225
346th Infantry Division, 95
352 Artillery Regiment, 38
352nd Infantry Division, 33,
43, 46, 47, 51, 67, 76, 94, 170
709th Fortress Division, 47
709th Infantry Division, 14, 16,
61, 95, 96, 99
711th Infantry Division, 37, 61
716th Infantry Division, 16, 31,
44, 46, 50-1, 58, 61, 63, 66,
67, 69, 87
736th Grenadier Regiment, 63
901st Panzer Grenadiers, 167

Adolf Hitler Platz, 36
Afrika Korps, 9
Aircraft – British
 Hawker Typhoon, 81, 178, 219
 Horsa gliders, 41
 Short Sunderland, 60, 74
 Supermarine Spitfire, 28, 138-9
Aircraft – German
 Dornier Do217, 28
 Focke-Wulf Condor, 86
 Focke-Wulf Fw190, 28, 53,
72, 241
 Heinkel He111, 147
 Junkers Ju52, 146
 Junkers Ju88, 28, 61
 Messerschmitt Me109, 28, 60,

71, 90, 131, 241, 246
Aircraft – US
 Boeing B17 Flying Fortress,
164
 Consolidated B24 Liberator,
59-60, 164
 Douglas DC3 Dakota, 41
 Lockheed P38 Lightning, 89,
90
 Martin B26 Marauder, 164
 North American P51 Mustang,
28, 72, 130
 Republic P47 Thunderbolt, 60,
166, 168
Alençon, 70, 186
Allied landings
 Italy, 7
 Sicily, 7
American Forces
 First Army, 164, 173, 186,
219
 Third Army, 185
 VII Corps, 96, 179
 VIII Corps, 101
 XV Corps, 186
 2nd Armored Division, 169,
172
 3rd Armored Division, 237
 9th Division, 99
 30th Infantry, 179
 82nd Airborne Division, 38, 41
 101st Airborne Division, 38,
41, 78
Amiens, 90
Anglo-American forces, 9
Arc de Triomphe, 231
Ardennes offensive, 248
Argentan, 70, 186
Army Group B, 72
Arromanches, 33, 48, 49
asset stripping in France, 7
Atlantic Wall, 6-7, 10, 12, 47,
49, 50, 65, 236

Auchinleck, Claude, 9
Avranches, 33, 165, 176, 178, 184, 185-6

'Baby Blitz', 29
Badinksi, Curt, 133
Bandomir, Gerhard, 140, 141
Barth, Joachim, 167
Bayerlein, Fritz, 25, 27, 57, 70, 71, 128, 167, 169, 170, 203
Bayeux, 48, 61, 70, 73, 105
bazookas, 27
Beck, *General* Ludwig, 144, 148-50, 151, 154
Beck, *Sturmmann* Oswald, 43
Bellengreville, 37
Bénouville, 41
Berchtesgaden, 40, 42, 146
Berghof, 113
Berliner Nachtausgabe, 93
Bernières, 44
Bittrich, Wilhelm, 111, 142
Block, *Major*, 43
Blöthner, Hans, 224, 237, 238-9
Blumentritt, Günther von 55, 143, 149, 153, 174, 181-2, 185, 195, 196, 197
Boardman, Captain Tom, 192
Boineburg-Lengsfeld, Hans von, 227-8
Böll, Annemarie, 1
Böll, *Gefreiter* Heinrich, 1, 5, 223
Bornert, *Fallschirmjäger* Johann, 209
Boulogne, 10
Bradley, General Omar Nelson, 164, 165, 172, 174, 181, 186
Braun, *Oberfeldwebel* Hans Erich, 81, 82-3, 206, 214, 215
Bren gun, 127
Brest, 30, 36, 58, 59, 182
Brinke, *Feldwebel* Edmund,

117-18
British Forces
  1st Northamptonshire Yeomanry, 192
  Second Army, 105
  3rd Division, 83
  6th Airborne Division, 41, 75
  22 Armoured Brigade, 79-80
  49th Division, 83
  Argyll and Sutherland Highlanders, 194
Brittany, 31, 33, 116, 173, 176, 180, 185
Buron, 70

Cabourg, 37
Caen, 16, 18, 25, 31, 37, 41, 48, 55, 57, 62, 63, 66, 69, 73, 79, 87, 96, 105, 106, 114, 117, 118, 119, 122, 138, 139, 160, 164, 189
Caen canal, 41
Cagny, 141
Calais, 10
Calvados, 33
Canadian Forces
  First Army, 189
  3rd Division, 51, 83
Canaris, *Admiral* Wilhelm, 159
Cap de la Hague, 101
Carentan, 36, 41, 63, 67, 78, 95
Carpiquet, 70
Catillon, 240
Caumont, 79, 81, 82, 164
Chambois, 209
Channel Islands, 16, 33
Chaumont, 217
Cherbourg, 33, 95-8, 99-100, 101-2, 106, 113, 164
Cherbourg peninsula, 16, 34, 36, 78, 91, 174
Chill, Kurt, 200
Choltitz, Dietrich von, 105,

263

116, 125-6, 134, 181, 228-30, 231-2, 232-5
Churchill tank, 120-1, 127, 211
Churchill, Winston, 117
Clifford, Alexander, 236-7
Cobra, 165, 166, 167, 175
Colleville, 53, 67
Cotentin, 165
Cotentin peninsula, 33, 38, 42, 47, 53, 61, 68, 73, 96, 97, 99-100, 101, 105, 170
Creil, 53
Cremer, Peter, 74-5
Crerar, Harry, 189
Crete, 26
Criegern, *Oberstleutnant* Friedrich von, 78-9
Cromwell tank, 80, 82, 127
Croydon, 184

Daniel, *Oberfeldwebel*, 138-9
Das Reich, 88
Der Pimpf, 249
Dessloch, Otto, 226-7, 230, 235
Dieppe, 5
Dietrich, *Oberstgruppenführer* Sepp, 84, 108, 141-3, 162, 185, 195, 197, 198, 226, 239, 250
Dischen, Richard, 141-2
Dollmann, *Generaloberst* Eugen, 20, 96, 109
Dollmann, *Generaloberst* Friedrich, 39, 108-9
Dombrowksi, *Rottenführer* Wolfgang, 238
Dönitz, *Grossadmiral* Karl, 13, 29, 30, 58-9, 75, 113, 151-2, 153, 159, 182, 183, 245
Dönitz, Klaus, 58
Dörner, Klaus, 102
Eberbach, Heinrich, 115, 118, 121, 139, 141-3, 175, 177,

180, 181, 185, 193, 196, 197, 200-1, 203, 226, 238, 244, 250
Ebner, Emil, 124, 164
Eisenhower, General Dwight D., 186, 198, 219, 229, 246, 247
El Alamein, 9
Elbeuf, 225
Enderle, *Gefreiter* Leo, 80
Engelke, *Oberst*, 238
English Channel, 53

Falaise, 186, 189, 195, 198-9, 200, 205, 218, 220
fall of Paris, 235-6
Feuchtinger, Edgar, 26, 55, 63, 69
Fey, Willi, 122
Fiebig, *Oberleutnant* Werner, 62
Fifteenth Army, 23, 90, 194, 225
Fifth Panzer Army, 185, 195, 209, 216, 218, 226
Finckh, Eberhard, 143
Fischer, *Leutnant* Wolfgang, 53-4
Flade, *Oberfähnrich* Hans-Ulrich, 28
Flak regiment 155, 90
France, 16, 25, 26
Freiwillige, 14
French Naval College, 30
Frerking, *Oberleutnant* Bernhard, 38, 45, 67
Freund, Leo, 217
Fromm, *Generaloberst* Fritz, 147, 148, 154
Front und Heimat, 161
Fullriede, Fritz, 239
Funck, *Freiherr* Hans von, 172-3, 177

Fürbringer, *Sturmmann*
  Herbert, 109, 120-2, 123,
  225-6
Fürst, Heinrich, 36

Galland, *General* Adolf, 184
Galtier-Boissière, Jean, 224
Gaumesnil, 192
Gause, Alfred, 125, 240
Gerhard Fieseler, 91
Geritzlehner, *Fallschirmjäger*
  Wolfgang, 41-2
German Army, 2, 3, 13, 26, 27
German, Paul, 199
German-Italian Army, 9
Gersdorff, *Oberst* Rudolf von,
  174, 180, 207, 211
Geyr von Schweppenburg,
  General Leo, 24, 65, 76-7, 90,
  112, 114, 250
Gockel, *Gefreiter* Franz, 2, 47,
  52
Goebbels, Joseph, 4, 16, 21,
  36-7, 42, 54, 86, 87, 88-9, 92,
  93-4, 99, 101, 102, 130-1,
  132, 150, 154, 155, 156, 159,
  202, 230, 232-3, 245, 248
Goering, *Reichsmarschall*
  Hermann, 13, 27, 28, 54, 113,
  146, 158-9, 183
Gold beach, 49, 50, 53, 61, 62,
  68
Graf, Josef, 209-10
Greisinger, Hans, 120
Groos, *Hauptmann* Hans, 60,
  72
Grossdeutschland guards
  battalion, 147, 150, 154
Gruppe Grünherz, 227
Gruppe Landwirt, 29
Guderian, *Generaloberst* Heinz,
  76, 124, 155, 157, 158, 172,
  177

Günther, *Sturmmann* Helmut,
  17, 170, 171

Haas, US Sergeant Hyman, 53
Haering, *Sturmmann*, 109
Hammer, *Leutnant* Alfred, 240-1
Hanf, *Leutnant* Gerhard, 129
Hansmann, *Obersturmführer*
  Peter, 48-50
Harmel, Heinz, 120, 131, 133,
  214
Hartdegen, *Hauptmann*
  Alexander, 71, 126
Hausser, *Obergruppenführer*
  Paul, 109, 111, 112, 113, 116,
  134, 142-3, 177, 180, 185,
  196, 197, 207, 208
Hayn, Friedrich, 38
Heidtmann, Wilhelm, 239
Heilmann, *Oberleutnant* Willi,
  129, 130, 227
Henderson, Horace, 67
Hengl, *General* Georg Ritter
  von, 223, 239
Hensel, Günther, 122
Herrmann, Hans, 234
Hesse, *Gefreiter* Helmut, 126
Heusinger, Adolf, 147
Hierl, Konstantin, 134
Hilfswillige, 14
Hill 112, 110, 111, 112-13,
  119, 120, 121
Hill 159, 198-9
Hill 168, 198-9
Hill 195, 194
Himmler, *Reichsführer SS*
  Heinrich, 15, 16, 109, 134,
  146, 154, 158
Hindenburg, Field Marshal
  Paul von, 157
Hitler Youth, 15
Hitler, Adolf, 3, 4, 5, 6, 7, 8,
  10, 13-14, 16, 17, 20-1, 23,

24, 31, 41, 42, 54-5, 76, 77,
86-7, 91, 95-6, 96, 97, 99,
113-14, 114, 116, 131, 135,
143, 145-6, 147, 149-50, 152-
3, 154, 155, 157, 159, 161,
175-6, 180, 183, 185, 196-7,
203-4, 223, 226, 228, 230-2,
234-5, 240, 243, 248-9
Höcker, Hans-Kurt, 238
Hoepner, Erich, 148, 154, 158
Hofacker, *Oberst* Caesar von,
145, 146, 148, 149-50, 153,
159, 249
Hofbauer, *Sturmmann* Walter,
178
Hoffmann, *Leutnant*, 75
Höflinger, *Hauptscharführer*
Hans, 192
Hohenstein, *Gefreiter* Adolf,
133, 244
Holstein, *Major* Prince, 212
Hörner, Helmut, 122-3, 156,
237-8
Hotel Meurice, 227, 230, 234

Italy, 10

Jacob, Alfred, 6
Jagdbomber, 1
Jagdgeschwader 1, 71
Jagdgeschwader 2, 53
Jagdgeschwader 26, 60, 72, 90
Jagdgeschwader 4, 241
Jagdgeschwader 53, 245
Jagdgeschwader 54, 227
Jagdkorps II, 27, 129, 183-4
Jagdwaffe, 28
Jägermann, Hans-Ulrich, 225
Jahnke, *Leutnant* Arthur, 48
Jobourg, 101
Jodl, Field Marshal Alfred, 11,
22, 27, 96, 145, 157-8, 181,
182, 196, 197, 230, 232, 235

Jünger, Ernst, 87
Juno beach, 50, 51, 57, 61, 68
Juvigny le Tertre, 178

Kaestner, *Oberst*, 238
Kaiser, *Oberfeldwebel* Herbert,
71
Kalinowsky, *Untersturmführer*
Eduard, 124
Kampfgruppe Rauch, 57
Kampfgruppe von Schlieben,
100
Kauffmann, Kurt, 165, 169
Keil, *Oberstleutnant* Günther,
101
Keitel, Field Marshal Wilhelm,
54, 114, 147, 148
Kempel, *SS
Panzerobergrenadier* Hans,
106
Kessler, *Oberst* Hans, 89
Klapdor, *Hauptsturmführer*
Ewald, 89, 109-10, 117, 120,
123, 195-6, 200, 201-2, 205,
208, 211-12, 213-14, 217,
218
Klein, Walter, 166-7
Kluge, Field Marshal Günther
von, 114, 115-16, 119, 135,
139, 142-3, 143, 144-5, 149-
50, 153, 159-60, 165-6, 167,
169, 174-5, 176, 180-1, 182,
185, 193, 195, 196, 197-8,
202, 203-5, 250
Knappe, Siegfried, 158
Knebelsberger, *Sturmmann* Leo,
206, 207
Köhn, *Oberst* Walter, 61-2
Koller, Karl, 183, 227
Koralle, 58
Korbacher, Manfred, 245
Kortenhaus, Werner, 17, 75,
95, 111, 140

Kraiss, Dietrich, 62
Krancke, *Vizeadmiral* Theodor, 13, 21, 29, 34, 74, 75, 151-2, 153
Kreipe, Werner, 182, 183, 226-7
Kreutz, *Standartenführer* Karl, 165
Kriegsmarine, 4, 13, 29, 30, 87, 158, 182
Krug, *Oberst*, 63
Kübel, *Unterscharführer*, 69
Küchler, Wolfgang, 93-4
Kufner, *Sturmmann* Ernst, 201

La Haye-du-Puits, 122
La Pallice, 58
La Rivière, 50
La Roche-Guyon, 22, 23, 39, 62, 114, 138, 149, 160, 198, 218, 229
Lammerding, Heinz, 110
Lang, *Hauptmann* Hellmuth, 22, 24, 51, 62
Langer, Karl-Heinz, 129-30
Laser, *Feldwebel* Heinrich, 198
Laska, Werner, 166
Le Mans, 39, 42, 56, 60-1, 66, 72, 108, 176, 181, 186
Le Mesnil-Tôve, 178
Le Quesnay, 82-3, 84
Lee, Private Alfred, 220
Lemcke, *Major* Gerhard, 127
Lengronne, 173
Les Invalides, 231
Leykauff, *Schütze* Jochen, 17
Liebeskind, Helmut, 62
life expectancy of a pilot in France, 129
life in France, 4
Lindner, *Hauptmann* Joachim, 1, 4-5
Lion-sur-Mer, 50, 57
London, 92, 93, 94

Lorient, 58
Luck, *Major* Hans von, 17-18, 37, 55, 57, 62, 140-1
Luftflotte 3, 12, 13, 28, 54, 90, 130, 183, 226, 233, 245
Luftwaffe, 4, 5, 11, 12, 13, 27-8, 54, 60-1, 72, 78, 87, 89-90, 97, 126-7, 129, 130-1, 133, 135, 158, 162, 178, 180, 181, 182, 183, 201, 226, 229, 231, 235, 239, 240, 245
Lüttwitz, *Freiherr* Hans von, 125, 126, 178
Lüttwitz, *General* Heinrich, 212-13

McKee, Alexander, 119
Maginot Line, 175, 237
Marbach, *Oberleutnant* Karl Heinz, 30
Marcks, *General* Erich, 16, 17, 33, 37, 38, 55-6, 58, 62, 78
Marinegruppe West, 13
Massenbach, *Oberstleutnant* Freiherr von, 238
Meimberg, *Hauptmann* Julius, 241
Meindl, *General* Eugen, 116, 164, 170-1, 172, 218
Meitzel, Bernhard, 106
Metz, 86
Meyer, *Standartenführer* Kurt, 42-3, 56, 63, 66, 69-70, 83, 84, 106, 108, 111, 112-13, 118-19, 138, 140, 190, 192-4, 199, 208-9, 247-8
Milch, Field Marshal Erhard, 91, 92
Misch, Kurt, 216
Möbius, *Hauptsturmführer* Rolf, 80
Model, Field Marshal Walter, 197-8, 202-4, 218, 225, 230-1,

232-4, 235, 240, 250
Mollière d'Aval, 1
Mont Ormel, 218-19
Montgomery, Field Marshal
  Bernard Law, 9, 53, 105-6,
  117, 139, 161, 186, 189, 198,
  224-5, 246-7
Moon, Private Ray, 52
Mortain, 178-9, 181, 186
Mouen, 111
Munich, 37
Mussolini, Benito, 10, 21

Nancy, 185, 218
Nantes, 185
*Nationalsozialistisches
  Führungsoffizier*, 14
Neuville-sur-Margival, 86
Normandy, 16, 17, 18, 23, 25,
  26, 31, 39, 40, 42, 54, 60, 67,
  73, 80, 88, 90, 105, 107, 116,
  127, 134, 135, 161, 168, 174,
  175, 176, 177, 180, 190, 196,
  200, 219, 223, 244, 246, 249
Notre Dame, 231
Nuremberg, 36
Nuremberg rallies, 9, 55

Obersalzberg, 36
Obstfelder, Hans von, 142
Oissel, 225-6
Olbricht, Friedrich, 151, 154
Omaha beach, 43, 45-7, 50,
  51-3, 61, 62, 67, 68, 76, 78
Operation Charnwood, 162
Operation Epsom, 105, 106,
  113, 162
Operation Goodwood, 139,
  141, 161, 162, 189
Operation Lüttich, 176, 177,
  179-81, 182
Operation Overlord, 79
Oppeln-Bronikowski, Hermann

von, 55-6, 57
Oradour-sur-Glane, 110
Organisation Todt, 6-7, 239
Osttruppen, 14, 61-2, 79, 95
Ouistreham, 49, 50, 68, 105

Padberg, Walter, 170, 217
Panzer Lehr Division, 25, 36,
  42, 56-7, 70, 71, 77, 79, 80,
  83, 95, 108, 134, 165, 166,
  168-9, 214, 226, 234
Panzergruppe West, 24, 76-7,
  90, 112, 114, 115, 125,
  202
Panzers
  Mark IV, 25, 26, 57, 69, 127,
  140
  Panther, 25, 26, 127, 178,
  194, 201
  Tiger, 25, 79-80, 120-1, 127,
  140, 192, 194, 201, 211
Paris, 4, 103, 223
Paris Chamber of Deputies, 231
Pariser Zeitung, 223
Pas de Calais, 11-12, 23, 31,
  33, 91
Patton, General George S., 185,
  186, 224-5
Paulus, Field Marshal, 101
Peenemünde, 91
Pemsel, *Generalmajor* Max, 26,
  33, 39, 42, 57, 58, 66-7, 109
Percy, 173
Périers, 168
Pflocksch, Gustav, 51
Philipsen, *SS Untersturmführer*
  Hannes, 11
Piat guns, 27
Pipet, Albert, 134-5
planned demolition of Paris,
  231-3
Pluskat, *Major* Werner, 2, 38,
  40, 43, 44

Plymouth, 184
Pock, *Sturmmann* Hellmuth, 56
Pontaubault, 173
Pöppel, *Oberleutnant* Martin, 36, 38, 39, 63, 67-8, 78, 89, 95
Port-en-Bessin, 73
Potigny, 193
Pretzel, Albert, 245
Prinz, *Obersturmführer*, 168
Pruller, Wilhelm, 250
Puttkamer, Karl Jesko von, 42
Pyle, Ernie, 166

RAF, 55, 97, 117, 179
Rangsdorf airbase, 147
Ranville, 41, 55, 57
Rauch, Josef, 57
Raymond, Corporal Dick, 216
Reichert, *Generalleutnant* Joseph, 37
Reichsarbeitsdienst, 15
Reichsrundfunk, 93
Remer, *Major* Otto Ernst, 150-1
Rennes, 34, 47, 185
Ribbentrop, Rudolf von, 34-5
Richter, *Generalleutnant* Wilhelm, 51, 58, 63, 87
Riegamer, *Untersturmführer*, 243-4, 247
Ritgen, *Major* Helmut, 25, 36, 57, 71, 128, 168-9, 237
Rivers
  Dives, 206, 209, 211-12, 213, 214, 219
  Odon, 108, 110, 161
  Orne, 23, 33, 41, 53, 55, 68, 75, 95, 105, 140, 141, 161, 202
  Sée, 173
  Selune, 173
Roeder, *Leutnant*, 124
Rome, 37, 42
Romer, *Grenadier* Helmut, 41

Rommel, Field Marshal Erwin, 8-10, 11-12, 16-17, 21, 22-3, 23-4, 27, 31, 34, 42, 43, 47, 51, 55, 62, 66-7, 68, 74, 75, 76, 77, 86-8, 90, 95, 96, 99-100, 113, 114, 115, 116, 119, 134, 135, 138-9, 143, 145-6, 159-60, 202, 204, 244, 249-51
Rommel, Lucie, 9, 22, 34, 51
Rommel, Manfred, 22
Roncey, 173
Rosen, *Leutnant Freiherr* von, 140
Rösing, Hans, 30
Rouen, 225, 247
Ruge, Friedrich, 10, 12, 115, 145-6
Rundstedt, Field Marshal Gerd von, 3-4, 5, 7, 11, 15, 21, 23, 25, 26, 31, 34, 39-40, 42, 58, 72, 74, 77, 86-7, 113, 114, 115, 143, 158, 250
Russia, 17

St Aubin sur Mer, 50
St Barthelemy, 178
St Germain, 196
St Germain-en-Laye, 3
St Honorine, 43, 53
St Lambert, 210-11, 213-15, 217
St Laurent, 53
St Lô, 33, 37, 62, 76, 105, 164, 165, 167
St Martin, 122
St Mère Église, 38, 39, 41, 42, 47, 68, 73
St Nazaire, 58
St Quentin, 60
St Sauveur, 100
Sattler, *Generalmajor* Robert, 96
Schimpf, *Generalleutnant* Richard, 128, 208

Schlachtgeschwader 4, 60, 71
Schlieben, *Generalleutnant* Karl
  Wilhelm von, 14, 47, 96-7,
  99-101
Schmundt, Rudolf, 97
Schnorchel boats, 29, 59
Schwalbe, Eugen-Felix, 225
Schwerin, *Generalleutnant* Graf
  von, 172, 178
Scott, Group Captain
  Desmond, 219
Seine Bay, 33, 38, 48, 53, 68,
  74, 105, 120, 164
Seventh Army, 23, 38-9, 42, 57,
  58, 66, 101, 108, 109, 112,
  114, 134, 174, 176, 180, 185,
  202, 208
Seventh Panzer Army, 216, 218
Severloh, *Obergefreiter*
  Heinrich, 2, 38, 43-5, 46, 52-3,
  62-3, 67
Sherman tank, 25, 51, 80, 101,
  127, 141, 192, 194
Sicherheitsdienst, 31, 73, 103,
  131-2, 148, 155, 156
Sicily, 10
Sieder, Heinz, 74
Sippenhaftung, 158
Slaughter, Sergeant Robert, 46
Speidel, *Generalmajor* Hans,
  39, 51, 86-7, 114, 144-5, 149,
  195, 231-2, 249
Sperrle, Field Marshal Hugo,
  12, 21, 54, 113, 226
SS *Verfügungstruppe*, see
  Waffen SS, 15
Stacey, Charles, 199-200
Stalingrad, 15
Stamm, *Untersturmführer* Fritz,
  124
Stauffenberg, *Oberst* Count
  Claus von, 138, 143-4, 146-8,
  151, 152, 154

Stegmann, *Generalmajor*
  Rudolf, 96
Steinbüchel, *Oberscharführer*
  Jupp, 178
Stober, Hans, 170
Stoob, Alfred, 237
Streng, *Hauptscharführer* Ernst,
  122, 126
strikes in Paris, 229
Stülpnagel, *General* Karl-
  Heinrich von, 144, 148-50,
  153, 249
Sword beach, 50, 55, 57, 61, 68

Tilly-sur-Seulles, 83
Tippe, *Unteroffizier* Erhard, 90
Tobruk, 9
Tractable, 198
Trautmann, Heinz, 120, 208
Tribulet, Madame Luce, 119
Trun, 220
Tychsen, *Obersturmbannführer*
  Christian, 170

U-boats
  U256, 59
  U309, 182
  U333, 74-5
  U413, 59
  U415, 30, 36, 59-60, 182
  U953, 30
  U984, 74
  U-Bootwaffe, 29
  US Air Force, 97
  USS *Nevada*, 44
  USS *Texas*, 44
Utah beach, 41, 47-8, 61, 63

Vasold, *Sturmmann* Karl, 70
Vierville, 53
Villacoublay, 227
Villers-Bocage, 79-80, 83, 84
Vogt, Robert, 49, 94
Völkischer Beobachter, 65-6,

72-3, 102, 103, 131, 155,
156-7, 235
Volksdeutsche, 14

Wacht am Kanal, 4
Wachtel, *Oberst* Max, 90, 91-2
Waffen SS, 15, 25, 68, 78-9,
109, 168, 173, 205
Wagner, Eduard, 159
Warlimont, Walter, 149, 175
Weapons
FZG76 flying bomb, 91
MG42, 27, 127
Nebelwerfer, 27, 111, 127
Panzerfaust, 27, 121, 190
Panzerschreck, 27, 121
V1, *Vergeltung 1* flying bomb,
93, 94, 113, 131, 132, 184, 236
Weber, Hermann, 241
Wehrmacht, 3, 4, 14, 25, 54,
55, 56, 76, 77, 87, 97, 99,
103, 105, 113, 125, 127, 154,
157, 158, 159, 169, 201, 233,
239, 244
Weidinger, *Sturmbannführer*
Otto, 110, 111, 180, 181, 217
Weidner, Hans, 168
Werkmeister, Erich, 122
Werner, *Oberleutnant* Herbert,
20, 30-1, 36, 59-60, 182-3

West Wall, 6, 175, 237
Western Front, 34, 105
Widerstandnest 5, 48
Widerstandsnest 62, 38, 43, 52
Wiegel, Robert, 98-9
Wietzorek, *Fallschirmjäger* Karl
Max, 17, 201
Witt, *Brigadeführer* Fritz, 69,
83
Wittmann, *Obersturmführer*
Michael, 79-80, 192
Witzleben, Field Marshal Erwin
von, 144, 149, 150-1, 154,
158
Wohlgemuth, *Oberscharführer*
Erich, 106
Wolff-Boenisch, Richard, 92,
156
Wolf's Lair, 10, 146-7, 149,
155, 230
Wolfschlucht II, 86, 95
Wulff, *Hauptmann* Theo, 235
Wünsche, Max, 112

Zeitzler, Kurt, 5, 54, 154
Ziegelman, *Oberst* Fritz, 46,
51, 76
Zimmermann, Bodo, 74
Zinssmeister, *Oberscharführer*
August, 108